Frieda R. Oetting

Wakarusa, Ind

1996

# German-American Names

# German-American
# N·A·M·E·S

George F. Jones

2nd Edition

1st Edition 1990
2nd Edition 1995
Copyright © 1990, 1995
Genealogical Publishing Co., Inc.
1001 N. Calvert Street
Baltimore, Maryland 21202
All Rights Reserved
Library of Congress Catalogue Card Number 95-76468
International Standard Book Number 0-8063-1481-8
*Made in the United States of America*

# Acknowledgments

I wish to thank Bertha Butler of the University of Maryland Computer Science Center for many years of expert and patient help in devising computer programs. One of these, a system of reverse-alphabetical listing, served to assemble the names in this book according to their last roots and thus shed much light on their meanings and relationships. I also wish to thank Carol Warrenton, likewise of the University of Maryland Computer Science Center, for composing the program for printing this book.

G. F. J.

# Der Schmidt.

# CHAPTER ONE

## Given Names - Significance and Origin

Many Americans with German names know the dictionary meaning of the corresponding German word without realizing that their name, being a name, may have an entirely different meaning. For example, the German dictionary tells us that the word *Kuss* means "kiss," but it does not tell us that the name Kuss is most often a shortened form of Dominicus and that, while the word *Mass* means "measure," the name Mass or Maas is usually a shortened form of Thomas, unless the first bearer of the name lived near the Maas (Meuse) River.        (1)

Unfortunately, onomastics (the science of names) is not an exact science, as is proved when experts disagree as to the meaning of a name. Only the parents of a child know what they think a name means, and often they do not know. While interning in an obstetrics ward, an acquaintance of mine once delivered a worn-out mountain woman of her tenth child. When the grateful woman asked him to think up a name, he suggested Decimus Ultimus; and she was delighted with the choice, which she did not understand. The name meant "the tenth and the last." He was right: he had tied her tubes.        (2)

When my wife's parents chose the name Joyce for their daughter, they probably associated it with "joy " and "rejoice," little realizing that it once denoted a Goth; and the same thing was repeated when Joyce named our daughter Jocelyn (little Goth). Such misunderstandings are called popular etymology or folk etymology, etymology being the study of *etyma* or roots of words. A good example of folk etymology is the common expression "planter's wart," which suggests that planters were most exposed to it, whereas it is really a "plantar wart" or a wart on the sole of the foot, as I learned recently.        (3)

Old Germanic names were misunderstood already a thousand years ago by scholars who tried to interpret them. For example, Ratmund was rendered as "counsel + mouth" instead of as "counsel + guardianship;" and Adalramus was rendered as "noble ram" instead of as "noble raven." This study will make every effort to avoid folk etymologies, but some are inevitable, and the author will appreciate hearing of any the reader might find.

(4)

Sometimes the researcher must risk an educated guess. For example, the German-American name Hass could derive from German *Hass* (hate) or from German *Hase* (hare), most certainly (but not absolutely certainly) from the latter, which is found in many American names such as Hashagen (hare hedge) and Hasenjaeger (hare hunter). A half century ago one of my sisters had a gentleman caller named Hass, who had the misfortune of having the first name Jack. When Jack Hass was spoken quickly, it said just what we brothers thought of him.

Sometimes the context makes it clear which of two homonymous roots is the correct one: in the name Sauerbier the root *sauer* means "sour," while in Sauerland it means "southern." Among the scores of homonymous root-pairs (having the same sound and spelling), we find *gehl* (yellow), *gehl* (swamp); *ger* (spear), *ger* (swamp); *han* (rooster), *han* (swamp); *reh* (roebuck), *reh* (marsh); and *sud* (muddy), *sud* (south). In some cases there are even triplets: *ahl* (eel), *ahl* (noble), *ahl* (awl); *dick* (thicket), *dick* (dike), *dick* (fat); and *hart* (strong), *hart* (stag), *hart* (forest). (5)

It is easy to define the term "German-American name," once we decide on the meaning of "German name"; for a German-American name is any name derived from the German language or its dialects, even if changes in pronunciation and spelling have rendered it unrecognizable. For our purpose, both Beam and Dice are German-American names, even if we do not easily identify them with Boehm and Theiss. (6)

Defining "German names" is somewhat more difficult. For example, the Netherlands were originally a part of the Holy Roman Empire (i.e. the German Empire); and the people there speak Low Franconian, Low Saxon, and Frisian. The first two of these are German dialects, while the third is an independent language, which is also spoken in Germany. Since Dutch is now a national language, we will not include obviously Dutch names such as de Gruyter and van Horn, even if they may have been borne for centuries by families in Berlin. (7)

On the other hand, even though Dreyfuss was a loyal Frenchman, his name (meaning "tripod") was German and is therefore included. When I first visited Paris, I rented a room from a woman who pronounced her name Oh-mess-air, which I took to be French. I later discovered that it was Haumesser, an

Alsatian word meaning "hackknife" or "meat-cleaver," so it is also included.

Also included are the names Kirchhoff and Stockmann, even though they are best known to us as the names of a Russian physicist and of the protagonist in Ibsen's *Enemy of the People* and also (with one *n*) of a precocious American economist who ridiculed Reaganomics. In other words, we are interested in the linguistic origin of the name, not in the nationality of its bearers. The word "German" refers to the German language, whether the name in question came from West or East Germany, Alsace, Switzerland, Austria, the South Tyrol, or any other German-speaking areas of Europe.     (8)

It is not always possible to ascertain from which language a name is derived: Horn could be German, English, Dutch, or Scandinavian. Therefore some American names discussed below may actually have been brought here by non-German families, but all do exist in Germany. A few well-known Latin and Greek names like Astor, Faber, Melanchthon, Mercator, Neander, Praetorius, Sartorius, and Stettinius are included because they have now become German names. There are also a few names of French origin, like Tussing for Toussaints, and a few names of Slavic derivation, like Kretschmer, Lessing, and Nietzsche. Some German-looking names appearing below may have been Slavic names shortened or germanized at Ellis Island by officials who knew German better than the various Slavic languages.     (9)

Because the word "philologist" will appear many times in this book, now might be a proper time to explain the word, even if it is hard to explain the profession. As the Greek roots *phil* and *logos* suggest, a philologist is one who loves words, one who cherishes them for their own sake, not for the sake of gain. No philologist ever became rich, not one ever built a bridge, removed a tumor, or won a battle; and it is difficult to explain what good they serve, unless, perhaps, to disabuse us of much misinformation. Nevertheless, some of the world's greatest minds have devoted themselves to this unproductive study, two splendid examples being Jacob and Wilhelm Grimm, scholars known to the public for their fairy tales but to the scholarly world for their collection of legal antiquities and, above all, for the "Grimms' Law," an explanation of the development of the various Germanic languages. The observations made by the

Grimm brothers and other philologists of their day make it
possible for us to understand the origin of German names, and
therefore their contributions will be described in some detail a
bit later.                                                    (10)

Most philologists write for each other, affecting an arcane
jargon to exclude everyone else. Unfortunately, this study will
have to use a few technical terms, but these will be explained.
At the Day of Judgment I shall have to confess to having
devoted a half century of my life to Germanic philology, whereas
I could have been serving my Maker in some more productive
way. However, unlike most Germanic philologists in their ivory
towers, I am aware that there are many perfectly decent,
hardworking, law abiding people out there who have never
studied Germanic philology. It is for them that this book is
written.                                                      (11)

"In the beginning was the word." St. John was not alone in
this belief; it was the opinion of most of his contemporaries,
especially of his Greek ones, who had a word for everything. It
was centuries before Goethe's Faust, as the first Modern Man,
refuted St. John and argued that "In the beginning was the
deed." Today most people would agree with the *New English
Dictionary* that a word is merely "Speech, utterance, or verbal
expression." The ancients, on the other hand, and not only
those of our culture, knew that a word was more than a mere
utterance. It was a living spirit with inherent power to do good
or evil, as is so evident in the blessings and curses of the Old
Testament. Noah's curse of Canaan and Isaac's blessing of Jacob
were not just words but were forces direct from Jehovah. Words
had power not only for the ancient Hebrews but also for the
ancient Germanic peoples, for whom an insult was a malevolent
spirit, a relentless demon that clung to a man until washed off
with blood.                                                   (12)

What has been said about words naturally holds for names
too, since they are proper nouns, even in the few instances
when they are formed like adjectives or verbs, as in the case of
Lionhearted or Lackland. The very term "proper nouns"
(*nomina propria*) is significant; for a name, be it given or
earned, is proper to, or the property of, the bearer. This is
especially evident in the German word *Eigennamen*, or "own
names." One's name is, of course, more than just a possession,

like land or gold; it is the immortal part of the person, as Othello's ensign Cassio avowed. It is the part that lives after the body dies, possibly borne by children of the deceased, or perhaps by many children of his admirers. Or perhaps his name is carved in stone or borne by a city or a symphony.      (13)

Even the Old Testament taught the value of a good name, and this is one reason that, during the Middle Ages, to be "nameless" (*namenlos* or *ungenant*) was most tragic. Proverbs 22:1 tells us that "A good name is rather to be chosen than great riches," and Ecclesiastes 7:1 preaches that "a good name is better than precious ointment." (Cf "to leave a living name behind," and "their bodies are buried in peace, but their name liveth for evermore.")      (14)

It has been said that "your name is who you are." Indeed, before social security numbers, a name was most people's only identity. This attitude is deeply ingrained in the Christian Church, which accepts a new member only when he receives a Christian name and ignores his surname; and it helps explain the emphasis on the Feast of the Holy Name on New Year's Day. In some cultures a change of name indicates a change in nature: the Indian youth receives a new name when he becomes a brave, and a British commoner receives a more fitting name when he is ennobled. When Lawrence Olivier was knighted, he became Sir Lawrence, not Sir Olivier.      (15)

That such obsession with names was only a holdover from ancient word-magic is suggested by the ease with which modern men can change their names, without any great metamorphosis in their person. Indeed, one does not even have to go to the legislature, as was necessary in my father's childhood. When his nextgate neighbors tired of being teased because of their name, which was Hogg, they changed it to Howard. The next day some jokester put a sign on their gate: "Hogg by name, and hog by nature, changed to Howard by legislature." What the public did not know was that Hog was a respectable name as long as it denoted the young of most animals, including sheep. A Highland lassie cared little whether her laddie called her "my little lamb" or "my little hog."      (16)

There are many tales of name changes, usually apocryphal but sometimes illuminating. From the '30s comes the tale of Franklin Delano Stink. When the judge agreed to let him change his name and asked which name he had chosen, he answered "Theodore Roosevelt Stink." Then there was the Mr. Murphy of South Boston who wished to change his name to O'Reily. When the judge asked why he wished to exchange one Irish name for another, he answered: "Venn I say my name iss Murphy, people aks me vut it vuss before it vuss Murphy."

(17)

The ancient Germans had no firm faith in a hereafter, despite what latter-day mythologists tell us about Valhalla, which must have developed late and probably through analogy with the Christian heaven. Long after they had become nominal Christians, Germanic warriors were far more concerned with their posthumous good name than with their souls. *Beowulf* is nominally a Christian poem; yet, when the hero dies, the poet is concerned not with his soul but only with his good name, for he eulogizes him as *leofgernost*, or "most eager for fame." (18)

This obsession with one's good name lasted throughout the Middle Ages. Despite Christ's injunction to turn the other cheek, men of honor preferred to risk their immortal souls in duels rather than risk their worldly honor by declining a challenge. Today we can say "Sticks and stones may break my bones but names can never hurt me," but in those days names hurt far more than mere broken bones. Turning the other cheek would have been incomprehensible to the ancient German, the medieval knight, or the Southern Gentleman, who knew that he would enjoy no respect or esteem if he failed to gain satisfaction for an insult. (19)

*The New English Dictionary* says that a name is "the particular combination of sounds employed as the individual designation of a single person, animal, place, or thing." It is to be noted that the name consists of sounds, not letters. Now that most people of the Western World are literate, we think of names as groups of letters, as in a signature. Yet even today the sound is foremost, extremely varied spellings are legally recognized only if they sound the same (*idem sonans*). MacIntire, McIntire, and McIntyre are the same name, even if differently spelled, as are Cramer, Craemer, and Kraemer. (20)

When the ancient Germans formed their names, they, like the ancient Hebrews, knew that a name was more than a mere designation: like a word, a name had inherent power and was part and parcel of the person himself. It was believed that a man's virtues were influenced by his name and were in turn transmitted to his namesake. This belief lasted long after the introduction of Christianity, and Christian parents continued to select godparents whose names would contribute to their children's virtue. (21)

Because the God of the Old Testament was created in man's image, He was a jealous God, especially jealous of His name; and it should be noted that He performed most of His great works "for His name's sake," or to enhance His reputation among the various tribal gods of the time. ("Thou shalt have none other god before me.") Woe unto anyone who took the name of the Lord in vain! In fact, the Hebrews dared not utter His name; they had to resort to all sorts of circumlocutions such as Adonai and Elohim. Sacred names are taboo in many other religions as well: for example, the Hairy Ainu of Hokaido are afraid to utter the name of the bear. The early Germans, who were also shamanists, must have shared this fear, for they avoided the inherited Indo-European name for "bear," which would have been similar to Latin *ursus*. Instead, they beat around the bush with words like *bruin* and *berin*, both of which meant "brown" and gave us names such as Bruno, Bernhard, and Bermann. It should be noted that the name Beowulf meant "bee wolf," a circumlocution for the bear, which relishes honey. (22)

With such a long tradition of name-magic behind us, it is not surprising that people are still so touchy about their names. Goethe was wise in saying that we should never make a play on a person's name. For some twenty-five years, whenever I have been introduced to someone, he was likely to answer with a hearty chuckle, "Oh, one of the Jones boys!" I have always tried to be diplomatic and laugh along with my tormentor, as if I had not been subjected to the same stupidity a thousand times before, realizing that he really thought he had said something clever and original. (Strangely enough, I still do not know who the Jones boys were.) (23)

How did names arise? According to the Bible, after God created Adam:

> Out of the ground the Lord God formed every
> beast of the field, and every fowl of the air; and

brought them unto Adam to see what he would
call them: and whatsoever Adam called every
living creature, that was the name thereof.

This occurred just before God created Eve from Adam's rib.
When Eve heard that Adam had named the hippopotamus hippopotamus, she asked why he had done so; and he answered
that it looked more like a hippopotamus to him than any other
animal God had shown him.                                   (24)

Just as one could injure his enemy by driving nails into
his image, one could gain power over him by abusing his name.
As Stith Thompson's *Motif-Index of Folk-Literature* proves, this
belief has been strong in all cultures, including our own. For
example, in the Grimm's tale of Rumpelstiltskin, the queen's
daughter gains power over her captor by learning his name.
Belief in the power over names still lingers in our subconscious
as either a positive or a negative factor. In discussing Johann
Adam Treutlen, the first elected governor of Georgia, Henry
Melchior Muhlenberg praised him for having Adam's natural
intelligence and ability to give a name to every animal. Despite
St. John's faith in the precedence of the word, many medieval
scholars agreed with Genesis that the thing preceded the name:
*Nomina sunt consequentia rerum* (names are the consequence
of things).                                                 (25)

To understand early German names, we must keep in mind
that the ancient Germans, like the Latins, Celts, Slavs, Greeks,
and many more peoples, were descended from one speech
community, one we now call the Indo-Europeans. When I was
in college, we learned that this linguistic community had
developed its language in India and had gradually spread it
westward to Europe. However, during the Hitler regime, when
the terms "Aryan" and "Indo-European" were confused and
abused, German philologists began to argue that the Indo-
Europeans, or Indo-Germans as they called them, first developed their language in eastern Central Europe, in what is now
more or less East Germany and Poland, from where they
gradually carried it eastwards into Iran (Parsee) and India
(Sanskrit), as well as into all of Europe, except where Finnish,
Estonian, Hungarian, and Basque are spoken.                 (26)

The languages resulting from these Indo-European invasions
in Europe were the Celtic languages in the west and south,

Latin and Greek in the south, the Slavic languages in the east
and south, and German in the old homeland and also to the
north. Perhaps the least changed of all these languages were
Old Prussian, Lithuanian, and Latvian, all of them near and
just north of the old cradle. This new theory, which smacked of
blatant racism, first met with ridicule; yet the linguistic
evidence has now convinced most philologists, be they ever so
anti-Nazi.                                                      (27)

The Germanic tribes, which were among the last to leave the
old homeland, were excellently described in the year 98 A.D. by
the Roman historian Cornelius Tacitus in a little area-study
called the *Germania*, which may have been the foreword to a
never-written history of the German wars. Tacitus describes a
barbarian culture centered mainly on war; and, as we shall see,
early German names bear him out. The language of the ancient
Germans was not recorded, but we can reconstruct it by
comparing words from old and modern Germanic languages,
and also by comparing Germanic names recorded in Greek and
Latin writings. From these we can learn much about the
ancient Germans' life-style. We know, among other things, that
they had cattle, horses, wagons, plows, grains, cloth, and a
means of inscribing words, names, and incantations.      (28)

All languages are in constant flux. Children do not speak
exactly like their parents and grandparents; and today we have
difficulty in understanding Chaucer, or even Shakespeare. The
remarkable thing is not that languages change, but that they
change so slowly. As the various Indo-European peoples left
their homeland, their dialects developed independently until
they became mutually unintelligible languages. It was the great
work of the Grimm brothers, especially of Jacob, to comprehend
and codify the mutations that distinguished the Germanic
languages from all other Indo-European languages. These
mutations are now known as the Germanic sound shift.   (29)

The phrase "sound shift" sounds ominous, like the Andreas
Fault, or the Tower of Babel, as if any moment we might not be
able to communicate. Actually, sound shifts occur so slowly that
the speakers who perpetrate them are unaware of the havoc
they are wreaking. There even seems to have been a sound
shift, although not yet recorded, since we Americans broke off
from our linguistic motherland: we pronounce words like "latter"

and "bitter" the same as "ladder" and "bidder." Some Americans deny obstreperously that they do so; but, if they didn't, they would sound like Englishmen with their "clipped accent." Imitating the Brothers Grimm, I will formulate the Jones law as follows: "In American English intervocalic voiceless dental stops have become voiced." Or, put simply, *t* has become *d* between vowel sounds. "Voiceless" stops like *p*, *t*, and *k* do not cause the vocal chords to vibrate as the voiced stops *b*, *d*, and *g* do. In "this" the *th* is voiced, in "thistle" it is not. A "stop" is a consonant that interrupts the breath, like *p*, *t*, and *k*, whereas a "spirant" is spoken while air is being exhaled as in the case of *th*, *f*, and *s*. An "affricate" combines a stop and its corresponding spirant, as in *pf* and *ts* (which is written as *z* in German). (30)

To explain the Germanic sound shift simply, yet sufficiently for our purpose, we might say that the voiceless stops *p*, *t*, and *k* became the voiceless spirants *f*, *th*, and *ch* (which soon became *h*), while the voiced stops *b*, *d*, and *g* became the voiceless stops *p*, *t*, and *k*, thus replacing the lost consonants. Consequently the Indo-European roots that gave the Latin words *piscis*, *tenuis*, and *cornus* also gave the English words *fish*, *thin*, and *horn* as well as the German words *Fisch*, *duenn*, and *Horn*, while Latin *turba*, *duo*, and *genu* are cognate with (related to) "thorpe," "two," and "knee." (31)

The language produced by the Germanic sound shift, which is called Proto-Germanic, was subsequently subdivided by various mutations into many Germanic dialects, including Alemannic, Anglian, Bavarian, Danish, Dutch, Frankish, Hessian, Norwegian, Saxon, Swedish, and Thuringian, as well as by many extinct languages such as Burgundian, Cimbric, Gothic, Lombard, and Vandal. Of the modern dialects, some have become national languages, such as Dutch and Flemish (from Low Franconian), and English from Anglian and Saxon. (32)

This might be a suitable time to remind the reader that one should distinguish between the words "German" and "Germanic" rather than confuse them as many genealogical societies do. The word "Germanic," like *germanique*, *germanico*, and *germanisch*, denotes all the languages resulting from the Germanic sound shift, including English, Dutch, Swedish, Pennsylvania Dutch, etc. Since English is a Germanic language, one cannot distinguish between the English and Germanic elements in Pennsylvania. The recent popularity of the word "Germanic" seems to have begun during the Hitler regime, perhaps because it sounded less Nazi than "German" did. Correctly speaking, the inhabitants of Tacitus' *Germania* should not be called "Germans," since the German nation did not develop until after the invasions of the fourth to the seventh centuries. However, since it is awkward always to say "Germanic" and "Germanic peoples," we will sometimes just say "Germans" and "ancient Germans." (33)

A language is a culturally independent dialect with its own rules. Pennsylvania German and Afrikaans, with only a million or two speakers each, are languages, while Bavarian and Swabian, with many millions of speakers, are only dialects of German. No one can complain that the Pennsylvanians are speaking incorrect German or that the Afrikaners are speaking incorrect Dutch; yet a speaker of standard German can scold a Bavarian or a Swabian for distorting the German language. We will soon see that many German and German-American names were taken from dialects and do not conform to standard German spelling or pronunciation. The dialect form of the name might be much older than the standard language and is not really a deviation, merely an alternate form not chosen by Luther and other language standardizers. Behm is merely a dialect variant of Boehm (Bohemian), whereas the American form Beam is a new development in both pronunciation and spelling. Because the vowels, like the consonants, varied from dialect to dialect, the names Naumann, Niemann, and Neumann are one and the same. (34)

The dialects sometimes caused differences in the meaning of names. Although *Fuss* means "foot" in standard German, the name Streckfus originally meant "Stretch leg," not "Stretch foot." Some South German colonists in Georgia told their pastor that one of his parishioners had suffered an injury to his *Fuss* when a bear he had treed and shot fell on him. The pastor reported in his journal that the man's foot had been injured, but later he was more specific, the man's thigh had been dislocated. I had a similar experience in Bavaria when a man's ski stuck in the wet snow and, with his foot held high up by the ski, he began screaming in his dialect *mein Fuoss ist gebroche, mein*

*Fuoss ist gebroche.* In trying to loosen his foot from the ski, I handled it ever so gently, while quite ignoring his thigh, even though it was really his femur that was broken.           (35)

Like the ancient Hebrews, but unlike the Romans, the Germans were content with one name, a name made of two syllables. We cannot call this name a "first" name, because there was no second one; and we cannot call it a "Christian" name, since the Germans were still heathens. Therefore we must call it a "given" name, or, for the present, just a "name." The Germanic system of name-giving seems to have been derived from Indo-European practices, for similar systems were used by the Celts and Greeks. Some scholars think this system was limited to the Celts, Greeks, and Germans; others think that it was once universal among the Indo-Europeans but was later discarded by many of the tribes after their dispersal. For our purpose such a dispute is irrelevant: it is enough to know that the ancient Germans, like the Celts and Greeks, chose names composed of two roots. For example, the Greek name Thrasybulos combines the concepts "brave" and "counsel," just as the German name Conrad does. The concepts, but not the Indo-European roots, were identical.           (36)

The roots used in primitive Germanic names were general concepts. For example, *\*rik* (cognate with Latin *rex* and *regnum*) could mean either "rule" or "ruler," as could the root *\*wald* (cognate with English "wield"). Likewise, *\*athel* could mean "noble," "nobility" or "nobleman." The asterisks (\*) in the above examples signify that the words have not been preserved in their given form but have merely been reconstructed or postulated from later linguistic evidence. A few Germanic name-roots survived intact long enough to be recorded more or less unchanged, for example, *\*athel* and *\*hrotho* appeared in many Anglo-Saxon names such as Aethelraed the Unready, king of Wessex, Aethelstan, king of Mercia, and Hrothgar, the lord and kinsman of Beowulf.           (37)

If these last three names had been preserved in southern Germany instead of in England, they would have appeared as *Edelrat, Edelstein,* and *Ruediger.* To understand these changes we must consider the High German sound shift, a second sound shift that followed the first almost a millenium later. This sound shift, also described by the Grimm brothers, distinguished the South German dialects from all the other Germanic languages. This High German sound shift, which altered most consonants, began soon after the Alemanni and Bavarians reached the Alps following the collapse of the Roman Empire.

(38)

The High German soundshift gradually spread northward into central Germany and affected standard German, while the North Germans clung to the unshifted consonants of the other Germanic languages such as Dutch and English. Thus the German dialects were divided into High German in the south and Low German in the north. Many of the names we shall discuss were North German and were therefore unaffected by the High German sound shift. On the other hand, with the increase of literacy and the spread of the High German written standard language into northern Germany, many Low German names have taken on standard spelling. For example, the spellings of Kock, Groote, and Schaper have often become Koch, Grosse, and Schaefer; and the names are pronounced accordingly.

(39)

Once a gentleman named Holthusen asked me the meaning of his name, and I explained that it meant "forest house," being the Low German form of Holtzhausen. He was highly indignant when I said "Low German" and assured me that his people had been perfectly respectable. What he did not understand was that "High German" refers to the southern highlands of Germany, while "Low German" refers to the low coastal plain in the north. Boats go down the Rhine in a northwesterly direction from Basel to Rotterdam and down the Elbe in a northwesterly direction from Dresden to Hamburg. Because maps often hang on walls with north at the top, we say "up north" and "down south," just as the Germans say "up in Schleswig" (*oben in Schleswig*) and "down in Bavaria" (*unten in Bayern*), so it is sometimes hard to remember that High Germany is in the south and Low Germany is in the north.

(40)

Of greatest interest to us in the High German sound shift are the changes of the new voiceless stops $p$ and $t$ (when initial) into the voiceless affricates $pf$ and $ts$ (written $z$) and the changes of $p$, $t$, and $k$ (when medial or final) into $f$, $s$, and $ch$ (pronounced as in Bach). Also important were the changes of the voiced stops *b*, *d*, and *g* to the voiceless stops *p*, *t*, and *k*. Because of this shift, the English words "plow," "hope," "toe," "water," and "break" are cognate with German *Pflug, hoffen, Zeh, Wasser*, and *brechen*; and English "door" is cognate with the High German word *Tor*. At the end of a syllable *k* was shifted to *ch* in all dialects; but at the beginning of a syllable it was shifted only in Switzerland, and there only in pronunciation, not in spelling, so it did not change the standard spelling of names beginning with *k*. As a result, "King" and *Koenig* are cognates, whereas in the Germanic root *\*rik* the final *k* was shifted in High German to *ch* (*rich*). This shift of *k* explains the different endings of English "book" and German *Buch*. The *b* and *g* shifted only in the Upper German dialects of the far south, where they are reflected in variants such as Pichler-Buehler and Kugel-Gugel. (41)

Simultaneously with the sound shift in some areas, and soon thereafter in others, the *h* was dropped before *l* and *r*, as it was also in English. Likewise, *w* was dropped before *r* as in English pronunciation, but not in spelling (Cf. "wretch" and *Recke*). Starting in the south a short time later was the change of *th* to *d* (*thing* became *ding*). The *th* in modern German names should always be pronounced as *t* because the *h* in the digraph *th* was introduced into spelling in the sixteenth and seventeenth centuries in an attempt to gain elegance, since *th* appeared in many words taken from the Greek via Latin. Therefore the *h* should be ignored in pronouncing German names like Walther and Goethe. (42)

Soon after the High German sound shift *sl*, *sm*, *sn*, and *sw* became *schl*, *schm*, *schn*, and *schw* so that *schlecht, schmal, schnee,* and *schwarz* are cognate with "slight," "small," "snow," and "swart." *St* and *sp* also acquired the *sh* sound, but it is not indicated in the spelling. By chance, many German-American names reverted to the older Germanic pronunciation through the influence of English, which had not gone through the High German sound shift. For example, Schwartz sometimes became Swarts, Schnell sometimes became Snell, and Stein was pronounced as Stein instead of as "Schtein." There were, of course, also changes in many vowels; but they played a lesser role in identifying names.

Both the Germanic sound shift and the High German sound shift were infinitely complicated, with many apparent exceptions, most of which were explained by the Danish philologist Karl Verner. The simplified account given here serves only to clarify those changes that will help explain the present forms of German names. For example, as a result of the High German sound shift there are many pairs of German names that are similar except that one of them (or its roots) was altered by the sound shift, while the other was not. Examples are the Low German names Dormann, Dierdorp, and Timmermann as opposed to the High German names Thormann, Tierdorf, and Zimmermann. (43)

It would be impossible, and certainly unrewarding, to try to reproduce all names under discussion in the exact form they had at a given date in their given area, because the changes took place at different times in different places. We will therefore give all German names in their classical Middle High German form, the form in which they appeared in South German literature from the eleventh through the thirteenth centuries. As a result of the High German sound shift, the Proto-Germanic roots *athel, *hari, *hrotho, *rik, and *theod became edel, her, ruod, rich, and diet. Therefore *Hludowics became Ludwig, *Hrothgar became Ruedeger, Hrothoberacht became Ruoprecht, Theodoric became Dietrich, and Hariman became Herman. (44)

Now that we have explained the origin of the roots used in German names, we might list some of them. It was mentioned that the Germans were a warlike people. Consequently, it is not surprising that their names often referred to war, weapons, and martial virtues, as well as to armies, victory, protection, and domination or rule. It is significant that the common German words Schwert (sword), Schild (shield), and Speer (spear), which were non-Indo-European, do not appear in old Germanic names. This confirms the theory that the old Germanic names were already composed in Indo-European times, before the Germans borrowed these three words, along with many maritime terms, from non-Indo-European neighbors. (45)

Among the name-roots designating battle were badu, gund, hadu, hilti, not, and wic, while wal designated a battleground. Among weapons we find bart (battle ax), bil, brand, and ecke (sword), *ger* (spear), *gies, giesel* and *ort* (point of spear or sword), *grim* (mask, helmet), *helm* (helmet), and *lind* and *rand* (shield). Among martial virtues we find *bald* (bold), *hart* (strong), *kuni* (brave), *mut* (courage), *neid* (hate), and *wille* (determination). *Macht* and *Megin* both meant "power" (as in "might and main"), as did *ellen* and *kraft*. *Diet* meant the folk, therefore Dietrich was the ruler of the folk, while Dietmar was famous among the people and *Dietbald* was brave among the people. *Liut*, related to English "liege," meant retinue and *volk* meant "people"; but, because all peoples were armed, *volk* also signified "army," as did *her*. It is to be noted that the ancient Germanic word for "folk" was the source of the Russian word *polk*, meaning "regiment."                                                          (46)

*Victory* was expressed by *sieg*, protection by *burg, fried, wart*, and *wern*, and guardianship by *mund*, while mastery or rule was suggested by *wald* and *rich*. Pride in possessions is suggested by *arbi* (inheritance), *od* (treasure) and *uodal* (inherited lands). Since fame, the purpose of life, was best won on the battlefield, we find the roots *hruod* (illustrious), *mar* (renowned), *brecht* (bright), and *luod* (loud or illustrious). *Regin* (mind, intelligence) and *rat* (both council and counsel) can be classed as military terms, since councils were usually councils of war. Among the few peaceful concepts we find E *(law), fruot* (wise), *hein* (home), *hold* (loyal to one's lord, cognate with "beholden"), *trut* (dear), *hug* (mind), and *win* (friend); and we also find *ans* and *god* (god) and *alb* or *alf* (elf).          (47)

Certain predatory animals and birds also deserved namesakes: *ar* or *arn* (eagle), *ram* and *hraben* (raven), *ber* (bear), *wolf* (wolf), and *lint* (dragon). Thus we get Arnold (*arn* + *hold*), Wolfram (*wolf* + *hraben*), Bermut (*ber* + *mut*). The wild boar (*ebur*), even though not predatory, was extremely brave and therefore offered the root found in Eberhart and many other names. Strangely, the harmless little hedgehog, the *igel*, also furnished the root in Igelhart, perhaps because of some shamanistic affinity, as was the case of *hirsch* (hart). Igelhart could, to be sure, derive from *igel* (hedgehog) and *hart* (stag), combining two creatures as are found in the names Wolfram (wolf + raven) and Arnolf (eagle + raven), but this is unlikely. The swan, although inoffensive, furnished the name-root *swan*, but at first only for women, as in Swanhild. The non-European lion, when finally introduced by the Bible and literature, and perhaps by royal menageries, supplied the first root in Leonhart, probably formed through analogy with Bernhart and Wolfhart. (48)

From the small sample of name-roots listed above we can make innumerable compounds, such as Albwin, Ansgar, Anshelm (St. Anselmus), Baldwin, Dietbald, Dietmar, Friedrich, Gunther, Hadubrand, Helmbrecht, Helmut, Heribrand, Hildebrand, Luther, Meinhart, Reinhart, Siegfried, Sigismund, Volker, Walther, Wernher, Willebald, and many more. Most of these roots could occupy either the first or the second place in the compound, for example, we find both Friedgund and Gundfried and Gundhild and Hildegunde. However, some, like *diet*, *edel*, and *sieg* could only occupy the first place, while some, like *mund* (guardianship), could only occupy the second. As a result, we find Siegmund and Dietrich but not Mundsieg or Richdiet. Two popular roots, *engel* and *land*, now mean "angel" and "land." If Engelhart was a pre-Christian name, then *engel* must have had another meaning, perhaps the tribal name "Angle." In Lambrecht *(landberacht)* and Roland *(Hrodoland)*, the root *land* must have had some meaning other than "land," perhaps "brave," or else it may have been corrupted from *nand* (risk). (49)

Not only men, but also women, bore warlike names, such as Gertraut (spear + beloved), Gerwig (spear + battle), Gundhilt (battle + battle), Hildegunde (battle + battle), Kriemhild (helmet + battle), Kunigunde (brave + battle), and Waltraut (battlefield + beloved). To be sure, Germanic women did not actually fight; but in his *Germania* Tacitus tells us how the women accompanied their men into battle and acted as cheer leaders, war being the chief sport of the time. Besides that, women could transmit warlike virtues to their sons through their names; for, as we have seen, names exerted a power of their own. Today most Germans assume that Rosamund and Roselind mean Rosemouth and Rosegentle; but, in actuality, they are composed of the root *hros* (warhorse) combined with *mund* (guardianship) and *lind* (dragon or shield). The name Roswitha is now usually interpreted as Rosewhite, whereas it really consisted of *hrodo* (famous) and *switha* (swift, brave). A medieval dramatist nun by that name was aware of the true meaning, for she called herself *Clamor Validus*. Familiar with Latin, the clerics assumed that Rosamunda came from *rosa munda* (pure rose) and referred to the Virgin Mary. We will, however, devote little time to feminine names because this study is concerned only with surnames, which patriarchal societies generally derive from male progenitors. Nevertheless, some feminine names and words did produce place names, which, in turn, formed surnames. For example, the Virgin Mary gave the city name Marienborn (Mary's spring), which in turn gave the surname Marienborner; and the Nonnengasse (convent alley) gave the surnames Nonngasser and Nunnengasse.                    (50)

In ancient days the two roots of an Indo-European name had usually reflected some mental association as in Adelbrecht (illustrious through birth), Wolfhart (as strong as a wolf), Sigismund (guardianship resulting from victory), and Dietrich (ruler of the people). In some cases the root *fried* would seem to contradict its partner, for example in Gundfried (battle peace) and Friedgund (peace battle). However, we should remember that war was the normal state: as Tacitus put it, a nation not at war was stagnating. Therefore we should not think that *\*frithu* (the earlier form of *fried*) had anything in common with the Christian concept of peace, rather it meant "protection" and even "defensive alliance." Consequently, Gundfried would suggest "security won through battle" and Friedrich would suggest "ruler of an alliance." Today most people think that a *Friedhof* (cemetery) is a place of peace, but actually it is a "protected yard," the German word *fried* in this context meaning "walled," as in *bergfried* (belfry). When I was a graduate student in Zurich, I took a room at a pension called the Friedegg (pronounced freet eck and meaning walled field). The other Americans knew it only as the Fried Egg.                    (51)

Whereas the name roots had once been meaningfully combined, in time the roots were chosen with no thought of logical connection. Each family had its favorite roots, which it attached at random to other roots, perhaps to those featured by the family with whom it was being allied through marriage. If a man named Wolfhart married a woman named Gertraut, they might name their son Wolfger, even though wolves do not use spears. Likewise, we find names like Arnolf (eagle + wolf) and Wolfram (wolf + raven), even though these creatures had

different virtues. Also, there were tautologies like Richwald (ruler + ruler) and Hildegunde (battle + battle). Eventually the roots were combined entirely mechanically. Some of the old Germanic roots eventually coalesced; both Gerwalt (spear + rule) and Gerhold (spear + loyal) became Gerold.          (52)
While Germanic names originally consisted of two roots, they were often shortened. For example, Adolf, Arnold, Bernhard, Gerhard, and Konrad could be shortened to Alf, Anno or Arnd, Benno or Bernd, Gert, and Kurt or Kunz. Likewise, Dietrich, Eberhart, Rudolf, and Uodalrich could give Dirk, Ewert, Rolf, and Uozo. Often a shortened form could have derived from any one of several longer forms: Otto might come from Otfried, Otmar, or Otward; Brand could have represented Hildebrand, Hadubrand, or Heribrand; and Wolf could have derived from Wolfbrecht, Wolfhart, or Wolfram. Often the shortened form of a name provided compound names. For example, Benshoff (Bernhard's farm) was derived from Bernhard via Benno. Names like Arnsdorf and Wolfshausen could mean "eagle village" and "wolf's houses," but they more likely mean "Arno's village" and "Wolf's village," being named for the founders rather than for animals.          (53)
The shortened form was often a pet name (*Kosename*), yet it was officially valid even in the case of emperors. Surprisingly, Attila, the scourge of God, was known by a pet name, it being a diminutive of the Gothic word *Atta*, "father." After passing through the High German sound shift, it became the name Etzel, which has been brought to America as a surname. While Attila was a bogeyman in Western Europe, the Etzel of German legend was a generous overlord, whom it was an honor to serve, a sort of Arthur and Charlemagne combined. Pet names are often so far removed from their base forms as to be unrecognizable. One could hardly guess that Peg is a pet name from Margaret or that Ted and Teddy are pet names from either Edward or Theodore. Such metamorphoses did not occur in one fell swoop. Margaret was shortened to Marg, Marg became Meg, and then Meg became Peg. Similar steps occurred in forming pet names like Theiss from Matthias (via Thiass and Thiess) and Bartel from Bartholomaeus. In time these pet names became surnames. Sometimes the shortened form is not immediately recognizable because it went back to an earlier

form of the name. The English name Hank and the German name Heink do not look like Henry and Heinrich, but they do look somewhat like the earlier forms Henrik and Heinrik. Likewise, Utley scarcely resembles Ulrich, whereas the older form Utli does have something in common with *Uod* in the older form *Uodalrich*.                              (54)

The very terms "pet name" and "shortened form" must be used advisedly. When one says Bill instead of William, it may show affection, but it may also show mere laziness, in which case it is actually only a shortened form. It would be difficult to ascertain the precise nature and degree of affection expressed by the names in the well-known lines, "Father calls me William, Mother calls me Will, Sister calls me Willie, but the fellows call me Bill." Heintzelein can hardly be called a "shortened" form of Heinrich. In my childhood gang there was a boy named John, but we called him Johnny with the Nubbin on the End of his Nose "for short." In the early stages of this book I used the term "pet name," but gradually I replaced it with the symbol < , meaning "derived from," thus leaving it to the reader to decide whether or not the shortened form indicated affection. It will be noted that pet names are often diminutives: a small man may refer to his wife as "the little woman" (*die Kleine*), where the diminutive denotes endearment, not stature. In German the main diminutives are *ke*, *kin*, and *je* in the far north, *chen* and *gen* in the central regions, *lein* and *le* in the south, and *li* in Switzerland.                              (55)

As the Roman Empire crumbled in the fifth and sixth centuries and the northern barbarians invaded Britain, Gaul, Spain, and Italy, they brought their names with them to the lands they conquered. The names of the invaders, as the ruling class, were soon adopted by many of the conquered populaces, with dire results for the names. Most of all, the Romanized Celts in France could not master the harsh consonants of the invaders' names and dropped many of them. Thus Henrik became Henri, Theodoric became Thierry, and Willihalm became Guillaume. Most of the names that we consider typically French today were once Germanic: Albert (Athalbrecht), Arnaud (Arnhold), Bertram (Berachtram), Gautier (Walthari), Louis (Hludowics), Renault (Reginwald), Robert (Hrothoberacht), Roger (Hrothgar), Roland (Hrotholand), and Thibault (Dietbald).

The same held for Italy, where we find Alberto, Arnoldo, Enrico, Gualtieri, Guido (Wido), Gulielmo, Leonardo (Leonhard), Ludovigo, Orlando, Ottone (Otto), Rinaldo (Reginwald), Ruggiero (Hrothogar), Umberto (Hunberacht or Helmbrecht), and a host of others. In Spain, the most common names, such as Alfonso (*athel* + *fons*, noble + ready) and Hernandez (*fardi* + *nantha*, journey + risk) were inherited from the Gothic invaders. (56)

After the Norman invasion of England in 1066, most Anglo-Saxon names (still clearly Germanic) were replaced by French cognates. These were no longer so clearly Germanic as they had been after being introduced into Gaul by the Frankish invaders. Instead of Hrothgar, Athelbrecht, and Reginwald, we therefore find Roger, Albert, and Reynold. (57)

# CHAPTER TWO

## Surnames - Their Need and Origin

As the population increased after the migrations, it became necessary to distinguish between the various individuals in the community who shared a common name. This could be done, among other ways, by reference to a person's parentage, his residence, a terrain or topographical feature near his dwelling, his profession, his employer, his appearance, or his behavior.

(58)

In Scandinavia, a man was often designated as the son of his father. Niel, the son of Lars, would be called Niel Larson, but his son Peer would be Peer Nielson, not Peer Larson. The same system of patronymics was once common in Germany. Arnold's son Berthold might have been designated Arnolds Berthold or Berthold Arnolds, just as Hinrich's son Hans might have been called Hans Hinrichs or Hans Hinrichssen. In the case of names like Arnolds and Hinrichs, the s eventually became a fixed part of the name and no longer suggested first generation descent. In other words, Heinz Hinrichs may have been the son of Hinrichs and the grandson of Hinrich, just as Felix Mendelssohn was the son of Mendelssohn, not of Mendel. Names sometimes indicated employment rather than descent, as in the case of the ecclesiastical names Pabst, Bischof, and Moench. The same was sometimes true of other names that could be mistaken for patronymics. While Hubers Hans, or Hans Huber, was probably Huber's son, he might also have been Huber's hired hand, as everyone in the village would know. (59)

As family names became fixed, Huber's Hans may have adopted the surname Huber and transmitted it to his children, even if they served other families. A similar phenomenon occurred in the American South after emancipation. The slaves had no surnames; they were known as "the Pinckney's Jim" or "the Middleton's Jupiter." As freedmen, these two may have become Jim Pinckney and Jupiter Middleton, unless they preferred to choose the names of neighboring planters. The surname Hubers could possibly come from the place name Hubers, a shortened form for Hubershof (Huber's farm). Although patronymics were the rule, there were a few cases of metronymics, or surnames from the mother, perhaps from a widow or an unwed mother. Examples are Elsohn (Else's son), Figge (Sophia's son), Grett (Margaretha's son), and Anneshansli (Anna's Hans). (60)

Noble families customarily assumed the name of their chief castle, as was the case of the Hapsburgs and Hohenzollerns. The owners of Wolkenstein Castle were the von Wolkensteins, or the Wolkensteiners. However, if they sold Wolkenstein Castle and moved elsewhere, they dropped their old appellative and took on the name of their new seat. Even humble people could sometimes be identified by the names of their residences: for example, the Josef who lived in Straatmannshaus was sometimes called Josef Straatmann, but only as long as he lived there. If he sold the house, the buyer received the name Straatmann along with the house. Already in the thirteenth century a German poet named Heinrich Hessler explained that Heinrich was his right name and that Hessler was the name of his house. It is understandable that the inventor of moveable type wished to be known by the name of his house, Gutenberg (good mountain), rather than by his true name, Gensfleisch (goose flesh). (61)

The name of the house sometimes appeared on a shield in front of the house with an illustration for the benefit of illiterates. These illustrations often had religious significance: not only the angel but also the eagle, lion, lamb, and ox had religious significance, they being the creatures that accompanied the four Evangelists in church art. If the house sign hung before a business establishment, it often designated the wares sold or the services rendered; and this explains many German names such as Fisch (fish) or Tuchscherer (cloth shearer). (62)

Sometimes a man was named for his place of business. If a tavern were called *zum Goldenen Loewen* (to the Golden Lion), *zum Rothen Hirsch* (to the Red Stag), or *zum Schwarzen Adler* (to the Black Eagle), the proprietor might have been called Loewe, Hirsch, or Adler. Regardless of the name of the establishment, the proprietor (*Wirt*) might be called Wirt or Wirth, or else Krug, Krueger, or Krieger, since the word *Krug* (pitcher) often designated a pub. Regardless of what the dictionary might say about the word *Krieger*, the name Krieger did not designate a soldier. Since taverners hung out a sprig of greenery to announce the arrival of new wine, they might be called Zweig (branch), or Busch (bush). According to popular wisdom, such advertisement should be unnecessary because "good wine needs no bush."                                                                    (63)

Many years ago a German colleague of mine named Busch, seeing my interest in names, suggested that I run an advertisement in the *New York Times* offering to interpret names. I did so; and the first request I received was from a widow named Busch. Suspecting that she might not care to have had a husband descended from tavern keepers, I answered that the name Busch could be either the sprig hanging in front of a tavern or else the *Helmbusch*, or crest on a knight's helmet. It is easy to guess which interpretation she preferred.          (64)

The words *Haus* (house) and *Haeuser* (the occupant of a house) provided many names. Since most people lived in houses, these simple words would have had little power of differentiation, so we can assume that the present names Haus, Haeuser, and Heuser are usually shortened forms of compounds such as Althaus (old house), Neuhaus (new house), or Scheraus (house where cloth or sheep are sheared). The American forester family Weyerhaeuser once lived in a house by a *Weiher* or fish pond (from Latin *vivarium*). Whereas the word *Haeuser* is now the plural of *Haus*, it used to denote the occupant, not the plural, of *Haus*. The plural used to be the same as the singular (*hus*), as is indicated by dative plural place names like Holthusen, Schaffhausen (sheep houses) and Niederhausen (lower houses). If one dwelled on a road, one might be called Gass, Gassner, or Gessner, or else Bahn or some name ending in *weg*.          (65)

In parts of Germany *aeu* and *eu* are pronounced like English "eye" (remember the Tannenbaum, a branch of which *freut* [gives joy] even in winter when it *schneit* [snows]). Therefore Haeuser is often pronounced Hizer, as in the case of James Lighthizer (from Leithaeuser), a county executive in Maryland, and also in the name Anhaeuserbusch, which recalls the ditty:

A boy fell off Anhaeuserbusch
And tore his pants to Schlitz.
He rose a sad Budweiser boy.
Pabst yes and Pabst no.

The baseball player Orel Hershiser's name derived from Hirschhaeuser, or "stag houses." Since the American name

Rukeyser would make no sense if divided into *ru* and *keyser*, it must have been Ruckheyser, meaning the occupant of a house on a ridge. (66)

As in the case of Rukeyser, families were often designated by the terrain features near which they lived, such as hills, dales, mountains, valleys, fields, and forests. If a Johann lived near a *buehl* (hill), he might be called Johann Buehl, or Buehler (and in America Beeler or Bealer). Or if, as was usually the case, the hill was more precisely defined, such as Kraehbuehl (crow hill), then the resulting name would be Kraehbuehl (in America, Craybill, Greybill, and some forty other forms). If a man lived at, but not on, the *Buehl*, he might be called Ambuehl (in America, also Ample). Another kind of hill is a *kofel*, a sort of monticule or projection jutting up from the slope of a mountain, which might give a man living on it the name of Kofler. If there were two such chimney-like projections, an upper one (*Oberkofel*) and a lower one (*Unterkofel*), they might furnish the names Oberkofler and Unterkofler or Oberkaufer and Unterkaufer. (67)

Far more numerous, of course, are names derived from *berg*, the commonest name for mountain. In addition to many families named Berg and Berger, there were far more named for specific mountains, such as Oberberg, Unterberg, Gruenberg, Silberberg, Koenigsberg, Heidelberg, and hundreds of others. In Switzerland, Austria, and Bavaria, where there are many mountains, names in *berg* and *berger* are especially frequent. The peak of the mountain was the *Horn*, as in Berghorn and Matterhorn, and the ridge was the *kamm* (comb) or the *ruecken* (back). (68)

The surnames based on terrain features or place names had at first been preceded by the preposition *von*, as in von Oberberg; but in time the preposition was dropped in most of Germany by all but the nobility and became a sign of rank. Commoners were satisfied with the name Oberberg or Oberberger. Nevertheless, some people, especially in Switzerland and along the Netherlands border, retained the *von* with no pretensions to nobility, as in the case of Von der Weit and Vonholt. Other prepositions, like *in* and *zu* were also usually dropped, though they occasionally remain as in Indorf and Inhoff. In dem Winkel (in the wooded valley) became Winkel or Winkler, and zem Stege (at the sty) became Steg or Steger. The name Austermuehle means "out of the mill," not "Oyster Mill." (69)

Sometimes the preposition was not entirely lost, as when zum Eichelsweg (at the acorn path) became Meichelsweg and when in den Eichen (in the oaks) became Neichen (just as in English "a nadder" became "an adder" and "an ickname" became "a nickname"). In the case of Admiral Zumwald the preposition has remained, as it has also in the names Vomberg (from the mountain) and Vormwald (before the forest). The preposition and article have regularly remained in Dutch names like Vandergrift, Vanderbilt, and van der Ren. Similar phenomena appear in English names like Attenborough and Atterbury, both meaning "at the borough." (70)

Since most flat lands in Germany are cultivated, the forests are largely on mountain ranges. As a result, the word *wald* (forest) usually designates a mountain range, as is the case of the Schwarzwald (Black Forest), Boehmerwald (Bohemian Forest), and Thueringer Wald (Thuringian Forest). In and near Austria a steep slope is a *Leite*, a word giving the names Leite, Leitner (Lightner in America), Hangleitner, etc. This name has an exact English equivalent in the name Banker, which denotes not a financier but a man who lives on a bank or slope. A person occupying a house on a *Leite* would be a Leithaeuser (the previously mentioned Lighthizer). Other names for slopes are *Fuhr, Gaeh, Gand, Halde, Ruetsche, Schief, Schrudde,* and *Stechen.* A man residing on or near a *Stade* (landing) might be called Stade, just as a man living near a bridge might be called Brueckner and a man living near a church might be called Kircher or Kirchner. (71)

There are relatively few name roots denoting forests.The most frequent is the root *wald* (cognate with English "wold" as in the Cotswolds). While *wald* always means "forest" in later names like Waldhausen, it must be differentiated from the older root *wald* meaning "rule," as in Walther (rule + army). A low or scrubby forest was a *busch,* as in Buschmann or Buschkirch (dweller or church in the low woods). A *horst* (cognate with the place-name root *hurst* in Lakehurst and Pinehurst) was a general word for a small forest or grove, whereas now it suggests an aerie or even a small military airbase, as in

*Fliegerhorst.* A *hain* or *hein* was a grove, as in Hainmueller and
Heindorf.                                                              (72)

A rocky summit or crag was a *Stein* (stone), which was a good
position for a castle, so we find castles with names like Steinfels
(stone cliff), Steinburg (stone castle), and Altenstein (old mountain). In most names of this kind the root *stein* refers to a
mountain, and therefore it is so translated in our appended list
even though, in some cases, the root *stein* could have referred
to the castle itself, which was inevitably built of stone. Logic
suggests that *Steinberg* means "stone mountain," whereas
*Bergstein* means "mountain rock." A man dwelling on or near a
*Stein* might be named Stein or Steiner (in America often Stine,
Stone, and Stoner). Whereas the ancient German fortress had
been made of wood, the medieval castle (*burg*) was always of
stone.                                                                (73)

In the name Steinert the last consonant is not part of the root:
it is merely an excrescent *t*, that is, a *t* that formed to interrupt
the *r*, which was still trilled in Germany at the time surnames
were being introduced. In some names the root *stein* does not
designate a cliff or crag, but merely a mineral substance, as in
Steinhauer (stone carver) and *Edelstein* (noble stone, jewel).
Other terms for hills, mountains, peaks, and ridges are *Boll,
Brink, Gipfel, Huebel, Huegel, Kamm, Knoll, Kopf, Kuppe, Nase,*
and *Stauf.*                                                          (74)

This might be an appropriate time to explain why there is so
often a dative ending on the adjective describing a terrain
feature, such as the *en* suffixed to the *alt* in the name Altenstein. This goes back to the previously mentioned days when
place names were still preceded by a preposition, as was
formerly the case in English tavern names such as "To the Red
Rose." Originally, one would have said "at the old stone" (*zum
alten stein* or *am alten stein*); and in both cases the place name
would end up as Altenstein. The same would hold of Breitenbach (*zum breiten bach,* "at the broad brook") and Neuemburg
(*zur neuen burg,* "at the new castle.")                              (75)

Names were suggested not only by hills and mountains, but
also by valleys, the most frequent root being the *Tal* (formerly
*Thal*) which is found in Rosenthal, Lilienthal, and Thalmann.
In Alpine regions a bowl-like valley is a *gruob*, and a man
dwelling in one might be dubbed Gruber. A narrow gorge is a

*Schlund,* so the Heinrich living in or near one may have been called Heinrich Schlund. (76)

People were often designated by the stream or creek on which they lived. As in the case of the name Berg, the name Bach (brook) was often a shortened form of a compound name. The appended list of names contains scores of compounds containing *bach,* examples being Auerbach, Bacher, Bachmann, and Rauschbach. In Pennsylvania the name Bach and its compounds are often written as Baugh because the English scribes knew the sound *ch* only in Scots names. These still retained the sound and indicated it with *gh,* whereas the sound had long since ceased in English and survived only in the archaic spelling of words like "through" and "though." Unfortunately, the first syllable of these Pennsylvania names with *baugh* are often corrupted beyond recognition. In Pennsylvania the names Bach and Bacher also appear as Pack and Packer. (77)

A *Bach* is sometimes larger than a brook: one would translate *Forellenbach* as "trout stream," rather than as "trout brook," just as a *Rauschbach* would be a "rushing stream" rather than a "rushing brook." An *Altmuehlbach* would surely be an "old mill stream" rather than an "old mill brook." In personal names, the ending *bach* was practically interchangeable with *becker.* A family living on the Winsbach could call itself either Winsbach or Winsbeker. (As we shall see, when standing alone the name Becker most often meant a baker.) The foot-crossing through a brook was a *furt* or *fort,* as in Frankfurt. (78)

The word *Ach,* which is cognate with Latin *aqua* (water) and designates a river, is found in many place names such as Charlemagne's capital Aachen and in Achebach and Anderach. This ending *ach* has now coalesced with the ending *ach* from *achi* (terrain) as in Steinach (stone terrain) and Dornach (thorny area) and also with *ach* from Latin *acum* (estate) as in Breisach and Andernach. Other words for streams are *born* and *bronn,* both of which appear in American names such as Aalborn (eel stream) and Bornemann (stream man). The word *brunnen,* which designated either a spring or a well, is found in the names Brunner and Brunnholtz. Many people took the name of the river near which they resided, as in the case of Johannes Tauber and Rembrandt van Ryn. An island in a river

is a *Werde* (also written Wert and Woerth), which is cognate
with the English root *worth*.                                    (79)
Although Germany has been well drained for the last few
centuries, it was, as Tacitus reported, a land of vast swamps. As
a result we find many name-roots referring to marshes, bogs,
and swamps such as *Bruehl, Bruch, Lache, Mar, Mies, Moor,
Moos, Ohl, Pfutze, Pfuhl, Schlade, Schlier, Siech, Seifen, Struth,*
and *Sutte.* Unfortunately, it is not possible to translate names
containing these roots precisely without knowing from which
areas their bearers came. For example, the word *bruch* (in Low
German spelled *brock, broek,* and *brook,* and cognate with
English "brook" and "brake") had various meanings, but it
usually meant a damp clearing in a swampy forest. Since that
definition is too cumbersome, we will translate it as "brake" as
in "canebrake." The same name, Bruch, can also designate a
quarry. The root *mar* meaning "swamp," as in Marbach and
Marburg, should not be confused with the root *mar* meaning
"famous," as found in Dietmar and Marbold. It is to be remem-
bered that a surname like Marbach may commemorate a place
that had long been drained before the name was assumed.(80)
   A marsh or bog is often indicated by a root meaning reeds or
bullrushes, as in the case of *riet* and *reth* in Riet and Rethmeyer. The concept of "marsh mountain" sounds contradictory,
yet we find it expressed by the names Hallenberg, Kellenberg,
Marberg, Mosberg, Morsberger, Moersberger and many more.
The name suggests a hill rising out of a marsh or swamp, as is
expressed by our Southern word "hammock" (for hummock).
However, in some areas there are actually marshes (*moor*) on
the tops of mountains, as in the Sauerland Mountains of
Westphalia. The word *mor* should not be confused with English
"moor," which usually denotes a dry heath, which in German is
a *Heide.*                                                         (81)
   To drain the many marshes, one had to dig many ditches and
build many dams and dikes (*dam, dick, diek*). The High German
cognate *Teich* means not the dike but the pond behind it, or any
pond. A *lache* can be a pond as well as a bog, and a *fizer* or
*fuetze* (from Latin *puteus*) could be either a pond or a puddle. A
*See* is not a sea, but a lake. In marshy areas the word *Berg* is
only relative. In Alpine regions it designates a sizeable pile of
rocks and earth, but on the North German coastal plain it

might be more modest, as in the case of Koenigsberg and Wittenberg. Similarly the root *brink* is translated here as "hill," while it may mean an area in a marsh elevated just enough to remain dry and arable. (82)

A large number of surnames may be based on river names even if they have other meanings as well. For example, the name Tauber could suggest the raiser or seller of pigeons, but it may also designate a dweller on the River Tauber. Like many other rivers in western and southern Germany, the Tauber may have derived its name from a Celtic word. Just as most American rivers have Indian rather than European names, many German rivers have pre-Germanic names, mostly Celtic, some of which, in turn, derived from earlier Ligurian names. The Germanic invaders learned the names of the streams, swamps, hills, etc. from the Celtic inhabitants of the areas they occupied, but they did not understand their meanings. Therefore they added the words for stream, swamp, and hill to the native name. This gave forms like *albach*, *ascbach*, and *erbach*, which were eventually folk-etymologized into Allenbach (eel brook), Eschbach (ash tree brook), and Erlbach (alder brook). Of course, some brooks named Allenbach, Eschbach, and Erlbach may have first been named by German-speaking people and therefore not be a case of folk-etymology. (83)

Many names were based on words for fields or pastures. The words *Acker* and *Feld* (field) supplied many American names such as Acker, Ackers, and Ackerman, as well as Feld, Felder, Feldman, and Rheinfelder. Low land, usually lying along a body of water, was an *au*, as in Reichenau on Lake Constance and also in the surnames Aumann and Aumueller. A man living on an *au* was an *auer*, as in Reitenauer and Rheinauer. Another word for meadow was *Wiese*, and a man living on it was a Wiessner or a Wiesmann. Only in Switzerland does one find *matt* (cognate with English mead and meadow), which designated a meadow that was mowed and is found in the surname Durrenmatt. The word *Weide* denoted a pasture, as in the name Fuellenweide (foals meadow); and so did the word *Anger*, as in names like Anger, Angermann, and Angermeyer. Smaller than a field is a *Garten* (garden), which may be a *Baumgarten* (orchard), two words that furnish many names such as Gaertner and Baumgaertner. If the field was fenced in, it gave names like Bantner, Bunde, and Painter.                                   (84)

One very common root is hard to define, namely, *eck* (corner), as in the previously mentioned *Friedegg*. Although the meaning "corner" is often acceptable, the root *eck* (or *egg*) often has a vague meaning of "place," as in the expression *in allen Ecken* (cf. "In every corner under the sun"), where no angle is implied. Therefore, it will be rendered as "place" in the following list. A man's name sometimes reflected the direction in which he lived from the major town, such as Nord (north), Nordhoff (northern farm), Ost (east), Ostberg (eastern mountain), Sudler (southerner), Sudhoff (southern farm), Westdorf (western village), and Westenfeld (western field).                          (85)

The reader is reminded that onomastics is not an exact science but sometimes requires an educated guess. While *eck* clearly means "corner" in the word *Eckstein*, the name Eckhof could mean either "corner farm," or more likely, "oak farm," the latter being more likely because of varients like Eichhof, Eickhof, and Eykhof. In the old Germanic name Eckhard, *eck* definitely means "sword."                                (86)

It will be noted that many surnames based on terrain features end with the agent suffix *er* (from Latin *arius*). This was especially common in South Germany, especially in Austria, with the result that, when the Salzburger Protestants were banished in 1731 and settled in East Prussia, the natives there assumed that all people whose names ended in *er* must be Salzburgers. Names like Acher, Bacher, Gruber, Kofler, and Steiner usually implied that the bearer was the proprietor of a farm at the said terrain feature: if he sold the farm, he left the name with it and took on the name of his new abode. The *er* ending often developed an excresent *T*, as in Bachert and Steinert.                                      (87)

In English it is easy to distinguish in writing between a terrain feature and a proper name, because only the latter is capitalized. For example, we say "he went to the white oaks," but also "he went to White Oaks." The difficulty in distinguishing between *Flurnamen* (terms for terrain features) and proper names is well illustrated in the boundary descriptions (*Markbeschreibungen*) found in medieval documents describing the lands donated to monasteries and other religious organizations. Most of these descriptions were written in Latin, only the terrain features and place names being left in German; the Wurzburg boundary descriptions are an exception, being written solely in German. In tracing the boundaries of the donated lands, these valuable documents name numerous terrain features that now appear in American names, including: *acha* (river), *berg* (mountain), *brunno* (spring), *buohha* (beeches), *clingo* (rapid stream), *furt* (ford), *gruoba* (round valley), *houc* (hill), *loh* (low forest), *ror* (reeds), *seo* (lake), *sol* (pond), *stein* (mountain), and *struot* (swamp). (88)

Rural people often derived their names from the kind of trees they lived among or near. If one of two Josefs lived near the oaks while the other lived near the linden, then the first might have been called Josef Eichner or Aichner and the second Josef Linde or Lindner. Similarly, a man named Erlenhaus must have lived in a house among the alders, while a man named Eschenbach may have lived on a brook with overhanging ash trees, if not one containing *Aesche* (graylings). A farmer living among the birches might be called Birkenmeyer, or just Birk, Birker, or Birkli. A man named Ulmer may have lived near the elms, unless possibly his forebears had come from the city of Ulm. The word *Tanne* (fir), which is found in names like Tannenbaum and Tanhoeffer, also appears as in Dannenbaum and Danhoeffer. Because firs are the dominant tree in some areas, the root sometime merely connotes a forest of any kind, not just of firs. Although the word *Kiefer* denotes both a pine tree and a jaw bone, the name Kieffer, as we shall see, most often meant a barrel maker. In the case of fruit trees and fruit, like Apfelbaum and Birnbaum, the name probably signifies the pertinent orchard owner or fruit dealer. Only a few names are derived from blossoms and flowers, such as Ahle (honey-suckle), Blum (flower), Eisenhut (monk's hood), and Mohn (poppy).(89)

When I was swimming on the University of Heidelberg swimming team shortly after the Berlin Olympics of 1936, the latest and most popular backstroke was the "Kieffer stroke." Seeing no connection with pine trees, we concluded that the stroke got its name from the fact that the swimmer had to thrust up his chin in order to lower his head and thereby raise his legs for a flutter kick. Years passed before I learned that the stroke was named for its innovator, an American swimmer at the '36 Olympics, who had inherited his name from some German barrel maker. And this leads us to names derived from professions.                                                                    (90)

The two oldest professions, for men, were hunting and fishing, which have given the names Jaeger and Fischer (Yeager and Fisher in America). In the late Middle Ages, when surnames were first being assumed, the fundamental profession was agriculture, which occupied about ninety-five percent of the population, rather than the five percent it occupies today in the developed nations. Consequently, many families were named Ackermann (field man), Bauer and Baumann (farmer), Felder or Feldmann (field man), and Pflug or Pflueger (plowman). The farmer's name might have derived from the nature of his farm. If he had one *huob* (hide of land), then he was a Huber; if he cultivated a *Schweighof* (cattle farm), then he was a Schweiger, Schwaiger, Schweighof, or Schweighofer (in America Swiger, Swiggert, or Swaggert, again with excrescent *t*). The name is not related to the noun *Schweiger*, meaning a silent man. A farmer might be named after the major crop he grew, such as Gerste (barley), Haffe (oats), or Weitzen (wheat). A husbandryman was often named for the kind of beast or fowl he raised: for example Gais (goat), Kalb (calf), Lamm (lamb), Ochs (ox), Stier (steer), Stehr (wether), and Ziege (goat) or Ante or Entemann (duck raiser), Huhn (chicken), and Gans or Goos (goose). As mentioned, all of these could have been house names with signs illustrating the occupant's profession.       (91)

Many families received their names from the word *Hoff*, which originally meant a farmyard. The ancient Germanic king, who was merely the foremost peasant of the kinship, also had a *Hof*, which was larger than the other *Bauernhoefe*. Eventually the king's court, or *Koenigshof*, became more elegant, with many a *Hofmann*, or courtier, in attendance, such as the *Hofmeister*, or steward of the royal household. These words are now spelled with one *f* to show that the *o* is long (as in "hope"); but they used to have double *f*, as still found in most American names derived from them, such as Althoff, Althoffer, Hoffmann, and Neuhoff.                                                                (92)

Perhaps the most common name designating a farmer was Meyer or Mayer, which also had many other meanings. The word derived from the Latin word *major domus*, or the keeper of the household. At first it referred to an important official who was more or less the business manager of the kingdom or the castle. Later it also referred to the bailiff who managed an estate or farm. Eventually it denoted any large farmer. Since this was the most usual meaning at the time that surnames were being formed, that is the way it is rendered in the appended list of names. A thirteenth-century Austrian tale called *Meier Helmbrecht* tells of a peasant lad who wished to become a knight but met a sad end. The story is misnamed, the lad is not a *meier:* his father, who is casually mentioned at the beginning, is the *meier*, a position the son would have inherited only at his father's death or retirement. (93)

The name Meyer was so common that it became the equivalent of *mann*, in fact, even interchangeable with it, so that a man could be called either Kuhlmann or Kuhlmeyer. In a few cases, the suffix *mann* still designated a vassal or follower. It will be seen that many Jews took the name Meyer, perhaps because of its similarity with the Hebrew name Meir, the name of a famous medieval scholar. Sometimes *mann* had no significance at all: Til and Tilmann were the same name, as were Litz and Litzmann, all of them having been derived from Dietrich and Ludwig. Likewise, *mann* and *er* were equivalent in names like Bacher--Bachmann, Felder--Feldmann, and Aicher--Aichmann. Names like Neumeyer and Neumann do not imply that the farmer was new but rather that he was the proprietor of the Neuhoff, or New Farm. Likewise, a Waldmeyer or Waldbauer did not have to live in a forest, he may have been the proprietor of the Waldhoff, which had once been in the woods before the surrounding forests had been cleared. Another word for farmer was *Hausmann*, literally "house man." That this word meant "farmer" was proved when the Dutch humanist Roelof Huysman latinized his name as Agricola. (94)

If a countryman owned no land, he may have been a *Schaefer* (shepherd), *Hirt* or *Hirte* (herdsman), or, in Switzerland, a *Senn*. Or else he many have been a *Holtzhacker* (woodcutter), *Kohlenbrenner* (charcoal burner), or *Aschenbrenner* (ash burner). There were many other professions open to landless people, such as finding wild honey (Zeidler) or gathering faggot (Ast). But this leads to the subject of more specialized trades. The ancient Germans lived in large family units, which provided most of their domestic needs. The non-warriors, meaning the women, children, elderly men, and serfs, not only farmed but also produced most of the goods and artifacts needed in their culture. Gradually, certain individuals became adept at certain crafts and supplied goods not only for their own family group but also for neighbors and even strangers, with the result that the craft became a full time profession. In this case the person practicing the profession often assumed the name of the trade he practiced. (95)

Because of constant warfare, smiths were essential for making and repairing weapons; and secret powers were ascribed to them so that the name Schmidt was held in awe. Later there were other smiths, such as the *Hufschmidt* (blacksmith), *Nagelschmidt* (nailsmith), *Blechschmidt* (sheet metal smith), and *Messerschmidt* (knife smith or cutler). As a consequence there were many names including the root *eisen* denoting the people who produced or sold iron. Among other surnames designating professions we find Brauer (brewer), Binder, Fassbinder, or Boettcher (cooper), Gerber (tanner), Reeper and Seiler (rope maker), Schneider and Schroeder (tailor), Schumacher (shoemaker), Wagner (wainwright), Weber (weaver), and Zimmermann (carpenter). In addition we find hosts and taverners (Wirth and Kruger) and musicians and entertainers such as Geiger (fiddler), Trommer (drummer), Harfner (harpist), Tanzer (dancer) and Gauckler (acrobat). (96)

As time passed, the trade could become more specialized, the brewer could be *Bierbrauer* (beer brewer) and the tanner could be a *Weissgerber* or a *Rotgerber*, depending on whether he cured white or red leather. This might be cut into straps or belts by a *Riemenschneider*, or strap cutter. As the weaver became more specialized, he might employ a *Scherer* or *Tuchscherer* (cloth shearer) to cut off the Irish pennants protruding from his cloth. While the tanner prepared raw hides, the *Kirschner* or *Kuerschner* (furrier) prepared fine furs. In all these cases the profession was originally in apposition to the person and required a definite article: Peter der Schuster (Peter the shoemaker), Hans der Schneider (Hans the tailor), etc. (97)

The ancient Germans built their houses of wood, as is proved by Germanic roots in American names like Ahle (awl), Hammer (hammer), and Naegel (nails). Other names from carpentry are

Drexler or Drechsler (turner), Tischler (cabinet maker), and Zimmermann (carpenter). The *l* in *Tischler* is not part of the root as it is in *Drechsler* and *Sattler* (saddler), which are composed of *Drechsel* and *Sattel* and the agent ending *er*. By error, names (and words) like Drechsler and Sattler were wrongfully divided into Drechs-ler and Satt-ler, thus causing people to think that *ler* was a functional agent-ending to be added to other roots like *tisch* (from Latin *discus*). The same faulty division was made of names like Gaert-ner (from *Garten*) and Oef-ner (from *Ofen*), thus producing a new agent-ending *ner*, which appeared in the recently mentioned names Lindner and Kirchner. As we have seen, the same phenomenon occurred in English when "a nadder" was erroneously divided into "an adder" and "an ickname" became "a nickname." (98)

Whereas most carpentry terms were of Germanic origin, the Germans did borrow the Roman word *scrinarius*, which designated a skilled joiner and later became the word and name Schreiner. In old Germanic sagas and ballads, the *burg* or borough was always made of wood, with the result that many feuds ended in a *Saalbrand* (hall fire), when the defenders chose to die in the flames rather than come out and surrender. After suffering raids from the Magyars in the tenth century, the Germans learned how to build stone fortifications like those of the Mediterranean and Arabic nations. (99)

Masonry was one of the most important skills learned from the Romans. The Latin word *murus* (wall) gave German *Mauer*, which in turn gave the word for a mason (*Maurer*), who might also be called a *Steinmetz*. (On the other hand, Hans Maurer may not have been a mason, he may have just lived on, or against, the city wall, in which case he would first have been called Hans auf der Mauer.) The Germans did, however, coin words from their own language for these imported skills: a stone cutter was a *Steinhauer* (stone hewer), a quarryman was a *Steinbrecher* (stone breaker), and a brickmaker was a *Steinbrenner* (stone burner). The ending *hauer* (cognate with English "to hew"), usually denoted someone who hacked or chopped, such as an Eisenhauer (metal cutter, armor smasher), Fleischhauer (butcher), and Holtzhauer (wood cutter); yet in some cases the basic meaning of to hack was lost and the ending *hauer* merely denoted a maker or manufacturer, as in Fadenhauer (thread-maker), Fasshauer (barrel maker), Haushauer (house builder), and Schildhauer, which means either the maker or breaker of shields.                                                                (100)

Upon occupying old Roman territory, the barbarian invaders learned many other skills they had never known or had practiced only crudely; and they often kept the Roman word, which in many cases went through the High German sound shift along with their native vocabulary. This was the case of the Latin word *cuparius* (barrel + maker), which gave the English name Cooper. Altered by the High German sound shift, it became Kuefer or, in southern dialects, Kiefer or Kieffer, as in the aforementioned "Kieffer stroke." When the Latin word *catila* (kettle) went through the soundshift, it came out as *kessel*, which gave the name Kessler (maker or repairer of kettles). Likewise, the Latin word *tegula* (tile) passed through the soundshift to become *Ziegel*, which gave the professional name Ziegler (tiler or brickmason).                              (101)

Perhaps Roman cooks were more skilled than German cooks, for the present German word for cook, *Koch*, is derived from Latin *coquus*, just as the name Pfister (baker) is derived from Latin *pistor*. The Germans also acquired two new words for "butcher": *Metzger* (from *matiarius*) and Metzler (from *macellarius*). A *Kellner* was the keeper of the wine cellar (*Keller*, from Latin *cellarium*). Tacitus tells us that the Germans had no wine, so they must have acquired all their art of viticulture from the Romans. The German word *Wein* was derived from Latin *vinum*, and the word *Winzer* (vintner) from *vinitor*, while the seller of wine, the *vinumcaupo*, ultimately gave the names Weinkauf and Weinkop. Tacitus makes it clear that, while the Germans had no wine, they did have beer. Nevertheless, the German word *Bier*, like English "beer," is derived from Latin *bibere* (to drink).                                              (102)

The name Mueller (from Latin *molinarius*) also reflects the Romans' more advanced technology, for the ancient Germans still had only the *quirn* (English "quern") or hand mill. Because there were so many kinds of mills, the name Miller was as common as the name Meyer. The millers often acquired their names from the spot along the stream where their mills were located, such as Aumueller (mill on the meadow), Waldmueller (mill at the forest), etc. Apparently meaningless miller-names may have been shortened forms. While a Weissmueller ground white flour and a Braunmueller ground brown flour, it is unlikely that Schwartzmueller ground black flour (even if his brown flour became blackbread). It is more likely that his mill stood on the Schwartzbach and that he had first been called the Schwartzbachmueller. (103)

Before the advent of store-bought clothes and shoes, tailors and shoemakers were in great demand and supply. The word *Schneider* originally meant "cutter," being analogous with the Old French word *tailleur*, from which we get "tailor." Another word for tailor was *Schroeder*, so that there are many American families named Schneider, Snyder, Shroder, and Schroeder (usually pronounced, and sometimes written, as Shrader). The most usual word for a shoemaker (and the source of the English word) was *Schumacher*, while the words *Schumann* and *Schubert* were also common. The Latin word *sutor* gave the German word *Schuster*. A man trained only to repair shoes, but not to make them, was a *Flickschuster*, which gives the American name Flick. As in the case of surnames based on place names and house names, professional names were not fixed initially. If Hans Schuster's son Heintz became a baker, he would become Heintz Beck or Heintz Becker, not Heintz Schuster. In time, however, professional names, like other names, became fixed and the cooper Carl Zimmermann may have inherited his name from his great-grandfather, the last carpenter in the family. Such non-correlation of names with their bearers must have been overlooked by the Englishman who was impressed by New York egalitarianism when he heard that a department store was being run by a lord and a taylor. (104)

When we speak of "Roman" arts and crafts, we should remember that the word is used in a general sense of everything from the Roman empire. The Romans were not the world's best craftsmen; they let their slaves, mostly foreigners, do much of their work for them. Therefore the "Roman" skills or sciences we praise may have come from Egypt, Cappadocia, Greece, Spain, or any other part of the far-flung Roman empire. For example, the Roman traders who visited the ancient Germans often came from Syria or Greece. Traders from the Roman world dominated trade in ancient Germany, just as the English and Scots did among the American Indians, who, like the ancient Germans, were warriors and disdained mercenary pursuits. Hence it is not surprising that the Latin word *caupo* (merchant), in its High German form *Kauf*, served as a root in the word *Kaufmann* (merchant). Later on, small retailers were Haacker, Hacker-mann, Hoeker, Haendler, or Kraemer, and the shopkeeper on the corner (Winkel) might have been called Winkel or Winkler. Often the merchants were given the names of the wares they sold.                                                    (105)

   Like the Roman wine seller (*vinumcaupo*), many medieval German merchants took their name from the wares they sold, for in the highly regulated and guild-minded commerce of the Middle Ages merchants usually specialized in a single item. A seller of pepper (from Latin *piper*) was Pfefferick or Pfeffer-mann, the seller of salt was Salzer, Selzer, or Saltzmann, and the seller of sugar was Zucker or Zuckermann, the word *Zucker* having come from Arabic via Spanish *azucar*. The seller of herrings (usually caught in the Baltic Sea and salted) was called Hering. Numerous items supplied names for the people who manufactured them, sold them, or used them. Typical of the resulting names are Beil (ax), Gabel (fork), Kamm (comb), Kunckel (distaff), Loeffel (spoon), Messer (knife), and Teller (dish). A Hutzler sold dried fruit. Whereas medieval merchants were usually specialists, we need not think that they always sold only one item. A fishmonger whose shield bore a pickerel may also have sold bass and perch. The artist may have chosen the most available fish as his model. Because craftsmen usually sold their wares in the front of their shop, we cannot really distinguish between craftsmen and shop keepers.          (106)

   Men who served in the military often gained their surnames from their military occupation or rank. At the time surnames were first being taken, most recruits became pikemen (*Landsknechte*, lansquenets), whereas the more fortunate ones became *Reuter*, or cavalrymen. The word *Reuter* and its synonym *Reiter* both came from the verb to ride (*reiten*), whereas the word *Ritter* first meant "trooper," being a member of a *rit* or cavalcade. In time *ritter* became the equivalent of French *chevalier* (knight) and was used only of the gentry. Those who served for pay were *Soeldner* (mercenaries, from Latin *solidarius*).                                              (107)

The crossbow (*Armbrust*, folk etymology from Latin *arca balestra*) was still an effective weapon and gave the name Armbruster to both the user and the manufacturer of the weapon. The same was true of the *bogener*, who could either shoot or make bows. The *panzer* and the *bruenner* were the makers, rather than the wearers, of armor. A soldier who excelled and survived might become a *Webel* (sergeant), *Faehnrich* or *Faenner* (ensign), a *Hauptmann* (captain), or *Oberst* (colonel), or even *Marschall* (*marah*, horse + *scalc*, servant). A man who served a knight was a *Schildknecht*, or squire (literally, "shield knight"). (108)

The foremost man in a rural village was the *Bauernmeister* or village head man, also called the *Schultz, Scholz,* or *Schultheiss*. A larger town would have a *Burgermeister* and council of *Ratherren,* which gives the American name Rather, as in the case of Dan Rather. A surname referring to the higher offices usually indicated not descent, but rather employment. A man named Kaiser (emperor) was probably in imperial service, while a man name Koenig (king) was probably in royal service, unless perhaps he was persistently the *Schuetzenkoenig,* or winner of the markmanship contest. Employment is also suggested by the names Herzog (duke), Graf (count), Vogt (governor), Probst (provost), and Witzthum (vice-governor), the last three of these being from Latin *advocatus, propositus,* and *vice-dominus*. In addition to the higher officials, there were many more modest public servants such as public criers (Bellmann), bell ringers (Glocke) and official weighers (Waeger or Wagemann). Some of these services were rendered by "dishonorable" people, those who had no legal standing, like the skinner (Schinder or Abzieher) and court bailif (Scherg). (109)

Employment obviously produced the names Pabst (pope), Bischof (bishop), Abt (abbot), Pfaff (priest), and Moench (monk), since clergymen did not leave legitimate children to carry on their names. On the other hand, the sextons Sigrist, Mesner, Kirchner, and Kuester (think of Custer's last stand) may have had families with surnames taken from their profession, as might a lay brother such as a Beghard (Beckhardt), Palmer, or mass attendant (Messmann). A Kentucky gentleman once named his sons Bishop, Commodore, Dean, and Major, with the result that later generations respected his family for having had so many titled members. (110)

The name Gott (God) was most often a shortened form of some name like Gottfried, Gotthelf, Gotthold, Gottlieb, or Gottschalk; but in some cases it may have been the nickname given to the actor who regularly played the role of God in a miracle play. Miracle plays may have contributed to the popularity of the names Adam and Eva, Maria Magdalena, Caspar, Melchior, and Balthasar (the Three Kings who brought gifts to Jesus), and other favorite roles in the plays. This was surely true of Puntzius (Pontius Pilate), who was hardly an exemplary character. (111)

People often gained their surnames from nicknames. (As mentioned, the word "nickname" is a false division of "an ickname," or an added name.) A common type of nickname comes from hair color or style, such as Red, Curly, Goldy, etc. In German we find the names Schwarz (brunet), Braun (brown haired), Roth (red haired), Weiss (blond), Krause, Kraus (curly), and Kraushaar (curly haired); and the name Gold may have sometimes referred to hair color, just as the name Kahl (bald) betokened the absence of hair. The name Rotbart, like its Italian form Barbarossa, could designate a man with either a red or a blond beard. As in the case of names from professions, all these nicknames had once been preceded by a definite article: Hans der Schwarze (Hans the brunet), and Klaus der Kraus (Klaus the curly haired). Nicknames could also result from the clothes one wore, especially if they were unusual or indicated the wearer's profession or status. Examples are Lederhos (leather breeches) and Bundschuh (laced footwear), both meaning peasant, Weisskittel (white smock), meaning miller or baker, and Gelbrock (yellow gown), meaning a Jew. People could also be teased about the food they ate, especially if it revealed their social status or rural tastes as in the case of turnips (Rueb), sour beer (Sauerbier), or porridge (Brey). (112)

Physical stature gave names such as Kurtz (short), Lang (tall), Gross (large), and Klein (small). and age gave names like Alt (old), Jung (young), Juengling (youth), and Greis (greybeard). A name like Kleinhans was appropriate when little Johnny was a child, but less so when he grew up and surpassed his father in height. I had two cousins called Big Julia, the mother, and Little Julia, the daughter, and Little Julia retained her name even after she had outgrown her mother. The physical cruelty of the Middle Ages is well attested by instruments of torture and by the popular merriment caused when they were used publicly, so it is not surprising that mental cruelty is suggested by some of the nicknames inflicted at that time. A man with a twisted body might be called Krumm (crooked) or Krumbein (crooked leg), one with arthritic joints could be called Steiff (stiff), one with a misshapen head might be called Breithaupt (broad head) or Groskopf (bighead), and one who squinted might be called Schiele (squint). Sometimes a nickname was facetious: a large man might be called Small, and vice versa. On Quadalcanal my troopers called me Curly (behind my back) because of my prematurely bald pate.                (113)

Kropf (goiter) was a fitting name for anyone so afflicted, and Spitznas suited anyone with a pointed nose, just as Finkbein (finch leg) suited a man with skinny shanks. A fat man might be called Feiss, Fett, or Dick (thick) or perhaps Bauch (belly). In fact, any part of the anatomy might suggest a nickname, provided it were sufficiently deformed or unusual, such as Nase (nose), Schnaebele (little snout, in America Snaveley), and Kehl (throat, unless he came from Kehl across the Rhine from Strassburg). Originally, such names had been prepositional phrases such as *mit dem bart* (with the beard), *mit dem bauch* (with the belly), and *mit der nase* (with the nose).                (114)

Nicknames could also result from personal behavior: a man might be serious (Ernst) or jovial (Froehlich), courtly (Huebsch) or crude (Rauh, Grob); or, if he vacillated, he might be called Wankel or Wankelmut. Even more vituperative were Greul (atrocity), Greulich (dreadful), and Grausam (cruel). Less frequent were positive terms, such as Schoen (beautiful), Klug (clever), and Kuhn (brave). Comical nicknames could also be taken from our furry and feathered friends, such as Fuchs (fox), Has (hare), Gans (goose), Fink (finch), Amsel (ousel, blackbird), and many others. Names were also suggested by fish, such as Aal (eel), Barsch (perch), Hecht (pickerel). In some cases the names of such creatures may have signified that the person involved trapped, raised, or sold them. This was true even of songbirds, for it was not unusual for four-and-twenty blackbirds to be baked in a pie, and thrushes and finches fared no better.

A man named Kaefer (beetle) may have had the perseverence of that insect, and a man named Frosch (frog) may have eaten frogs, as Frenchmen do in American fancy. Even extinct animals such as the *Wissent* (bison) and *Auer* (aurochs) survive as surnames.                                                      (115)

Nicknames were sometimes imperatives, such as Bleibtreu (Remain loyal!), Fuerchtegott (Fear God!), Haltdichwohl (Keep well!), Hoerauf (Stop it!), Kaufdasbier (Buy the beer!), Streckfuss (Stretch a leg!), Schwingschwert (Swing the sword!), and Siehdichum (Watch out!). Such names were often given to new guild members at their initiation. Some of these imperative names were commands given in tasks no longer known to us. For example, Schudrein means "Shove it in!," but we do not know what was being shoved into what. If Samuel Clemens had not told us, we would not know the meaning of "Mark Twain."                                                      (116)

Some nicknames derived from a man's favorite expression, as was the case of Jasomirgott (so help me God!), as Henry II, the first duke of Austria, was called because he used that oath so often. Similarly derived names may include Garaus (bottoms up!), Fruehauf (early up!), Glueckauf (safe return!, probably a miner's term), Gottbehuet (God forbid!), Herr Gott (Lord God), and Amen. The names of small coins sometimes serve to suggest parsimony or miserliness, examples being Dreier (thrupence), Grosch (penny), and Heller (worthless coin). On the other hand, a large coin like a Gulden (guilder), Mark (mark), or Thaler (reichsthaler) might suggest magnanimity. Many names were "initiation names," names given to new members when they joined a guild or brotherhood. These could be complimentary like Goldfuss (gold foot) or defamatory like Ochsenreiter (ox rider), or Galgenschwank (gallows bird).                        (117)

Some nicknames lasted for a long time, long after the reason for them had been forgotten. One of my fellow Boy Scouts rightfully acquired the name Asparagus Tips, which plagued him for years but was, fortunately, not passed on to his children to the third and fourth generation. Having run out of supplies on a mountain hike and half starved, we resolved to send a relief party down to the valley to find food. With many empty stomachs and only a few dollars, we could not decide between baked beans and hominy grits with gravy. At that point our

the result that a bachelor is called a *Hagestolz*. The root *hag* (hawe) appears in many names like Hashagen (hare hedge), Hagenbeck (enclosure brook), and Hagedorn (hawthorn); and a man living in a *hag* might be called Hagen, Hager, Hagmann, Hagemann, or even Hackmann. The Low German root *rode*, meaning a clearing, is found in Minnegerode and Wernigerode, while its High German equivalents *reit* and *reut* are found in Reitenbach and Reutlingen. (125)

A name often misunderstood is Roland, of whom there is a statue in Bremen holding a gigantic sword. Most people assume that it commemorates the hero of the *Chanson de Roland* (from *\*Hrotho* and *\*land)*, but this was not the case. Roland was not a name: it was a corruption of the legal term *rodoland*, or "reclaimed land." If a ruler undertook to clear *(roden)* unclaimed and uncultivated land, he could assert jurisdiction over it. To attest his juridical rights over this *rodoland*, he might stake his claim by erecting a marker, often in the shape of a man holding a sword as a symbol of jurisdiction. Because of the popularity of the hero Roland, people supposed that the markers represented him; and thus we have another case of folk etymology. A whole category of names derived from the act of clearing land, among which are *brand, reut, rod, sang,* and *schwand*. The name Waldbrand does not denote a forest fire, but a clearing in the woods. In America the root *schwand* sometimes appears as *schwang,* as in the name Neiswanger and Neuswanger (new clearing).(126)

In addition to the place names ending in *dorf, heim, hagen, rod,* and *reut,* there were also many towns, especially in Switzerland, that ended in *weil* (also written *weiler, wil,* and *wyler*. These derived from the Latin word *villa,* which meant a large farm or estate and gave us the word "village." The first component of names ending in *weil* was often the name of the owner. For example, Wittenweil was a Roman villa appropriated by a Germanic invader named Witto, whose descendants were later called Wittenweiler. Among American names stemming from *weil* we find Weil, Weiler, and Hofwyl. At some time, already in Switzerland, names like Ebers-wil were wrongly divided and resulted in forms like Eber-schwil or Eberschwyl. Another root designating a town that is largely restricted to Switzerland is *ikon* (from *inghofen*), which is found in Ruemlikon, Rueschlikon, Russikon, Stallikon, Fuellikon, and many

more. A less common ending, found mostly in  north central
Germany is *leben*, originally meaning "inheritance" but later
just meaning property in general, as in Eisleben. The Slavic
root *witz*, meaning village, appears in names like Bonnewitz.
(127)
*Inghofen* is not the only ending that has been mutilated. By
tracing successive documents mentioning a place, we find that
they have often dropped many unstressed syllables, so that from
Udilscalckesberge all that remains is Uschelberg. Similar
contractions occur in England, even if not always indicated by
the spelling. When an American stated that he was going to St.
Magdalene Church to catch a bus for Lancashire in order to call
on Lord Cholmondeley, his British friend corrected him,
pronouncing the names as Maudlin, Lancsha, and Chumly.
When the Englishman said he would like to see Niagara Falls,
the American corrected him with "Niffels." Because some long
German names like Hruodinesheim, Autmundistat, and
Heribrachtshusen have been shortened to Rudisheim, Umstadt,
and Herbstein, we cannot always be certain of the etymology of
place names unless they appear in very old documents.   (128)
   As Tacitus mentioned, the ancient Germans did not care to
live in cities; during the invasions they often camped around the
old Roman settlements and left the inhabitants at peace. The
result was that many South German cities, towns, and villages
retained their names, even if these names were sometimes
altered by the High German sound shift and by the inability of
the invaders to pronounce them properly. Most of these names
were Celtic names that had long been latinized, such as
Turicum (Zurich), Tavernae (Zabern), and Moguntia (Mainz).
These Romanized Celtic place names provided the American
names Zuricher, Zaber, Maintzer, and Mentzer.          (129)
   There were also genuine Latin names such as Confluencia
(Koblenz, at the confluence of the Rhine and Moselle) and
Colonia Agrippina (Koeln, a colony named in honor of Nero's
mother, which we call Cologne).                        (130)

# CHAPTER THREE

## Christian Names

As we have seen, early German names were all pagan and mostly warlike. Names containing the roots *ans* and *god*, like Ansgar (god + spear) and Godwin (god + friend), referred to pagan gods. While the Germanic names were the most popular ones in Western Europe throughout the Middle Ages, Christianity introduced new names, mostly of Hebrew, Greek, and Latin origin. These names, often those of saints, were first found in the monasteries, where the monks shed their warlike Germanic names in favor of names more pleasing to God. Gradually, some of these names were assumed by royalty also; and we find rulers named John (Jehan, Jean, Johann, Jan, etc.), Georg, Stephan, and Philip. Some Christian names joined the older pagan names more easily because they resembled them. For example, Philip could have been confused with Filibert (very bright), Simon with Siemund (*sigi*, victory + *mund*, guardian), and Pilgrim with Biligrim (*bil*, sword + *grim*, helmet). Later converts often received names such as Christ, Christian, Karst, Kirst, and Kressmann, names which should protect their bearers from the devil. The devil, incorporating the qualities of Satan and of various pagan gods, became a very important personage with many names and circumlocutions such as Helmann, Helmeister, and Deubel. (131)

The names of saints gradually took root also among secular people who, following ancient pagan beliefs, wished to gain the personal support of certain saints by naming their children for them, since namesakes had a moral claim on the protection of the people for whom they were named. The Virgin Mary's name was so popular that it was even borne by men, as in the case, later, of Karl Maria von Weber, Rainer Maria Rilke, and Erich Maria Remarque. (Few people know that Voltaire's real name was Marie Francois Arouet.) (132)

Despite the intrusion of saints' names, the old Germanic names still predominated until the Counter Reformation of the sixteenth and seventeenth centuries. In a group of ballads by a thirteenth-century Austrian poet known as Neidhart von Reuwenthal, we find many rustic names. The first fifty-seven names are Adelber, Adelheit, Adelhune, Adelmar, Ave, Berchtel,

Diethoch, Eberhart, Elena, Engelbolt, Engelmar, Engelprecht, Eppe, Ermelint, Etzel, Frideger, Friderich, Friedliep, Friderun, Gisel, Giselher, Gotelinde, Gozbrecht, Gumprecht, Gunthart, Gundrat, Hadwig, Heilken, Hilde, Hiltburg, Hiltrat, Holengaere, Irenwart, Irmgart, Kuenzel, Randolt, Kuenegunde, Kuenz, Megenbolt, Liuthart, Megenwart, Richilt, Ruoze, Ruoprecht, Sibant, Sigehart, Uodalhilt, Uolant, Uoze, Vrena, Vriderun, Vromuot, Walfrit, Waregrim, Werenbolt, Wierat, and Willebolt. It will be noted that all but three of these peasants have old Germanic names, mostly expressing warlike concepts, and most of these names were composed of the roots discussed earlier. Only Ave, Elena, and Vrena (St. Verena) have any Christian significance.                                                    (133)

Among the most popular holy names were those of certain popes, including Adrian, Alexander, Benedict, Clement, Fabian, Hildebrand, Johannes, Mark, Martin, Nicholas, Paul, Stephen, Urban, and Victor. A modern German named Hildebrand probably owes his name to Pope Hildebrand rather than to the hero of the old German *Lay of Hildebrand*, who had to fight his own son. Many of these foreign names gave two sets of derivatives. The common people followed native speech patterns and stressed the first syllable, whereas the Church retained the Latin accent. Thus we get JOhann and JoHANNES, from which arose Jahn, Jahnke, and Jantz as well as Hans, Hannes, and Hansel. Likewise, Jacobus gave both Jack and Kopp.        (134)

After Luther revolted against Rome, most of his followers limited themselves to the names of scriptural saints such as Andreas, Johannes, Marcus, Matthaeus, Lucas, Petrus, and Paulus, while dropping the names of local and otherwise dubious saints. In place of the discarded saints, they often chose the names of Old Testament characters such as Abel, Abraham, Adam, Benjamin, Daniel, David, Jacob, Joachim, Jonas, Samuel, and Solomon. All of these were the source of German-American surnames in numerous variants. Because Old Testament names began to smack of heresy, they were forbidden in 1574 by the Synod of Tournai in France.                                      (135)

Meanwhile, during the Counter Reformation, the Roman Catholic Church required all parents to name their child for a saint, which was usually the saint on whose day it was born. Consequently, most of the old Germanic names fell into disuse,

except for those of popular emperors such as Carl, Conrad, Friedrich, Heinrich, Leopold, Ludwig, Otto, Siegmund, and Wilhelm. Among the most popular masculine saints in Germany, as elsewhere in Europe, were Johann, Joseph, Matthaeus (or Matthias), Sebastian, and the archangels Michael and Gabriel. It is not clear why the archangels Raffael and Uriel were less popular. Once a child had a hagiographic name, the parents could add a secular one too; and this custom continued in Protestant lands, as in the case of Johann Wolfgang Goethe.
(136)

While most of the saints had Aramaic, Greek, or Latin names, there were some Celtic and even a few Germanic names on the list. Among the latter the Germans cultivated Conrad (brave + counsel), bishop of Augsburg, Meinrad (power + counsel), abbot of Einsiedeln, Oswald (god + rule), an Englishman, Rupertus (usually Ruprecht, from *hrodo + beracht*, famous + bright), who established Christianity in Salzburg, and Hubertus (mind + bright), the patron saint of hunters. Very popular was St. Francis of Assisi, whose name, derived from Germanic *frank*, appears in German as Franz or Frantz, but is pronounced Frantz in both cases. Less popular was St. Anselmus (god + helmet), also an Italian. Among the saints who contributed names to many German-American families were Anthony (Thoeni, Denny), Bartholomaeus (Bart, Bartel), Marcus (Merk, Merkel), Martin (Marti, Maertens), and Matthias (Matt, Matz, Thiess, Thyssen, and, in America, Tyson and Dyson.)
(137)

Christianity brought a slight softening of manners: to use Nietzsche's terms, a *Herrenmoral* (master morality) gave way somewhat to a *Sklavenmoral* (slave morality); and the ethics of the monastery were gradually imposed on society at large. Old names took on new meanings, while new names were introduced. The adjective *vrum* had once denoted effectiveness, a *vrumer ritter* was a capable knight, a *vrumer bauer* was a productive peasant, and a *vrumer munich* was a pious monk. Gradually the word dropped its first two meanings and kept only the last, and thus the name Frommhold, instead of meaning "effective and feudally loyal," took on the new meaning "pious and dear" for all classes. *Tuechtig* and *bieder*, which once meant doughty in battle, acquired for some people the

meaning of capable and diligent, for example in business. In the
new bourgeois society, respectability was more important than
fame, so people adopted names like Ehrenmann (man of honor),
Ehrlich (honest), and Ehrsam (respectable).                    (138)

Gutmann, like French *bonhomme* and English Goodman,
first meant "landowner" but was gradually understood to mean
"good man." Among these new Christian names were Sanftmut
(gentle disposition) and Demut (humility), which had literally
meant "servant-disposition" (from *thius*, servant, and *mut*,
disposition). The name is pronounced "day moot" in German,
but is pronounced mostly as DeMUTH in America. This is one
of the many cases in which the English sound *th* (thorn), long
since dead in Germany, has been falsely introduced into
German-American names. Since it is more Christian to serve
than to be served, we begin to find names like Diener (servant)
and Dienst (service). The christianizing of German culture is
shown in place names like Marienborn (Mary's well) and
Theresienstadt (Theresa's city), which in turn became surnames. The Swiss city and surname Frauenfeld, which is now
interpreted as "Field of our Lady," may have originally been
Fronfeld "the field of our lord," or field where the peasants could
perform their corvee service, or *Frondienst* (cf. *Fronleichnam*,
Corpus Christi). However, most names like Frauenmann,
Frauenhof, etc. do designate men or farms belonging to a
convent.                                                        (139)

The names Gottfried, Gotthelf, Gotthilf, Gotthold, Gottlieb,
Gottlob, and Gottschalk, which had once belonged to the
monasteries, gradually crept out into the world and became
especially popular in Lutheran parsonages, where they were
joined by new coinages like Fuerchtegott (fear God), Ehregott
(glorify God), Leberecht (live right), Christfried (Christ peace),
and Himmelreich (kingdom of heaven). The old name Friedrich
(ruler of the *frithu*) was interpreted as "Prince of Peace" and
was equated with the Hebrew name Solomon. Ulrich Zwingli
misinterpreted his first name as Huldreich (full of grace),
whereas it had actually been Uodalrich and had meant "rich in
allodial (inherited) lands," again a case of folk etymology.(140)

During the period of humanism in the sixteenth century,
scholars often signed their Latin writings with Latinized names.
Georgius Agricola, the great humanist, was actually named

Bauer; and the ancestors of the pencil manufacturing family Faber derived their name from the Latin word for smith, their name having been Schmidt. The map maker Gerhard Kremer signed his Latin maps with his Latin name, Mercator, while Francis Praetorius, the founder of Germantown, bore a latinized form of Schultheiss. In like manner Fischer (fisherman), Weber (weaver), Schumacher (shoemaker), Jaeger (hunter), and Schneider (tailor) gained prestige by calling themselves Piscator, Textor, Sutor, Venatus, and Sartor, or, the even more elegant, Sartorius. The prestigious ending *ius* was quite superfluous in Praetorius and Sartorius, since the Latin forms were complete as Praetor and Sartor. (141)

Some Latinists latinized their names by retaining or adding the suffix ending *us*, which was still commonly used until modern times in Biblical names like Petrus, Paulus, Martinus, etc. It should be noted that the common German name Christ is not blasphemous, since it merely means "Christian," the Lord's epithet always being Christus. Hans, the son of Martinus was Hans Martini, that being the Latin genitive, not an Italian name as is sometimes believed. In like manner, Paulus' son Niklas was Niklas Pauli or Pauly, while Jacobus' son Heinz was Heinz Jacobi or Jacoby. Scholars with names ending in *e* preferred the ending *ius*. The pastor of the Georgia Salzburgers bore the name Boltzius, a latinization of either Bolte or Boltze, while a con-artist who fleeced him called himself Curtius, although his real name was Kurtz. A Moravian teacher who served in Georgia and Pennsylvania was named Schulius, surely from Schule. The name Stettinius came from Stettin on the Baltic. (142)

Some scholars were not satisfied with mere Latin names but preferred Greek ones, such as Neander for Neumann (new man). This was the case of Luther's friend Melanchthon, who incorrectly interpreted his name Schwarzerd as "Black earth." Actually the name may have been only Schwarzer (brunet), to which an excrescent *T* had been added. Excrescent *T*s appear in numerous names, among which are Braunert, Craemert, Daubert, Dickert, Dobert, Pabst, Obst, and Schweigert. Some people were named for the day of their births, such as Freitag (Friday), Sontag (Sunday), Maytag (May Day), and Oster (Easter). Obviously, descendants of such people bore those names without being born on those days. It is possible that a man named Freitag received his name because he owed corvée service on Fridays.                                                    (143)

Many German names had originally been French, often Huguenot. Literate French immigrants could preserve the correct spelling of their names because they associated with educated people who understood them, as was the case of the family of the German author Friedrich Heinrich Carl de La Motte Fouqué. On the other hand, the names of the working-class and peasant immigrants were usually germanized, and one would scarcely recognize Tussing as a rendering of Toussaints. In one instance the reverse took place: the accent on the North German name Guder Jan (Good John) was shifted to the second syllable, forming the name Guderian, which is usually assumed to be French. German names were sometimes gallicized when Germans settled in francophone areas, examples being Blancpain, Chupart, and Grenier from Weissbrodt, Schubart, and Greiner.                                          (144)

In the South German language area the Romance-speaking Celts survived the Germanic invasions and lived alongside the invaders, even to the present in the Engadin. The first Celts the Germans met when crossing the Rhine were the Volcae, which gave them the noun *walch* and the adjective *welsch*. In England the Saxons gave the cognate word *welsh* to the Celts of Wales. When the Volcae became romanized, the Germans on the Continent began to use the word *welsch* to designate Romance-speaking people, as the German Swiss still call their French-speaking countrymen. Because the romanized Celtic pockets remained among the Germanic invaders, we find place names like Wallensee, Wallenstein, and Wallis, where the older inhabitants survived.                                              (145)

The number of germanized Slavic names is high everywhere east of the Elbe, which served as a linguistic frontier between Germans and Slavs after the latter had occupied the lands abandoned by the former during their migrations westward and southward. Ever since the thirteenth century there had been a persistent *Drang nach Osten* (drive toward the east), which was finally reversed in 1944 at the Battle of Stalingrad. During the drive toward the east the Germans had often retained, even if altered, Slavic names such as Bogatzky, Cernak, Kretschmer,

Lessing, Nietzsche, and Leibnitz. They also kept many East
German place names such as Berlin, Breslau, Danzig, Dresden,
Fehrbellin, and Leipzig, which have given us American surnames. Many names could be of either Germanic or Slavic
derivation. If they are frequent in western Germany but rare in
the east, then they are probably Germanic; if they are frequent
in the East but rare in the West, then they are probably
Slavic.                                                                                        (146)
     There are not really any German-Jewish names. There are
Hebrew names, such as Chaim, Cohen, Levi, and Me'ir, the last
of which, as mentioned, may have predisposed some Jews to
adopt the name Meyer. A few German-language names were
borne mainly by Jews, such as Langrock and Gelbrock, which
referred to the long and yellow garments they were required to
wear. Otherwise, there is no distinction between the names
borne by Christians and Jews, except that certain names were
more frequently adopted by the latter. In many of our Eastern
inner-cities, names like Evans, Davis, Robertson, White,
Williams, Wilson, etc. are borne mostly by blacks; yet they
remain British, not African, names.                              (147)
     Within the Jewish community, or ghetto, simple names
usually sufficed; if not, the father's name could be added.
When the Jews were emancipated at the end of the eighteenth
and beginning of the nineteenth centuries, they were required
to take surnames for the purpose of taxation. If they had their
choice many chose common German names that began with the
same consonant as their "holy" or "synagogue" name. Thus,
Menachem might choose Mendel just for its initial sound, and
Nathan might choose Nadler for the same reason, not because
he made needles. Some merely re-arranged the letters, so that
Lewi became Weil. Even after assuming gentile-sounding
*Decknamen* (cover names), religious Jews still considered their
synagogue names to be their true names, for which they felt an
emotional attachment. When given a choice, some Jews chose
romantic names such as Morgenthau (morning dew), Blumenthal (flower valley), Lilienthal (lily valley), Rosenberg (rose
mountain), Silberstein (silver stone), and their like. Although
Americans often consider such names to be Jewish, they are
straight German names, for such names were current in
sentimental novels at the time that Jews were taking civil

names. The name Rosenkranz (rosary) is certainly more appropriate for a Catholic than for a Jew, and the name Rosenberg was borne by the Nazi ideologist who wrote *The Mythos of the Twentieth Century*. Shakespeare was not suggesting Jewish descent when he named two of Hamlet's colleagues Rosencrantz and Guildenstern. Some "fantasy" names were composed with as little logic as were many of the ancient Germanic names composed of two unassociated roots. Examples of typical *Fantasienamen* are Feinstein, Goldfein, Himmelfarb, Loewenstern, and Morgenroth.                                (148)

Like their gentile neighbors, the Jews often took the name of their trade, so many bore names like Kuerschner or Kirschner (furrier), Kraemer (shopkeeper), Schlechter (slaughterer), or Wechsler (money-changer). On the other hand, the chosen name did not necessarily designate trades associated primarily with the Jews, for we also find Ackermann, Bauer, Forster, Gaertner, Gerber, Jaeger, Wirth, and Zimmermann. When required to assume surnames for purposes of taxation, the Jews often used their house names, by which many families had been known for generations. Typical examples were Adler, Drache, Fisch, Fuchs, Gans, Hecht, Mandelbaum, Rose, Rosenstock, and Rothschild. Many Jews took the names of cities, often of large and imposing cities like Frankfurt and Hamburg, without having ever lived there.                                                              (149)

It is said that the Jews often had to bribe the officials to obtain desirable names. A tale, surely apocryphal but no less significant, tells of a Jew who was in the tax collector's office for a long time while getting his name. When he finally emerged, his friends asked what name he got. "Schweiss" (sweat) was his answer. "Very good," his friends remarked. "Yes, but the *w* cost me half my fortune!" Since puns cannot be translated, the story should be altered in English: he received the name Shirt, but the *r* cost him half his fortune. To know what names the German Jews received or selected, one has only to look at any list of donors to cultural and charitable undertakings. When I was studying at Heidelberg, the main building, which had been donated by American benefactors, bore a large bronze plaque listing the names of the donors, more than half of whom were clearly Jewish. When I arrived there in 1936, all Jewish professors had just been dismissed.                        (150)

# CHAPTER FOUR

## The Americanization of German Names

In looking through the following list, it will be noted that, while German-American names differ widely from the standard written form of the German words, they differ far less from the dialect variants brought to this country. Nevertheless, many names did become altered significantly through English influence.When the immigrants boarded their ships at Rotterdam, the English captains had difficulty in writing their manifests or ships lists. Knowing no German, and unfamiliar with German dialects, the scribes wrote down the names as they heard them, sometime in the form of the English names most resembling the sound. In this way Theiss, Weiss, and Weidmann became Dice, Wise, and Whiteman, while Albrecht, Leitner, and Leithaeuser became Albright, Lightner, and Lighthizer. The reason that so many eighteenth-century German immigrants could not sign their names and merely made an X was not that they were illiterate, because Protestant Germans had a higher literacy rate than their British contemporaries. The reason was that they could write only in German script, which the British authorities could not read. It occasionally appears that the immigrants tried to spell their names but did so with the German sounds of the letters. If a man named Diehl spelled his name as *"day, ee, ay, ha, ell,* the scribe may have understood it as Deahl. (151)

In a few cases the writer of the ship list gave up and asked the meaning of the name; and thus Becker, Koch, Schneider, Soeldner, and Zimmermann became Baker, Cook, Taylor, Soldier, and Carpenter. Often the translation was advantageous. When two brothers named Zwetschen (plum) stood in separate lines at Castle Garden (prior to Ellis Island and therefore used by most German immigrants) they were handled by different clerks. One, being conscientious, struggled with the unfamiliar name and wrote it Tsvetshen. The other soon gave up and asked the meaning, and then he assigned the name Plum. It is not hard to guess which brother was more successful in business in America. (152)

In the eighteenth century it was customary to translate Christian names, just as we still do today in the case of royal

names when we say Frederick the Great and William the
Second instead of Friedrich der Grosse and Wilhelm der Zweite.
Common names like Johann, Georg, and Wilhelm were regularly anglicized into John, George, and William; but the scribes
failed to recognize the roots of some names. Therefore they
failed to see that Ruprecht was the equivalent of Robert and
that Ludwig was the equivalent of Lewis, and the result was
that they sometimes rendered them as Rubright and Ludowick.
The same situation could occur in the case of surnames that
were identical with Christian names: Paulus Franz might
become Paul Francis and Johann Wilhelm might become John
Williams. Sometimes only a part of the name was translated, as
in the case of Newbauer, Newhart, and Blackwaelder (for
Schwartzwaelder).                                          (153)

Only a few German first names have taken root in the United
States, most of them still being found in families who cherish
their German heritage. Among those that are still popular are
Carl, Ernst, Herman, Hubert, and Otto, all of which also serve
as surnames. Among girls' names we find Heidi, Gretchen,
Liese, and Minna. A test of whether or not such names have
really taken root is their presence or absence in non-German
families, for example, among our African-American populace.

                                                            (154)

It should be noted that, while the first few generations of
Germans in America continued to choose German first names
to honor their parents and grandparents, later generations
joined the mainstream in naming their children for national
heroes and non-German friends. The reverse was also true: the
black mayor of Baltimore is named Kurt Schmoke, and a lovely
black bank teller in Savannah, Georgia, is named Zeagler (from
Ziegler). My own grandfather, who had no German blood and
bore the surname Meldrim, was christened Peter Wiltberger in
honor of his father's commanding officer.                 (155)

In a few cases the German immigrant willfully changed his
name for professional reasons. The dancer Frederick Austerlitz
preferred to perform under the stage name Fred Astaire, which
sounded more elegant to American ears after World War I; and
Allan Konigsberg and Doris Kappelhof acted under the names
Woody Allen and Doris Day. It has been mentioned that
religious Jews cherished their synagogue names more than their

cover names, and that explains why it was easy for some of them to discard their cover names and choose more suitable ones after reaching America. (156)

Some Germans tried to gain prestige by giving a French flavor to their names, French being fashionable at the time. August Schoenberg, a Jew, translated his surname to Belmont and thus entered circles formerly closed to him. Some people merely shifted the accent to the second syllable to make it sound French. A few North Germans whose names ended in an *e*, like Bode (messenger) and Gode (good), had already added an acute accent (Bodé, Godé) so that South Germans would not drop the final vowel. In America such names were thought to be French and were pronounced, and sometimes written, as Boday and Goday. In Charleston the early Lutheran silversmith Johann Paul Grimké left many "Huguenot" descendants named Grimké. (157)

A name like Dusel (pronounced DOOzel and meaning "silly") sounds very French when the accent is shifted to the second syllable and the name is pronounced as DuSELLE, and the same is true of Mandel (almond) and Mantel (coat) when they are pronounced ManDELLE and ManTELLE (which Mickey Mantle did not choose to do). The same principle was at work in the change of accent in the word "tercel," meaning a thrice-moulted male falcon. The word should be accented on the first syllable, but the automobile manufacturer knew that the car would be more stylish if pronounced TerCELLE. Even the seventeenth-century English composer Purcell suffers his name to be murdered by Francophiles as PurCELLE. (158)

Some immigrants altered the spelling of their names to preserve the correct pronunciation, which would have been mispronounced if they had kept the original spelling. Families named Erhardt, Gerhardt, and Igelhard saved the correct sound (the true component of a name) by changing the spelling to Earhardt, Gearhard, and Eagleheart. Many German-American names deviated greatly from the standard German form without being americanizations. The apparently "wrong" letters may not have resulted from American pronunciation or spelling: they may represent a dialect variant or a relic of a bygone age. For example, Rhylander and Schwytzer are not American corruptions: they are the authentic Swiss forms of those names. It is

evident that names like Mince, Minehart, Rice, Tice, and Troy
are American phonetics for Maintz, Meinhart, Reiss, Theiss, and
Treu. On the other hand, it is not always possible to ascertain
whether names like Isemann, Wigel, and Wiler are corruptions
of the standard forms Eisemann, Weigel, and Weiler or whether
they derive directly from old dialect forms. The same is true of
the use of umlauts, which varied greatly from region to region.
Sometimes the corruption of a German name was due to a false
breaking of the name, as we have seen in the case of Ebers-wyl
and Eber-schwyl. Roth-schild (red shield) has become Rothschild, which has no meaning. Rat-her (council gentleman) has
become Ra-ther, a rather meaningless name; and the Kraushaar (curly hair) Auditorium in Baltimore is often pronounced
Kraw-shower. (159)

World War I extinguished, or hopelessly disguised, many German names. Because British propaganda convinced most Americans that the Germans cut off the hands of all Belgian boys and
impaled little girls on the projections of the Gothic cathedrals,
some German Americans renounced their origins in order to
escape public opprobrium, and even sauerkraut had to take on
the name "liberty cabbage." I was born during "the War to End
all Wars," and for years afterwards we knew scarcely any
Germans. Among our acquaintances the Ottos were Norwegians,
the Balls were Alsatians, the Altstaetters were Swiss, and the
Holsts were Danish. Some others had rectified their spellings
from Schmidt to Smith and from Henrichsen to Henderson.
Strangely, German shepherd dogs remained German, except
when they were called police dogs, and Dachshunds remained
"dash hounds." (160)

The chief value of the appended list of German-American
names for genealogists is to help them continue their search of
a family's antecedents when the line seems to come to an end.
A friend of mine in Atlanta was proud of his descent from a
prominent New England family named Capp. However, when he
tried to document the descent, the line came to an abrupt halt
in the mid-nineteenth century in Ohio and could not be pursued
until it was discovered that the father of the earliest known
Capp had previously been named Kapp. Therefore, if a genealo-
gist comes to the end of an Anglo-Saxon line, it may be worth
his while to search under the nearest German names. (161)

To be sure, not every Miller used to be a Mueller, in fact the spelling Miller was common in South Germany and Switzerland, as in the case of Johnny Weissmiller, the original Tarzan. In many cases the source of an apparently Anglo-Saxon name must have been Continental, usually German, because the name does not appear, or seldom appears, in England. Among these are Albright (Albrecht), Fulbright (Vollbrecht), Height (Heyd, Heid, or Heidt), Lightner (Leitner), Lighthizer (Leithaeuser), Yonce (Jantz), and Youngblood (Juengbluet, not young blood but young blossom). It is generally known that Firestone was an anglicization of Feuerstein, but it has not been mentioned that Firestone's greatest rival, Goodyear, may have had a similarly formed name. I have never known an Englishman named Goodyear, but Johannes Gutjahr of Linzingen arrived in America aged sixteen in 1864, just as Rudolf Feuerstein had done one year earlier; and it is likely that other Gutjahrs had arrived before Charles Goodyear vulcanized rubber.     (162)

# CHAPTER FIVE

## Suggestions for Using the Name-list

In searching for a German-American name, particularly an early one, the reader should keep several things in mind. Being unfamiliar with German names, the English ship captains sometimes wrote them phonetically. Thus they sometimes spelled the sound represented in German by *ie* as "ee" or "ea", as was the case with Keefer and Keafer for Kiefer and with Reeser and Reaser for Rieser. Unfamiliar with the trigraph *sch*, the scribes usually wrote only "sh" as in English. Thus Schneider appears as Shnyder (or Snyder), Schultz as Shults, and Schueler as Shiele. In searching for a German-American name beginning with *sh*, the reader is advised to search under the *sch* spelling, since the *sh* list has been greatly shortened to avoid unnecessary duplication.                                                    (163)

The digraph *pf*, unfamiliar to the scribes, appeared as *f*, as in Fleeger and Fleager for Pflueger and in Fister for Pfister. Whereas there had been only a few German surnames ending in *s* (indicating the genitive case), the English scribes often added a spurious *s* to German surnames, so that Bauer, Meyer, and Hyde (Heidt) also appeared as Bauers or Bowers, Meyers or Myers, and Hydes. Perhaps the scribes heard of these families mentioned in the plural, as in the case of the Smiths or the Blacks, and thought the *s* to be part of the name.       (164)

Umlauts, the diacritical marks over *a*, *o*, and *u*, were seldom used by German Americans and therefore do not appear here. They were originally the letter *e* superimposed over the vowel to modify its pronunciation, changing an *a* to *e* (rhyming with "say"), an *o* to the vowel sound in "girl" or "hurt," and the *u* to the sound of a French *u* (or, in South German names, to the sound *ee*). Instead of being superimposed, the *e* could follow the vowel, as in names like Goethe and Goetz; and that is the method used in the following list, even when the Standard German name has umlaut, as in the case of Schoen instead of Schön. In many cases the umlaut was eventually dropped. Therefore, when seeking a name with an *ae*, *oe*, or *ue*, the researcher should also search under *a*, *o*, and *u*, and vice versa. There is also a correlation between *e* and *oe*. A Germanic *e* like that in "hell" and "twelve" may be rounded to *oe* (*ö*) in German, as in the case of *Hoelle* and *zwoelf*. The reverse also appears: Goetz becomes Getz and Boehm becomes Behm.               (165)

The following compilation was begun in the naive belief that it could be complete, or even almost complete. Although not of German descent, I have competed for half a century against German thoroughness and have striven for *Vollstaendigkeit*, or completeness. Innocently expecting to find all German-American names, I have added list after list; yet, like Achilles, whenever I have almost caught up with the tortoise of completion, the tortoise has moved on; and now the list, still incomplete, is as much as my readers, or my publisher, will bear. While this is a partial list, I cannot claim that it is an impartial list, for I have included all eligible friends, acquaintances, and colleagues lest they think I did not have them in mind while compiling the list. Originally based on eighteenth- and nineteenth-century ship manifests, this list also includes German names from American telephone books, newspapers, and TV programs.               (166)

Although this study cannot pretend to list all the thousands of American variants of German names, it is hoped that the reader can deduce most unlisted names by observing the various roots and the way they are combined in the names that are listed. For example, the name Auerstein is not listed (because I have found no American by that name), but the roots are found in Auerbach and Steinfeld and many other names so that the reader should be able to ascertain the meaning without finding the exact name itself. Likewise, the index sometimes refers to paragraphs (not pages) in the introduction that do not list the precise name in question but which do explain related names.               (167)

If the researcher cannot find a name where it belongs alphabetically, he should look for several lines above and below. Also, he should remember that, because of the High German sound shift, *b*, *d*, and *g* are sometimes interchangeable with *p*, *t*, and *k* and *p* and *t* are sometimes interchangeable with *pf*, *f*, and *z*. Also, many names can begin with either *C* or *K*, *T* or *Th*, or *Sch* or *Sh*.               (168)

The reader will note that the translations often do not concur with modern dictionaries. Since most surnames were adopted in the fourteenth to the seventeenth centuries, they were based on older meanings of the roots, often as they appeared in Middle

High German. For example, since there were still no street cars, umbrellas, alarm clocks, or computers, the names Schaffner, Schirm, Wecker, and Rechner are rendered as "steward," "protection," "waker," and "teller" rather than as "conductor," "umbrella," "alarm clock," and "data processor." It will also be noted that many German-American names, especially of the earlier families, differ in spelling from modern German forms of the same names. This is because in the nineteenth and early twentieth centuries many German families altered the spelling of their names to concur with current orthographic reforms, which attempted to simplify and standardise spelling. The early immigrants, being safely in America, were unaffected by these reforms. Therefore many American families still use the older spellings; for example, we still find the spellings Carl, Schwartz, and Cunckel in place of the newer spellings Karl, Schwarz, and Kunkel. (169)

Every effort has been made to avoid folk etymology, or the popular but mostly incorrect interpretations of the names, but instances surely appear. The English renditions are merely transliterations, not interpretations. The reader is free to interpret a definition such as "marsh dweller" as "a person who lives near a marsh," " at a marsh," or "in a marsh," as he sees fit. The reader is reminded that fr means "from," the symbol < means "derived from," and OT and NT mean Old and New Testament. (170)

In the case of surnames derived from place names, space has sometimes been saved by explaining only the place name. The item "Altdorf, Altdorfer (old village)" explains the place name Altdorf as "old village"; it is assumed that the reader will understand that an Altdorfer is an inhabitant of that place. The same is true of "Frankfurter" (the Franks' ford), which explains only the name of the city, not that of the inhabitants. Places sufficiently populated to appear on maps and in gazetteers are marked with a raised 122, which follows the entry unless there may be confusion, in which case the 122 follows immediately after the pertinent name. It will be noted that old Germanic names like Eckhard and Anslem are rendered as (sword + strong) and (god + helmet) to indicate that there need be no conceptual relation between the two roots. Some names seem to be listed twice; for example, Forstreiter (forest rider, gamekeeper) is listed separately from Forstreiter (dweller in a forest clearing). Although the two appelations share the same spelling and pronunciation, they have different sources and different meanings and are therefore treated as separate names. (171)

## Foreword to Revised Edition

I wish at this time to thank all the reviewers who judged the first edition of this work favorably and all the readers who sent letters suggesting additional names, all of which, I hope, appear below. I also wish to thank all those who bought copies and thus encouraged the Genealogical Publishing Company to publish this revised and expanded edition.

George Fenwick Jones

# Der Müller.

Reminder: Numbers following items refer to paragraphs, not to pages, of the introduction. OT and NT = Old and New Testament, fr = from, < = derived from.

## A

Aach, see Ach
Aachen (city) 79, 122
Aal, Aahl (eel) 115, 106
Aal, Ahl (awl, cobbler) 98
Aalborn, see Ahlborn
Aargauer, Aargeyer (fr Aargau, Swiss region on the Aar) 121
Assheim (carrion hamlet) 123
Abaler, see Abele
Abbriter (from the clearing) 69, 124
Abbuehl (from the hill) 69, 67
Abderhalden (from the slope) 69, 71
Abel, Abell, Abels (brother of Cain) 135, 122
Abel 53 < Albrecht
Abel 53 (diminutive for Abraham)
Abele (poplar tree, fr Latin *albus*) 89
Abelmann (dweller near the poplars) 89
Abend (evening, one who lives toward the south) 85
Abendroth (evening red) 148
Abendschein, Abenschein (evening glow) 148
Abendschoen, Abenschoen (as beautiful as the evening) 148
Abenroth (Abbo's clearing) 124, 126
Abens (pre-Germanic river name) 23
Aberbach, see Auerbach
Aberholt (hostile, offensive) 115
Aberle, Aberly < Albrecht, see also Aeberli
Abert < Albrecht

Abich 53 (left, averse) 115
Abich < Albrecht
Abicht, see Habicht
Able, see Abel
Ableiter, Ableitner 122 (fr the slope) 69, 71
Abraham (OT name) 135, 122
Abrecht, see Albrecht
Abram, Abrams 164 (OT name) 135
Abscherer, see Scherer
Abschlag (steep slope) 71
Abschlag (excise collector) 109
Abt, Abts (Abbot, fr Latin *abbas*) 110
Abtsreiter, Abstreiter (abbot's clearing) 110, 125, 126
Abzieher (skinner) 96, 109
Abzug (gully, drain) 79
Abzug (copy-sheet, printer) 96
Ach, Ache, Achen, Acher (river, cog. Latin *aqua*) 79, 122
Achebach, Achenbach 122 Achenbacher, Achenback (brook coming fr a spring) 79, 77
Achen (fr Aachen) 79, 122
Acher (dweller on a river), see also Acker
Achilles (Greek name)
Achim 53 < Joachim
Achmann (dweller on a river) 79, 94
Achsteller (stable on a stony terrain) 79
Achterholt (behind the forest) 69, 72
Achterkirchen (behind the church) 69
Achtermann (dweller behind [the village, hill, etc.]) 69, 94
Achtung (attention) 117
Achtziger (eighty-year-old, born in the year '80)
Ackenbach, see Achebach
Acker 122, Ackers 164, Ackert 74 (field) 84

Ackerhaus (house on a field) 84,
  65
Ackerhof (small farm) 84, 92, 122
Ackerknecht (field hand) 84, 95
Ackermann, Akermann (farmer)
  84, 91, 94
Ackmann, see Achmann
Acuff, see Eichhoff
Adalmann, Addleman 159, see
  Edelmann
Adam, Adams 164 (husband of
  Eve) 135, 111
Adami (son of Adam) 142
Adamsweiler (Adam's village)
  135, 127
Ade, Adde, see Adam
Adelbald (noble + bold) 47, 46
Adelberg 122, Adelberger (noble
  mountain) 47, 68
Adelbert, see Albrecht
Adelbrich, Adelbrecht (noble +
  bright) 47, 51
Adeler, see Adler
Adelhart, Adehart, Adelhardt
  (noble + strong) 47, 46
Adelheid, Adelhyt (noble + qual-
  ity) 47, 133
Adelheim (noble hamlet) 47, 123,
  122
Adelmann, Adelman (nobleman)
  47, 94
Adelsberg, Adelsberger (fr
  Adelsberg, nobility mountain)
  47, 68, 122
Adelsdorfer, Adelsdoerfer (fr
  Adelsdorf, nobility village) 47,
  123
Adelstein, see Edelstein
Ader (vein, well)
Ader (crossbow string) 108
Adich 53, Adichs 164, Adix <
  Adolf
Adleberg 159, see Adelberg
Adleman 159, see Adelman

Adler 122, Adeler (eagle, fr noble
  + eagle, often a house name 48,
  63, 149)
Adolf, Adolph (noble + wolf) 46,
  48
Adoremus (Let us adore Him)
  116, 138
Adrian (Christian saint, name of
  pope) 134
Advent (fr church calendar) 143
Aeberli, Aeberlj, Aberley, see
  Eberle
Aebischer (dweller near ash trees)
  89
Aegidi (St. Aegidius) 131
Aelbragt, see Albrecht
Aeppli (little apple), see Apfel
Aeschbach (brook among ash
  trees) 89, 79
Aeschbach (brook containing
  *aesche* [graylings]) 79, see
  Aschenbach
Aescher, Aeschlimann 94 (dweller
  near ash trees) 89
Afeld, Afeldt, Affeldt (river field)
  79, 91
Aff (ape) 115, 116
Afferbach, Afflerbach (appletree
  brook) 89, 77
Affolter (apple tree) 89
Agatstein, Agetstein (agate,
  magnet) 73
Agede, see Eigenter
Agilbert (sword + bright) 46, 47
Agricola (Latin for farmer) 141
Agtermann, see Achtermann
Ahl (eel, catcher of, or dealer in,
  eels) 106, 115
Ahl, see Ahle
Ahlbach (eel brook) 115, 77, 83,
  122
Ahlberg (noble mountain) 47, 68
Ahlborn (nobly born) 47
Ahlborn (eel spring) 79
Ahlbrand, see Albrand
Ahle (awl, shoemaker) 98

Ahle (honeysuckle) 89
Ahlemann, see Alemann
Ahler 55, Ahlers 164, Ahlert 74 <
    Albrecht
Ahlfeld, Ahlfeldt (honeysuckle
    field) 89, 84, 122
Ahlhorn (place name) 122
Ahlinger (fr Ahling) 122
Ahlmann (dweller at a fen or
    swamp) 80, 94
Ahlstrom (eel stream) 115, 78
Ahn, Ahner (grandfather or
    ancestor) 119
Ahn (dweller at a fen) 80
Ahn 53 < Arnold
Ahneman (kinsman) 119, 94
Ahorn (maple) 89, 122
Ahrbeck (eagle brook) 48, 77, 122
Ahrberg, see Arberg
Ahrenbeck (eagle brook) 48, 78
Ahrenberg 122, see Arberg
Ahrend, Ahrends, Ahrens, see
    Arend, Arends
Ahrendorf, Ahrensdorf, see
    Arendorf
Ahrenholtz, see Arenholtz
Ahrenhorst (eagle hurst) 48, 72
Ahrens, Ahrend, Ahrendt, Ah-
    rends, see Arnd
Ahrensfeld (eagle field) 46, 84,
    122
Ahrensmeyer (dweller at the
    Ahrenshoff, Eagle Farm) 92, 93
Aich 122, Aicher, Aichner
    (dweller among the oaks) 89
Aichach (oak place) 89, 79, 122
Aichbichler (oak hill) 89, 67
Aichel, Aichele (acorn), see Eichel,
    Eichelmann
Aichelberg (acorn mountain) 89,
    68, 122
Aiching (belonging to the oaks)
    89, 123, 122
Aichmann (dweller among the
    oaks) 89, 94

Aichroad 159 (oak clearing) 89,
    124
Aidt, see Eid
Aierstock (ovary!? Nickname for
    egg dealer?)
Aigel, see Eigel
Aigner, see Eigne
Aik, see Aich
Aikenbrecher (oak cutter) 89, 95,
    100
Ainbinder (cooper) 96, see Ein-
    binder
Airheart 159, Airhart, see Erhard
Aisch (river name) 83
Aisenberg, see Eisenberg
Aisenstark (as strong as iron) 115
Aisner, see Eisner
Aist (place and river name) 122,
    83
Aker, Akermann, see Acker,
    Ackermann, also Eckert
Aker, Akers 164 (metal container
    for liquids) 106
Akkerman, see Ackerman
Aland (a kind of fish) 115, 122
Alb, see Alp
Albach, see Ahlbach
Alban (St. Albans) 131
Albaugh 159, see Ahlbach
Albeisser, see Altbuesser
Alber, Albers (poplar tree, fr
    Latin *albulus*) 89
Alberg, Alberger, Albirger 159 (fr
    Adelberg, noble mountain) 46,
    68
Albersheim (poplar hamlet) 89,
    123
Alberstein (poplar hill) 89, 73
Albert, Albertus 141, see Albrecht
Alberti, Alberty, son of Albert 59,
    142
Albinus (Latin: white) 141
Alborn, see Ahlborn
Albrand (noble + sword) 46, 47
Albrecht, Albracht, Albraecht
    (noble + bright) 47, 47

Albrechtsdorf (Albert's village) 47, 123

Albright 159, 162, Albrite 159 < Albrecht

Albwin (elf + friend) 48, 48

Aldag (weekday, also Adaldag, noble day)

Alder, Alders 164, see Alter

Alderfer 159, see Altdorfer

Aldhaus, see Althaus

Aldorf, see Altdorf

Aldorfer, Alldorfer (fr Aldorf 122), see Altdorfer

Aldhaus, see Althaus

Aleberger, see Alberger

Aleman, Alleman, Allman, Alemann (a German, fr French *allemand*) 121

Alexander (name of a pope) 134

Alf 53, Alfs 164, Alfing 55 < Adolf

Alfers 53, 164 < Adolf

Algeier, Algeir, Algeyer, Algire 159, Algyer 159 (fr Allgaeu in Austria) 121

Alkire 159, see Algeier

Allbach, Allenbacher, see Ahlbach

Allbring 53, Albrink < Albrecht

Alldach, see Aldag

Alldorfer, see Altdorfer

Allemann 122, Allman, Allimann, Allimang, see Aleman

Allenbach, Allebach, Allenbaugh 159 (eel brook) 77, 83, 151

Allendorf (old village) 123, 122

Allendorf (river village) 79, 123

Aller, Allers 164 (name of river) 83

Allerhand (all kinds of, exclamation) 117

Allerheiligen (All Saints) 143

Allgeier, Allgaier, Allgire 159, see Algeier

Allhelm, Alhelm (noble + helmet) 47, 46

Allman, Allmang, see Aleman

Allmendinger (fr Allmendingen, public common) 122

Allp, see Alp

Allschbach, Allschpach, Allspach, see Alsbach

Alltschul, Alltschuler, see Altschul

Alltstatt, Alstadt, see Altstatt

Allwein, Allwin, Allwine 159, see Alwin

Alm (alpine pasture) 84

Alman, Almann, see Aleman

Almende (common forest or pasture) 84

Almstedt (alpine meadow 84, Almsteadt 151)

Alp (fr Alpe 122, alpine pasture) 84

Alpaugh 159, see Ahlbach

Alpenbaur (peasant on the mountain pastures) 84, 91

Alper, Alpers 164, Alpert 74, Alphart (elf + strong) 47, 46

Alper, Alpers 164, see Albrecht

Alperstein (Albrecht's mountain) 73

Alphart, see Alper

Alps 164, see Alp

Alrich (noble + rule) 47 + 47

Alsbach 122 (pre-Germanic river name + *bach*, brook) 83

Alspach (eel brook 77, 122), see Ahlbach

Alsentzer (fr Alsenz) 122

Alstadt, see Altstadt

Alster (river at Hamburg) 83

Alster (magpie) 89

Alt, Altz, Ault, Alter (old man, the elder, senior) 113

Altaker (old field) 84

Altbuesser (shoe repairer) 96, 104

Altecken (old corner, old field) 85

Altemeyer, Altemeyer (previous owner of a farm) 93

Altemueller (fr the *Altmuehle*, old mill) 93, 94

Alten (place name) 122
Altenbach (old brook) 77, 122
Altenberg, Altenberger (old mountain) 68, 122
Altenburg, Altenburger (old castle) 73, 122
Altendorf (old village) 123, 122
Altenhein (old grove, or old hamlet) 123, 122
Altenhoefer (fr Altenhoefen) 122, 92
Altenhoff 122, Altenhoefer, see Althoff
Altenstein (old mountain) 73, 122
Alter, Alther, Alters 164,
Alterman 94 (old man, senior) 113
Altevogt (old governor) 112, 109
Altfather 159, see Altvater
Altfeld (old field) 84
Altgelt (old money) 117
Altgenug (old enough) 117
Althans (old Johnny, John the elder) 113
Althaus, Althauser (old house) 65, 122
Altheinz (Heinrich the elder) 113
Altherr, Alther (old master) 113
Althoff, Althof 122, Althoffer (old farm, old court) 92, 122
Altholz (old wood) 72, 122
Althous 159, Althouse 153, see Althaus
Altig, Altik, see Aldag
Altland 122, Altlandt (opposed to Neuland, or land recently reclaimed fr forest or swamp) 126
Altman, Altmann (old man) 113, 94
Altmark (German province, old march, old boundary) 120
Altmeister (senior guildsman) 113
Altmeyer (fr the Althoff) 92, 94, see Altemeyer

Altmuehl (corruption of pre-Germanic word for "swamp water") 83
Altmueller, see Altemueller
Altoff, see Althoff
Altona (fr pre-Germanic word for swamp, folk-etymologized to "all too near," town near Hamburg, cf. Too Nigh in Georgia) 122
Altorffer, see Altdorfer
Altreith, Altrith, Altruth (old clearing) 125
Alts 164, see Alt
Altschuh (old shoe, cobbler) 106
Altschul (old school, old synagogue)
Altstadt, Altstaedt, Altstaetter (old city) 122
Altstein (old stone, old mountain) 73
Altvater (grandfather, patriarch) 113
Altwobner (old weaver) 113, 96
Altz (fr pre-Germanic river name) 7, see Alt, Alts
Altweg (old path) 65
Alumbaugh 159, see Allenbach
Alvater, Alvather, see Altvater
Alwin (noble + friend) 47, 47
Alzheim, Alzheimer, Altesheim (old hamlet) 123
Amacker, Amacher (at the field) 69, 84
Aman, Amann, see Amman
Amand, see Amend and Aman
Ambach 122, Ambacher (on the brook) 69, 77
Amberg 122, Amberger (on the mountain) 69, 68
Amberman, see Ammermann
Ambinder, see Ainbinder
Amborn, Ambron (at the spring) 69, 79
Ambrister, Ambrust, Ambruster, see Armbrust

Ambros, Ambrose, Ambrosius 141
(St. Ambrose of Milan) 131
Ambrosi (son of Ambrose) 142
Ambrust, Ambruster, Ambrister
159, see Armbrust
Ambuehl (at the *Buehl* or hill) 69,
67, 122
Amburn, see Amborn
Amecker (fr Amecke 122, at the
corner) 69, 85
Ameis, Ameise (ant) 115
Ameis (deforested area) 71
Amelsberg (mountain of the
Amelungs), see next entry
Amelung, Ameling (a Germanic
tribe or dynasty) 120
Amen (Amen) 117, see Amman
Amend, Amende, Amendt, Ament,
Amment (at the end of the
road, field, etc.) 69
Amenhauser, Ammenheuser,
Ammenhewser 159, see Am-
menhauser
Amereihn, see Amrhein
Amerman, see Ammerman
Amersbach (yellow hammer
brook) 77
Ametsbichler (fr Ametsbichl, ant
hill) 67, 122
ˈAmhyser (at the houses) 69, 65,
66
Amman 94, Aman,
Ammeister (Amtmann, official)
109
Ammen (nurses, see also Amman)
Ammend, see Amend
Ammenhausen (the nurses'
houses, the officials' houses)
65, 122
Ammer (yellow-hammer) 89
Ammer (pre-Germanic river
name) 83
Ammerheim (yellow-hammer
village) 89, 123
Ammerheim (village on the
Ammer) 83, 123

Ammermann (bucket maker, fr
Latin *amphora*) 94, 96, 101
Ammlung, see Amelung
Ammon, Amon (OT name) 135,
see also Amman
Ampel (swinging lamp, fr Latin
*ampulla* 106), or see Ambuehl
Ample 159, see Ampel
Amrein, Amrain, Amrhein,
Amrhine 159 (on the Rhine) 69,
83, 122
Amrain (on the footpath) 69, 72,
65
Amsbacher, Amsbaugh 159
(dweller on the Amsbach,
inhabitant of Amsbach) 83, 122
Amsel, Amsl (ousel, blackbird,
fond singer) 115, 106
Amspacher, see Amsbacher
am Stein (on the crag) 69, 73, 122
Amtag (by day) 143
Amthor (at the gate) 69
Amtman (official) 94, 109
Amueller, see Aumueller
Amweg (on the path) 69, 65, 122
Anacker (without a field) 84
Anacker (on the field) 69, 84
Anbinder, see Ainbinder
Ancker (butter, butter maker) 96
Anczel 53 < Johann
Andenrieth (at the reeds, marsh)
69, 81
Anderach (on the river) 69, 79
Andereas, Anders, see Andreas
Andereck, Andereg, Anderich (at
the corner) 69, 85
Andermath (on the meadow) 69,
84
Anderschat (in the shade) 69
Anders, Andersen (son of An-
dreas) 59
Anderwiese (at the meadow) 69,
84
Andlau (pre-Germanic river name
in Alsace) 83
Andoni, see Anton

Andreas, Andrae, Andrea, An-
dres, Andress, Andries (St.
Andrew) 135
Andresen, Andresson, Andrewsen
159 (son of Andreas) 59
Anfeld (on the field) 69, 84
Anfeld (without a field) 84
Anfeld (fr Anfelden) 122
Anfield 153, see Anfeld
Angebrant (field cleared by fire)
84, 126
Angel, Angels 164, Angell (fish-
hook, hinge, Angle), see Anger
Angel (pre-Germanic river name)
83
Angelbach, Angelbeck (fishing
brook, or see Engelbach) 77
Angelberger (fr Amelberg 122),
see Engelberg
Angenendt (dweller at the end) 69
Anger 122, Angert 74 (small
meadow, pasture) 84, 122
Angerbauer (small farmer) 84, 91
Angerhoffer (small farmer) 84, 92
Angermann (dweller on the
meadow) 84, 94
Angermayer, Angermeier, Ang-
ermair (farmer dwelling on or
at a pasture) 84, 93
Angermueller (miller on the field)
84, 103
Angersbach (meadow brook) 84,
77, 122
Angerstein (field marker) 84, 73,
122
Angle 159, see Angel
Angst (fear) 115
Angst (dweller in narrow part of
valley) 76
Angstmann (executioner) 109, 94
Angstmann (timid man) 115, 94
Anhaeuser (fr Anhausen 122, at
the houses) 69, 65
Anhalt (German city and state)
121, 122
Anhorn (at the peak) 69, 68, 122

Anhut (without guard) 115
Anhut (hatless) 122
Ankerberg (mountain on the
water) 68
Ankerbrand (clearing on the
water) 126
Anmuth (grace) 115
Annacker, see Anacker
Annbacher (St. Anne's brook) 131,
77
Annen 53 (short for Annenberg,
etc.)
Annenberg (St. Anne's mountain)
131, 68, 122
Anneshansli 55 (little Hans, son
of Anna) 60
Annewallt, see Anwalt
Anno 53 < Arnold
Anoker 159, see Anacker
Ansbach (fr Ansbach 122, brook of
the gods, or *ans* pre-Germanic
word for "river") 48, 77, 83
Anschutz, Anschuetz (one who
turns on the water at a mill)
Ansel, Ansell, Anssel, Ansler, see
Anselm
Anselm, Anshelm, Anselmus 141
(god + helmet) 47, 48, 46, 131,
137
Anselmi (son of Ansel) 142
Anske 55 (little god) 47
Ansorge (without worry) 115
Anspach, Anspacher, Anspack (fr
Anspach 122, god + brook) 47,
47
Anstadt, Ansteadt, Anstet < St.
Anastasius 131
Anstadt (town on the *Ans*, pre-
Germanic river name) 83
Anstein (at the mountain) 69, 73,
122
Anstine 159 (fr Anstein) 122
Answald (god + rule, god + forest)
47, 46, 72

Ante, Antemann 94 (dweller on the boundary, at the end), see Amend

Antemann (duck raiser) 91, 94

Antenberg (duck hill) 115, 68

Antenbrink (duck hill) 115, 74

Anters 53, Antes, Anthes < Andreas

Antli, Antley 159 (little duck) 91, 115

Antlitz (face, countenance)

Anton, Anthon (St. Anthony) 131

Antoni, Anthoni (son of Anton) 142

Antwerck (siege machine, mechanic) 108

Antzengruber (fr Anzengrub) 122

Anwalt (attorney) 109

Apel, Appel, Apelt 74 (apple) 89, 105

Apelberg (apple hill) 89, 68

Apelman, see Appelmann

Apfel (apple) 89, 105, 122

Apfelbach, Apfelbeek (apple brook) 89, 77, 122

Apfelbaum (apple tree) 89

Apfelhaus (apple house) 89, 65

Apitz 53, Apitsch < Albrecht

Apke 53, 55 (little Albrecht)

App 53 < Albrecht

Appel 122, Appelt 74, Appelbaum, see Apel, Apfelbaum

Appel (pre-Germanic river name) 83

Appelbome, see Apfelbaum

Appeldorne (apple thorn) 89, 122

Appelmann (apple grower or seller) 89, 106, 94

Appelstein (apple seed) 89, 151

Appenzeller, Appenzellar 159 (Swiss fr Canton Appenzell) 121

Appert 53 < Albrecht

Apple 53, 159 < Adelbert, see Appel

Applefeld 159 (apple field) 89, 84

Applegarth 159 (apple orchard) 89, 84

Appler (apple grower or seller) 89

April (April) 143

Arb (heir, see Erb) 47

Arbaugh 159 (fr Arbach 122, eagle brook 48, 77)

Arbaugh (fr *ar*, pre-germanic word for "river") 83, 77

Arbegast, see Arbogast

Arbeiter, Arbetter (worker) 91

Arbengast, see Arbogast

Arberg (eagle mountain) 48, 68

Arberg (mountain on the Aar) 83, 68

Arbesman (heir) 47

Arbogast (heir + guest, name of a saint) 47, 131

Arbor, Arbort 74 (Latin, arbor) 141

Arburg (eagle castle) 48, 73

Arcularius (Latin, casket maker) 141

Arehart 159, see Erhard

Arenberg, see Arensberg

Arend 53, Arends 164, Arendt, Arenth, Arentz, Arens, see Arnold

Arenholtz (eagle forest) 48, 72, 122

Arensberg, Arensberger (eagle mountain) 48, 68, 122

Arenstein, see Arnstein

Arfmann (heir) 46, 94

Argabright 159, Argenbright, Argubright < Erkanbrecht, genuine + bright) 46, 151

Argire 159, Argauer, see Aargauer

Arisman 159, see Ehrismann

Arlt 53 < Arnold

Armbrust, Armbruester, Armbreast 159, Armbreaster (crossbow, fr Latin *arcuballista*) 108

Armel, Aermel (sleeve, tailor) 104

Armenbeter (one who prays for poor) 138

Armentraut 159, Armentrout (friend of the poor) 138

Armgast (poor stranger) 120

Armistead 159 < Armistaed (place name) 122

Armknecht (poor servant) 138

Arnau (eagle meadow) 46, 84

Arnbuehl (eagle hill) 46, 67

Arnd 53, Arndt < Arnold

Arndorf (eagle village) 46, 123, 122

Arndt, see Arnd

Arnheim (eagle hamlet) 46, 123

Arnhelm (eagle + helmet) 46, 46

Arnhoff (eagle farm) 46, 92

Arnholt, Arnholtz, see Arnold

Arno 53 < Arnold

Arnold, Arnolt, Arnolds 164, Arnoldus 141 (eagle + loyal or eagle + rule) 48, 58, 47

Arnoldi (son of Arnold) 142

Arnreich (eagle + rule) 46, 47

Arnsdorf, Arnsdorfer, see Arndorf

Arnsmeyer (occupant of the Arnshoff, eagle farm, Arnold's farm) 93

Arnstein (eagle mountain) 46, 73, 122

Arnswald (eagle forest) 48, 72

Arnt, see Arnd

Arnulf (eagle + wolf) 46, 48

Arnwine 159 (eagle + friend) 48, 48

Arold, see Arnold

Aronstein, see Arnstein

Arnt, see Arnd

Arzberger (fr Arzberg 122), see Erzberger

Arzt, Artz, Arts 159 (doctor, fr Latin *arciater*) 96

Asbach, Asbacher (pre-Germanic *as*, meaning "water" + *bach*, brook) 83

Asch, Asche, Ash 159 (ash tree, ash forest, see Esch) 89, 122

Asch (ashes, ash burner) 95

Asch (vessel) 106

Aschbacher (fr Aschbach 122), see Eschbach

Aschberg, Ascheberg, Aschberger (ash tree mountain) 89, 48, 122

Aschemeier (farmer among the ash trees) 89, 93

Aschenbach (ash tree brook) 89, 77

Aschenbrenner (burner of ashes, perhaps for soap or potash) 95

Aschendorf (ash tree village) 89, 123, 122

Aschenmoor (ash fen) 89, 80

Ascher, Aschman 94, Aschmann (maker of tanner's lime, soap-maker's ash) 95

Asendorf (grazing village) 122

Ash 159, Ashe, see Asch

Ashauer 159 (ash tree cutter, dweller on a meadow in the ash trees) 89, 95

Ashbaugh 159, Ashbaugher, see Aschbacher

Ashenfelter 159 (ash tree field) 84

Asher 159, see Ascher

Ashman 159, see Asher

Asman 53, Asmann, Assmann, Asmus, Assmus < St. Erasmus 131

Aspe, see Espe

Aspeck, Aschbeck (ash brook) 89, 77

Aspel (fen) 80

Aspelhof (farm on a fen meadow) 80, 92

Aspel (fen) 80

Aspelmeyer (fr the Aspelhof, fen farm) 80, 93, 94

Aspinwall < Espenwald (aspen forest) 89, 72

Assenmacher (wainwright) 96

Assheim (carrion hamlet) 123, 122

Ast (branch, wood cutter, difficult person) 95, 115, 122

Astheim (east hamlet) 85, 123, 122

Astholz (branch wood, faggot gatherer) 95

Astor (astor, fr the Greek 9, or perhaps *Aster*, magpie 89, or *astore*, Italian: hawk 89)

Astroth (branch clearing) 126

Aswalt, Answald, see Oswald

Atterholt, Atherholt (at the forest) 69, 72

Atz, Attz (donkey) 115

Atz 53 < Albrecht)

Atzbach (pre-Germanic *at*, river + *bach*, brook) 83, 77, 122

Atzel, see Elster

Atzelstein (magpie mountain) 73

Atzman (follower of Albrecht) 94

Atzrodt, Atzrott (donkey clearing) 126

Au, Aub, Aue (meadow, usually shortened fr compound word) 84, 122

Aubel 53 < Albrecht

Auberg (meadow hill) 84, 68

Aubitz 53 < Albrecht

Aubrecht, see Albrecht

Auburg, Auburger (castle on the meadow, or castle at Au) 84, 73, 122

Auch, Auchmann 94 (night shepherd) 95

Auchenbach, Auchenbaugh 159, Auchinbaugh 159, see Achebach

Auchtmann, see Achmann

Aue, Auen, see Au

Auenbrugger (dweller near the bridge at the meadow) 84, 71

Auer (dweller on a meadow, usually shortened fr compound word) 84

Auer (auerochs) 115

Auerbach 122, Auerback (brook through meadow, possibly bison [*auerochs*] brook, or else based on pre-Germaic *ur*, muddy water) 84, 77, 115, 122

Auerhahn (grouse) 84, 115

Auerswald (meadow wood) 84, 71

Auerweck (meadow path) 84, 65, Auerweck (meadow village, fr Latin *vicus*) 84, 123

Aufderheide (on the heath) 69, 81, 122

Auffahrt (Ascension Day) 143

Auge, Augen (eye, eyes) 114

Augenbaugh 159, see Achebach

Augenstein (St. Augustine) 131

Aughinbaugh 159, see Achebach

Augsburg, Augspurg, Augsburger (Swabian city) 122

August, Augustus (Latin, Augustus) 141

Augustin, Augustinus 141 (St. Augustine) 131

Aul, Auler, Aulner (pot, potter, fr Latin *olla*) 96

Aulbert, see Albert

Auld, see Alt

Aule (jackdaw) 115

Aulebach, Aulenbacher (fr Aulenbach) 122

Aulenbaecker (potter) 96

Aulmann (potter) 96, 94

Ault, see Alt

Aulthaus, see Althaus

Aultland, see Altland

Auman, Aumann (meadow man) 84, 94

Aumiller, see Aumueller

Aumueller (fr the Aumuehle, mill on the meadow) 84, 103

Aungst 159, see Angst

Aurich (place name) 122

Ausdemwalde (out of the forest) 69, 71

Ausderau (out of the meadow) 69, 84

Ausdermuehle (out of the mill) 69

Ausfresser (glutton) 115

Ausheim (outside the village) 69, 124

Ausherman 159, see Ascher

Auslander (outlander, foreigner) 120

Auspurger, see Augsburg

Aust, Austen, Austin (St. Augustine) 131

Auster, see Oster

Austerlitz (town in Bohemia) 122

Austermann (easterner) 85, 94

Austermuehle, see Ausdermuehle

Austrich, Austria 153, see Oestrich

Auwaerter (meadow guard) 96

Averbach, see Auerbach

Averhart, see Eberhard

Avig 159, see Ewig

Awalt 159, see Ewald

Awert 159, see Eber

Ax, Axe, Axt 74, Axmann 94 (ax, ax maker, carpenter) 96

Axel 53 < Absolon (OT name, Absalom) 135

Axelbaum (axel shaft, wainwright) 96, 106

Axelmann (cartwright) 96, 94

Axelrad, Axelrod (axle wheel, cartwright) 106

Axt 74, Axtman 94 (ax, woodcutter) 95

Ay, Aye, Ayer, see Ei, Eier

Ayd, Aydt, see Eid

Ayrer, Ayers 164, see Eier

Ayzenberg, see Eisenberg

Azenweiler (donkey village) 127

Azman (donkey man) 115, 94

**B**

Baacke, Baake, see Baak

Baaden, Baader, see Baden, Bader

Baak (horse, horse dealer) 106

Baar 122, see Bahr

Baart, Baartz, see Bart

Baas (master, chief, boss)

Baasche, see Basch

Baase, see Base

Babbes, Babst 74, Babest, see Pabst

Baccus, see Backhaus

Bach 122, Bache, Bachs 164 (brook, dweller on a brook) 77

Bacharach, Bachrach (city on the Rhine) 122

Bachaus, see Backhaus

Bachdold, Bachdolt, see Bechtold

Bache (brood swine, female wild boar) 91, 115

Bachenheimer (fr Bachenheim 122, brook hamlet) 77, 123

Bacher, Bachert 74, Bachner, Bachart 74 (dweller on a brook) 77, 87, 122

Bacher (wild boar) 115

Bacher (Jewish, *bachur*, Talmud student) 147

Bachhoffen, Bachofen 122, see Backof

Bachhuber (farmer on the brook) 77, 92

Bachmann, Bachman (dweller on the brook) 77, 94

Bachmeyer, Bachmeier, Bachmaier, Bachsmeyer (farmer on a brook) 77, 93

Bachmeyer (occupant of the Bachhof, brook farm) 77, 93

Bachner, see Bacher

Bachrach, see Bacharach

Bachtel, Bachtell, Bachtler, see Bechtel

Bachstein (brook hill, brook stone) 77, 73

Bachstein, see Backstein

Bachthal (brook valley) 77, 76, 122
Bachus, see Backhaus
Back, see Baak
Back 159, see Bach
Back, Backe (jowl) 114
Backebrandt (baker's fire, baker) 96
Backer, Backert 74, see Bacher, Becker
Backhaus, Backhus, Backhuas 159 (bakehouse, bakery) 65, 122
Backhoffer, Backhofer, see Backof
Backler (baker) 96
Backley 159, see Bechtle
Backman, Backmann (baker) 96, 94
Backmeister (master baker) 96
Backner (baker) 96
Backof, Backoff, Backofen, Backoven (baker's oven, baker) 96
Backstrom (brook stream) 77, 78
Backus, see Backhaus
Bacmeister, see Backmeister
Badder, see Bader
Badecker, see Boettcher
Badedorfer (bath village) 96, 123
Bademann (bath attendant) 96, 94
Baden (baths, any one of many South German places) 121, 122
Badenhamer, Badenheimer (fr Badenheim 122, bath hamlet) 123
Bader (bath attendant, surgeon) 96
Badertscher (surgeon) 96
Badmann, Badner, see Bademann
Baecher, see Becher
Baechle 53 (little brook) 77
Baechtel, see Bechtel
Baeck 122, see Becker
Baecker 122, see Becker
Baedeker, see Boettcher

Baehler, see Buehler
Baehm, see Boehm
Baehr, Baehre (bear) 48
Baehring, Baehringer, see Behrens
Baehrle 53 (little bear) 48
Baehrmann, see Berman
Baehrwolf (bear + wolf) 48, 48
Baender, see Bender
Baeninger, see Peninger
Baenisch, Baensch, see Benisch
Baenk (bench, bench maker) 96, 106
Baentzler 53 < St. Benedictus 131
Baer, Baehr (bear, usually a shortened form) 48
Baer (wild boar) 48
Baerenburg (bear castle) 48, 73, 122
Baerenreuth (fr Berenreuth 122, burned clearing) 126
Baerger, see Berger
Baerhold (bear + loyal) 48, 48
Baeringer, see Behrens
Baerli 53, Baerley 159 (little bear) 48
Baerman, Baermann (bear man, bear trainer) 48, 96, 94
Baerstein (bear mountain) 48, 73
Baertlein 55 (little beard) 114
Baerwald (bear forest) 48, 71
Baesler, see Basler
Baetger, see Boettcher
Baetje, Baetjer, see Boettcher
Baetz, see Betz
Baeumer, Baeumler (expert on fruit trees) 89, 96
Baeuml 53 (little tree) 89
Baeurele, Baeurlein, Baeuerlein (little peasant) 91, 55, 122
Baeyerlein 55, see Baeuerl
Baez, see Betz
Bagger (dredger) 96
Bahl 53, Bahle, Bahls 164, Bahlmann 94, Bahler < Baldwin

Bahn, Bahne, Bahnlein 55 (path,
track, road) 65
Bahner, Bahnert 74 (weaver's
tool, weaver) 106
Bahnke 55 (little path) 65
Bahnmueller (miller on the path)
65, 103
Bahr (bear) 48
Bahre, Bahremann 94 (stretcher
bearer) 96
Bahrenburg, see Barenburg
Bahrlein 55 (little bear) 48
Bahsel, see Basler
Baier, Baierman 94, see Bayer
Baierlein 55, Baierline 159, see
Bayerle, Baeurele
Baiersdorf 122, see Bayersdorf
Bail, Baile, Bailer, Bailor 159,
Baylor 159, see Beil, Beiler
Bain, see Bein
Bair, see Baer, Bayer
Baisch 53 < St. Sebastian 131
Baitmann 94, Baitz, Baizner
(falconer) 91
Bakenhus 122, see Backhaus
Baker, Bakker, see Becker,
Bacher
Balcer, see Baltzer
Balch (kind of game fish) 115, 106
Balck, see Balk
Bald, Balde, Baldt, Balt (bold 46,
river name 83)
Baldauf, Balldauf, Balduf (brave
+ wolf) 48, 117
Baldauf ("soon up," perhaps a
greeting to miners) 117
Baldhauer, see Waldhauer
Baldinger 122 (fr Balding, be-
longing to Baldwin) 46, 59
Baldrick (bold + rule) 46, 47
Baldwin, Baldewin (brave +
friend) 46, 48, 50
Balk (beam, carpenter) 96
Ball, Balls 164 (ball, dance,
hunting sound)
Ball 53, Ballmann 94 < Baldwin

Ballauf, see Baldauf
Ballenberg, Ballenberger (fr
Ballenberg) 122
Ballenger, Baller 53 < Baldwin
Ballenhausen (town name) 122
Ballerstadt (fr Ballerstaedt) 122
Balling 53, 55, Ballinger < Bald-
win
Ballman 53, 94, Ballmann <
Baldwin
Balmer, Ballmer, Ballmert 74
(dweller under a cliff, see also
Palmer)
Balmtag (Palm Sunday) 143
Balsam (balsam) 106, 115
Balser 53, Balsor 159 < Balthasar
Balsinger, see Bellsinger
Balter 53 < Balthasar
Balthasar, Baltasar, Balthhauser,
Baltzar, Baltzaer (one of the
Three Kings) 131, 111
Balthauer, see Waldhauer
Baltz, Balz, Baltze, Baltzer,
Baltzel, Baltzell, Baltzer,
Baltzar, see Palts, Paulser,
Balthasar, Baldwin
Bambach 159, see Bombach
Bamberg, 122, Bamberger, Bam-
esberg (fr Bamberg)
Bancalf 159, see Bannkauf
Band (hoop maker) 106
Bandel, Bandell, Bandele, Bandli
(ribbon maker) 106
Bandhagen, Bandhaken (cooper's
hook, cooper) 106
Bandholt, Bandtholtz (wood for
barrel hoops, cooper) 96, 106
Baner, Banner, see Bahner
Bang, Bange, Bangs 164, Banger,
Bangers 164, Bangert 74
(timid) 115
Bangart, Banghart, Bangerth, see
Baumgart
Banholtz (proscribed forest) 72

Bank 122, Banke, Banker, Banks 164 (bench, workbench, bench maker) 106
Bankamper (field on a road) 65, 84
Bankard, Bankhart, Bankerd, Bankert (illegitimate child) 119
Bankwirt (taverner) 96
Bann (ban) 122
Bannat (Banat, German area in Hungary) 121
Banne, Bannmann (crowd, mob)
Banner (banner, ensign) 107
Bannerman, Bannertraeger (ensign) 107, 94
Banninger (fr Banningen) 122
Bannkauf (proscribed sale)
Bansch, Banscher, Baensche (pot belly) 114
Banse, Bansen (store room, granary, woodpile)
Bantel, Bantell, Bantle 159, Bantli 55 (little band, ribbon maker) 106
Bantel 53 < St. Pantaleon 131
Bantner (dweller in a fenced area) 84
Bantz, Banz, Banzel 55 (small child)
Banwarth (forest guard) 65, 47
Banzer, see Panzer
Baptista, Baptiste, Baptisto (John the Baptist) 131
Baranhardt, see Bernhard
Barb (kind of river fish) 115, 106
Barbel 53, Baerbel < Barbara 60
Barbelroth (Barbara's clearing) 126
Barch (barrow hog) 91
Barchell (fr Barchel) 122
Barchmann (swineherd) 95, 94
Barcket (weaver of Barchend, rough cloth) 96
Bard, see Bart
Bardelman, see Bartel

Bardenhagen (halbard enclosure) 123, 122
Bardenwerter (halbard maker) 108
Bardman, see Bartmann
Barenbaum, see Birnbaum
Barenburg (bear castle) 48, 73, 122
Barfuss (barefoot, Barefoot Friar) 114, 110
Barg (castrated swine) 91, see Barmann
Bargar, Barger, see Berger
Bargfeld 122, see Bergfeld
Barghoff, see Berghoff
Bargmann, Bargman, see Bergmann
Barmann (swine castrator) 95, 94
Barhausen (bear houses) 48, 65
Barhorst (bear hurst) 48, 72
Baringer, see Baehringer
Bark, Barke 122 (birch tree) 89
Bark, Barke (ship, boatman) 96
Barkamp (bear field) 48, 84
Barkdoll, see Bergdoll
Barkewitz (mountain village) 127
Barkhaus, Barkhausen 122, Barkhauser, Barkhouse 153, Barkhouser, see Berghaus
Barkheimer, Barkhimer 159, see Bergheimer
Barkhorn, see Berghorn
Barkmann, see Bergmann
Barmann (half-free peasant) 91, 94, see Bermann
Barnd, see Bernd
Barner, see Berner
Barnhard, Barnhardt, see Bernhard
Barnhaus 122, Barnhauser (bear house) 48, 65
Barnheart 159, see Bernhard
Barnholt, see Bernholt
Barnhouse 153, Barnhouser 159, see Barnhaus
Barnscheier (bear barn) 48

Barnstein (fr Barnstein 122), see
Bernstein
Barnstorf (bear village, or
Bernhard's village) 48, 123, 122
Baron, Barron (warrior, baron)
107
Barr (cash) 115
Barrabas (NT name) 111
Barringer < Berenger (bear +
spear) 48, 46
Barsch, Barss (perch) 115, 106
Barsch 53 < Bartholomaeus
Bart, Barth, Barthel 55, Bartz 74
< Bartholomaeus, Barthold,
Bartolf, etc.
Bart, Barth (beard, barber) 112,
96
Barte (butcher's ax, butcher) 106
Bartal 159, see Bertel
Bartasch (fringed purse) 106
Bartel, Bartels 164, Barthels,
Barttel, Bartelmes < Barthol-
omaeus
Barth 122, see Bart
Barthel, see Bartel
Barthelm (battle-ax + helmet) 46,
46
Barthelmes, see Bartolomaeus
Bartholomaeus, Bartholomae,
Bartholome, Bartholomes,
Bartholomei, Batholomy,
Bartholomus (St.
Bartholomew) 131
Bartholt (battle-ax + loyal) 46, 48
Bartkuss (beard kiss) 112
Bartle 159, see Bartel
Bartlebaugh 159 (Bartel's brook)
77
Bartling (fr Bartlingen) 122
Bartmann (thick stone jug) 106
Bartmann (beard wearer) 112, 94
Bartol, Bartold, see Bartholt,
Bartholomaeus
Bartolomaeus, see Bartholomaeus
Bartosch, see Bartasch

Bartram (battle-ax + raven) 46,
48
Barts 164, see Bart
Bartsch 53 < Bartholomaeus
Bartscher, Bartscheer, Bartsche-
rer (beard shears, barber) 96
Barttel, see Bartel
Bartz 53, 164, Barz, see Bart,
Bartholomaeus
Barzmann 53, 93 < Bartholo-
maeus
Basch (sharp, as of spice) 115
Base, Basemann 94 (cousin,
gossip) 119
Basel 122, Basler, Bassel (fr
Basel) 122
Bass (boss) 109
Basse (one-masted boat) 122
Basselmann, see Basel
Bassler, see Basel
Bast 53, Bastian, Bastien < St.
Sebastian 131
Bast (hunting term, breaking up
of stag) 91
Bastert (bastard) 119
Bate (help), see also Pate
Bates 159, see Betz
Bateman 159, see Bethmann
Bath, see Bad
Bathmann, Batmann (bath
attendant) 96, 94 Batt
(emolument), also St. Beatus
131
Batten, Battenberg, Battenfeld
(place names fr *bat*, swamp
water) 80, 122
Battermann (wooden spade) 106
Battermann (boaster) 115, 94
Battist (John the Baptist) 131
Batts 159, Batz, Batze, Batzer,
see Patz
Batty 159, see Battist
Bau (construction, cultivation)
122
Bauch (belly, glutton) 114

Bauer, Bauers 164, Baur, Bau-
erdt 74 (farmer) 91, 149
Bauerfeld, Bauersfeld (peasant
field) 91, 84
Bauerle 55, Bauerlein, Bauerlien
159, Bauerline 159 (little
peasant) 91
Bauermann (same as Bauer) 91,
94
Bauermeister, Bauernmeister
(village head) 109
Bauernfeind, Bauernfiend 159
(peasant enemy, probably
initiation name) 117
Bauernschub, Bauernshub 159
(peasant overcoat) 112
Bauers 164, see Bauer
Bauerschmidt, Bauernschmid
(village smith) 91, 96
Bauersfeld, see Bauerfeld
Bauershaefer (peasant oats) 91,
92
Bauerwein (peasant wine) 91, 102
Baugh 159, Baugher, Baughman,
see Bach, Bacher, Bachmann
Baughman 159, see Baumann
Baughtall 159, see Bechtold
Bauhaus (shelter at construction
site) 65, 122
Bauholzer (seller of building
wood, builder in wood) 72, 106
Bauk, Bauker (drum, drummer)
96, 106
Bauknecht (construction helper)
96
Bauknight 159, see Bauknecht
Baum, Baums 164 (tree) 89, 122
Baumann (tenant, see Bauer) 91,
94
Baumbach (tree brook) 89, 77,
122
Baumberger (fr Baumberg 122,
tree mountain) 89, 68
Baumbusch (tree busch) 89, 72
Baumeister (builder, agricultural
manager) 96

Baumel 55 (little tree) 89
Baumer, Baumert 74 (horticul-
turist) 84, 143
Baumer (manager of, or dweller
near a toll gate)
Baumgaert, Baumgaertner (or-
chard, orchardist) 84
Baumgarden, Baumgarten 122,
Baumgardner, Baumgartner,
Baumgarthner, Baumgartel,
Baumgarner, Baumgart (or-
chardist) 84
Baumhard (strong as a tree) 89,
46
Baumhard (uncultivated, tree-
studded area) 89, 84
Baumhof, Baumhoefer (tree farm)
89, 92, 122
Baumiller (miller at a *Bauhof*)
103
Baumler (tree guard) 89, 96, see
also Baumer
Baummer, see Baumer
Baumoehl (tree cutter) 95, see
also Baumohl
Baumohl (olive oil seller) 106
Baumrin, Baumrind (collector of
bark for tanning) 95
Baumstark (strong as a tree) 115
Baumstein (tree stone) 89, 73
Baumwoll (cotton) 105, 106
Baur, see Bauer
Baurmeister, Bauernmeister
(village mayor) 109
Baus, Bausch, Bauscher (bolster)
106
Baus (bruise, swelling) 114
Bausch, see Busch
Bauschenberger (bush mountain)
72, 68
Bauth, Bauthe, Bauthner
(building, beehive) 95
Bauthz (fr Bautzen) 122
Baverungen 159, see Beverungen
Bawman 159, see Baumann

Bayer, Bayr, Beyer, Bayermann 94 (Bavarian) 121
Bayerfalck (Bavarian falcon) 120, 91, 115, 62
Bayerhoff (Bavarian farm) 122, 121, 92
Bayerle 55, Bayerlein 55 (little Bavarian, see Baeuerle) 120
Bayersdorf (Bavarian's village) 120, 123
Baylor 159, see Beiler
Bayrle, see Bayerle
Bazermann, see Patz
Beacher 159, see Buecher
Beachler 159, see Buechler
Beadenkof 159, Beadenkoef, Beadenkopf, see Biedenkopp
Beagle 159, see Buegel
Beahm 159, see Boehm
Beahmesderfner 159 (Bohemian villager) 122, 123
Beal 159, Beals 164, Beall, see Buehl
Bealefeld 159, Bealefield 153, see Bielefeld 122
Bealer 159, Beeler 159, see Buehler
Beam 159, Beamer, see Boehm, Boehmer
Beamsderfer 159, Beamesderfer, see Beahmesderfner
Bean 159, Beane, see Bohn, Bohne
Bear 159, Bearman, see Baehr, Baehrmann
Beardorf 159 (bear village) 48, 123, 151
Beaver 153, see Bieber
Bebel, Bebler, Beber (something or someone small) 113
Bechelmeier (fr the Bechelhof, little brook farm) 77, 93, 92, 94
Becher, Bechermann 94, Bechler (maker of mugs, fr Latin *bicarium*) 106

Becher (tarheeler, tar maker, fr Latin *pix*) 95
Becher (dweller on a brook) 77
Becher, Bechler (drinker, tippler) 115
Bechhoffer (pitch farm) 92
Bechlinger (fr Bechlingen) 122
Bechmann (tarheeler, tar maker) 95, 94
Bechold, see Bechthold
Bechstein (pitch stone) 73
Becht, Bechte, Bechtel, Bechtler (New Year revelry), see also Bechthold
Bechthold, Bechtolt, Bechtoll, see Berchthold
Beck (brook) 77, 122
Beck, Becks 164, Becke (baker) 96
Beck (snout) 114
Beck (basin, Latin, *bacinum*) 106
Beckel (helmet) 108
Beckelheimer 55, Beckelhimer 159 (fr Beckelheim 122, little brook hamlet) 77, 123
Beckemeyer (brook farmer) 77, 93
Beckenbach (Becco's brook) 77
Beckendorf (brook village) 77, 123, 122
Beckenholt (brook wood) 77, 72
Becker, Beckert 74 (baker) 96, 104, 143
Becker (dweller on a brook) 78
Beckerbach, see Beckenbach
Beckermann, Beckmann (baker) 96, 94
Beckeweg (brook path) 77, 65
Beckhardt (Beghard, lay brother) 110
Beckler (tippler) 115
Becklin 55, Beckley 159, see Boekle
Beckman, Beckmann (baker) 96, 94
Beckmann (dweller on a brook) 77, 94
Beckner, see Becker

Beckolt, see Berchtold

Beckstein (brook stone) 77, 73, 122

Beckstein (brick maker) 100, 122

Beckstrom (brook stream) 77, 78

Beech 159, see Buech, Buecher

Beechener 159, see Buechner

Beehler 159, see Buehler

Beek (brook) 77

Beeker 159, see Buecher

Beekmann, see Bachmann

Beel 159, see Buehl

Beeler 159, Beehler, see Buehler

Beem 159, Beemer, see Boehm, Boehmer

Beer, Beermann, see Baer, Baermann, Bier, Biermann

Beer, Beers 164, see Ber, Behr, Bier

Beerbach (bear brook, boar brook) 48, 77, 122

Beerbohm (pear tree) 89

Beerends, see Behren

Beermann, see Baehrmann

Begabock 159, see Beckenbach

Begemann (dweller on the Bega) 83, 94

Begstein, see Beckstein

Begtel, Begtoll, see Bechtel

Behagel (affable) 115

Behl, Behle, Behler, Behlert 74, see Buehl

Behling (fr Behlingen) 122

Behm, Behme, Behmer 34, see Boehm

Behn, Behne, Behner, Behnemann 94 < Bernhard

Behnke 55, Behnken (little bear), or < Bernhard

Behr, Behre, Behrs 164 (bear, boar), or < Bernhard

Behren 53, Behrens 164, Behrend, Behrendt < Bernhard

Behringer (fr Behringen, the descendants or people of Behr) 123, 122

Behrmann (bear + man, bear trainer) 48, 94

Behrman, Behrmann (beer handler) 96, 94

Behrnhard, see Bernhard

Behse, see Besen

Beichel 55, Beichl (little belly) 114

Beichler, Beichmann 94 (slope dweller) 71

Beichter (confessor) 110

Beidel, see Beutel

Beidelmann, Beidelman, see Beutelmann

Beiderwieden (by the willows) 69, 89

Beier, Beiermann, see Bayer

Beierlein, see Baeuerlein, Bayerlein

Beigel, see Buegel

Beightel 159, Beightol, see Beichtel, Bechtol

Beights 159, see Beitz

Beil, Beiler (ax maker or seller) 106

Beilfus (ax foot) 114

Beiling (fr Beilingen) 122

Beilke 55 (little ax) 106

Beilstein (ax stone, old hunting grounds) 73

Beimel, Beimler, see Baeumel, Baeumler

Bein, Beine, Beinn, Beinle 55 (leg, bone) 114

Beinhauer (butcher, not leg hacker) 96

Beinhorn (river name, swamp corner) 80, 83

Beinike 55 (little bee) 115

Beinkampen (by the fields) 69, 84

Beinstein (by the mountain) 69, 68, 122

Beischwanger (adjacent clearing) 126

Beisel, Beissel, Beissler (tool for splitting wood) 106

Beisner (one who hunts with falcons) 91

Beispiel (example)

Beisser (falconer) 91

Beitel 122, Beittel, Beitle 159, Beitler, Beitelmann (purse maker) 106, see Beutel, Beutler, Beutelmann

Beitz, Beitzel, Beitzell (falconer) 91

Beker, see Becker

Bekmann, see Beckmann

Beler 159, Beeler, see Buehler

Belfield 153, see Bielefeld

Belitz (place name) 122

Bell, Belle (part of a ship)

Bell, Belle (white poplar) 89

Beller (watch dog, quarreler) 115

Belling, Bellinger (fr Belling) 122

Bellmann (public announcer) 109, 94

Bellner (public announcer) 109

Belman, Bellmann, see Bellmann

Belmont 157, see Schoenberg

Beltz, Belz, Beltzer, Beltzner, see Peltz

Beltzenhagen (place name) 123, 122

Bemer 159, see Boehmer

Bence 159, see Bentz

Benck, see Benk

Bendel (ribbon maker or seller) 106, 106

Bendel, Bendler (barrel hoop maker, cooper) 96, 106

Bender, Benders 164, Bendert 74 (cooper) 96

Benderoth (swamp clearing) 80, 126

Bendewald (swampy forest) 80, 71

Bendex, Bendix < St. Benedict 131

Bendt < St. Benedict 131

Benedict, Benedick (St. Benedict) 131

Beneke 53, Bennecke < Bernhard

Bener 53 < Bernhard

Benesch, Bensch, Benisch < Czech, Benedict 146

Bengel (club, fool) 115

Bengert, see Benkert

Benhof, Bennhoff (Bernhard's farm) 92, 122

Benighoff, see Benninghoff

Benisch, see Benesch

Benjamin (OT name) 135

Benk, Benke, Benker, Benkert 74 (bench, cabinet maker, from Benk 122) 96

Benkert, Benkart (bastard) 119

Benner, see Bender

Benning 53, 122 < Bernhard

Benninghoff, Benninghof 122, Benninghove (peat bog farm) 80, 92

Benno 53 < Bernhard

Benroth, Benrath 122 (a city, stream clearing) 126

Bensch, see Benesch

Bense, Bensen 122, Benser, Bensing, Bensinger (place where bullrushes grow) 81

Bensel, Benseler (dweller among the reeds) 81

Benshoff (reed farm) 92

Benshoff (Bernhard's farm) 53, 92

Bensing, Bensinger, see Bentzinger

Benson, see Bentzen

Bentell, Bentels 164, see Bentler

Bentheim (name of city, marsh hamlet) 122

Bentler < St. Pantaleon 131

Bentli, Bentley 159, see Bantli

Bentsen, son of Bentz 59

Bentz 53, Benz, Benze, Benzel 55, Bentzel < Bernhard or Benedict

Bentzen, son of Bentz 59

Bentziger, Bentzing, Bentzinger (fr Bentzingen) 122

Benzelius 141, see Bentzel

Benzenhof 122, Benzenhoffer,
  Benzenhafer 159 (reed farm)
  81, 92
Benzinger, see Bentziger
Beohmer 159, see Boehmer
Ber, see Baer
Berach (bear river) 48, 83
Berbisdorf (Berbi's village) 123,
  122
Berch, see Berg
Berchelbach, Berckelbach (birch
  brook) 89
Bercher, see Berger and Bircher
Berchner, see Bergner
Berchtel, see Berchthold
Berchthold (bright + loyal) 46, 46
Berchthold < Berchtwald (bright
  + rule) 46, 46
Berck, see Berg
Berckhaeuser, Berckheiser 66,
  Berckhyser 66 (occupant of
  mountain house) 68, 65
Berdahl (bear valley) 48, 76
Bere 53, Berele 55 < Bernhard
Berenbach (bear brook) 48, 77,
  122
Berenberg 122, Berenberger (bear
  mountain, berry mountain) 48,
  68
Berend, Berends 164, Berents,
  see Baehrend
Berenger (bear + spear) 48, 46
Berenhaus (bear house) 48, 65
Berenholtz (bear forest) 48, 72
Berenstecher (boar castrator) 95
Berfeld (boar field) 48, 84
Berg, Berge, Bergs 164, Bergen
  (mountain) 68, 82
Bergbauer (mountain farmer) 68,
  91
Bergdoll 159 (mountain valley)
  68, 76
Bergdoll, see Berchtold
Bergenbach (mountain brook) 68,
  77
Bergenslott (mountain castle) 68

Bergenstine 159 (fr Bergenstein
  122, mountain stone) 68, 73,
  151
Bergenthal (mountain valley) 68,
  76
Berger (mountain man) 68
Bergfeld (mountain field) 68, 84,
  122
Bergh, see Berg
Berghaus (mountain house) 68,
  65, 122
Berghauser, Berghaeuser, Berk-
  haeuser, Berckheiser 66,
  Bergheiser 66 (fr Berghausen
  122, house on a mountain) 68,
  65
Bergheimer (fr Bergheim,
  mountain hamlet) 68, 123, 122
Berghof, Berghoff, Berghoeffer
  (mountain farm) 68, 92, 122
Berghorn (mountain peak) 68, 68
Berghuis, see Berghaus
Bergk, see Berg
Bergkirch (mountain church) 68,
  122
Bergland (mountain country) 68,
  49
Bergler, Bergner (mountain man)
  68
Bergmann, Bergman (miner,
  mountain man) 68, 96, 94
Bergmeister (mine supervisor) 68,
  96
Bergner (mountain man, miner)
  68, 96
Bergschmidt (mountain smith) 68,
  96
Bergschneider (mountain tailor)
  68, 104
Bergstein (mountain stone) 68,
  73, 122
Bergstrasser 122, Bergstresser,
  Bergstrosser (dweller on a
  mountain road, fr Bergstrasse)
  68, 65

Bergstrom (mountain stream) 68, 78

Bergtold, Bertoll, see Berchtold

Bergweiler (mountain village) 68, 127, 122

Berhart, see Bernhard

Bering, Beringer (fr Beringen 122; see Behring)

Berk, Berke, see Berg and Birck

Berkelbach (birch brook) 89, 77

Berkemeyer, see Berkmeyer

Berkenbusch (birch bush) 89, 72

Berkenfeld (birch field) 89, 84

Berkenhauer (birch chopper) 89, 95

Berkenkamp, Berkenkaempfer, Berkenkemper (birch field) 89, 84

Berkenmayer, see Berkmeyer

Berkenstock (birch trunk) 89

Berker, see Berger

Berkhausen, see Berghaus

Berkheim 122, Berkheimer (birch hamlet) 89, 123

Berkhof, Berkhoff, Berkoff (fr Berghof, mountain farm) 89, 92, see Berghoff

Berkholtz (birch wood) 89, 72, 122

Bergholtz (mountain forest) 68, 72, 122

Berkman, Berkmans 164, see Bergmann

Berkmeyer, Berkmeyer (fr the Berkhoff) 68, 93, 92, 94

Berkner (mountain man, miner) 68, 96

Berkstresser, see Bergstrasser

Berlanstein 159 (pearl mountain) 68

Berlein 55 (little bear) 48

Berlin, Berliner (German city) 122, 146

Berman, Bermann, Bermant 74 (bear trainer) 48, 22, 94

Berman (swineherd) 95, 94

Bermut (bear + disposition) 48, 114

Bern 122, Berne, Berner, Berns 164 (fr Bern)

Bernard, see Bernhard

Bernauer (fr Bernau, swamp meadow) 80, 84, 122

Bernd 53, Berndt, Berends 164 < Bernhard

Berner (Swiss fr Bern) 122

Bernfeld (swamp field) 68, 80, 84

Bernhard, Bernhardt, Bernard (bear + strong) 22, 48, 46

Bernhardi (son of Bernhard) 142

Bernheim, Bernheimer (swamp hamlet) 68, 123

Bernheisl 55, see Berninghaus

Bernholt (bear + loyal) 48, 48

Bernholt (bear forest) 48, 72

Bernholt (bear + loyal) 48, 48

Berning (belonging to the bear) 48, 59

Berninghaus (Berning's house) 65, 122

Bernolt, see Bernholt

Bernsohn (son of the bear, son of Bern) 48, 59

Bernstein (amber) 106, 122

Bernstein (bear mountain) 48, 73, 122

Bernt 53, see Bernhard

Bernwinkler (bear + wooded valley) 48, 76

Berodt (bear clearing) 48, 126, 122

Bersch, see Barsch

Berstein (bear mountain) 48, 73

Berstroser 159, see Bergstrasser

Bert 53, Bertz 164 < Bertram, Berthold, etc.

Bertel 53, Bertell, Bertels 164 < Berthold

Bertha < Brecht ...

Berthel, see Bertel

Berthold, Bertholdt, Bertold,
Berthhoud (brilliant + loyal)
46, 48

Bertling, see Bartling

Bertman, see Bartmann

Bertoldi, son of Bertholdus 142

Bertram, Berteram, see Bartram

Bertrand (brilliant + shield) 46,
47

Bertsch 53, Bertschi < Berthold,
etc.

Bertz, Berz, see Bert

Berwage, Berwanger (fr Ber-
wangen, bear field) 48, 71, 122

Berwald (bear forest) 48, 71

Besch 53 (St. Sebastian) 131

Beschorner (shorn one, clergy-
man) 112, 110

Besel (broom maker) 96

Besemann (broom maker) 96, 94

Besinger, see Bessing

Besner (broom maker) 96

Besold 159, see Betzold

Besse (swamp) 80

Besser, Bessert 74 (better, collector of fines)

Bessing, Bessinger (fr Bessingen)
122

Bessmann (repairman) 96, 94

Best (best) 115

Best 53 < St. Sebastian 131

Beste (river name, muddy water)
83

Bestenholtz (for Westenholtz,
western forest) 85, 72

Besterfeldt (west field) 85, 84

Betenbaugh 159, see Bittenbach

Bethge 55, Bethke, Betke <
Bertram

Bethman, Bettmann (payer of
landlord's "requests") 109, 94

Betram, see Bertram

Betrand, see Bertrand

Bettendorf (town name) 123, 122

Bettenhausen (tenant house) 65,
122

Better, Bettermann 94 (rosary,
rosary maker) 106

Bettger, see Boettcher

Betz 53, Betts 159, Bates 159,
Pates 159 < Bernhard

Betzinger, Betzner (fr Betzingen)
122

Betzold, Petzold, Betzel, Betzler <
Peter 131

Beuchel (little belly) 114

Beucher, Beuchert 74, see Buecher

Beuckelmann 94, see Buechner

Beuel (bruise) 114, 122, see Beul

Beuer, Beuermann 94 (peasant)
91

Beuerle, see Baeuerle

Beuke, see Buche

Beul, Beuler, see Buehl, Buehler

Beulshausen (place name) 65, 122

Beumler, see Baeumler

Beunde (private fenced-in area)
84

Beurlein 55, see Baeuerlein

Beusch, see Baus

Beuschlag, see Beyschlag

Beuschlein 55 (little bush) 89, 72

Beutel (purse, sack, purse maker)
96

Beutel (wooden club)

Beutelmann (purse maker) 96, 94

Beutelsbach, Beutelspacher (fr
Beutelsbach, sack brook) 77,
122

Beuthler, Beutler (purse maker)
96

Beutner (honey gatherer) 95

Beverung, Beverungen (a city, the
people on the Bever) 122, 123

Beyder (possibly short for name
like Beiderwieden) 69

Beyer, Beyers 164, Beyern, see
Bayer

Beyerle 55, Beyerlein, Beyerling,
see Bayerle, Baeuerle

Beyermeister, see Bauernmeister

Beyersdorf (Bavarians' village) 121, 123, 122, see Bayersdorf

Beyl, Beyhl, see Beil

Beylstein, see Beilstein

Beyrer, see Bayer

Beyrodt (adjacent clearing) 125

Beyschlag (small piece of a field) 84

Beyschlag (illigitimate child of a ruler) 119

Beyth (hesitation) 115

Bez, see Betz

Bezold, see Betzold

Bibelhimer 159 (Bible hamlet) 123

Biber, see Bieber

Bicher, Bichert 74, see Buecher

Bichell, Bichler, see Buehl, Buehler

Bickel 53, Bickell < Burkhart, see Pickel

Bicksler (box maker) 96, 151

Biddel 159, Buettel (beadle) 109

Biddenbach, see Bittenbach

Biddinger (fr Bidingen) 122

Biddle 159, see Biddel

Biderman 159, see Biederman

Biebel, Bieble 159, Biebel (Bible)

Bieber (beaver) 115

Bieberbach (beaver brook) 77, 122

Bieberbach (swamp-water creek) 80, 77

Biecheler, Biechelar, see Buechler

Biedekopp, Biedenkopf (boundary lookout) 122

Biedenbach, Biedenback (fr Biedenbach 122, boundary brook) 77, 122

Biedenbuender (boundary fence) 84

Biederkep, see Biedekopp

Biederman, Biedermann (doughty man, respectable citizen) 138, 94

Biegel, Biegler (ax maker) 96, see Buegler

Biegeleisen (stirrup, pressing iron) 96

Biehl, Biehler, see Buehl, Buehler

Biehlmueller (hill miller) 67, 103

Biel, Bieler, Bieller, see Buehl, Buehler

Bielefeld (city name) 122

Biemann (bee keeper) 95, 94

Bien, Bienemann 94, Bieneman (bee keeper) 95

Bienenfeld (bee field) 84

Bienert 74 (bee keeper) 95

Bienfang (bee catcher) 95

Bienkorb (beehive) 95

Bienlein 55 (little bee) 115

Bienstein (bee stone) 73

Bienstock, Bienenstock (beehive, beekeeper) 95

Bier, Bierr (beer, brewer) 96, 106

Bierach (beaver river, bear river) 83, 122

Bierbach (mud creek) 80, 77

Bierbaum 122, see Birnbaum

Bierbrauer (beer brewer) 97

Bierenbaum, see Birnbaum

Bierenberg (pear mountain) 89, 68

Bierhagen (bear enclosure), 48, 123

Bierhagen (pear tree enclosure) 89, 123

Bierkenbeyl (birch ax) 89, 96

Bierley 159, see Bayerle

Bierman 94, Biermann, Biermeyer 93, Bierwirth (taverner) 96

Biernbaum, see Birnbaum

Biersack (taverner) 96

Biersack (beer belly) 114

Biersdorf (beer village) 123, 122

Biersdorf (swamp village) 80, 123, 122

Bierstadt (place name, swamp city) 80, 122

Bierwage (beer wagon, beer distributor) 96

Bierwirt, Bierwirth (beer host) 96, also < Berwart (bear + guardian 46, 47)

Biettel, see Buettel

Bigel, Bigler, see Buegel, Buegler

Bihl, see Buehl

Bihlmeier, Beylmeyer, see Buehlmayer

Bilauer (hill meadow) 67, 84

Bilderbach, Bilderback, Bilderbeck, see Wilderbach

Bildstein 122, see Wildstein

Bile 159, see Buehle

Bilfinger (having six fingers) 114

Bilfinger (fr Bilfingen) 122

Bilger, see Pilger

Bilheimer, see Buehlheimer

Bilig, see Billig, Bille

Bill, Bills 164 (hill) 67

Billauer (swamp meadow) 80, 84, see Bilauer

Bille, Biller, see Buehl, Buehler

Bille (battle ax) 108

Billerbeck (hill brook) 67, 77, 122

Billheimer, Billhimer 159, see Buehlheimer

Billig (fair, as in *recht und billig*) 115, 122

Billing, Billings 164, Billinger (fr Billing 122, hill dweller) 68

Billman, Billmann, see Buehlman

Billmann (maker or user of battle axes) 107, 108, 94

Billmeyer, Billmeier (hill farmer) 67, 93

Billmire 159, Billmyer, see Billmeyer

Billroth (hill clearing) 67, 126

Billstein (hill stone) 67, 73

Billstone 159, see Billstein

Bilse (henbane) 89

Biltz, Bilitz, Bilz, see Piltz

Bimeler 159, see Baeumler

Binau (bee meadow) 84, 122

Bince 159, see Bintz

Bindbeutel (fastenable purse) 96, 106

Bindel (bundle)

Binder, Bindermann 94, Bindler (sheaf binder, cooper, bookbinder) 96

Bindschaedler (cooper) 96

Bindseil (cord maker, roper) 96, 106

Binebrink (bee hill) 74

Bineke, Bineker, see Beneke

Binfield 153, see Bienefeld

Bingel, Bingle 159, Bingley 159, see Bengel

Bingen, Binger (city on the Rhein) 122

Binkert, see Benkert

Binning, Binninger, Bininger (fr Binningen 122), see Benning

Binnix < St. Benedict 131

Binstock (rush stem) 81, see Bienstock

Binswanger (fr Binswangen, reed field) 81, 126, 122

Bintz, Bintzel (fr Binz 122, bull rushes) 81

Birbaum, Birenbaum, see Birnbaum

Birch, Birchen, see Birk

Birchbauer, Birchbaver 159 (fr the Birchhof, birch farm) 89, 91, 94

Birchler, Birchner (dweller among the birches) 89

Birchwil (birch village) 89, 123

Birck, Birk, Birke (birch) 89

Birckelbach (birch brook) 89, 77

Birdsong 152, see Vogelsang

Birely 159, see Bayerle

Birgel (place name) 122

Birger, see Berger

Birk, Birkel 55, Birkelein 55 (little birch) 89

Birk 53 < Burkhart

Birkborch (birch bark) 89, 73

Birkelein 55, see Birk

Birkenbach (birch brook) 89, 77, 122
Birkenberg (birch mountain) 89, 68
Birkenfeld (birch field) 89, 84, 122
Birkenhauer (birch cutter) 89, 95, 100
Birkenstock (birch trunk) 89
Birkenthal (birch valley) 89, 76, 122
Birkholt (birch wood) 89, 72, 122
Birkholz, Birkholtzer (birch wood) 89, 72, 122
Birkle 55 (little birch) 89
Birkle 55 < Burkhard
Birkmann 94, Birkmeyer 93, Birkmaier, Birckenmayer (farmer among the birches) 89
Birkner, see Birchler
Birman, see Berman
Birnbach (pear tree brook) 89, 77, 122
Birnbaum (pear tree) 89, 122
Birner 159, see Berner
Birstaedt 159, see Bierstadt
Birtha 159, see Bertha
Birx, see Birck
Bisant, Biszant (Saracen coin)
Bischberg 122, see Bischoffsberger
Bischoff, Bischof, Bischop (bishop) 59, 110
Bischoffsberger, Bischopberger (bishop's mountain) 110, 68
Bishof 159, see Bischoff
Bisinger (fr Bising) 122
Bismark, Bismarck 122 < Bischofsmark (bishop's boundary)
Bisschop, see Bischoff
Bissel, Bissler (bite, small quantity)
Bisser (fr Bissen) 122
Biswanger 159 (adjacent clearing) 126
Bitel, see Buettel

Bitinger, Bittinger (fr Bittingen) 122
Bitman, see Buettner
Bitner, see Buettner
Bittel, see Buettel
Bittenbach (barrel brook) 77
Bittenbender (barrel maker) 96
Bitter, Bitterlich (bitter, bitterly) 115
Bitter (public announcer, beggar) 109
Bittermann (barrel maker) 96, 94
Bittle 159, see Buettel
Bittmann 94, see Buettner
Bittner, see Buettner
Bitz, Bitzel (fenced area) 84, 122
Bitzelberger (fenced hill) 84, 68
Bitzer (dweller on the Bitiz) 83
Bixler (box maker) 96
Black 153, see Schwartz
Blacker, Blackert 74, Blackner, Blackman 94 (bleacher) 96
Blackwelder 153, see Schwarzwaelder
Blaetterlein 55 (little leaf)
Blahut (blue hat, show-off) 112, 115
Blaich, Blaicher, Blaik (bleacher) 96
Blakmann, see Blech
Blamberg (place name) 122
Blancke, Blank, Blanke (white, clean)
Blancpain 144, see Weissbrodt
Blankemeier, see Blankmeyer
Blankenbaker 159, Blankenbeckler (baker of white bread) 96
Blanckenberg (white mountain) 68, 122
Blankenburg (white castle) 73, 122
Blankenheimer (fr Blankenheim, white hamlet) 123
Blankenhorn (white peak) 68
Blankensee (white lake) 82, 122

Blankfeld (white field) 84

Blankmann (white man, bleacher) 96, 94

Blankmeyer (fr the Blankhof, white farm) 93, 94

Blankner (bleacher) 96

Blass, Blasse, Blasser, Blaser (bald 112)

Blass (pale) 114

Blass 53, Blasse < St. Blasius 131

Blatman, Blatner, see Blatter

Blatt (leaf) 89

Blatt (hunter's decoy call) 91

Blattberg (leaf mountain) 68

Blattberg (swamp mountain) 80, 68

Blatter, Blatterman 94, Blattermann, Blattner (armor smith) 108

Blatz, Blatzer (wedge for breaking stone) 106

Blatz, see Platz

Blau, Blauer, Blauert 74 (blue) 112

Blau, Blauer, Blauert 74 (credulous) 115

Blaufeld (blue field) 84, 122

Blaumen, see Blumen

Blaustein (blue stone, blue mountain) 73, 122

Blaxberg 159, see Blocksberg

Blay, see Blei

Bleacher 152, see Bleicher

Blech, Bleche, Blecher, Blecker, Blechmann 94, Blecman, Blechschmidt (sheet metal, tinsmith) 96, 106

Bleck, Bleckmann 94, Bleckenschmidt, see Blech

Bleeker (bleacher) 96

Blei (lead, lead worker) 96, 106

Blei (kind of fish) 105, 115

Bleiberg (lead mountain, lead mine) 68

Bleibtreu (Remain true!) 116

Bleich, Bleicher, Bleichner (pale) 113

Bleich (bleacher) 96

Bleier, Bleiler (lead worker) 96

Bleiker, see Bleicher

Bleistein (lead stone, pencil) 96

Blekmann, see Bleck

Blendermann (prestidigitator) 96, 94

Blendermann (swamp dweller) 80, 94

Blenker, Blenkner (dweller in a barren spot)

Blesch (blow)

Bless, Blesse (blaze, bald head), also < Blasius

Blessing 53 < Blasius

Bleucher, see Bleicher

Bley, Bleyer, see Blei, Bleier

Bleystein (lead mountain) 73

Bligh 159, see Blei

Blimke, see Bluemke

Blimline 55, 159 (little flower) 89

Blimmer (little flower) 89

Blind, Blinder (blind) 114

Blitstein 159, see Blitzstein

Blitz, Blitzer (lightning)

Blitzstein (lightning mountain) 73

Blob, see Blau

Bloch, Block, Bloech, see Block

Blocher (jailer) 109

Block (block, trunk, stocks)

Bloede (weak, shy) 115

Bloem, Bloemen, Bloemer, Blom, Blohm (flower seller) 89, 106

Blomeyer (flower farmer) 89, 93

Blond, Blondell, Blonder (blond) 112

Bloom, Bloomer, see Bloem

Bloomberg, see Blumberg

Bloomfield 153, see Blumenfeld

Bloomgarden 153, see Blumgaertner

Bloomingdale 153, see Blumenthal

Bloss, Blosse, Blosser (bare, naked, unarmed) 113

Bloss 53 < Blasius

Blotenberg, Blottenberger (swamp mountain) 80, 68

Blotkamp (swamp field) 80, 84

Blotner 159, see Blatner

Blough 159, see Blau

Blubaugh 159, Bluebaugh 159 (blue brook) 77

Blubaum 159 (blue tree) 89, 151

Blucher, Bluecher (Slavic place name) 122, 146

Bluefeld 153, see Blaufeld

Bluehe (blossom) 89

Bluehtner (flower seller) 106

Bluemel 55, Bluemelein (little flower) 89, 106

Bluementhal, see Blumenthal

Bluemke 55 (little flower) 89, 106

Bluestein 153, Blustein, Bluestone 152, see Blaustein

Bluh, see Bluehe

Bluhdorn (blossom thorn) 72, 89

Blum, Blume, Bluem, Bluhm, Blumen (flower) 89, 106

Blumbach (flower brook) 89, 77

Blumberg, Blumenberg (flower mountain) 89, 68

Blume, see Blum

Blumenauer (flower meadow) 89, 84, 122

Blumenberg, see Blumberg

Blumenfeld, Blumenfeldt, Blumfeld (flower field) 89, 84, 147, 122

Blumenschein (flower brilliance) 89, 147

Blumenstein (flower mountain) 89, 73, 147

Blumenstiel (flower stem) 89

Blumenthal (flower valley) 89, 76, 147, 122

Blumer, Blumert 74, Blummer (flower seller) 89, 106

Blumingdale 152, see Blumenthal

Blumlein (little flower) 55, 89

Blumner (flower seller) 106

Blunt (blond) 112

Bluntschli (fat man) 114

Blusten 159, see Blaustein

Bluth (blood)

Bluth (blossom) 89

Bly 159, see Blei

Blyer 159, Blyler, see Bleier

Blyman 159, see Bleimann

Blyweiss 159 (lead white)

Boarman 159, see Borman

Boas, Boaz (OT name) 135

Bobenheisser 66 (upper house, see Oberhaeuser)

Bobenhyser 66, see Bobenheisser

Bobenrieth (upper marsh) 81

Bober (dweller by the Bober) 83

Bobst, see Pabst

Bock, Bocks 164, Bocker (buck, often a house name) 149, 62

Bock (beach tree) 89

Bockhaus, see Backhaus

Bockman, Bockmann (dweller among beech trees) 89, 94

Bockmiller (fr the Bockmuehle, beech mill) 89, 103

Bockner, see Buechner

Bod, Bode (messenger), 96, 157, see also Boede

Boday 157 < Bode

Bodefeld (swampy field) 80, 84

Bodeke, see Boettcher

Bodemeyer (farmer in the swamp) 80, 93

Boden (soil, bottom, valley) 76

Bodenbender (cooper) 96

Bodenberger (valley mountain) 76, 68

Bodener (valley dweller, cotter), 76 see also Buettner

Bodenheimer (valley hamlet) 76, 123

Bodenschatz (duty on wine)

Bodensieck (valley swamp) 76, 80

Bodenstein (valley stone) 76, 73, 122
Bodiker, Bodker, see Boettcher
Bodmer (tabulator) 96
Bodmer (dweller on the plain)
Bodner, Bodnar 159, see Bodener
Bodtker, see Boettcher
Boeck, Boecker, Boeckh, Boeker, Boekel, Boekl, see Bock, Beck, Becker
Boecker, see Boettcher
Boeckman, Boeckmann, see Beckmann
Boede, Boedde (wooden tub) 106
Boedeker, see Boettcher
Boeger, Boegner, see Bogener
Boehl, Boehler, Boehling, Boehlke 55, see Buehl, Buehler
Boehler (cloister official) 139
Boehm, Boehme, Boehmer, Boehmlein 55, Boem (Bohemian) 34, 121, see also Baeumer
Boehme (pre-Germanic river name) 83
Boehne, Boehner, Boehnert 74 (bean dealer) 105
Boehning, see Benning
Boehnisch, see Benesch
Boehnlein 55, Boehneke 55 (little bean)
Boehringer, see Behringer
Boeke (beech) 89
Boekel 55, Boeckl, Boekle, Boeklin, Buckley 159 (little buck)
Boeker, see Boettcher
Boekman, Boeckmann, see Beckmann, Buchmann
Boelker (howler, bellower) 115
Boelker 53 < Baldwin
Boellner see Bellner
Boender, see Bender
Boener, see Behner
Boening, Boenning, see Benning
Boer, Boeren, Boern, see Bauer
Boerger, Boergert 74 (burgher)

Boerghausen, see Burghause
Boermann (peasant) 91, 94
Boerner, see Berner
Boernstein, see Bernstein
Boerries 53 < St. Liborius 131
Boesch 53, see Sebastian
Boese, Boesser (angry, mean) 115
Boese (small stag) 91
Boessel (place name) 122
Boessner (repairman) 96
Boettcher, Boetcher, Boether, Boettge, Boettger, Boetjer, Boettiger (barrel maker, fr Latin *apoteka*) 96
Boettinger, see Boettcher
Boettner, see Buettner
Bogener, Bogner, Bognar 159 (bowman or bow maker) 108
Bogensberger (bow mountain) 68
Bohde, see Bode
Bohl, Bohle, Bohlen, Bohls 164, Bolsen (plank)
Bohlander, see Polander
Bohlen 53, Bohler, Bohling, Bohlinger, Bohlmann 94 < Baldwin
Bohltz, see Boltz
Bohm, Bohmer, see Boehm, Boehmer
Bohmann, see Baumann
Bohmfalk (tree falcon) 89
Bohn, Bohne, Bohner (bean dealer) 106
Bohn 53, Bohne < St. Urbanus 131
Bohnenberg (bean hill) 68
Bohnenstengel (bean stalk)
Bohnsack (bean sack) 96, 106
Bohr 53 < St. Liborius 131
Bohrer (borer) 96
Bohrmann, see Bormann
Bohrmester, see Bauernmeister
Bohse, see Boos
Bokmann, see Buchmann
Boland, Bolandt, Bolander, see Poland, Polander

Bolderman, see Poldermann
Boldt (bold) 46
Boldt (bolt, crossbow bolt) 108
Bolenbaugh 159 (fr Bolenbach, swamp brook) 80, 77
Bolender, see Polander
Boler, see Bohlen
Boll, Bolle (hill) 67
Boll (river name, swamp water) 83
Bollack, see Pollak
Bolle (plump person) 114
Boller, see Bohlen
Bollhorst (hill hurst) 67, 72
Bolling 112, Bollinger (hill dweller) 67, see also Buhle
Bollman, Bollemann (small heavy-set youth) 114, 94
Bollmann (dweller on a hill) 67, 94
Bollwagen < Baldwin
Bollweg (hill path) 67, 65
Bollwinkel, see Bullwinkel
Bolner (hill dweller) 67
Bolte, Bolter, Bolth, Bolten, see Boltz
Boltz, Boltze, Bolz, Boltzius 141, Poltz (bolt, maker of crossbow bolts 108, also < Baldwin
Boman, see Bauman
Bombach, Bomback, Bombeck (swamp brook) 80, 77
Bomberg, Bomberger (fr Bomberg 122, tree mountain) 89, 68
Bomert 74, see Baumer
Bomgartner, see Baumgaertner
Bomhardt (tree forest) 89, 72
Bomhoff (tree farm) 89, 92
Bomstein (tree stone) 89, 77
Bonacker (bean field) 84
Boner, see Bohner
Bongart, Bongartz, see Bomgartner
Bonhag, Bonhage (forbidden enclosure) 123
Bonhoff (bean farm) 92

Bonmueller (bean miller) 103
Bonn, Bonner (inhabitant of Bonn) 122
Bonner, see Bonn
Bonnewitz (place name, swamp village) 127
Bonsack (bean sack) 96, 106
Bontrager (bean carrier)
Bontz, see Buntz
Boode, see Bote
Book ..., see Buch ...
Booker, see Bucher
Bookhultz, see Buchholtz
Bookman, see Buchman
Bookmiller, see Buchmueller
Bookoff, see Buchhoff
Bookstein (beech mountain) 89, 73
Boom, see Baum
Boonce, 159, see Buntz
Boone, see Bohne
Boor (peasant) 91
Boos (wicked, evil) 115
Boot, Boote, see Bote
Booterbaugh 159, see Butterbaugh
Booth, see Bote
Borch, see Burg
Borchart, Borchardt, Borchert, see Burkhart
Borcher, Borchers 164, see Burger, Burkhart
Borcherding (belonging to Borcher) 59
Borchgrave, see Burggraf
Bordemann (lace maker) 96, 94
Bordner (gate keeper) 96
Bordorf, see Borgdorf
Borenstein, see Bernstein
Borg, Borger, see Burg, Buerger
Borg (swamp) 80
Borgdorf, see Burgdorff
Borgfeld (swamp field) 80, 84
Borgenicht ("Don't borrow," or "I don't borrow") 116
Borger (borrower)

Borger (castle dweller) 73
Borgfeld (castle field) 73, 84
Borggreve, see Burggraf
Borghard, see Burkhard
Borgholte (castle wood) 73, 72
Borgmann, Borgman (castle man, burgher) 73, 94
Borgmeier (castle bailif) 73, 93
Borgstrom (castle stream) 73, 77
Borgstrom (swamp stream) 80, 77
Boris, see Borries
Bork, Borke (bark, bark gatherer) 95
Bork, see Burg, Burkhard
Borkholz (castle wood) 73, 72
Borkmann, see Borgmann
Bormann 53 < St. Liborius 131, see also Bornemann
Born, Borne, Borner, Borns 164 (spring) 79
Borneman, Bornemann (spring + man) 79, 94
Bornfiend 159, see Bauernfeind
Borngesser (spring road) 79, 65
Bornhausen (spring house) 79, 65, 122
Bornheim (spring hamlet) 79, 123
Bornhoefte (spring farm) 79, 84
Bornholt, Bornholtz 164 (spring forest) 79, 72
Bornhorn (spring peak) 79, 68
Bornhorst (spring hurst) 79, 72
Bornkessel (spring kettle) 79
Bornman, see Bornemann
Bornscheuer (spring barn) 79
Bornsdorf (spring village) 79, 123, 122
Bornstein (spring mountain) 79, 73, see Bernstein
Borrus 53 < St. Liborius 131
Borsch 53, Borscher < St. Liborius 131
Borsdorf, see Burgdorf
Borst (bristle) 114, 106
Bortner, see Pfortner
Bortz, Borz, see Portz

Bosch, Bosche (bush, brush, branch) 72
Boschert 74, Boschmann 94, Boschenmeyer 93 (dweller in the bush) 72
Bose, see Boos
Bosemann (evil man) 115
Boskind (naughty child) 115
Bosler, see Basler
Bosman, see Bosemann
Boss (barrow hog) 91
Bossard, Bosshard, see Bussart
Bosse 53 < Burckhart
Bosshard, Bosshart, Bossert (Strike hard!) 116, also see Bussart
Bossler, Bossle, see Basler
Bossner (striker, ten pin player)
Bostian 159, see Bastian
Bote, Both, Bothe, Bott (messenger) 96, 157
Bottcher, see Boettcher
Botterbusch (butter bush) 89
Bottich, Bottiger (barrel, barrelmaker, fr Latin *apotheca*) 96
Bottmann (court messenger) 109, 94
Bottner, see Buettner
Bottomstone 153, see Bodenstein
Botts 159, Botz, Botzler (bogeyman) 115
Botzenhard, Botzenhart (scarecrow, bogeyman) 115
Botzmann (scarecrow, bogeyman) 115, 94
Bouch 159, see Bauch
Bouerman 159, see Bauermann
Bough 159, see Bau, Bauch
Bougher 159, Boughers 164, see Bauer, Bauers
Boughman 159, see Bachmann, Baumann
Boughner 159, see Bachner
Boughtall 159, see Bechtold
Bouknight 159, see Bauknecht
Bouman 159, see Baumann

Bounds 159, see Buntz
Bouse 159, see Bauss
Bousman 159, see Baussmann
Bouthner 159, see Bauth
Bouwkamp 159 (cultivated field) 84
Bowden 159, see Boden
Bower 159, Bowers 164, see Bauer
Bowerfind 159, see Bauernfeind
Bowerman 159, see Bauermann
Bowermaster 159, see Bauernmeister
Bowersack 159, Bowersock, Bowersox (peasant bag) 91
Bowker 159, see Bauker
Bowman 159, see Baumann
Bowmaster 159, see Baumeister
Bowscher 159, Bowsher 159, see Baus
Boyer, see Bayer
Bozman, Bozemann, see Botzmann
Braaten, Braatz (roast, cook) 96
Brabant (province in Belgium) 121
Brach (fallow land) 122
Brachfeld (fallow field) 84, 122
Brachmann (dweller on a fallow field) 94
Bracht (river name) 83, 122, see Brecht, Pracht
Brack, see Brach
Bracke (small hound, huntsman) 91
Brackbill (fallow hill) 67
Brackhahn, Brachhahn (plover) 115
Bracklein (small hunting dog)
Brackmann (hunter leading hounds) 91, 94
Bradenbaugh 159, see Breitenbach
Bradt, see Brot
Braeger, Brager, see Prager
Braendel 53, 55 < Hildebrand

Braeuer (brewer) 96
Braeuniger, see Brauninger
Braeutigam (bridgroom) 119
Braf, Brafman, Braffmann, see Bravmann
Brager, see Prager
Brahm, Brahms 164 (swamp) 80
Brahm, Brahms 164 < Abraham 135
Brahm (broom plant) 89
Braid, Braidman, see Breit, Breitmann
Brake, Bracke (fallow, brackish)
Brakebill, see Brackbill
Brakebusch (fallow scrub land) 72
Brakefield 153, see Brachfeld
Brakenhoff (fallow farm) 92
Brakhage (fallow enclosure) 123
Brakmann, see Brachmann
Brambeck (thorn brook, swamp brook) 80, 77
Bramer (hornet, see also Bremer)
Bramkamp (thorn field) 84, 122
Brammeyer (fr the Bramhoff, thorn farm) 93, 94
Bramstedt (thorn place)
Brand 53, Brandes 164, Brandt, Brant (sword) 46, also < Hildebrand
Brand, Brant, Brandt (forest clearing) 126
Brandau (clearing meadow) 126, 84, 122
Brandecker, Brandegger (fr Brandeck 122, clearing) 126, 85
Brandeis, Brandies 159, Brandis (cauterizing iron) 106
Brandel, see Brander
Brandenberg 122, see Brandenburg
Brandenburg, Brandenburger (fr Brandenburg) 121
Brandenstein (torch mountain) 73, 122
Brandenstein (burned-off mountain) 126, 68

Brander, Brandner (occupant of a clearing) 126
Brander, Brandler (distiller) 96
Brandes 53, 164 < Hildebrand
Brandhaver 159, Brandhover, see Brandhoff
Brandhoff (cleared farm, burned off farm) 126, 92
Brandhorst (burned off hurst) 126, 72, 122
Brandjes, Brandl, see Brander
Brandland (burned off land) 126
Brandl, see Brandel
Brandmueller (miller at the burned clearing) 103, 126
Brandner, Brandtner, Brantner (occupant of a forest clearing, fr Branden) 126
Brandstaedter, Brandstetter (cleared place, burned off place) 126, 122
Brandstein (brick) 106, 122
Brandt, see Brand
Brandwein, Brandtwein, Brantwein (brandy, distiller) 96, 106
Brandywine 159, see Brandwein
Branoff, see Brandhoff
Brant, Brantl 55, see Brand
Brasch, Brash 159 (impudent) 114
Brasch 53 < Ambrosius 131
Brasse (broom plant) 89
Bratfish 152 (fried fish) 115, 105
Bratmann, see Brotmann
Bratt (roast, cook) 96, 106
Brauch, Braucher (use, custom)
Braucht 159, see Pracht
Brauer, Braue (brewer) 96
Braukhoff, Brauckhoff (brake farm) 80, 92
Braumann (brewer) 96
Braumbart (brown beard) 112
Braumueller, see Braunmueller
Braun, Brauns 164, Braune, Braunert 74 (brown, fr Braunau) 112

Braunbach (brown brook) 77
Braunbeck (brown brook) 77
Braunbeck (baker of brown bread) 104
Braunberg, Braunberger (brown mountain) 68
Braunfeld (brown field) 84
Braungart (brown garden) 84
Braungreber, see Brungraeber
Braunhof (well farm) 92
Brauning, Brauninger (having brown hair) 112
Braunmueller, Brownmueller 159 (miller of brown meal) 103
Braunscheidt, Braunscheidel (brown log)
Braunschweiger (person fr Brunswick, "Bruno's village," fr Latin *vicus*) 121, 122
Braunspan (brown chip)
Braunstein (brown stone) 73
Brauntuch (brown cloth) 105, 106
Braunwald, Braunwalde (brown forest) 72
Braus, Brause, Brausen (noise, confusion) 115
Brautigan, see Braeutigam
Brautlacht (wedding, wedding song)
Bravmann (well-behaved man) 115, 94
Bravermann (brewer) 96, 94
Brawn 159, Brawner, see Braun
Bray, see Brey
Braymer 159, see Bremer
Breakfield 153, see Brachfeld
Brech, Brecher (breaker, flax breaker) 95
Brechbill, Brechbiel, Brechbuel, see Brackbill
Brecht (bright) 47
Brecht 53 < Albrecht
Brecht (a clearing) 125
Brechtel 53, 55 < Brecht, Albrecht
Brecker, see Brecher
Brede, Breden (swamp) 80

Bredehoef (marshy farm) 80, 92
Bredehoeft, Bredehoft, see Breithaupt
Bredekamp (marshy field, broad field) 80, 84
Bredemeyer (marsh farmer) 80, 93
Bredenburg (marsh castle) 80, 73
Bredhorst (marsh hurst) 80, 72
Bredt, see Brett
Bredthauer, see Brethauer
Breeback (marsh brook) 80, 77
Breemer, see Bremer
Bregenzer (fr Bregenz, town and river name) 83, 122
Brehm, Brehmer (deer fly, see also Bremer)
Breidenbach 122, Breidenbeck, see Breitbach
Breidenbaugh 159, see Breitbach
Breidenstein 122, Breidenstine 159, see Breitenstein
Breier, see Braeuer
Breigher 159, see Braeuer
Breiner, Breighner 159 (pottage maker), 112, see Breun
Breining, Breininger, see Brauning
Breit, Breiter (broad) 113
Breitacker (broad field) 84
Breitbach 122, Breitenbach, Breitenbaecher (fr Breitbach 122, broad brook) 77
Breitbart (broad beard) 112
Breitbart (broad battle-ax) 46
Breitenbach 122, see Breitbach
Breitenberger (fr Breitenberg 122, broad mountain) 68
Breitenbuecher (broad beeches) 89
Breitenecker (broad place) 85
Breitenfeld (broad field) 84
Breitenstein (broad stone) 73, 122
Breitfus (broad foot) 114
Breithaupt (broad head) 114
Breithof (broad farm) 92

Breitmann (fat man) 114, 94
Breitmeyer, Breitmier 159 (occupant of the Breithoff, broad farm) 93
Breitmoser (broad marsh) 80
Breitschneider, see Brettschneider
Breitschwerd, Breitschwerdt (broadsword) 108
Breitstadt (broad city)
Breitstein (broad stone) 73
Breitwieser (broad meadow) 84
Breivogel (porridge eater) 112
Brem, Bremer, Bremehr, Bremen, Bremmer, Bremermann 94 (fr Bremen, swamp) 122
Bremhorst (gadfly hurst) 72
Brendel 53, 55, Brendl, Brendle 159, Brendler < Hildebrand
Brennecke (burned field) 85
Brenneisen (poker, brand) 106
Brenner 122, Brennermann 94 (burner of charcoal, etc., or distiller of brandy) 95
Brennholtz, Brenholts 159 (firewood) 72, 105
Brennwald (burned forest) 72
Brentz 122, Brentzer, Brentzel, Brentzinger (dweller near the river Brenz) 83
Breslau, Breslaw, Breslauer, Bresslauer (fr Breslau 122)
Breslow, see Breslau
Bresler, Bressler, Bresslers 164, see Breslau
Breth (board, board cutter) 98
Brethauer, Bretthauer (board cutter, cabinet maker) 98, 100
Brethholz (board, board sawyer) 98, 105
Brethower 159, see Brethauer
Brett, Bretz 164 (board) 105, see also Bretzel
Brettschneider, Brettscheider (board sawyer, cabinet maker) 98

Bretzler (pretzel maker, fr Latin *bracillum*) 96
Breuel (swamp) 80, see Brauer
Breuer, see Brauer
Breun, Breune, Breuner, see Braun, Braune
Breuning, Breuninger, see Brauning, Brauninger
Breusscher (dweller on the Breusch 83), see Preuss
Brewbaker 159, see Brubach
Brewer 153, see Brauer
Brey (pottage) 112
Breyer, Breyere, see Braeuer
Breymayer, Breymeyer (brewmaster) 93
Brezler, see Bretzler
Briar 159, see Braeuer
Brickbauer, see Brueckbauer
Brickel 55, Brickell (little bridge)
Bricker, Brickerd 74, see Bruecker
Brickhouse 159, Brickous, see Brueckhaus
Brickhus, see Brueckhaus
Brickmann, see Brueck
Brickner, see Brueck
Bridenbach 159, Bridenbaugh 159, see Breitbach
Bridner 159 (dweller on the Briede) 83, see Breitner
Briedenstein 159, see Breitenstein
Briefel 55 (little letter)
Brieger (fr Brieg) 122
Briel, Brieler (fr Briel) 122, see Bruehl
Brier 159, see Breuer
Briest 122, see Priest
Brigenz, see Bregenzer
Briggeman, Briggemann, Brigermann, see Brueggemann
Brigger, see Bruecker
Brighoff (farm at the bridge) 92
Bright 159, see Brecht

Brightbill 159 (broad hill) 67, 151, see also Brechbill
Brightman 159, see Breitmann
Brightstein 159, see Breitstein
Brigman, Brigmann, see Brugge
Brik, see Brueck
Brill (eye glass) 114, 106, 122
Brinckerhoff (farm on raised ground) 74, 92
Brine 159, Briner, see Braun, Brauner
Bringenberg (grassy mountain) 68
Bringhurst (grassy hurst) 72, 151
Bringmann, see Brinkmann
Brink 122, Brinke, Brinck, Brinks 164, Brings (grassy raised ground) 74
Brinker, Brinkmann 94, Brinkmeyer 93, Brinkmayer, Brinkmeier (small farmer) 74
Brinkerhoff (small farm) 74
Brinkschulte (village mayor) 74, 109
Brintzenhoff (prince's farm) 92
Britenstein 159, Britenstine 159 (swamp mountain) 80, 73, see Breitstein
Broadbeck 159 (bread baker)
Brobeck (bread baker) 104
Brobeck, see Brombeck
Broberg, see Bromberg
Brobst, see Probst
Broch 122, Brochmann 94 (brake dweller) 80
Brocht, see Pracht
Brock (brake, swamp) 80, 122
Brockdorf (brake village) 80, 123
Brockelhorst, Brochelhurst, Brockelhurst (brake hurst) 80, 72, 122, Brockelmann (fr Brockel) 122, 94
Brockhage, Brockhagen 122 (brake enclosure) 80, 123
Brockhaus, Brockhausen 122, Brockhus (brake house) 80, 65
Brockhoff (brake farm 80, 65, 122

Brocklebach 159 (brake brook) 80,
77
Brockman, Brockmann (brake
dweller) 80, 94
Brockmeyer, Brockmeier (brake
farmer) 80, 93
Brockner (brake dweller) 80
Brockschmidt (brake smith) 80,
96
Brocksmith, see Brockschmidt
Brod, Brode, Brodt, Brodte
(bread, baker) 96
Brodbaeker, Brodbeck (bread
baker) 96
Broeder, see Bruder
Broek, see Brock
Broemm, see Brehm
Broening, see Brening
Broenner, see Brenner
Broenstein, see Braunstein
Brohm, see Brahm
Broich, see Brock
Brokhus, see Brockhaus
Brokman, see Brockmann
Bromann (swamp dweller) 80, 94
Brombach 122, Brombeck (swamp
brook) 80, 77
Bromberg, Bromberger (swamp
mountain) 80, 68
Bromberg (thorn mountain) 68,
122
Bromer (swamp dweller) 80
Bronner (dweller near a well) 79
Bronstein (spring stone) 79, 73
Brook, Brooks 164, see Bruch,
Brock
Brooker (brake dweller) 80
Brookhard (brake forest) 80, 72
Brookhover, Brookover, see
Brockhoff
Brookland (marshy ground) 80
Brookmann, see Brockmann
Brookmeyer, see Brockmeyer
Brosi 53, Brosius < St. Ambrosius
131
Broth (bread, baker) 96

Brotman, Brotmann, Brotzmann
(baker) 96, 106, 94
Broun 159, Brouner, see Braun,
Brauner
Brouse 159, see Braus
Brower 159, Brouwer, see Brauer
Brown 159, Browner, see Braun,
Brauner
Browning 159, see Brauning
Brownstein 159, see Braunstein
Brubach, Brubaker, Brubacher,
Brubeck (swamp brook) 80, 77
Bruch (quarry) 122
Bruch (bog, swamp) 80, 122
Bruchmann (quarry worker) 96,
94
Bruchman, Bruchmann (bog
dweller) 80, 94
Bruckhard, see Burkhard
Bruck 122, Brucker, Bruckmann
94, Bruckmeyer 93, Bruckner
(dweller by a bridge) 71
Bruckbauer, see Brueckbauer
Bruder (brother) 119
Brueck, Bruecker, Brueckner
(dweller by a bridge, bridge
builder) 71
Bruecker, Brueckmann 94, Bru-
eckner (dweller near bridge) 71
Brueckhaus (house near a bridge)
71, 65, 122
Brueckhoff (farm at the bridge)
71, 92
Bruegge, Brueggemann 94,
Bruegemann, Bruegger, see
Bruecker
Brueggermeyer (farmer at the
bridge) 93
Bruehl (scrub-covered marsh) 80,
122
Bruekbauer, Brueckenbauer
(bridge builder), 96
Bruekbauer (farmer near bridge)
71
Bruening 53 < Bruno
Bruennings 164 (fr Bruening) 122

Bruenner (maker of burnies) 108
Bruens, see Bruns
Brugge, Bruggeman, Brugge-
mann, Brugger, see Bruecker,
Brueckmann
Bruhn, see Bruno, Braun
Bruich, see Bruch
Brumann, see Braumann
Brumback, Brumbaugh 159, see
Brombach
Brumm, Brummer (loud noise,
maker of loud noise) 115
Brun, Brune, Bruner, Brunert 74,
see Braune
Bruner, see Brunner
Brungard, Brungardt (well
garden) 79, 84
Brungreber, Brungraber, Brun-
graeber, see Brunnengraeber
Brunhoefer (well farm) 79, 92, see
also Braunhof
Bruning, Brunjes < Bruno
Brunk 53, 55, Brunke, Brunken,
Brunker < Bruno, see also
Prunk
Brunkhorst (swamp hurst) 80, 72
Brunn 122, Brunner (person
living near a spring or well)
77, see Bruenner
Brunnengraeber (well digger) 79
Brunner (dweller by a well) 79
Brunner (burnie maker) 108
Brunnholtz, Brunnsholtz (forest
by a spring) 79, 72
Bruno, Brunno (brown, bear) 22
Bruns, Brunsmann 94 (brown),
see also Bruno
Brunst (ardor, heat) 115
Brunstetter (well site) 79
Brupbacher 159, see Brubacher
Brusch (low growth, backwoods)
72
Bruschmueller (brush miller) 72,
103

Bruschweiler, Bruschwiler,
Bruschwiller (brush village) 72,
123
Brushwiler 159, see Bruschweiler
Brust (breast) 114
Bruun, see Brun, Bruhn
Bryl, see Brill
Bryner 159, see Breiner
Bryte 159, see Breit
Bube (boy, servant)
Bubeck (butterfly)
Buberl 55 (little boy)
Bubikon (town in Switzerland)
127, 122
Bubp, see Bube
Buccolz 159, see Buchholtz
Buch, Buchs 164, Buchler,
Buecher, Buechner (dweller
near the beeches) 41, 89
Buchalter, see Buchhalter
Buchbinder (bookbinder) 96
Buchdahl (beech valley) 89, 76
Buchdrucker (book printer) 96
Buchel 55, Buchal 159, Buchle
(little beech) 89
Buchel 55, Buechel (little book)
106
Buchenmeyer, Buckenmayer, see
Buchmeyer
Buchenwald 122, see Buchwald
Bucher 122, Buchert 74, see
Buechner
Buchhagen (beech enclosure) 89,
123, 122
Buchhalter (bookkeeper) 96
Buchheimer, Buchhiem 159
(beech hamlet) 89, 123
Buchhoff (beech farm) 89, 92
Buchholtz, Bucholz (beechwood)
89, 72, 122
Buchler, see Buechler
Buchman, Buchmann, Buchman,
Buchner (dweller near the
beeches) 89, 94

Buchmeyer, Buchmaier, Buchmoyer (fr the Buchhoff) 89, 93, 94

Buchmueller (miller near the beeches) 89, 103

Buchoff, see Buchhoff

Bucholz, see Buchholtz

Buchsbaum (boxwood) 89

Bucht (corral)

Bucht (bay)

Buchwald, Buchwalter (beech wood) 89, 71, 122

Buck, see Bock, Buche, Burkhard

Buckbinder 159, see Buchbinder

Buckel, Buckelman 94, Buckleman 159 (humpback) 114

Bucker, Buckert 74 < Burkhart

Buckhalter 159, see Burkhalter, Buchhalter

Buckhard 159, Buckert, Bucker < Burkhard

Buckhaults 159, see Buchholtz

Buckholtz 159, Buckholz, see Buchholtz

Buckler (shield, fr Latin *buccula*) 108

Buckman 159, see Buchmann

Buckmeyer 159, Buckmeier, Buckmeir, see Buchmeyer

Buckner 159, Bucknor 159, see Buechner

Buckreus 159 (beech branch) 89

Buckwalter 159, see Buchwald

Budde (cooper) 96

Buddemeier, Buddemeyer, Buddemyer (bog farmer) 80, 93

Buddenbohm, Buddenbohn (bog tree) 80, 89, 122

Buddenbrook (bog brake) 80, 80

Buddenhagen (bog enclosure) 80, 123, 122

Budecker, Budicke, Budke (cooper) 96

Budelman, Budelmann (purse maker) 96, 94

Buechel 55 (little book)

Buechel 55 (little beech) 89

Buechel, Buechler, Buehler (hill dweller) 67

Buechenau (beech meadow) 89, 84, 122

Buecher, see Buechner

Buechner, Buechler (dweller among beeches) 89

Buecker 159, see Buechner

Buedel, see Buettel

Buegler (stirrup maker) 96

Buehl, Buehler, Bueler (fr Buehl 122, hill) 41, 67

Buehlheimer (hill hamlet) 67, 123, 122

Buehlmayer, Buehlmeyer (hill farmer) 67, 93

Buehlman, Buehlmann (hill dweller) 67, 94

Buehr, Buehre, Buehrer, Buehrmann, see Bauer

Buekler, see Buckler

Buel, Buell, Bueller, see Buehl

Buenger, see Binger

Buerger (castle dweller, burgher) 73

Buergi 55, Burgy, see Birck

Buerhaus (peasant house) 91, 65, 122

Buerk, Buerkie 55, 159 (peasant) 91

Buermann, see Bauermann

Buesche, Buescher, see Busch, Buscher

Bueschel (bundle)

Bueschner (bush dweller) 72

Buetefisch (plaice, fishmonger) 115, 106

Buettel (beadle) 109

Buettel (homestead)

Buettemeyer (householder) 93

Buettler, Buettner (barrel maker, fr Latin *buttis*) 96

Buetzel (scarecrow, bogeyman) 115

Buetzenberger, see Pitzenberger

Bugher 159, see Bucher
Buhl, Buhle, Buhler, Buhlert 74,
  Buhlman 94, Buhlmann (lover,
  suitor, see also Buehl)
Buhr, Buhrmann 94 (peasant) 91
Buick (beech) 89
Bulger (Bulgarian) 121
Bullerich (shouting, screaming)
  115
Bullermann 53, 94 < Baldher
  (bold + army) 46, 46
Bullhausen (bull houses) 65, 91
Bullinger, see Bollinger
Bullwinkel (attic space)
Bulman, see Buhlmann
Bultman, Bultmann (mattress
  seller) 106, 94
Bultmann (dweller on a hill) 72,
  94
Bumann, see Baumann
Bumbaugh 159, see Bombach
Bumgardner, Bumgartner,
  Bumgarner, see Baumgaertner
Bummel (stroll, promenade)
Bunce 159, see Buntz
Bunde (fenced meadow) 84, 122
Bundschuh (laced boot, peasant
  revolt) 112
Bungartz, see Baumgart
Bunger, Bungerts 74, 164
  (drummer) 96
Bunt, Bunte, Bunter (colorful)
  115
Bunte (fish box)
Buntrock (coat of many colors
  112, kind of crow 115)
Bunts 159, see Buntz
Buntz, Bintz (sleeping birth)
Buntz (fat man) 114
Burack, Buracker (peasant's field)
  84
Burch, see Burg
Burchard, Burchhards 164,
  Burckhardt, see Burghart
Burck, see Burg
Burdorf 122, see Burgdorf

Buresch, Buresh (Slavic: peasant)
  146
Burg (fortress, castle) 46, 73, 122
Burgard, Burgartz 164, see
  Burkhard
Burgdorf (castle village) 73, 123,
  122
Burgemeister, see Burgermeister
Burger, Burgers 164, Burgert 74
  (burgher, castle dweller,
  townsman) 73
Burgermeister (mayor) 109
Burggraf (burgrave) 109
Burghalter (castellan) 73, 109
Burghard, Burghardt, Burghart,
  see Burkhart
Burghauser, Burgheiser 66 (fr
  Burghausen 122, castle houses)
  73, 65
Burgheimer (castle hamlet) 73,
  123, 122
Burgherr (castellan) 73
Burghof (castle courtyard) 73, 92,
  122
Burgholder, see Burkhalter
Burgman, Burgmann (burgher)
  73, 94
Burgtorf, see Burgdorf
Burgunder (Burgundian) 121
Burgwin (protection + friend) 47,
  48
Burhard, Burhart, see Burkhart
Burhorst (peasant forest) 91, 72
Burkard, Burkart, see Burkhard
Burker, Buckert 74, see Burger
Burkhalter, see Burghalter
Burkhamer, Burkheimer, see
  Burgheimer
Burkhard, Burkhardt, Burckhart
  (protection + strong) 47, 46
Burkhoff, Burkoff, see Burghoff
Burkholder, see Burkhalter
Burkman, see Burgman
Burkhouse 153 (castle house) 73,
  65, 151

Burkmeyer, Burkmire 159 (castle bailiff, castle farmer) 93

Burmann, see Bauermann

Burmeister, Burmester, see Bauernmeister

Burnemann, see Bornemann

Burrichter (village magistrate) 109

Burt (birth, burden)

Busch, Busche (bush, tavern-keeper) 72, 63

Buschel, Buschell (bunch, bundle)

Buscher, Buschert 74, Busching, Buschling (dweller in the bush) 72

Buschgans (bush goose) 72, 115

Buschkemper (bush field) 72, 84

Buschman, Buschmann, Buschmeyer (farmer in the brushland) 72, 93, 94

Buse (pocket)

Bush ..., see Busch ...

Bushart 159, Busshart, see Bussard

Bushbaum 159 (bush tree) 72, 89, 151

Bushert 159, 74 see Buscher

Bushman 159, Bushmann, see Buschmann

Bushrod 159 (bush clearing) 72, 126, 151

Bushyeager 159 (bush hunter) 72, 91, 151

Buskirk (bush church) 72

Buss, Busse (penitence, penance, fine, see also Busch)

Bussard, Bussart (soaring hawk) 115

Busse 53 < Burkhard

Busser (one doing penance)

Busser, Bussler, Bussmann 94 (repairman) 96

Bussman, Bussmann (heavy drinker) 115, 94

Bussmann (handyman) 95, 94

Buterbaugh, see Butterbaugh

Butke, see Boettcher

Butner, see Buettner

Butt (plaice, fishmonger) 115

Butts 159, see Butz

Butter (butter dealer) 105, see also Butz

Butterbaugh 159 (butter brook) 77

Butterbaum (butter tree) 89

Butterbrot (buttered bread) 112

Butterfuss (butter foot) 114

Butterhof, Butterhoff (butter farm) 92

Butterweck (butter role, baker) 96

Buttmann (paice dealer) 106, 94

Buttner, see Buettner

Butz, Butze, Butzer, Butzner, Butts 159 (scarecrow) 114, also < Burkhard

Buxbaum (boxwood) 89

Byer 159, Byers 164, see Bayer

Byerly 159, Byerley, see Baeuerle

Byler 159, Beyler, see Beiler

Byrle 159, see Bayerle

Byroade 159 (by the clearing) 69, 126

# C

Note that most early German American names that formerly began with "C" are spelled with a "K" in later importations, so names should be sought under both spellings. A few Upper German names beginning with "C" begin with a "G" in standard German and are so listed.

Cabel, Cabell, Cabler, see Kabel, Gabel

Cace 159, see Kaes

Cade, see Kade

Caemmerer, see Kaemmerer

Cagle 159, see Kegel

Cahler, see Kahl, Koehler

Cahn, see Kahn
Calb, see Kalb
Caldmeyer (fr the Kalthof, cold
farm) 93, 94
Calk, see Kalker
Call, see Kall, Gallus
Callbaugh 159, Callbeck, see
Kaltenbach
Callenius (Latin for Callen) 142
Calp, see Kalb
Camman, see Kamm
Camp, Campe, Campen, see
Kampe
Camper, see Gamper, Kamper
Canegieser, see Kannengiesser
Campf, Campher, Camphor 159,
see Kampf, Kaempfer
Canisius (probably Latin for
Hund) 142
Cansler 159, see Kantzler
Cantor (Latin, singer) 142
Cantzler, see Kantzler
Canz, see Ganz
Capehart 159, see Gebhard
Caplan (chaplain) 110
Capp, Cappe, Cappes 164, see
Kapp
Cappel, Cappele, Cappelmann 94
(person fr Cappel) 122
Carbaugh 159, Carbauh, Carbach,
Carbeck (possibly carp stream)
115, 77, 151
Carber, see Gerber
Carcher, see Karch
Carcker, see Karcker
Carhart 159, see Gerhard
Carl, Carle, Carel, Carll, Carls
164, Carolus 141 (man)
Carlberg (Charles' mountain) 68
Carling (follower of Charles) 123
Carlsen, son of Carl 59
Carman, see Garmann
Carner, see Garner
Carsten, Carstens 164, Carsten-
sen (Christian) 131

Carthaeuser (Carthusian 110, or
fr Carthausen 122)
Cartman, see Gaertmann
Carver, see Gerber
Casch 53 < Karl
Casman, see Kaesemann, Gas-
mann
Casner, see Gessner
Caspar, Casper, Caspers 164,
Casperl 55 (one of the Three
Kings) 131, 111
Caspari (son of Caspar) 142
Cassel, Cassell, Casseler, Castle
159 (fr Cassel, fr Latin *castel-
lum*) 121, 122
Castleman 94, 159, see Kassel
Castner, see Kastner
Castor (Latin, beaver, patron
saint of Koblenz) 141, 131
Catz, see Katz
Caufman, Cauffmann, Caughman
159, 94, see Kaufmann
Caulberg, see Kalberg
Caulk, see Kalk
Caup, see Kauf
Cayce 159, see Kaes
Caylor 159, Cayler, see Kehler,
Koehler
Cedarbaum 159 (cedar tree) 89
Cerf (French, stag) 144
Cellarius (Latin, cellar master)
141
Centner, see Zentner
Chorengel (choir angel)
Chresman 159, see Kressmann
Chrisman 159, see Christmann
Christ (Christian) 131, 142
Christbaum (Christmas tree) 143
Christer (Christian) 131
Christfried (Christ peace) 139
Christgau (Christian district)
Christhilf (Christ's help) 139
Christi, Christy 159 (son of
Christian) 139, 142
Christian (Christian) 131
Christiani (son of Christian) 142

Christman, Christmann (Christian), see Kressmann Christof, Christoff, Christoffel, Christoph (St. Christopher) 131

Chrypfius (Gryphius, griffin) 141, 142

Chrysler, see Kreisel

Chupart 144, see Schubart

Chur (person fr Chur in Switzerland) 122

Claas, Classen, see Clas

Clabaugh 159, see Kleebach

Clain 159, see Klein

Clap, Clapp, see Klap, Klapp

Clas, Class, Clasen, see Nicolaus

Clatenbaugh 159, Clattenbaugh, Clatterbaugh, Clatterbuck, see Gladbach

Clauer, see Glauer

Claus, see Klaus

Clausey 159, Clawsey, see Klause

Clause, Claussen (hermitage, cell) 122

Clausenius 141, see Klaus

Clauser, see Klause

Clawes 53 < Niklaus

Claybaugh 159, see Kleebach

Clayman 159, see Klehmann

Claypool 159, Claypoole, see Kleepuhl

Cleaver 159, see Cleve

Cleh, see Klee

Clem, see Klemm

Clemens, Clementz, Clement (name of pope) 134

Clemmer, see Klemmer

Cleve (fr Cleves) 121

Clever, see Kleber

Clevenstine 159, see Kliebenstein

Click, Clickner, see Glueck

Cline 159, Clien 159, see Klein

Clinedienst 159, Clinedinst, Clindist, see Kleindienst

Clinefelter 159, see Kleinfeld

Clingenpeel 159, see Klingenbuehl

Clinger, see Klinger

Clingman, Clingermann, see Klingmann

Clise 159, see Gleis

Cloates 159, see Klotz

Clocke, Clocker, see Glocke, Glocker

Clodfelter (log field) 84

Clontz 159, see Glantz

Closs, Closse, see Kloss, Klosse

Clostermann, see Klostermann

Clotfelter, see Clodfelter

Clouse 159, Clouser, Clowser, see Klaus, Klause

Clower 159, Clowers 164, see Glauer

Clutts 159, Clutz, see Klott

Coal 159, Coale, see Kohl

Cobach, Cobaugh 159 (cow brook) 77

Coben, see Koben

Cober, see Kober

Coberg (German principality) 121

Coble 159, see Goebel

Coblenz, Coblenzer, see Koblenz

Coch, see Koch

Coen 53, Coene, Coenen < Conrad

Coerper, see Koerber

Coder 159, see Koeder

Coffelt, Coffield 153 (cow field) 84

Coffer, see Koffer

Coffman, see Kaufmann

Cogle 159, see Kugel

Cohen, Cohn (Hebrew: priest) 110, see also Kuhn

Cohnen, see Koehn

Cokenour 159, see Kochenauer

Colb, see Kolb

Colbeck, see Kohlbecker

Colberg, see Kohlberg

Coldiron 153, see Kalteisen

Cole, see Kohl

Colefelt, Colfelt (cabbage field) 84

Colhower 159, see Kohlhauer

Colehaus 159, Colehouse 153, see
 Kohlhas
Coleman, see Kohlmann, Kuhl-
 mann
Colflesh 159, see Kalbfleisch
Colhower 159 (coal digger)
Collar 159, Coller, see Kohler,
 Koller
Collin 53 < Nickolaus
Collin (place name) 122
Collitz (place name) 122
Collmann, Colman, see Kohlmann
Collmeyer, see Kohlmeyer
Colmar (fr Colmar in Alsace) 122
Colter, see Kolter
Comb 152, see Kamm
Compher 159, see Kaempfer
Conkel, Conkle 159, see Kunckel
Conrad, Conrads 164, Conradt,
 Conrath, Conradus142 (brave +
 counsel) 36, 46, 46, 136
Conradi, Conrady, son of Con-
 rad(us) 142
Conselman 159, see Kuenzelmann
Conz 159, see Kunz
Conzelman 159, see Kuenzelmann
Cooble 159, see Kuebel
Coogle 159, see Kugel
Cook 152, see Koch
Cool 159, Cooll, see Kuhl
Coolbaugh 159, see Kuhlbach
Cooler 159, see Kuhler
Coolmann 159, see Kuhlmann
Coomer 159, see Kummer
Coon 159, Coons 164, Coonce 159,
 164, Coonts, see Kuhn, Kuhns
Coope (merchant, fr Latin *caupo)*
 105
Cooper 159, see Kupfer, Kuper
Cooperman 94, 159, see Kupfer-
 mann
Cooperstein 159 (copper moun-
 tain) 151
Coopman, see Kaufmann
Coos 159, see Kuss
Copeman 159, see Kaufmann

Copenhaver, Copenheaver, see
 Koppenhaver
Copman, see Kaufmann
Coppel, Coppele, see Koppel
Coradi, see Konradi
Corber, see Koerber
Corbman 94, see Koerber
Cordes, see Kordes
Corenblith, see Kornblith
Corfman 94, see Korff
Cornbach (corn brook) 77
Cornberger (fr Cornberg 122,
 grain mountain) 68
Cornblath, Cornblatt, see Korn-
 blatt
Cornbrook, Cornbrooks 164 (grain
 brake) 80
Cornelius (Roman name [crow],
 name of pope) 141, 134
Cornell, see Cornelius
Cornfield 152, see Kornfeld
Cornman, see Kornmann
Cornmesser (grain measurer) 109
Corthes, Cortes, see Cordes
Cost, see Kost
Coster, see Kuester
Cott, Cottman, see Gott, Gott-
 mann
Cotz 159, see Goetz
Couchenuour 159, Coughenour,
 see Gauchenauer
Coughman 159, see Kaufmann
Cougle 159, see Kugel
Couler 159, see Kuehler
Coulter 159, see Kolter
Coun 159, see Kuhn
Counce 159, see Kuntz
Councel 159, Council, Counsul,
 Counselman 94, Councilman,
 see Kuenzel, Kuenzelman
Counterman 159, Countryman,
 see Guenthermann
Counts 159, see Kuntz
Couts 159, Coutts, see Kauz
Crabbe (crab)
Crabill 159, see Kraebuehl

Crable 159, see Kraehbuehl
Craemer, Cramer, Cramert 74,
see Kraemer
Craesman 159, see Kressmann
Craft, see Kraft
Crall, see Kral
Cram (retail trade, huckster's
cart) 105
Cramer, see Kraemer
Crance 159, see Krantz
Crank, see Krank
Crass, see Grass
Cratsar 159, see Kratzer
Cratz, see Kratz
Crawf 159, see Graff
Craumer 159, Crawmer, see
Kraemer
Craus, see Kraus
Cravenstine 159, see Graffenstein
Craver, see Graeber
Craybill 159, Crebil, see Kraeh-
buehl
Creager 159, see Krueger
Creamer 159, see Kraemer
Crebbs, Crebs, see Krebs
Creger 159, Creeger, Cregar, see
Krueger
Creek 159, see Krueg
Creiner 159, see Greiner
Creitz, Creytz, Creitzer, see
Kreutz, Kreutzer
Cress, Cresse, see Kress, Kresse
Cressman, Cressmeyer, see
Kressman
Creutz, Creutzer, see Kreutz,
Kreutzer
Crever 159, see Grueber
Crews 159, see Kruse
Creyts, see Kreutz
Crickenberger 159, Cricken-
burger, see Krueckenberger
Crickman 159, see Kruegmann
Crider 159, Cridler, see Kreider
Crigger, see Krueger
Crimm, see Grimm
Criner 159, see Greiner

Cripe 159, see Greip
Crisman, Crissmann, see Kress-
mann
Crist, Criste, Cristner, see Christ
Crites 159, Critz, Critzer, Crizer,
Critzman, see Kreutz,
Kreutzer, Kreutzmann
Croesman, Croessman, see
Kressmann
Croft, see Craft
Croll, see Groll, Kroll
Crombach, see Grumbach
Crombholts 159, see Krumbholtz
Cromer 159, see Kraemer
Cromm, see Krumm
Cron, Crone, see Kron, Krone
Cronauer, see Gronau
Cronberger, Cronenberg, Cron-
enberger, Croneberge, see
Kronberg
Cronemeyer (royal bailiff) 93, 109
Cronjager (royal hunter) 91
Cronk 159, see Krank
Cronkite 159, see Krankheit
Cronmiller (crown miller) 103
Cronrad, Cronrath (crown coun-
cil), see Konrad
Crow 153, see Kraehe
Crosman 159, see Grossmann,
Kressmann
Crossbart (big beard) 112
Crosse, Crossman, see Grosse,
Grossmann
Crossman, see Kressmann
Crounse 159, see Krantz
Crouse 159, see Kraus
Croushore 159, see Kraushaar
Crout 159, see Kraut
Crouthamel 159 (herb hamlet)
123
Crowder 159, Crouther, see
Krauter
Crownen 159, see Kronen
Crowninshield 159, see Kronen-
schild

Croyter 159, Croyder, see
Kraeuter
Crueger, see Krueger
Cruess, see Gruess
Cruise 159, see Kruse
Crull, see Krull
Crum, Crumm, see Krumm
Crumbacker, Crumbaker, Crum-
baugh 159 (crooked brook) 77
Crumling (misshapen person) 113
Crump, see Krumm
Crupe 159, see Krup
Cruse 159, see Kruse
Crusse 159, see Gruss
Crute 159, see Kraut
Cryder 159, see Kreider
Cryer 159, Cryor, see Kreier
Crynes 159, see Grein
Crytzer, see Kreutzer
Cuffman 159, see Kaufman
Cugel, see Kugel
Cuhn, see Kuhn
Culler, see Koller, Koehler
Culman, Cullmann, see Kuhl-
mann
Culp, see Kulp
Cumberbatch 159, Cumberpatch,
see Kummerbach
Cunkel, see Kunkel
Cunrad, Cuonrad, Cunred 159,
see Conrad
Cunradi, son of Cunrad 142
Cuntz, Cunz, see Kuntz
Cunzeman, see Kuntzemann
Cuper, see Kupfer
Curland, Curlander (fr the Kur-
land) 121
Curtius 141, see Kurtz
Custer, see Kuester
Cutchall 159, see Gottschalk
Cutlip 159, see Gottlieb
Cyfret, Cyphert, see Seyfert

**D**

A name beginning with "D" in one
dialect may begin with a "T" in
another and be so listed below.

Daab (swamp) 80
Dachenhausen, Dachhausen
(thatched houses) 65
Dacher (thatcher, roofer) 96
Dachhausen, see Dachenhausen
Dachler, Dachl, see Dacher
Dachler (swamp dweller) 80
Dachs (badger, badger hunter)
115, 91
Dachslager (badger lair)
Dackerman 94, Dackermann,
Dackman, Dackmann, see
Dacher
Daegen, see Degen
Daehnert < Degenhard
Daehnick 53, Daehnike, Daehnke
< Degenhard
Daeneke 53, 55 < Degenhard
Daengler, see Dengler
Daescher, Daeschner, see Taes-
cher
Daeuber, see Taeuber
Daeubler, see Taeubler
Daeumler (thumb, Tom Thumb)
113
Dafner, Daffner (taverner, fr
Latin *taberna*) 96
Dagenbeck (baker who bakes
daily) 96
Dagenhart 159, see Degenhart
Dagher, see Dacher
Dahl 122, Dahle 122, Dahler,
Dahlmann 94, Dallmann
(valley man, see Thalmann) 76
Dahlberg (valley mountain) 76, 68
Dahlheim, Dahlheimer (fr Dahl-
heim 122, valley hamlet) 76,
123
Dahlhoff, Dalhoff (valley farm)
76, 92

Dahlinger (fr Dahlingen) 122
Dahlke 55 (little valley) 76
Dahlmann, see Thalmann
Dahlmeyer, see Thalmeyer
Dahm 53, Dahms 164, Dahme,
   Dahmer < Adam, 135
Dahm 53 < Damian 131
Dahm (dweller near the Dahme
   River) 83, 122
Dahn, Dahne (forest) 72
Daichler, see Deigler
Daigel, Deigle, see Deigler
Daimler (thumb screwer) 96
Dalhoff, see Dahlhoff
Daller (moist, cool place) 80
Dallmeyer, see Thalmeyer
Dallwig, see Dalwig
Dalman, see Thalmann
Dalmeyer, see Dahlmeyer
Dalsheimer, Dalshimer 159,
   Dalsemer (valley hamlet) 76,
   123
Dalwig (valley village) 76, 123
Dam 53 < St. Damian 131
Dam 53, Dame, Damser < Adam
   135
Dam (stag)
Daman, Damen, see Dahm
Damewald, see Dannewald
Damkoehler (forest collier) 89, 95
Damm 122, Damme, Dammes 164
   (causeway, dike) 81
Dammann, Dammermann
   (dweller on or near dike) 81
Dammann 53 < Thomas
Dammermut (dike, causeway,
   dweller on the dike) 81
Dammeyer 93, Dammeier, Dam-
   myer (farmer on or at the dike)
   81
Dampf (steam)
Damrosch (forest slide) 89, 71
Dan (forest, fir) 89, 71
Danaker, see Danecker
Danbach (brook through firs) 89,
   77

Dance 153, see Tanz
Dancel 159, see Dantzel
Dandorf (fir village, forest village)
   89, 123
Danecker, Danecke, Danegger
   (place in fir trees) 89, 85, see
   Tannecker
Daneman, Danemann (forest
   dweller) 89
Danenhauer, Danhaur (fir
   chopper, wood cutter) 89, 95,
   100
Dange 53 < St. Anthony 131
Dangel, Dangle 159 < Daniel 135
Dangler, see Dengler
Danhower 159, see Danenhauer
Danick, Danicke, see Danecke
Daniel, Daniels 164 (OT name)
   135
Dankelmann 94 (marsh dweller,
   cf. English "dank") 80
Dankelmeyer (marsh farmer) 80
Danker, Dankers 164, Dankert <
   Dankwart 48, 47
Dankmar (thought + famous) 48,
   47
Dankmeyer 93, see Dankelmeyer
Dankwart (thought + guard or
   watch) 48, 47
Danmeyer, Danmyer 159 (forest
   farmer) 89, 93
Danmiller (forest miller) 89, 103
Dannecke, Dannecker, Dannec-
   ker, Dannegger, see Danecker
   or Denecke
Dannenbaum 122, Dannebaum,
   see Tannenbaum
Dannenberg (forest mountain) 89,
   68, 122
Dannenfeld, Dannenfeldt, Dan-
   nenfelder, Dannenfeltzer (forest
   field) 89, 84
Dannenfelser (wooded cliffs) 89,
   84
Dannenmann (forest dweller) 89,
   94

Danner, Dannermann 94 (forest dweller) 89
Danner < Giessendanner
Dannewald, Damewald, see Tannenwald
Dannewitz (fr Danewitz 122, forest village) 89, 127
Dannhaeuser 122, see Tannhaeuser
Dannhoeffer, see Tannhoeffer
Danninger (fr Danningen) 122
Danoff, see Dannhoeffer
Dannwolf (forest wolf) 89, 48
Dansberger (forest mountain) 89, 68
Dansicker 159, see Dantziger
Dansler, see Densler
Dantz, Dantzer, Dantzler (dancer) 96
Dantzenbecker, Tanzenbecker (dancing brook) 77
Dantzic, Dantzig, Dantziger (Baltic city) 122
Dantzler, see Dantz
Danz, Danzer, Danzel, see Dantz
Danzig, Danziger, see Dantzic
Dapfer, see Tapfer
Darmstadt, Darmstaet, Darmsteadt, Darmstaedter (fr Darmstadt) 122
Dasch, Dascher, Dasher 159, Dashner, see Taescher
Dasinger (fr Dasing) 122
Dattelbaum (date tree) 89, 149
Datwyler, see Dettwiler
Daub, Daube, Dauber, Daubert 74, Daubner, see Taub, Taube
Daube (barrel stave, cooper) 96
Daubenberger (dove mountain) 115, 68
Dauberman, see Taubermann
Daublein 55 (little dove) 115
Daudt (swamp, reeds) 80
Dauer (duration)
Dauer (barrelstave maker) 95

Dauernheim (place name) 123, 122
Daum (thumb, short person) 113
Daumenlang (thumb long) 113
Daumer (thumbscrew, torturer, tool for cutting rock) 106
Daun, Daunn (goose down, dealer in feathers) 106
Daun (down, swamp) 80, 122
Dauner (swamp dweller) 80
Dausch (mother swine) 91
Daymude 159, see Demuth
David, Davit (OT character) 135
Davids, Davidssohn (son of David) 59
Deaderick 159, see Dederick
Deagler 159, see Diegler
Deahl 159, see Diehl
Dealbone 159 < Thiel Bohn
Deamer 159, see Dietmar
Deamud 159, see Demuth
Deaner 159, see Diener
Deangler 159, see Dengler
Deardorf 159, Deardorff, see Tierdorf
Dearholt 159, animal forest 72
Dearman 159, see Diermann
Dearstine 159 (animal mountain) 73
Deasel 159, see Diesel
Deatrich 159, see Dietrich
Deats 159, see Dietz
Debald, Debold, Debolt, see Dietbald
Debelbesin, see Teufelbiss
Deboer (the peasant) 91
Debold, Deboldt, see Dietbold
Debs 53 < Matthias
Dechan, Dechant (tithing man, tithe collector) 109
Decher, Dechert 74 (roofer) 92, 143
Decher (set of ten, tenth child)
Deck, Decke (blanket) 106
Deckdenbron (Cover the well!) 116

Decker, Deckert 74, Deckner (thatcher, roofer) 96

Deckler, Deckelman 94 (maker of bedclothes) 96

Deckman, Deckmann (thatcher) 94, 96

Dedekind 53 < Dietrich

Dedemeyer (Dietrich + farmer) 93

Dederer (stutterer) 114

Dederick, Dedrich, Dedrick, see Dietrich

Deeck 53, Deeken < Dietrich

Deemar 159, Deemere, see Dietmar

Deener 159, see Diener

Deer ..., see Tier ...

Deering, see Thueringer

Dees 53, 159, Deese, see Thiess

Deeter, see Dieter

Deetje, 53, 55 Deetjen < Dietrich

Deets 159, Deetz < Dietrich

Defenbau 159, Defenbaugh, Defibaugh, Deffibaugh, Deffinbaugh, see Tiefenbach

Defriece 159, see Devries

Degen (thane) 46

Degen, Degener (dagger, dagger maker) 108

Degenhardt, Degenhart (thane + strong) 46, 46

Degenkolb (hero + club) 46

Degering 53, Degerink < Degenhard

Degner, Degener (dagger maker) 108

DeGraffenried, see Graffenried

Degrote, Degroot, DeGroat 159 (the large) 113

Dehle 53, Dehles 164, Dehls 164, Dehler < Dietrich

Dehlenbeck (Dietrich's brook) 77

Dehlke 53, 55 < Dietrich

Dehm, Dehmann 94, Dehmert 74 < Thomas, Damianus 131

Dem 53 < Damianus 131

Dehn, Dehne, Dehner, Dehnert < Degenhard

Dehrenbach (animal brook) 77

Dehrenkamp (animal field) 77

Deibel (devil) 131

Deibert < Dagebert

Deibler, see Teubler

Deich, Deicher, Deichert 74 (dweller on a dike) 81

Deichgraber, Deichgraeber (ditch digger, dike digger) 81

Deichgraff (dike supervisor) 109

Deichman, Deichmann, Deickmann, see Teichmann

Deichmiller, Deichmueller (pond miller, miller on the dike) 81, 103

Deicke, Deickman 94 (dweller at or on the dike) 81

Deigler (maker of wooden water pipes) 96

Deimling, see Daeumling

Deinert, Deinhart, see Degenhard

Deininga 53, Deininger < Degenhard

Deinlein 53, 55 < Degenhard

Deis 159, Deise, see Theiss

Deisinger (fr Deising in Bavaria) 122

Deisler (wainwright) 96

Deisroth (manure clearing) 126

Deiss 159, see Theiss

Deissel (wainwright) 96

Deist, Deister, Deistler (wooded ridge) 72

Deisterberg (wooded mountain) 68

Deistermann (dweller on a wooded ridge) 72, 94

Deisteroth (clearing on a wooded ridge) 72, 125

Deitsch, Deitscher, Deitschman 94, Deitch 159, see Deutsch

Deitelbaum, see Dattelbaum

Deiter, Deitrich, Deitrick, see Dieter, Dietrich

Deiter, Deitrich, Deitrick, see
Dieter, Dietrich
Deitz, Deitzel, see Dietz, Dietzel
Deken 53 < Dietrich
Dekker, Dekher, see Decker
Delinger, Dellinger, see Dillinger
Demback (Tom's brook) 77
Demke 53, 55, Demeke, Dempke
< Thomas
Demm 53, Demme < Thomas
Demmler, Demler (glutton) 115
Demuth (humility) 139
Denbeck (fir brook, forest brook)
89, 77
Denburg (forest castle) 89, 73
Dencker, Denker (thinker, left-
handed person) 114
Dencler 159, see Dengler
Denecke 53, 55, Denicke < Deg-
enhard
Dener 159, see Diener
Dengler (one who repairs blades
by hammering them) 96
Denhard, Denhardt < Degenhard
Denk (left, left handed) 114
Denker, see Dankwart
Denlein, see Dennelein
Denmeyer (fr the Denhoff, forest
farm) 89, 92, 93
Dennard < Degenhard
Denner, Dennler, see Tanner
Denneger 53 < Degenhard
Dennelein 55, Dennerlein (little
fir tree) 89
Dennemann (dweller among the
firs) 89, 94
Dennenberg 122, see Tannenberg
Dennewitz 122, see Dannewitz
Dennstedt, Daennstaedt (forest
place) 89
Denny 159, sometimes < Thoeni
Densler (dancer) 96
Dentz, Denz, Dentzer, Denzer, see
Tants, Tantz
Dentzel, Dentzler (dancer) 96
Deobald, see Dietbald

Depfer, see Tepper
Deppendal, Dependahl (deep
valley) 76
Deppisch, Deppish 159 (foolish)
115
Derenberger (animal mountain)
68
Derenkamp (animal field) 84
Derflinger 159 (villager) 123
Derhammer (fr Derheim) 122, 123
Derheim (animal hamlet) 123
Derick 53, Derrick < Dietrich
Derling 159, see Deuerling
Dermeyer (occupant of the
Derhoff, animal farm) 93
Derrenbacher (animal brook) 77
Derrenberger, see Derenberger
Derring, Derringer, see Thuer-
inger
Dersch (foolish) 115
Derst 159, see Durst
Derwart (game warden) 96
Derwin (animal friend) 48
Desch, Descher, Deschner, see
Taescher
Deschler, Deschner, see Taescher
Desel 159, see Diesel
DeShong (French, Deschamps, fr
the fields) 144
Dessau, Dessauer (German city)
122
Dester, Destler, see Textor,
Dexter
Detenbach (swamp brook) 80, 77
Deter, Deters 164, Detert 74,
Dettermann 94, Detterer <
Diethard
Detje 53, 55, Detjen, see Dietrich
Detmer < Dietmar
Detmold (place name, "people's
assembly" or else "swamp
place") 46, 80, 122
Detner, Detters 164, see Dettner
Detrich, see Dietrich
Dettelbach (swamp brook) 80, 77,
122

Detter, Dettermann, see Dettner
Dettmann (swamp dweller) 80, 94
Dettmar, Dettmer, see Dietmar
Dettmeyer (swamp farmer) 80, 93
Dettner, Dettler (swamp dweller) 80
Dettweiler, Dettwiler, Detwiler (swamp village) 80, 127
Detzel 53, 55 < Dietrich
Detzner (manurer) 95
Deubel (devil) 131
Deuber, Deubler, Deubert 74, see Tauber, Taubert
Deubner, see Taubner
Deuchler (maker of wooden water pipes) 96
Deuerling (darling) 115
Deurer, see Duerer
Deutermann (expounder) 94
Deutsch, Deutscher, Deutschman 94, Deutschmann, Deutch (German) 121
Deutschendorf (German village) 121, 123
Devilbiss 159, De Villbiss, see Teufelbiss
Devriend (the friend)
Devries (the Frisian) 121
Dewalt, Dewald < Dietwald (people + rule) 46, 46
Dewitz (Slavic place name) 146, 122
Dexter (Latin, right hand), see also Textor
Deyck, see Deich
Deys, see Theiss
Diamant (diamond)
Dibert < Dietbrecht
Dice 159 < Theiss
Dichmann, see Dickman
Dick 122, Dicke 122, Dicks 164, Dix, Dicker, Dickert 74, Dueck (dweller near a thicket) 142
Dick, Dicker, Dickert 74 (fat, thick) 114, 143
Dickerhoof, see Dickhoff

Dickhaut, Dickhout (thick skin) 114
Dickhoff, Diekhof, Dieckhof, Dyckhoff (dike farm) 81, 92
Dickman, Dickmann, Dickermann, see Teichmann
Dickmer, see Dickmeyer
Dickmeyer (dike warden) 81, 93
Diebald, see Dietbald
Dicks 53 < Benedictus 131
Diebel, see Teufel
Diebert, see Dietbrecht
Diebold, Dietbolt, see Dietbald
Dieck, Diecks 164 (dweller on or near the dike) 81
Dieckhaus (dike house) 81, 65, 122
Dieckmann, Diekmann, see Teichmann
Diederich, see Dietrich
Diefenbach, Dieffenbach, Dieffenbacher, see Tiefenbach
Dieffenthal (deep valley) 76
Diegel, Diegler, Diegelman 94 (potter) 96
Diegmann, see Teichmann
Diehl, Diehle, Diehlmann 94, Diel (wall or floor of planks)
Diehl 53 < Dietrich
Diehlbeck, see Dillenbeck
Diehm 53 < Dietmar
Diekmann, see Teichmann
Diel (swamp brook) 80, 77
Diele (board, board sawyer) 96
Diemer, see Dietmar
Diener (servant) 139
Dienhart < Degenhard
Dienst (service, servant) 139
Dienstag (Tuesday) 143
Diepolt, see Dietbald
Dier, see Tier
Dierauer (animal meadow) 84
Dierbaum (animal tree) 89
Dierdorf 122, Dierdorff, Dierdorp (swamp village) 80, 43, 123, see Tierdorf

Dischong, see DeShong
Dishman 159, see Tischmann
Ditmann, see Dietman
Ditmar, Dittmer, see Dietmar
Dittenbrand (swamp clearing) 80, 126
Dittenhafer, Dittenhoefer, Dittenhoffer (swamp farm) 80, 92
Dittmann (swamp dweller) 80, 94
Dittmann, see Dietmann
Ditter, see Dieter
Dittmar, Dittmer, see Dietmar
Dittrich, see Dietrich
Ditz, Ditzel, Ditzell, see Dietz, Dietzel
Divilbiss 159, Divilbess, Divilplease, see Teufelbiss
Diwall, see Dietbald
Dix 53 < Benedictus, also see Dick
Doarnberger 159, see Dornberger
Doarnfeld 159, see Dornfeld
Dober, Doberer, Dobert 74 (pigeon raiser or seller) 115, 143
Doberstein (dovecote mountain) 73
Dobert < Theodoberacht (folk + bright) 46, 46
Dobler, Dobeler, Doebeler, see Tobler
Dochman, see Tuchmann
Dochterman, see Tochtermann
Dock (kind of fish, fishmonger) 115
Dock (dry dock)
Dockstade (fish landing) 71
Dockweiler (marsh village) 80, 127
Doctor (teacher, professor) 96
Dode (swamp, reeds) 81
Dodenhof (swamp farm) 81, 92
Doderer (stutterer) 114
Doebberstein, see Doberstein
Doebel, Doebler, Doebling, see Tobler
Dorf (village, villager) 123

Doefler, see Dorfmann
Doehl 53, Doehle, Doehlen, Doehler < Adolf
Doehl, Doehle (place names) 122
Doehling (fr Dehling in Wurttemberg) 122
Doehrer, Doehrling, Doehring, see Thueringer
Doelfel 53, 55 < Adolf
Doell, Doelle, Doeller (marsh water, dweller in a marsh) 80
Doelling (kind of perch, fishmonger) 115
Doellinger (fr Doelling) 122, see also Doehling
Doellinger, see Doehling
Doemling < Domarich (judgment + rule) 46
Doenges 53 (fr Anthonius) 131
Doeninger (dweller on damp terrain) 80
Doepfer, Doepner (potter) 96
Doerer 53 < Theodor 131
Doerflein 55 (little village) 123, 122
Doerfer, Doerfling, Doerflinger (villager) 123
Doering (Thuringian, "heringnose" attributed to Thuringians) 121, 113
Doerle 55 (little door, dweller by city gate)
Doermer (tower keeper, fr Latin *turris*) 96
Doerner (thicket dweller) 72
Doerr, Doerre (dry) 115
Doerrer, Doerrmann 94 (dryer) 96
Doetsch, see Deutsch
Doggendorf (bulldog village) 123
Dohl, Dohle 122, Dohlen, Dohler, Dohlert 74 (daw) 115
Dohm 53, Dohme, Dohmke < Thomas 131
Dohnke 53, 55 < Anton 131
Dohrman, Dohrmann, see Thormann

Dohrn, see Dorn
Dolch (dagger) 108
Dold 53, Dolde < Berthold
Doleman, see Dollmann
Doles 159, 164, see Dohl
Dolf 53, Dolfi, Dolfs 164 < Adolf
Doll, Dolle (mad) 115
Doll (valley) 76
Dollenberg (valley mountain) 76, 48, 122
Doller, Dollar 159 (valley dweller) 76
Doller, Dollar 159, see Thaler
Dollfuss (club foot) 114, or < Adolphus or Rudolfus
Dollinger, Dolinger (fr Dolling) 122
Dollmann (madman) 115, see Tollmann
Dollmann (valley dweller) 76, 94
Dolmetsch (Slavic: interpreter) 146
Dolph 53, see Adolf
Dom, Dohm, Dohme, Dohmer (dweller near a cathedral)
Domaas 53 < Thomas 131
Dome, Domes, Dohm, Dohme < Thomas 131
Domhoff (cathedral court) 92, 122
Donat, Donatt, Donath < St. Donatus 131
Donawerth, fr Donauwerth (city on Danube island) 79
Dondorf, see Dandorf
Donecker, see Danecker
Donge 53, Donges, Dongis < St. Anthonius 131
Donhauser, see Tanhauser
Donnenberg, see Tannenberg
Donner (thunder, thunderer)
Donnewitz, see Dannewitz
Dopmann (potter) 96, 94
Doppler (gambler)
Doremus < Adoremus (Let us adore [Him]!) 117
Dorenfeld (thorn field) 72, 84

Dorf, Dorff, Dorfman 94, Dorffmann, Dorfler (villager) 123
Dorman, see Thormann
Dorn (thorn, thicket) 72, 122
Dornbach (thorny brook) 72, 77, 122
Dornberger (thorn mountain) 72, 68
Dornburg (thorn castle) 72, 73, 122
Dornbusch, Dornbush 159 (thorn bush) 72, 72, 122
Dornfeld (thorn field) 72, 84
Dornheim (thorn hamlet) 72, 123, 122
Dorp (village) 123, 122
Dorr, see Thor
Dorsch (codfish seller) 115, 106
Dorst, see Durst
Dorward, Dorwarth, see Thorwart
Dosch, Dosche, Dosh 159 (bush, tavern keeper) 96
Doster (thyme seller, spice seller) 106
Dotter (egg yolk)
Dotterweich (yolk soft) 115
Doub 159, see Taub
Dower 159, see Dauer
Dowhauer 159, see Tauhauer
Downer 159, see Dauner
Drach, Drache (dragon, house name) 62, 149
Drachenbert (Bert of the Dragon House) 62, 149
Drachman (occupant of the Dragon House) 62, 149, 94
Drachsel, Drachsler, see Drechsler
Drake, see Drach
Drakenfeld (dragon field) 84
Drayer 159, see Dreher
Dreber 53 < Andreas 131
Drechsel, Drechsler, Drexler (turner) 98
Drees 53 < Andreas 131
Dreher (potter) 96

Dreher, see Drechsler

Dreier (thrupence) 117

Dreier (potter) 96

Dreifus, Dreifuss, Dreyfuss (tripod) 8

Dreifus, Dreyfuss (fr Trier) 122

Dreisbach, Dresbach, see Troestbach

Dreiss (swamp water) 80

Dreiser, Dreist (audacious) 115

Dresch, Dresh 159, Drescher, Dreschler (thresher) 95

Dresden, Dresner (fr Dresden) 122

Dresselhaus (fr Dresselhausen 122, turner's house) 96, 65

Dressel, Dressler, Dresler, see Drechsel

Dreus 53, Drewes, Drewing < Andreas 131

Drexel, Drexler, see Drechsel

Dreyer, Dryer 159 (turner, see Dreier) 96

Dreyfus, Dreyfuss, see Dreifuss

Driebenbach (murky brook) 77

Driehaus (fr Driehausen) 122

Dries 53, Driesslein 55 < Andreas 131

Driesch (uncultivated field) 84, 122

Drieschbach (pasture brook) 84, 77

Driessheim (pasture hamlet) 84, 123

Driessler, see Drechsel

Droege (dry)

Droegmyr 159 (dry farmer) 93

Drommelhausen, Drommelhauser (drummer houses) 65

Drost, Droste (steward) 109

Druckenbrod, see Trockenbrod

Drucker, Druecker, Druker 159 (cloth presser) 96

Drucker (printer) 96

Drusch (uncultivated, as of land)

Drussel (trunk, snout) 114

Drutz (defiance) 115

Dryer 159, see Dreier, Dreyer

Dubendorffer, Diebendoerfer (swamp village) 80, 123

Ducker (diving duck, devil) 115

Dude (bagpiper) 96

Duden (blockhead) 115

Duden 53 < Ludolf

Dudenhoffer, Dudenhoefer (fr the Dudenhoff, Ludolf's farm) 92

Dueffenbach, see Tiefenbach

Duehring, see Duering

Duemmling (mute, fool) 115

Duenn (thin) 115

Duensing (Duden's swamp) 80

Duerbeck (dry brook) 77

Duerenberger (region in Austria, dry mountain) 121

Duerer (door keeper) 96

Duering, Dueringer (Thuringian) 121

Duermueller (water miller) 103

Duerr (dry, skinny) 114

Duerrbaum (dry tree) 89

Duerrenmatt (dry meadow) 84

Duesenberg (silent mountain) 68

Duetsch, Duitscher, see Deutsch

Duffner (fr Teufen in Wurttemberg) 122

Dulde 53 < Berthold

Dumbaugh 159 (fr Dumbach 122) 77

Dumler (inexperienced) 114

Dunbaugh 159, see Danbach

Dundorf, see Dandorf

Dunge 53 < St. Anthonius 131

Dunger (manure)

Dunger (dweller on a hummock)

Dunkel, Dunkle 159 (dark) 113

Dunkelberg (dark mountain) 68

Dunker, see Dunkel

Dunkhorst (low-hill hurst) 68, 72

Dunmire 159, Dunmyer, see Danmeyer

Durcholtz (through the forest) 69, 72

Durenberger, see Durrenberger

Durer, see Duerer

Durholtz (dry wood)

Durlach (dry pond) 80

Durlach (principality on Rhein) 121, 122

Durman, see Thurmann

Durnbaugh 159 (dry creek) 77

Durner, see Turner

Durr, see Duerr

Durrenberger, see Duerenberger

Durschlag (colander, sieve) 106

Durst (thirst) 115

Durst (daredevil) 115

Dusel (silly, cf. English "dizzy") 115

Dusenberry 159, see Duesenberg

Dussel, Dussler (stream near Dusseldorf) 83

Dusseldorf (German city), 122, 124

Dussing (ornamental belt 106), see also Tussing

Dusterhoff (dreary farm) 92

Dutweiler 122, see Dettweiler

Dyce 159, see Theiss

Dyckmann, see Teichmann

Dyson 159, see Theissen

Dyssgen 53, 55 < Dietrich

## E

Eagel 159, Eagle, Eagler < *Igel* (hedgehog) 48, 159

Eagleburg 159 (hedgehog castle) 48, 73, 159

Eaglehart 159, see Igelhart

Eakel 159, Eakle 159, see Eichel

Eaker 159, Eakers 164, see Eicher

Ealy 159 (Eli, OT name)

Earhart 159, Earhardt, Earehart, see Erhard

Earl 159, Earle, Earley, see Erle

Earlbeck 159, see Erlenbach

Earman 159, see Ehrmann

Earnest 159, see Ernst

Earnhard 159, Earnhardt, see Erhard

Earp 159, see Erb

East 152, see Ost

Eastberg 153, see Ostberg

Easter 152, see Oster

Eastwood 153, see Ostwald

Ebbeke 53, 55, Ebbeling < Eggebrecht

Ebbert 53, Ebberts 164 < Eggebrecht

Ebbinger, Eppinger (fr Ebbingen, plain), also see Eggebrecht

Ebbinghause, Ebbinghauser (house on the plain) 65

Ebel 53, Ebele, Ebell, Ebelein 55, Ebelt 74 < Albrecht

Ebelding (belonging to Ebel) 59

Ebeling 53, 55, Ebelke < Ebel 59

Eben, Ebener, Ebner (whiffletree)

Eben, Ebener, Ebner (fr Eben 122, dweller on a plain)

Ebenhack (level enclosure) 123

Ebensberger (mountain on a plain) 68

Eber, Ebers 164, Ebert 74, 143 (wild boar) 48, or < Eberhard

Eberbach, Ebersbacher, Eberbeck (reed brook) 81, 77

Eberding (fr Eberding 122, belonging to Ebert 59)

Eberhagen (wild boar enclosure) 48, 123

Eberhard, Eberhardt, Eberharde, Eberhards 164, Eberhart (wild boar + strong) 48, 46

Eberl 55, Eberle, Eberlet, Eberli, Eberly, Eberlein, Eberlin, Eberling (little wild boar) 48, or < Eberhard

Eberman (wild boar hunter, Eber's vassal) 48, 94

Ebersbacher, Eberspacher (fr Ebersbach 122, boar brook) 48, 77

Ebersberg, Ebersberger (fr Ebersberg 122, boar mountain) 48, 68

Eberschwein (wild boar) 48

Eberschwyl (boar village) 48, 127

Ebersmann (Eber's vassal) 48, 94

Eberstein (boar mountain) 48, 73, 122

Ebert 53, 74, Eberts 164, Eberth, Ebertz, see Eber, Eggebrecht

Ebertsbach (Ebert's brook) 48, 77

Eberwein, Eberwine 159 (boar + friend) 48, 48

Ebinger (fr Ebing 122, see also Eppinger)

Ebinghausen (place name) 65, 122

Ebler 53 < Albrecht

Ebner, see Eben, Ebener

Ebrecht (law + brilliant) 47, see also Eggebrecht

Ebright 159, see Ebrecht

Ebstein, see Epstein

Eccard 159, see Eckhard

Eccles 159, 164, see Eckel

Eche, Echeman, see Eiche, Eichmann

Echerd, Echard, see Eckhard

Echt (lawful, genuine) 115

Echternacht (name of Swiss town) 122

Eck, Ecken, Ecker (fr Ecke 122, corner, place) 86

Eckard, Eckhardt, Eckhart, see Eckhard

Eckbert (sword + bright) 46, 47

Ecke, see Eckehard

Ecke (peak) 68

Eckeberger (oak mountain) 89, 68

Eckeberger (sword + protection) 89, 68

Eckel, Eckell, Eckels 164, Eckelt 74, see Eickel

Eckel, see Ekel

Eckelhof (oak farm) 89, 92

Eckelmann (dweller among the oaks) 89, 94

Eckelmeyer (fr the Eckelhof, oak farm) 89, 93, 94

Eckenauer (oak meadow) 89, 84

Eckenfelder, see Eckfeld

Eckenrode, Eckeroth (oak clearing) 89, 125

Eckensberger, Eckensbarger, see Eckeberger

Ecker (river name) 83, see Acker

Eckerd, Eckert, Eckardt, see Eckhard

Eckerle 55 (little field) 84

Eckermann (dweller on the Ecker) 83, 94, see Ackermann

Eckert, see Eckhard

Eckes 164, see Eck

Eckfeld, Eckfield 153 (oak field) 89, 72, 122

Eckhard, Eckehard, Eckhardt, Eckert (sword + strong) 46, 46

Eckhaus (corner house) 85, 65, 122

Eckhoff (oak farm) 89, 92, 122

Eckholt, Eckholdt (oak forest) 89, 72, 122

Eckholt (sword + loyal) 46, 48

Eckinger, Eckler, Eckner, Eckmann 94 (dweller on the corner) 85

Eckmann, see Eckinger, Eichmann

Eckmeyer (fr the Eckhoff, oak farm) 89, 93, 94

Eckner, see Eckinger, Eichner

Eckrich (sword + rule) 46, 47

Eckroad 159, Eckrodt, Eckrote, Eckroth (oak clearing) 89, 126

Eckstein, Eckstine 159 (corner stone) 89, 73

Eckstrut (oak swamp) 89, 80

Eckwart (sword + guard) 46, 47

Edel, Edell, Edele, Edeler, Edler, Edeling, Edling (noble) 47

Edelberg (noble mountain) 47, 68

Edelblute (noble blood) 47

Edelbrock, Edelbrook (noble brake) 47, 80

Edelen (noblemen) 47

Edelheiser (noble houses) 47, 65, 66

Edelman, Edelmann (nobleman) 47, 94

Edelmeyer (fr the Edelhof, noble farm) 4, 93, 94

Edelmut (noble disposition) 47, 115

Edelsberg (noble's mountain) 47, 68, 122

Edelstein (jewel) 38, 47, 74

Eden, Edens 164 (Eden)

Edenbaum (tree of Eden) 135, 89

Edenfeld, Edenfield 153 (Eden field) 84, 135

Eder, Ederle 55, Edert 74 (dweller on barren soil) 122

Eder (dweller near the Eder) 83

Edgar (treasure + spear) 47, 46

Eding, Edinger, see Ettinger

Edler, see Edel

Edmund, Edmunds 164 (treasure + guardian) 47

Edsell, Edsall, see Etzell

Edward, Eduard, Edwards 164 (treasure + guardian) 47, 47

Efeldt (place name) 122, 84

Effert < Everhard 122

Effinger (fr Effingen) 122

Effler, Effner, Effland (dweller among the elms) 89

Effler (smith, tool repairer) 96

Efland, see Effler

Egbert, Egbertsen 59 (sword + brilliant) 46, 47

Ege, Egge (harrow) 106

Egeberg (harrow hill) 68

Egel (leech, bloodsucker) 115

Egelberg (swamp mountain) 68

Egenberger, see Eckenberger

Egenhoeffer (oak farm) 89, 92

Eger 122, Egert 74 (fr the Eger) 83

Eggebrecht (sword + bright) 46, 47

Eggelmann 53, 94 < Eggebrecht

Eggemann 94, Eggermeyer 93 (harrower) 95, see also Eckmann

Eggenberger 122, see Eckeberger

Egger, Eggers 164, Eggert 74 (harrower) 95, Egger < Agiheri (sword + army) 46, 46

Eggert, see Eckhard and Eggebrecht

Eggs 164, see Eck

Eghard, see Eckhard

Egiloff (sword + wolf) 46, 48

Eginhard (sword + strong) 46, 46

Egli, Eglin (kind of perch) 115

Egli (a place in Switzerland) 122, see Egloff

Eglisau (perch meadow, place in Switzerland) 84, 122

Egloff, see Egiloff

Egloffstein (Egloff's mountain) 68, 73

Egmont (sword + protection) 46, 47

Egner, Egnert 74, see Eigen, Eigner

Egolf, see Egloff

Ehard, see Ehart

Ehardi (son of Ehard) 142

Ehart (law + strong 47, 46), see also Erhard

Ehebrecht (law + bright 47, 46), see also Eggebrecht

Eheman, Ehemann (lawful husband) 47

Ehinger (fr Ehingen) 122

Ehle, Ehlen, Ehles 164 (alder) 89, see also Ehrler

Ehler, Ehlers 164, Ehlert 74, Ehrlermann 94 (sword + army) 46, 46

Ehly, see Ely

Ehren (honors)

Ehrenheim (honors hamlet) 123

Ehrenkranz (wreath of honor)
Ehrenmann (man of honor) 138, 94
Ehrhard, see Erhard
Ehrlerding (belonging to Ehrler) 59
Ehling, Ehlinger (fr Ehlingen) 122
Ehly (Eli, OT name)
Ehman, Ehmann, see Ehemann
Ehnert < Eginhard
Ehninger (fr Ehningen) 122
Ehr, Ehren (honor, honors) 47
Ehregott (Glorify God!) 116, 140
Ehrenbeck, Ehrbaker 159 (swamp brook)) 80, 77
Ehrenberg, Ehrenberger (fr Ehrenberg 122, honor mountain, swamp mountain) 47, 68, 80
Ehrenbrink (honor hill, swamp hill) 47, 74, 80
Ehrenfeld (field of honor) 47, 84
Ehrenfried (honorable peace) 47, 51
Ehrenhard (honor + strong) 47, 46
Ehrenhaus, Ehringhouse 159 (honor house) 65, 149
Ehrenmann (man of honor) 47, 94, 138
Ehrenpforten (glory portals) 47
Ehrenpreis, Ehrenpries 159 (prize of honor) 47
Ehrenreich (rich in honor, realm of glory) 47, 46
Ehrenspeck, see Ehrenbeck
Ehrensperger, see Ehrenberg, Ahrensberger
Ehres Ehresmann, Ehrismann, see Ehrenmann
Ehrhard, Ehrhardt, Ehrheart 159, see Erhard, Erhardt
Ehrich, Ehrichs 164, see Erich, Erichs
Ehrig, Ehrick 159, see Erich

Ehringer (fr Ehringen) 122
Ehrle, see Erl
Ehrlich, Ehrlichs 164,
Erlicher, Ehrlick 159 (honest) 138
Ehrling, Ehrlinger (fr Erlingen) 122
Ehrman, Ehrmann, see Ehren-mann
Ehrmannstraut (honored man's beloved) 94
Ehrmannstraut (the beloved of Irmin, the chief god)
Ehrreich (rich in honors) 47, 46
Ehrsam (respectable) 138
Ehrstein (honor stone) 47, 73
Ei (egg, egg seller) 106
Eib (yew, crossbow) 89, 108
Eibach (fr *ib*, pre-Germanic word for brook) 77, 122
Eibel 53, 55, Eibl, Eibner, Eibling < Albrecht
Eiben, Eibner (yew tree) 89, 122
Eiberger (yew mountain) 89, 68
Eich, Eiche, Eicher (oak) 89
Eichach, Eichacher (fr Eichach 122, oak river, oak forest) 89, 79
Eichacker (oak chopper) 95
Eichbach (oak brook) 89, 77, 122
Eichbauer (oak farmer, occupant of the Eichhoff, oak farm) 89, 91
Eichbaum, Eichelbaum (oak tree) 89
Eichberg 122, Eichenberg, Eich-berger (oak mountain) 89, 68
Eichborn (oak spring) 89, 79
Eichel (acorn)
Eichel (pre-Germanic river name) 83
Eichelberg, Eichelberger (fr Eichelberg 122, acorn moun-tain) 68
Eichelhart (acorn forest) 89, 72
Eichelkraut (acorn herbs) 89

Eichelmann (acorn gatherer) 89, 94
Eichelsbeck (acorn brook) 77
Eichelstein (acorn mountain) 73
Eichen (oaks) 89, 122
Eichenauer (oak meadow) 89, 84, 122
Eichenberg 122, Eichenberger, see Eichberg
Eichenbrunn 122, Eichenbrunner (oak well) 89, 79
Eichenfeld (oak field) 89, 84, 122
Eichenfels (oak cliffs) 89
Eichengruen, Eichengrien 159 (oak green) 89
Eichenlaub (oak foliage) 89
Eichenmeyer, Eichenmoyer (fr the Eichhoff, oak farm) 89, 93, 94
Eichenmueller (miller at the oaks) 89, 103
Eicher, Eichert 74, Eichler (dweller near the oaks) 89
Eichfelder (oak fields) 89, 84, 122
Eichhacker (oak chopper) 95
Eichhammer (oak hammer) 89, fr Eichheim (oak hamlet) 122
Eichhauer (oak chopper) 95, 100
Eichhoff (farm surrounded by oaks) 89, 92, 122
Eichholm (oak island) 89
Eichholtz, Eichholz (oak wood) 89, 72, 122
Eichhorn (squirrel) 115
Eichhorst (oak hurst) 89, 72, 122
Eichler, Eichinger, Eichlinger, see Eicher
Eichmann, Eichermann, see Eicher
Eichmeyer (fr the Eichhoff, oak farm) 89, 93, 94
Eichmueller, Eichmiller (miller in the oaks) 89, 103
Eichner, see Eicher
Eicholz, see Eichholtz
Eichorn, see Eichhorn

Eichstadt, Eichstaedt, Eichstedt (oak city, oak place) 89
Eichstein (oak mountain) 89, 73
Eichwald (oak forest) 89, 72
Eick ..., see Eich
Eick, Eicke, see Eich, Eiche
Eickel, see Eichel
Eickelberg, Eichelberger (acorn mountain) 89, 68
Eickenberg (oak mountain) 89, 68
Eickhammer, see Eichhammer
Eickhoff 122, see Eichhoff
Eickholt 122, see Eichholtz
Eickmann, see Eichmann
Eickmeier, see Eichmeyer
Eid, Eide (oath)
Eidam, Eydam (son-in-law) 119
Eidel, see Eitel
Eidelberg 122, see Heidelberg
Eidelmann, see Edelmann
Eidemiller (miller on the Eide) 83, 103
Eidenberg (mountain on the Eide) 83, 68
Eidenwald (forest on the Eide) 83, 72
Eidenweil (village on the Eide) 83, 127
Eidinger (fr Eidingen) 122
Eidler, see Edler
Eidman (oath taker) 94
Eier, Eiers 164, Eyers, Eirler, Eierman 94, Eiermann (egg seller) 105
Eif, Eife (fr Eife) 122
Eifel, Eifler (fr the Eifel region) 121
Eifert 74, Eiffert (zeal) 115
Eifrig (zealous) 115
Eigel, see Egel
Eigelbach (leech brook) 77, 122
Eigen, Eigner (fr Eigen 122), see Eigenmann
Eigenberg (private mountain) 68
Eigenbrod, Eigenbrode, Eigenbrodt (one's own bread)

Eigenbrun (private well) 79
Eigenheer (independent land-
owner, freeholder) 109
Eigenholt (vassal + loyal) 48
Eigenholt (private forest) 72
Eigenmann (serf, vassal) 94
Eigner, Eigert 74 (smallholder)
Eik ..., see Eich ...
Eike (oak) 89
Eikenberg, see Eichenberg
Eikenberry 159, see Eickenberg
Eiker, see Eicher
Eikhoff, Eikof, Eickhoffe, see
Eichhoff
Eikmann, see Eichmann
Eikmeyer (fr the Eikhoff, oak
farm) 89, 93, 94
Eikner, see Eichner
Eikstein (oak mountain) 89, 68
Eiland, Eilander (island)
Eilbach, Eilbacher (rapid stream)
77
Eilbach (swamp brook) 80, 77
Eilberg (place name, swamp
mountain) 80, 68, 122
Eildeberger, see Eidelberger
Eiler, Eilers 164, Eilert 74,
Eilermann 94 (hurrier), see
also Euler, Eilhart
Eilertsen (son of Eilert) 59
Eilhart (sword + strong) 46, 46
Eimer (bucket, fr Latin *amphora*)
106
Eimer (sword + famous) 46, 47
Eimke (little bucket) 55
Einaugler (one-eyed) 114
Einberg (place name 122, swamp
mountain) 80, 68
Einbinder (book binder) 96
Einbrod, see Eigenbrod
Einegger 122, Einecker (owner of
private field) 84
Einert, see Einhardt
Einfalt (simplicty) 115, 139
Einfeldt, Eigenfeld 122 (private
field) 84

Einhardt, see Eginhard
Einhaus (private house) 65, 122
Einholt, see Eigenholt
Einhorn (unicorn, a house name)
62
Einig (united)
Einiger (single, solitary) 115
Einmueller (independent miller)
103
Einolf (sword + wolf) 46, 48
Einsiedler (hermit 110, fr Ein-
siedeln, hermitage 122)
Einspruch (objection, protest)
Einstein (place encompassed by a
stone wall) 73
Eirich, see Eurich
Eis (ice)
Eis (iron, ironmonger) 96
Eischberger (ice mountain) 68
Eischberger (iron mountain) 68
Eisdorfer (ice village) 123, 122
Eise, Eisele, Eiseley 159, Eiseler,
Eiselen, Eiselt 74, Eiseman 94
(iron monger) 96
Eiseman, Eisenmann, see Eise
Eisen (iron, ironmonger) 96
Eisenach 122, Eisenacher (Ger-
man city, iron springs) 79
Eisenauer (fr Eisenau 122), see
Eisenhauer
Eisenbach (iron brook) 96, 77, 122
Eisenband (iron band) 106
Eisenbart < Eisenberacht (iron +
bright) 96, 46
Eisenbeil (iron axe) 96, 106
Eisenbeis, Eisenbeiss (iron bite,
bully) 115
Eisenberg, Eisinberg 159, Eisen-
berger (fr Eisenberg 122, iron
mountain) 96, 68
Eisenbiss, Eisenbiess, see Eisen-
beis
Eisenbrand (iron fire, smith) 96
Eisendraht (iron wire) 96, 106
Eisenfeld (iron field) 96, 84, 122
Eisenfels (iron cliff) 68

Eisenfress (iron eater, turbulent
    person) 115
Eisengrein (iron + mask, helmet)
    46
Eisenhand (iron hand) 114, 115
Eisenhard, Eisenhardt, Eisenhart
    (iron + strong) 96, 46
Eisenhaub (helmet) 108
Eisenhauer (iron hacker, perhaps
    based on Fr. Taillefer) 100
Eisenhauser (iron house) 65
Eisenhaut, see Eisenhut
Eisenhoefer (iron yard) 96, 92
Eisenhour 159, Eisenhower, see
    Eisenhauer
Eisenhut, Eisenhuth, Eisenhueter
    (fr Eisenhut 122, iron hat,
    helmet, helmet maker) 96, 108
Eisenhut (monk's hood, a flower)
    89
Eisenklam (iron clamp) 106
Eisenkolb (iron club)
Eisenloeffel (iron spoon) 106
Eisenlohe, Eisenlohr (iron flame,
    smith) 96
Eisenman, Eisenmann (iron-
    monger) 96, 94
Eisenmann (jailer) 109, 94
Eisenmenger, Eisenmenger
    (ironmonger, fr Latin *mango*)
    96
Eisenmeyer (fr the Eisenhof, iron
    farm, ice farm) 93, 94
Eisenrauch (iron smoke, smith)
    96
Eisenreich (rich in iron)
Eisenring (iron ring) 106
Eisenschmid, Eisenschmidt (iron
    smith) 96
Eisenstadt (iron city, iron place)
    122
Eisenstein (iron stone, iron
    mountain) 73
Eisentraut, Eisentrout 159 <
    Isandrut, iron + beloved) 60
Eisenzoph (iron top)

Eiser, Eisert 74 (iron worker) 96
Eisermann, see Eisenmann
Eisfeld, Eisfelder, Eisfeldt (ice
    field) 84, 122
Eisgrau (iron grey) 112
Eisgruber (iron miner) 96
Eisinger (fr Eising) 122
Eisler, see Eiser
Eisloeffel, see Eisenloeffel
Eisman, Eismann (ironmonger)
    96, 94
Eisner (ironmonger) 96
Eiss, see Eis
Eiswald (iron forest) 72
Eiswald (ice forest) 72
Eit, Eith (oath)
Eitel, Eitler (empty, having no
    first name)
Eitemiller (miller an the Eite) 83,
    103
Eitermann (dweller among the
    nettles) 89, 94
Eiting, Eitner (fr Eiting) 122
Eitner (burner, stoker, smelter)
    96
Ekard, Ekhard, Ekhardt, Ekert,
    see Eckhard
Ekel 112, Ekels 164 (disgust)
Ekelberry 159, see Eichelberg
Eken (oaks) 89
Ekenhoffer (oak farm) 89, 92
Ekenroth, Ekerroth (oak clearing)
    89, 126
Ekert, Ekhard, see Eckhard
Ekestein, see Eckstein
Ekman, see Eckmann
Elbaum (alder tree) 89
Elbe, Elbthal (German river, Elbe
    valley) 83
Elbeck, Elbek (alder brook) 89, 77
Elberg (alder mountain) 89, 68
Elbers 164, Elbert, Elberth,
    Elbrecht (sword + bright) 46,
    47
Elbing (fr Elbingen) 122
Elbrecht, see Elbers

Eldemann, see Eltermann
Elenzweig (alder branch) 89
Elermann, see Ellermann
Elers, see Ehlers
Elert 74, see Eller
Elfenbein (ivory) 106
Elfers 164, Elfert 74 < Alfheri, elf + army) 48, 46
Elflein 55 (little elf) 48
Elfring 53, Elfringer (son of Elvert)
Elg, Elger, Elgert 74, Elgart (foot path) 65
Elhardt, see Eilhart
Eli (OT name) 135
Elias (OT name) 135
Eliasberg (Eli's mountain) 135, 68
Elich, Elik, Eliker (lawful) 115
Eliel (OT name) 135
Eling, Elinger, see Elling
Elkmann (elk + man) 94
Elkmann (swamp man) 80, 94
Ell, Ells 164 (yard, measure)
Ellbrecht, see Elbrecht
Elldorfer (alder village) 89, 123
Ellekamp, see Ellenkamp
Ellemann, see Ellermann
Ellen (prowess) 115
Ellen (alders) 89, 122
Ellenbach, Ellenbeck (alder brook) 89, 77
Ellenberg, Ellenberger (fr Ellenberg 122, alder mountain) 89, 68
Ellenbogen (elbow) 114, 122
Ellenburg (alder castle) 89, 73
Ellenkamp (alder field) 89, 84
Eller, Ellers 164, Ellern, Ellert 74 (dweller by the alder trees) 89, 122
Ellerbach (alder brook) 89, 77
Ellerbrock, Ellerbrake 159, Ellerbruch (alder brake) 89, 80, 122
Ellerkamp, see Ellenkamp
Ellermann (grandfather) 119, 94

Ellerrot (alder clearing) 89, 126
Ellestad (elder place, alder shore) 89
Ellewin, see Alwin
Ellg, see Elg
Ellgass (alder street) 89, 65, 122
Elling 122, Ellinger (foot path)
Ellinghaus, Ellinghausen, Ellinhuyzen (fr Ellinghausen 122, house on foot path) 65
Ellingrod, see Ellroth
Ellmer, see Elmer
Ellner (dweller among the alders) 89
Ellrich (prowess + strong) 46
Ellroth (alder clearing) 89, 126
Ellwanger (fr Ellwangen) 122
Ellwanger (alder field) 89, 84
Ellwanger (fr Ellwangen, elk trap)
Elm, Elms 164, Elman 94 (dweller among the elms) 89
Elm, Elms 164 (swamp) 80
Elmendorf (elm village) 89, 123, 122
Elmer, Elmar (sword + famous) 46, 47
Elmer, Elmar (noble + famous) 46, 47
Elmshaeuser (swamp houses) 89, 65
Elpert, see Albrecht
Elrich, Elrick (noble + rule) 46, 46
Elrod, see Ellroth
Elsass, Elsasser, Elsaesser, Elsassor 159 (Alsatian) 121
Elsbach, Elsbacher (shad brook, swamp brook) 80, 77, 122
Else, Elsen, Elser, Elsner (dweller on the Els) 83
Elsenbach (alder brook) 89, 77
Elsenheimer (alder hamlet) 89, 123
Elsensohn (Else's son) 60

Engelbert, Engelberth, Engelberts
164, Engelbrecht (angel +
bright, Angle + bright) 49, 47
Engeler, see Engler
Engelfried (angel + peace) 138
Engelhart, Engelhardt, Engel-
hart, Engelharth, Engelhaart
(angel + strong, Angle +
strong) 49, 46
Engelhaupt (angel head) 62, 149
Engelhaus, Engelhausen (angel
house) 65, 149
Engelhoff (angel farm) 92, 122
Engelke 53, 55, Engelken, Eng-
elking, see Engelbert
Engelkraut (angel herb) 89
Engelman 94, Engelmann (oc-
cupant of Engelhaus 65 or
Engelhoff 92
Engelman 53, 94 < Engelbert)
Engelmann (Englishman) 121, 94
Engelmeyer (fr the Engelhoff,
angel farm) 93, 92, 94
Engels, see Engel
Engelsberg, see Engelberg
Engelskirche (angel church) 71,
122
Engemann (dweller in a narrow
valley) 76, 94
Engenhoefer (narrow farm,
swamp farm) 92, 76
Enger, Engers 164, Engert 74 (fr
Engen 122)
Engermann, see Engemann
Engesser, Engass (dweller on a
narrow street) 65
Enghause, Enghausen, Eng-
haussen, Enghauser (narrow
house) 65
Enghaus (house on a swamp) 76,
65
Enker (anchor, house name) 62
England, Englander, Englaender
(Englishman) 121
Engle.... 159, see Engel...
Englebach 159, see Engelbach

Englebrecht 159, see Engelbert
Englehart 159, Englehardt, see
Engelhart
Englehaupt 159, see Engelhaupt
Engleman 159, see Engelman
Engler, Englert 74, Englerth
(Angle + army) 46, 49
Engler, Englert 74, Englerth
(dweller in house *zum Engel*)
61
Engli 55 (little angel)
Englischer (Englishman) 121
Engman, Engmann, see Enge-
mann
Engmeyer (fr the Enghof, narrow
farm) 93, 92, 94
Engnoth (difficult straits) 76
Engstrand (narrow beach)
Engwall (narrow wall)
Enk, Enke, Enker (hired hand) 95
Enkel (grandchild) 119
Ennesfeldt (Enno's field) 84
Enninger (fr Enning 122)
Enrick, see Heinrich
Ensel, Enslin 55, Ensslin, Enslein
< Anselm 131
Ensinger (fr Ensingen) 122
Ent, Ente, Enten, Entemann,
Entenmann 94 (duck raiser) 91
Entermann (duck raiser) 91, 94
Entner, see Ent
Entstrasser (dweller across the
road) 69, 65
Entz, Enz, Enzman (fr Enz or fr
the Enz) 122, 83
Entzbacher, Entzenbache (fr
Enzenbach) 77, 122
Enzinger (fr Enzingen) 122
Ep 53, Epp < Eberhard
Epelbaum, Epelboim, see Apfel-
baum
Epenstein, Eppenstein, Epstein,
Eppstein, see Epstein
Eple, Epple, Eppli (little apple)
53, 55, 89

Eppel, Epple, Eppler, Epler,
Eppelmann, see Appel, Apfel
Eppelsheim, Eppelsheimer (fr
Eppelsheim 122, apple hamlet)
89, 123
Epperle 53, 55, Epperley 159 <
Eberhard 53
Eppert 53 < Eggebrecht
Epping, Eppinger (fr Epping) 122
Epps 53 < Eberhard
Eprecht, Epprecht (law + bright)
47, 47), see also Eggebrecht
Epstein, Epsteine, Epstien 159
(wild boar stone) 48, 73
Erard, see Erhard
Erasmi (son of Erasmus) 142
Erb 122, Erbe, Erber, Erbin,
Erben (heir, inheritance) 47
Erb 53 < Erwin
Erb, Erbe, Erbes 164, Erbsen
(pea) 105
Erbach 122, Erbacher (swamp
brook) 80, 77, see Erdbach
Erblich (inheritable)
Erbsland (inherited land) 47
Erck, see Erk
Erd 53 < Erhard
Erd, Erde (earth, or fr *ard*,
swamp) 80
Erdbach, Erdesbach (earth
stream, swamp stream) 80, 77,
122
Erdbrink (earth + grassy hill) 74
Erdel (arable land) 84
Erdenbrecht (earth + brilliant) 47
Erdheim (swamp hamlet) 80, 123
Erdman 94, Erdmann (earth
man, modeled on Hebrew
*Adam*) 135
Erdmeyer (swamp farmer) 93
Erdroth (swamp clearing) 126
Erenheim (honor hamlet) 123
Erfmeyer, Erffmayer (farmer on
the water) 80, 93
Erfurt 122, Erffurth, Erfuerth
(German city)

Ergelet (grape bucket, fr Latin
*arca*) 106
Ergenbright 159 < Erkanbrecht
(genuine + bright) 46
Ergler (grape picker) 95
Ergott (Glorify God!) 117, 140
Erhard, Erhart, Erhardt (honor +
strong) 47, 46
Erich, Erichs 164, Erig, Erick
(law + rule) 47, 47
Eriksen (son of Erick) 59
Erischmann, see Ehresmann
Erismann, see Ehresmann
Erk 53 < Erkenbrecht
Erkenbrecht (genuine + brilliant)
47
Erkmann 53, 94 < Erkenbrecht
Erl, Erle (alder) 89
Erlach (swamp pond) 89, 81, 122
Erlanger (fr Erlangen) 122
Erlebach, Erlbeck (alder brook)
89, 77, 122
Erlemann (dweller among the
alders) 89, 94
Erlen, Erler (alder) 89, 122
Erlenbach 122, see Erlebach
Erlenheiser (inhabitant of house
among the alders) 89, 65, 66
Erlewyn, Erlwein (freeman +
friend) 48
Erlich, Erlichman, see Ehrlich,
Ehrlichmann
Ermann, see Ehrmann
Ermattinger (fr Ermattingen) 122
Ermel, Ermling, Ermeling (sleeve,
tailor) 96, 106
Ermut (honor + disposition) 115
Erna 53, Erne < Arnold
Ernest, see Ernst
Ernesti (son of Ernest) 142
Ernhut (guardian of honor) 138
Ernsperger, Ernsberger, see
Arnsperger
Ernst, Ernest (vigor, earnestness)
115
Ernstein 122, see Arnstein

Ernsthausen (Ernst's houses) 65, 122

Ernte (harvest) 143

Erp, see Erb

Erpenbach, Erpenbeck (heirs' brook) 47, 77

Erpenstein (heirs' mountain) 47, 68

Errmann 159, see Ehrmann

Ertz, see Erz

Ertel, Ertell, Ertle 159, Ertelt 74 < Ortlieb

Ertzberger (ore miner, man fr Erzberg) 96, 122

Ervin, see Erwein

Erwein, Erwin (honor + friend) 47, 48

Erz (ore, miner) 96, 106

Erzbischof (archbishop) 110

Erzgraeber (ore miner) 96

Esbach 122, see Eschbach

Esbrandt (clearing in the ash trees) 89, 126

Esch, Esche (ash tree) 89, 122

Eschauer (fr Eschau 122, ash meadow) 89, 84

Eschbach, Eschenbach, Eschbacher, Eschelbach, Eschbeck, Eschelbeck (fr Eschenbach 122, ash tree brook, or fr pre-Germanic river term 83) 89, 77, see Aeschbach

Eschborn (ash tree spring, or see Eschbach) 89, 79, 122

Eschelmann, see Escher

Eschenbrenner, see Aschenbrenner

Eschenfelder (fr Eschenfelden 122, ash tree field) 89, 84

Eschenhagen (ash tree enclosure) 89, 123

Eschenmosen, Eschenmoser (ash bog) 89, 80

Escher, Eschler, Eschmann 94 (fr Escher 122, swamp) 80

Eschmeyer (farmer among the ash trees) 89, 93

Eschrich (rich in ash trees) 89

Eschwege (path through the ash trees) 89, 122

Eselkopf (donkey head, house name) 114, 62

Esenberg (ash mountain) 89, 68

Esendal (ash dale) 89, 76

Eser (back pack, also see Escher)

Eshbach 159, see Eschbach

Eshelmann 159, see Eschelmann

Esher 159, Eshler, see Escher

Eshman 159, see Escher

Esler, see Escher

Eslin, Esslin (jenny) 91

Eslinger (fr Eslingen) 122

Esner, see Eschner

Espe, Espen (aspen) 89, 122

Espenhain (aspen grove) 89, 72, 122

Espenschade (aspen shade) 89

Espenscheid, Espenschied (aspen log) 89

Espich (aspen bush) 89

Ess (forge, hearth, smith) 96

Essel, Esselmann 94 (fr Essel) 122

Essendorf (forge village, chimney village, swamp village) 80, 123, 122

Essenfeld (forge field, swamp field) 80, 84

Essenhaven (forge farm, swamp farm) 80, 123

Esser, Essers 164, Essert 74 (axel maker, wainright) 96, 106

Esser (glutton) 115

Esserwein (wine drinker) 115

Essig, Essich (vinegar, fr Latin *acetum* 105

Essig (pre-Germanic word for swamp) 80

Esslin, see Eslin

Essling, Esslinger (fr Esslingen) 122

Essner (forge worker, hearth worker) 96
Ester, Esters 164 (OT name) 135, 122
Esterling (easterner) 85
Estermann (field man) 96, 94
Estermann (Ashkenazic metronym for Esther's husband) 60, 94
Estermyer 159 (fr the Esterhof, eastern farm) 85, 93
Estinghausen (eastern houses) 85, 65, 122
Estreicher, see Oestreich
Estrich (flooring, parquet layer) 96
Etchberger 159, see Etschberger
Etel ..., see Edel
Etsch, Etschmann 94 (Adige, dweller on the Adige) 83
Ettenhoffer, Ettenhuber 122 (farmer on the Ett) 83
Etter (dweller on the Ett, dweller in a wattled enclosure) 83
Ettinger (fr Ettingen, village on the Ett) 83, 122
Ettlinger (fr Ettlingen, village on the Ett) 83, 122
Ettwein < Otwin (wealth + friend) 47, 48
Etzel, Etzler (pet name of Attila the Hun) 54
Eubel 53 < Albrecht
Eugel (little eye) 114
Eulbacher (swamp brook) 77
Eulbeck (swamp brook) 77, 122
Eulberg (owl mountain) 68
Eulberg (swamp mountain) 80, 68
Euler, Eulers 164, Eulert 74, Eulner (potter) 96
Eurich (sword + rule) 46, 47
Eva (wife of Adam) 135
Ever ..., Evers ..., see Eber..., Ebers
Everet 159, see Eberhard

Everhard, Everhardt, Everhart, see Eberhard
Everman, see Ebermann
Eversburg (boar castle) 48, 73, 122
Eversfield 153 (wild boar field) 48, 84
Eversmann (Ever's vassal) 94
Eversmeier (fr the Evershof, Ever's farm) 73, 94
Everstein 122, see Eberstein
Evert, Everts 164, Evertz, see Ebert
Ewald, Ewalt (law + keeper, priest) 47, 47
Ewart, Ewartz 164 (guardian of the law, priest) 47, 47
Ewers 164, Ewert, Ewertz, see Eber, Ebert
Ewig (eternal) 138
Exler, Exner, see Oechsler, Oechsner
Exley 159, see Oechsele
Ey, Eyer, see Ei, Eier
Eyb (pre-Germanic river name) 83, see Eib
Eybel, see Eibel
Eyc, Eych..., see Eich...
Eychler, see Eicher
Eyck (oak) 89
Eyckhof (oak farm) 89, 92
Eydam (father-in-law) 119
Eydelman 159, see Eitelman
Eyder (eider) 105, 106
Eyer, Eyermann, see Eier, Eiermann
Eygenbrod, see Eigenbrod
Eyler, see Eiler
Eymann (egg man) 105, 94
Eyrich, see Eurich
Eyring, see Eurich
Eysel (iron monger) 96
Eysemann, Eysenman, see Eiseman
Eysen ..., see Eisen
Eytel, see Eitel

Eyth, see Eid
Ezell, Ezzel, see Etzel

**F**

Faas < Gervasius, Servatius 131, see Fass
Fabal, Fabel < St. Fabian 131
Faber, Fabert 74, Fabor (Latin: smith) 141
Fabian (name of pope) 134
Fabricius, Fabritzius (Latin name for Schmidt) 141
Fabrikant (manufacturer) 96
Fach (compartment, pigeonhole, fishtrap) 106
Fach (swamp water) 80
Fachler (swamp dweller) 80
Fack (swine) 91
Fackert 74, Fackeret (flax breaker) 95
Fackert (joyful) 115
Fackler, Fakler (torch bearer)
Fackler (flax breaker) 95
Fadem (thread, tailor) 96
Fadenhauer (thread maker) 96, 100
Fader (dweller in a fenced area) 84
Faecher (fan) 106
Faehner, Faehnrich (ensign) 107
Faelten, see Felten
Faerber (dyer) 96, 122
Faernbacher, see Farbach
Faesch 53, Faesche < St. Servatius 131
Faessle, Faessler (cooper) 96, 106
Faeth, Faetke 55, see Fader
Faeustlin 55 (little fist, little dog)
Faff, see Pfaff
Fahenstock, see Fahnenstock
Fahl, Fahle, Fahler, Fahler (pale, swamp) 80
Fahlbusch (pale bush, swamp bush) 80
Fahlfeder (pale feather)

Fahlteich (swamp pond) 80
Fahn (swamp) 80
Fahn < Stephanus (St. Stephen) 131
Fahn, Fahnen (flag) 108
Fahnestock (flag staff)
Fahr, Faehr (ferry landing, ferryman) 122, 96
Fahrbach, Fahrenbach, Farenbach (*vornebach*, before the brook) 69, 77
Fahrencorn (before the grain field) 69
Fahrenhorst (before the hurst 69, swamp hurst 80) 72, 122
Fahrenwald (before the forest 69, swamp forest 80) 71
Fahrmann (ferryman) 96
Fahrmeyer (fr the Fahrhoff, ferry farm) 93, 94
Fahrner (fr Fahrn) 122
Faid (shirt, shirt maker) 96
Faigel, Faigle 159 (timid) 115
Fainberg, see Feinberg
Fairbaugh 159, see Fahrbach
Fairchild 152, see Schoenkind
Faiss, Faist 74, Faister, see Feiss, Feist, Feister (fat, corpulent) 114
Fakler, see Fackler
Falbausch, see Fahlbusch
Falk, Falke, Falck (falcon, falconer, fr Latin *falco*) 91, 115
Falkenau (falcon meadow, swamp meadow) 91, 84, 122
Falkenberg (falcon mountain) 68, 122
Falkenburg 122, Falkinburg 159 (falcon castle) 73
Falkenhahn, Falkenhain (falcon's grove) 72
Falkenheimer (falcon hamlet) 123
Falkenklous 159 (Klaus the falconer) 91
Falkenmeyer, Falenmayr (fr the Falkenhoff, falcon farm) 93, 94

Falkenstein 122, Falkenstine 159
   (falcon's crag) 73
Falkewitz (falcon village) 127
Falkner, Falker, Falker (falconer)
   91, see Volker
Fallentin (St. Valentine) 131
Falsenmayer (cliff farmer) 93
Falten 53 < St. Valentine 131
Falter (butterfly) 115
Falter (apple tree, fr *apfelter*) 89,
   122
Falter (portcullis, gatekeeper) 96
Falz, see Pfalz
Fandrich (ensign) 108
Fang, Fanger, Fangman, Fang-
   mann 94 (catcher) 96
Fannacht, see Fasnacht
Farabaugh 159, see Fahrenbach
Farb (color)
Farbach, see Fahrbach
Farbenblum (colored flower) 89
Farbenstein (colored stone,
   jeweler) 73, 96
Farber, Farbman 94, see Faerber
Farenholtz (before the forest) 69,
   72
Farenhorst, see Fahrenhorst
Farenwald (before the forest) 69,
   72
Farinholt, see Farenholtz
Farn, Fahrne (fern) 89
Farnbacher, see Fahrbach
Farrenkopf (steer head) 62, 113,
   149
Farver, see Faerber
Fascher (bandager) 96
Fasching (Mardi Gras, Carnival)
   143
Fasel (draft animal) 91
Fasenfeld (pheasant field) 84
Fasman, Fassmann (barrelmaker)
   96, 94
Fasnacht, Fassenacht, Fastnacht
   (Mardi Gras, Shrove Tuesday)
   143

Fass, Fasse, Faas (vat, barrel,
   barrel maker) 96, also pet
   name for Servatius, Gervasius
Fassbach (barrel brook) 77
Fassbinder, Fassbender, Fass-
   bindler (barrel maker) 96
Fasshauer (barrel maker) 96, 100
Fassel, Fassell, Fassler (barrel
   maker) 96
Fassnacht, see Fasnacht
Fatthauer, Fathauer, see Fass-
   hauer
Fatz 53 < St. Bonifatius 131
Fatzenbacher (St. Boniface brook)
   77
Fauch, Fauck, Faucker (bellows,
   smith) 96, 106
Fauenbach (peacock brook) 115,
   77
Fauerbach, see Feurbach
Faught 159, see Vogt
Faul, Fauler, (lazy) 115
Faulbach (stagnant brook) 77, 122
Faulert 74 (dweller near stagnant
   water)
Faulhaber, Faulhaffer (noxious
   oat-like weed) 89
Faulhuber (farmer near stagnant
   water) 91
Faulker 159, see Volker
Faulkinberry 159, see Falkenberg
Faulkner, see Falkner
Faus, Fausel, Fauser (puffed up)
   115
Fausnacht, Fausnaugh 159, see
   Fasnacht
Faust, Fausten (fist, little dog)
   114, 115
Faut 159, Fauth, Fautz, Fautzen,
   Fautzer, Fautter, see Vogt
Fawler 159, see Fauler
Fawst 159, see Faust
Fay < St. Sophia 131, 60
Faygenblat 159 (fig leaf) 148
Fayler, see Feil
Faynshteyn 159, see Feinstein

Fayst, see Feist
Fazenbacher, see Fatzenbacher
Fearer 159, see Fuehrer
Feaster 159, see Pfister
Fecher, see Faecher
Fechheimer (fr Fechheim) 122
Fechler, Fechner (furrier) 96
Fecht, Fechter, Feght 159, Feght-
mann 94, 159, Fegter 159
(champion) 96, 107
Feckel 53, 55 < Frederick, Frie-
drich
Fedder, see Vetter
Feder, Federer, Federler, Fed-
ermann, Feddermann 94
(feather seller, goose down
dealer, pillow maker) 106, 96
Feder, see Vetter
Feder (scribe) 96
Federbush 159 (crest on helmet)
Federkeil (quill, scribe) 96
Federlein 55 (little feather)
Federspiel (trained raptor, fal-
coner) 91
Fee 159, see Vieh
Feer 159, Feehr, see Fehr
Feerer 159, see Fuehrer
Feffer, see Pfeffer
Feger, Fegert 74 (cleaner, bur-
nisher) 108
Fegler, Feglear 159, Feggeler, see
Feger
Fegt ..., see Fecht...
Fehl, Fehle, Fehler (swamp
dweller) 80
Fehlbaum (swamp tree) 80, 89
Fehn (swamp) 80, 122
Fehr, Feehr, Feer (ferryman) 96
Fehrenbach, Fehrenbacher,
Fehrbach (fr Fehrenbach 122,
swamp brook) 80, 77
Fehrenecke (fir field) 89, 85
Fehrenkamp, Fehrkamp (fir field)
89, 84
Fehrhof (ferryman's homestead)
92

Fehrlinger (fr Fehrlingen) 122
Fehrmann (ferryman) 96
Fehsenfeld (spelt field) 91, 84
Fei < St. Sophia 131, 60
Feichtner 159, see Fechner
Feidler, see Pheidler, Fiedler
Feierabend (quitting time) 117,
122
Feierstein, Feiersten, see Feuer-
stein
Feiertag (holiday) 143, 117
Feig, Feige, Feigel, Feigelman 94
(doomed to die, cowardly) 115
Feige, Feigel, Feigl (violet) 89
Feigenbaum (fig tree) 89
Feight 159, see Veit
Feigmann (coward) 115, 94
Feil 122, Feiler, Feilner, Feihl,
Feillmann 94 (file, file maker)
96
Feil (violet) 89
Feilenschmidt (file smith) 96
Feilinger (fr Feilingen) 122
Fein (fine, elegant) 115
Feinberg (fine mountain) 68, see
Weinberg
Feinblatt (fine leaf) 89
Feinblum (fine flower) 89
Feind, Feindt (enemy)
Feinglas (fine glass, glazier) 96
Feingold (goldsmith) 96
Feinleib (fine loaf, baker) 96
Feinman, Feinmann (elegant
man) 115, 94
Feinstein (fine mountain) 73
Feinstein (precious stone, jeweler)
96
Feinster 159, see Finster, Fenster
Feintuch (fine cloth, weaver) 106,
96
Feirtag, see Feiertag
Feiss (fat) 114
Feist, Feister (fat, fertile) 114
Feistenau (fertile meadow) 84,
122

Feit, Feitel, Feitler, Feith, Feitz,
Feiz (St. Vitus) 131
Felbach (swamp brook) 80, 83, 77
Felbaum (willow tree) 89
Felbinger (fr Felbing) 122
Feld, Feldt, Felder, Felders 164,
Felden (field) 84
Feldbach (field brook) 84, 77
Feldbaum (field tree) 84, 89
Feldbausch, see Feldbusch
Feldberger (fr Feldberg 122, field
mountain) 84, 68
Feldbursch (field lad) 84
Feldbusch (field bush) 84, 72
Felder, Feldner (fieldman, far-
mer) 84, 91
Felderstein, see Feldstein
Feldhamer, see Feldheim
Feldhaus 122, Feldhausen (field
house) 84, 65
Feldheim 122, Feltheim, Feld-
heimer (field hamlet) 84, 123
Feldhofer (fr Feldhof 122, field
farm) 84, 92
Feldkamp (field field) 84, 84, 122
Feldman, Feldmann (field man,
farmer) 84, 91, 94
Feldmeier (field farmer) 84, 93
Feldmesser (surveyor) 84, 96
Feldmueller (field miller) 84, 103
Feldner, see Felder
Feldpausch, see Feldbusch
Feldscher, Feldsher 159 (army
surgeon) 96, 108
Feldschuh (field shoe, bootmaker)
96, 112
Feldstein (field stone) 84, 73
Felgemacher (felly maker, cart-
wright) 96
Felger, Felgenhauer (felly maker,
cartwright) 96, 100
Felhauer, see Felger
Felinger (fr Feling) 112
Felix (Latin, joyful) 115, 141
Felk 53, Felkel 55, Felker, Felk-
ner < Volkmar

Fell, Felle, Fellman 94, Fellmann,
Feller, Fellner, Fellers 164,
Felleret 74, Fellermann
(worker in hides) 96, 106
Fellenbaum (Fell the tree!,
lumber-jack) 116
Fellenstein (Hew the rock!,
quarryman) 116
Felman, see Fell
Felmar < Volkmar
Felner, see Fell, Feldner
Fels (cliff, crag) 68
Felsberg (cliff mountain) 68, 122
Felsch (false) 115
Felscher, see Feldscher
Felsecker (cliff field) 68, 85
Felsen (cliffs) 68
Felsenberg (cliff mountain) 68
Felsenstein (cliff mountain) 68, 73
Felsenthal (cliff valley) 68, 76
Felsenheld (cliff hero)
Felser, Felsing, Felsinger (fr
Felsen 122, cliff)
Felt, Felts, Feltz, see Filtz
Feltberger, see Feldberger
Felten, Feltkin 55 < St. Valentin
131
Felter, see Felder
Felthaus (field house) 84, 65
Feltheim, see Feldheim
Feltmacher (felt maker) 96
Feltman, see Feld
Feltmeyer (field farmer) 84, 93
Feltner, see Felder
Feltz, see Filtz
Feltzmann, see Feldman
Feltzner, see Felder
Fendrick, see Faehnrich
Fenhagen (marsh enclosure) 80,
123
Fenkel (spice dealer, fr Latin
foeniculum) 106
Fenker (millet dealer) 106
Fenkhoff (millet farm, fr Latin
panicum) 92

Fenn 122, Fennemann 94 (bog dweller) 80
Fenner (ensign) 107
Fennhof, Fennhoff (fen farm) 80, 84
Fennig, see Pfennig
Fennigwerth (pennyworth) 117
Fenster, Fensterer, Fenstermacher, Fenstermaker, Fenstamaker 159 (window maker, fr Latin *fenestra*) 96, 106
Fensterwald, see Finsterwald
Fentz, Fenzel, see Wentzel
Ferber, Ferbert 74, see Faerber
Ferch (fir tree) 89
Ferdig, see Fertig
Ferdinand, Fernantz (Gothic: journey + risk) 56
Feredag, Feredag, see Feiertag
Ferembach, Ferenbach, Ferenback 159, see Fehrenbach
Ferg, Ferge, Ferger, Ferges 164 (ferryman) 96
Ferhman, see Fehrmann
Ferhorst, see Fahrenhorst
Ferkel, Ferkler (shoat) 91
Ferman, see Fehrmann
Fernbach, see Fehrenbach
Ferne (glacier) 68
Fernhaber, see Firnhaber
Fernholtz, see Fahrenholtz
Ferrenbach, see Fehrenbach
Fersch, see Pfirsich
Ferschbach (swamp brook) 80, 77
Fersner, see Foerstner
Ferst 159, see Fuerst
Ferster 159, Ferstner, Ferstermann, see Foerster
Fertig (ready to travel) 115
Fertner 159 (see Pfoertner)
Fesenfeld (spelt field) 91, 84, 122
Fesmeier (spelt farmer) 91, 93
Fessel, Fesseler, Fessler, Fesler (fetter maker) 96, 106
Fessel (barrel maker) 96
Fest (firm, fat) 114

Fester 53, Festerling 55 < Sylvester 131
Festerman (vespers singer) 110
Feter, Fetter, see Vetter
Fett, Fette (fat, fertile) 114
Fetter, Fetters 164, Fetterle 55, see Vetter, Vetterli
Fetterhof (fertile farm) 92
Fettig, Fetting, see Fett
Fetting (wing)
Fetz, Fetzer (executioner, quarreler) 115
Fetz 53 < St. Boniface 131
Feucht, Feuchter (damp, moist) 122
Feucht (fir tree) 89, 122
Feuchtenberger (fir mountain) 89, 68
Feuchtenwange, see Feuchtwange
Feuchtner (dweller by the firs) 89
Feuchtwange (swamp field) 80, 84
Feuer, Feurer (fire, fireman) 96
Feuerbach 122, Feurbach (swamp brook) 80, 77
Feuerberg (swamp mountain) 80, 68, 122
Feuereisen (fire iron, poker) 106
Feuerhacken (poker) 106
Feuerhardt, see Feuerherd
Feuerherd (fire hearth, smith) 106
Feuerleim (fire clay) 106
Feuerlein 55 (little fire, smith) 96
Feuermann (fireman, stoker) 96
Feuermann (flint dealer) 106
Feuerstein, Feuerstine 159 (flint dealer) 106
Feurer (stoker) 96
Feurmann (stoker) 96
Feust, Feustel, Feustle 159, see Faust
Fey, Feye, see Fay
Feyerabend, see Feierabend
Feyerbaugh 159, see Feurbach
Feygelman, see Feig
Feyl, see Feil

Fichandler 159, see Fischhaendler
Ficht 122, Fichtel, Fichter,
 Fichtner (dweller among the fir
 trees) 89
Fichtelberg (fir mountain) 89, 68
Fichtmeyer, Fichtemayer (farmer
 in the fir trees) 89, 93
Fick 53, Ficke, Ficks 164, Ficken,
 Ficker, Fickert 74 < Friedrich
Fickenscher (Cut the purse!) 116
Fickus (fig, fr Latin *ficus)* 89
Fickweiler (Friedrich's villa) 127
Fidel, Fidler, Fidelman, see
 Fiedel, Fiedler
Fieber (fever) 113
Fiebig, Fiebiger, see Viebig
Fiedel, Fiedler, Fiedeler, Fiedel-
 man (fiddler) 96, 106
Fiedelmeyer (occupant of the
 Fiedelhoff, fiddle farm) 93
Fliederer (fletcher) 108
Fiege, Fiegner (overseer) 96
Fiegenbaum, see Feigenbaum
Fiehmann 159, see Viehmann
Fieken, Fiekers 164, Fiekert 74 <
 Sophia 60
Fieldhouse 153, see Feldhaus
Fienberg 159, see Feinberg
Fierer 159, see Fuehrer
Fierschnaller (four buckles) 112
Fierstein 159, see Feuerstein
Fiess (violent person) 115
Fiessler, Fiesler (womanizer) 115,
 see Fuessler
Fiester 159, see Pfister
Fietzen < St. Vincent 131
Fifer 159, see Pfeifer
Figge (son of Sophia) 60
Fighte 159, Feight, see Veit
Fikus (fig, Latin *ficus)* 89, 141
Filbert < Volkbrecht
Fildhut (felt hat, peasant) 112
Filer 159, see Feiler
Filibs, see Phillips
Filtz (pasture) 84

Filtz (course farmer) 115, cf.
 "wool hat" and *filtzgebur*
Filtzer, Filzer (hatter, felt maker)
 96
Filtzinger (fr Filtzing) 122
Filtzmeier (farmer by a high
 marsh) 80, 93
Finck, see Fink
Finckel, see Finkel
Finckelstein, see Finkelstein
Finckenstedt (finch city) 122
Findeisen (bloodletter) 96
Finder, Fintler (finder in a mine)
 96
Findling (foundling) 119
Fine 159, see Fein
Fineberg, Fineblum, Fineman,
 Finestone, see Feinberg, Fein-
 blum, Feinman, Feinstein 159
Finfrock (five gowns) 112
Finger, Fingern (finger 114, also
 ring maker 106)
Fingerhut, Fingerhuth, Finger-
 hood 159 (thimble, tailor,
 thimble maker) 106
Fingernagel (finger nail) 114
Finglas 159, see Feinglas
Finister 159, see Finster
Fink, Finke, Fincke, Finken,
 Finks 164 (finch, carefree
 person) 115
Finkbein, Finkbeiner, Finkbiner
 159 (finch + fenced area)
Finkbein (finch leg) 114
Finkel, Finkle 159, Finkelman 94
 (blacksmith 96), see also
 Fuenkel
Finkelstein (sparkling mountain,
 pyrite) 68
Finkemeyer, see Finkmeyer
Finkenauer, Finknauer (finch
 meadow) 84
Finkenbeiner, see Finkbein
Finkenstein (finch mountain) 68
Finkernagel 159, see Fingernagel

Finkmeyer (fr the Finkhof, finch farm) 93, 94

Finkstedt (finch city) 122

Finkweiler (finch hamlet) 123, 122

Finsterbusch (dark bush) 72

Finsterwald (dark forest) 72

Finzel < Wentzel, Vincentius 131

Firebaugh 159, see Feuerbach

Fireman 159, see Feuermann

Firestone 152, Firestine 159, see Feuerstein

Firkel 159, see Ferkel

Firmwald, see Vormwald

Firne, see Ferne

Firnhaber (last year's oats) 106

Firor 159, see Fuehrer

First (mountain ridge) 68, see also Fuerst

Firstenberg, see Fuerstenberg

Firstman, see Fuerstmann

Firstnau (ridge meadow, prince's meadow) 84

Fisch (fish) 62, 106

Fisch, see Fischer

Fischauer (fish meadow) 84

Fischbach, Fischbeck (fish stream) 77, 122

Fischbein, Fischbein, Fishbein 159 (whale bone, not fish leg!) 106

Fischborn (fish stream) 79, 122

Fischel, Fischell, Fischelt 74, see Fischer

Fischer, Fisscher (fisherman, fishmonger) 91, 105

Fischgrund (fish bottom, fishing hole) 91

Fischhaber 159, Fischhof (fish farm) 92

Fischhaendler (fish monger) 106

Fischlein 55 (little fish)

Fischler (swamp dweller) 80

Fischner, see Fischer

Fischmann 94, Fischner (fishmonger) 91, 105

Fischmeyer (fr the Fischhof, fish farm) 93, 94

Fise 159, see Feise

Fishbach 159, Fishbeck, Fishbaugh 159, Fishpaugh, Fishpaw (fish brook) 77, 155

Fishbein 159, Fishbone, see Fischbein

Fisher 153, see Fischer

Fishter 159, see Fichter

Fisler, Fissler, see Fuessler

Fister, see Pfister

Fite 159, see Veit

Fitschner 53 < Friedrich

Fitten (place name) 122

Fitter, Fitterman, see Vetter, Vetterman

Fitts 159, Fitz, Fitze, Fitzell, Fitzer, Fitzner (artistic weaver, tailor) 106

Fitzberg, Fitzenberg, Fitzenberger (pond mountain) 81, 68

Fitzenreiter (pond clearing) 81, 126

Fitzlert 74, see Fitts

Fizner (dweller near a pond) 81, see Fitts

Flach, Flacher (flat, plain)

Flachmueller 103, Flachmeyer 93 (miller, farmer on the Flach) 83, 103, 93

Flachs, Flaxman (flax, flaxenhaired) 112

Flachs (flax grower or dealer) 91, 106

Flachsbart (flaxen beard) 112

Flachshaar (flaxenhaired) 112

Flacht (woven fence) 84

Flack, see Flach

Flack (swamp) 80

Flacks 159, see Flachs

Flad, Fladd, Flade (flat cake, cake baker) 96, 112

Flaechsner (flax dealer) 106

Flaesch, see Fleisch, Flaschner

Flagel 159, Flagler, see Flegel, Flegler
Flagge (flag, colors)
Flaks 159, see Flachs
Flamholtz (fire wood, wood cutter or dealer) 96, 106
Flamholtz (swamp forest) 80, 72
Flamm (flame, blacksmith) 96
Flammenkamp (swamp field) 80, 84
Flammer (smith) 96
Flanders (a Belgian province, a mercenary fr there or who served there) 121
Flanz (crooked mouth) 114, see also Pflantz
Flaschenriem (flask strap) 106
Flaschner (bottlemaker) 96
Flashhauer 159, see Fleishhauer
Flashman 159, see Fleischmann
Flashner 159, see Flaschner
Flath, Flather, Flater, Flathman, Flathmann 94 (swamp dweller) 80
Flaum, see Pflaum
Flautt (flute player) 96
Flax, Flaxman, see Flachs
Fleager 159, see Pflueger
Fleagle 159, see Fluegel
Flechner (basket weaver) 96
Flechsenhar (flaxenhaired) 112
Flechsner, see Flaechsner
Fleck, Flecke (speck, spot, stain, cobbler, tailor) 96, 104
Fleckenstein (spotted mountain) 68
Fleckner (cobbler, tailor) 96
Fleckner (fr the Fleckhof, stain farm)
Fleddermann (cake baker) 96, 94
Fleegle 159, see Fluegel
Fleetmann (dweller by running water) 94
Fleg, see Pfleger

Flegel, Flegler (flail user or maker, thresher, fr Latin *flagellum*) 106
Fleig (fly, lively person) 115
Fleisch, Fleischer, Fleischmann 94, Fleischner (butcher) 96
Fleischbein (flesh leg, meat bone, butcher) 96
Fleischer (butcher) 96
Fleischhacker (butcher) 96
Fleischhauer, Fleischouer 159 (butcher) 96, 100
Fleischhaus, Fleishhous 159 (butcher shop)
Fleischman, Fleischmann, Fleishman 159 (butcher) 96
Fleischner (butcher) 96
Fleisener 159, see Fleischner
Fleisher 159, Fleishmann, see Fleischer, Fleischman
Fleiss (industry, diligence) 115, see also Fleisch
Fleissner (fr Fleissen), see Fleischner
Flekstein, see Fleckstein
Fleming, Flemming, Flemmings 164 (Fleming, Flemish mercenary) 121
Flender (flighty person) 115
Flensberg (fr Flensberg) 68, 122
Flersheim, see Floersheim
Flesche, Flescher, Fleschmann, see Fleisch, Fleischer, Fleischmann
Fleschner, see Fleischner, Flaschner
Flesher 159, Fleshman, Fleshow, see Fleischer, Fleischmann, Fleischhauer
Flettner (dweller near rushes) 81
Flettner, see Floetner
Flexer, Flexner, see Flaechsner
Flick, Flicker, Flickner (patch, short for *Flickschuster*, cobbler) 104, 106
Flickinger (fr Flicking) 122

Flieder (elder, lilac) 89
Fliedner (bloodletter) 96
Fliegel, see Fluegel
Flieger (restless person) 115, see
Pflueger
Flinchbaugh 159 (pebble brook)
77
Flink, Flinke, Flinkman (quick,
nimble) 115
Flintenfeld (flint field) 84
Floch, Flock (flake)
Flockshaar, see Flachshaar
Floerscheim (fr Floersheim) 122
Floetner (flute player) 96
Flohr 53, Flor < St. Florian 131
Florey, Flory < St. Florian 131
Florian < St. Florian 131
Florscheim, see Floerscheim
Florschutz (field guard) 96
Flossman (rafter) 96
Flott, Flotz (river, pond) 79, 81
Flottmann (dweller on a river) 79
Flougar 159, see Pflueger
Flucht (flight)
Fluck, see Fluegge
Fluegel (wing, jutting piece of
land) 84
Fluegge, Fluegger, Flueggert 74
(fledged, lively) 115
Fluers (field guard) 95
Flug, Fluge (flight), see also Pflug
Flugel, see Fluegel
Flugfelder (plowed field) 84
Fluh (steep stone slope) 71
Fluhr, Flur (meadow) 84
Fluhrer (field guard) 95
Fluke, see Flug
Flumenbaum, Flumbaum (plum
tree) 89
Fluss (river) 83
Fluth (flood) 77
Focht 159, Fochtmann, see Vogt
Fock 53, Focke, Focken < Volk-
wart, Volker, etc.
Fockeroth < Volkerodt (folk +
clearing) 126

Fockhausen < Volkhausen (folk +
houses) 65
Foederer (furtherer)
Foehr, Foehrs 164 (fir tree) 89
Foehrkolb (fir club) 89
Foelix, see Felix
Foelke, Foelker, see Voelke,
Voelker
Foerg (ferryman) 96
Foerst (pre-Germanic river name)
83, see Fuerst
Foerstel, Foerstler, see Foerster
Foerster, Foerstner, Foerster-
mann 94 (forester) 96
Foerstermann (fr Foerster in the
Harz 122) 94, see also Foerster
Foertsch, see Pfirsich
Foertschbeck (peach brook) 89, 77
Fogel 159, Fogal, Foegel, Fogaler,
Fogler, see Vogel, Vogler
Fogelman 159, see Vogelmann
Fogelsanger 159, Fogelsong, see
Vogelsang
Foght 159, see Vogt
Fohl (foal, young horse) 91
Fohlk, see Volk
Fohn, Foehn (south wind) 91
Fohr (fir) 89
Fohr (ferryman) 96
Fohrman, see Fuhrman
Fohrbach (fir brook) 89, 77
Fohring, Fohringer (fir) 89
Foht 159, see Vogt
Folck, Folk, Folke, Folker, Folkert
74, see Volk, Voelker
Folckemer, Folckemmer, Folke-
mar, see Volkmar
Folendorf, Folenweide, see
Fuellendorf, Fuellenweide
Folger (follower)
Folk, Folke, see Volk
Folkart 74, see Volker
Folkman, see Volkmann
Foll, Follen (foal) 91
Follendorf (foal village) 123

Foller, Foeller < Volkhart (folk +
  strong) 46, 46
Follhart, see Foller
Follman, see Volkmann
Follmeyer (foal farmer)
Folmer, Follmer, Fulmer, see
  Volkmar
Folter (torturer) 96
Folter (portcullis)
Foltin < St. Valentin 131
Foltmann (torturer) 96, 94
Foltz, Folz < Volkmar
Fooks 159, see Fuchs
Foos 159, Foose, see Fuss
Forbach 122, Forbeck, see Fahr-
  bach
Forch, Forchel (fir) 89
Forchenbach (fir brook) 89, 77
Forchenbach (trout stream) 77
Forchheimer, Forchhenner (fr
  Forchheim 122, fir hamlet 123)
Forchner (dweller among the firs)
  89
Forcht (fear) 115
Forchtenicht, see Fuerchtenichts
Fordemfeld (in front of the field)
  69, 84
Fordenbach, Fordtenbacher, see
  Vorbach
Forderer, see Foerderer
Forellun (trout) 115
Foremann, see Formann
Forgang, see Vorgang
Forhel (trout) 115
Forhoff, Fornnoff, Fornhof, see
  Vorhoff
Fork, Forke, Forkel 55 (pitchfork)
  106
Formann (drayman) 96
Formhals (before the pass) 69
Formwalt, see Vormwalt
Fornadel (fir needle) 89
Forner (dweller among the ferns)
  89
Forsberg, see Forschberge

Forsch, Forschlern, Forschner,
  see Forst
Forschberge, Forshberge 159
  (forest mountain) 72, 68
Forschlager (forest lair) 72
Forscht, see Forst
Forsh 159, see Forsch
Forsman, see Forst
Forst 122, Forster, Forstmann 94,
  Forstner (forester, dweller in
  the forest) 72
Forster (see Foerster)
Forstreiter, Forstreuter (forest
  clearing) 72, 126
Forstreiter, Forstreuter (forest
  rider) 72
Fortenbaugh 159 (brook with
  ford) 78, 77, 155
Forth, see Furth
Forthofer (farm at the ford) 78, 92
Forthuber (farmer at the ford) 78,
  91
Fortkamp (field at the ford) 78,
  84
Fortman, Fortmann (dweller at
  the ford) 78, 94
Fortmeier (farmer at the ford) 78,
  93
Fortmueller, Fortmuller 159
  (miller at the ford) 78, 93
Fortner, Fortney, see Pfortner
Fortwengler, see Furtwanger
Fosbrink (fox hill) 74
Fosbrok, Fosbroke, Fosbrook (fox
  brake) 80
Fosburg (fox castle) 73
Fosler, Fossler, see Vossler
Fosnaught 159, Fasnot, see
  Fasnacht
Foss, Fosse, Fosz, see Voss
Foster, see Forster
Fourhman 159, see Fuhrmann
Foust 159, see Faust
Fout 159, Fouts, Foutz, see Faut
Fowl 159, Fowle, see Faul, Faule
Fox 153, see Fuchs

Fraalich 159, see Froehlich
Frack (full dress) 112
Fraenkel 55, Fraenkle 159 <
  Frank
Fraenzel 55 < Franz 131
Frage, Frager (food dealer) 106
Fralich, Fralick, Fraley 159,
  Fraleigh 159, see Froehlich
Frambach, see Frombach
France 159, Frances, Francis, see
  Frantz
Franck, Francke, see Frank,
  Franke
Franckfurther, see Frankfurter
Franckhauser, Frankhuyse (the
  Franks' house) 121, 65
Frank, Franke, Franken, Franks
  164 (Franconian) 120. Franken
  may be short for Frankenberg,
  etc.
Frankel 55, Frankle 159, Frankl
  < Frank
Frankenbach (Franks' brook) 121,
  77
Frankenberg, Frankenberger,
  Frankenberry 159 (Franconian
  mountain) 121, 68
Frankenfeld, Frankenfelder (fr
  Frankenfeld 122, the Franks'
  field, or Frank's field) 121, 84
Frankenfield 153, see Franken-
  feld
Frankenheim (the Franks' ham-
  let) 121, 123
Frankenstein (Franconian
  mountain) 121, 73
Frankenthal (Franconian valley)
  121, 76, 122
Frankfelder, see Frankenfelder
Frankford, see Frankfurter
Frankfurter, Franckenfurther (fr
  Frankfurt) 122
Frankl, Frankle 159, see Fraenkel
Frankland (Franconia) 121
Frankouse 159, Frankhouser (the
  Franks' houses) 121, 65, 155

Franks, see Franck
Franz, Frantz, Frantzen, Fran-
  sen, Franssen (St. Francis) 131,
  137
Franzmann (Frenchman) 121
Fras, Frass (glutton) 115
Fratz (grimace, rascal, glutton)
  115
Frauenberg (Mountain of Our
  Lady) 139, 122
Frauendienst (service of the
  ladies)
Frauendoerfer (fr Frauendorf 122,
  Our Lady's Village) 139
Frauenfelder (fr Frauenfeld 122,
  "Field of our Lady," or "corvée
  field") 139
Frauenholtz (convent woods) 139
Frauenknecht (servant to Our
  Lady's convent) 139
Frauenpreis (praise of ladies)
Frauenschu (maker of ladies'
  shoes) 96, 104
Frauenstadt (City of Our Lady)
  139
Frauke 55, Fraucke (little lady)
Fraumann (vassal of or worker at
  a convent) 139
Fraunfelder, see Frauenfelder
Fraundorf, see Frauendoerfer
Fraunhoffer (convent farm) 139,
  84
Fraunholtz (probably Fronholtz,
  corvée forest) 139
Fray, see Frey
Frayberg, see Freiberg
Fraylick 159, Fraylich, see
  Froehlich
Frease 159, see Fries
Freburger 159, see Freiburger
Frech (impudent, bold) 115
Freck, Frecker, Freckmann 94
  (bold), also < Friedrich
Frede, Freder (fr Frede 122,
  swamp) 80, also < Friedrich
Fredekin 55 (little Friedrich)

Fredenstein (peace stone) 73
Frederic, Frederik, Frederica, see
    Friedrich
Fredericki, son of Frederick 142
Fredericksen (son of Fredrick) 59
Fredhoff 159, see Friedhoff
Fredrica, see Friedrich
Freeauf 159, see Fruehauf
Freeberger 159, Freeburger, see
    Freiberger, Freiburger
Freebour 159 (free peasant) 151
Freed ... see Fried ...
Freed 159, Freede, see Friede
Freedberg 159, Freedbergh,
    Freedburg, see Friedberg,
    Friedburg
Freedlander 159, Freedlender (fr
    Friedland) 121, 151
Freedman 159, see Friedmann
Freehauf 159, see Fruehauf
Freehof 159, see Friedhof
Freehold 159, see Freiholt
Freeland 159, see Friedland
Freehling 159, see Fruehling
Freemann 159, see Freimann
Freemire 159, see Freimeyer
Frees, Freese, Freeze 159, Free-
    sen, Freesemann (Frisian) 121
Freesmeyer (Frisian farmer) 121,
    93
Frei, Freie, Frey (free) 115, 109
Freiberg, Freiberger (fr Freiberg
    122, tax exempt mountain) 68
Freiburger (fr Freiburg) 122
Freid ..., see Fried ...
Freidag, see Freitag
Freidel 159, see Friedel
Freidenberger 159, see Freud-
    enberger
Freidenstein 159, see Freud-
    enstein
Freier (wooer)
Freihauf, see Fruehauf
Freihof (independent farm) 84,
    122

Freiholt, Fryholtz (public forest)
    72
Freihuber, see Freihof
Freilich, Freligh 159 ("freely! to
    be sure!") 117, see Froelich
Freimann 94, Freiling (freedman)
Freimueller (tax exempt miller)
    103
Freimut, Freimuth, see Freyer-
    muth
Freind, Freint, see Freund
Freinstein, see Freudenstein
Freis, Freise, Freisen (Frisian),
    see Fries
Freistat, Freishtat 159 (free city)
    122
Freistueler, Freisthuhler, Freis-
    tuler (official of Vehmgericht)
    109
Freitag (Friday) 143
Freivogel (free bird, outlaw) 109
Fremd, Fremder (stranger) 120
Fremdling, Froembdling (stran-
    ger) 120
Frendt 159, see Freund
Frenkamp (swamp field) 80, 84,
    see Fehrenkamp
Frenkel, see Fraenkel
Frens, Frenz, Frenzel 55 < Franz
Frenssen (son of Franz) 59
Frentz, Frenzel 55 < Franz
Frerich, Frerichs 164, see Frie-
    drich
Frese, Fresen, see Fries
Fress (glutton) 115
Fretz, see Fritz
Freud, Freude, Freuden (joy) 115
Freudenberg, Freudenberger (fr
    Freudenberg, joy mountain) 68,
    122
Freudenberger (one who has seen
    the *Mons Gaudium*)
Freudenburg (joy castle) 73, 122
Freudenhammer (fr Freudenheim
    122) 123

Freudenreich, Freudenrich (joyful) 115

Freudenstein (joy montain) 73, 122

Freudenthal (joy valley) 76, 122

Freudhafer (joy farm) 92, 159

Freudig (joyful) 115

Freund, Freundt, Freint, Freundel 55 (friend)

Freuntlich, Freunlich (friendly)

Frevel (theft)

Frey, Freye, Freyer (free) 109

Freyberger (fr Freyberg 122, free mountain), see Freiberger

Freyburger (fr Freyburg 122, free castle), see Freiburger

Freydel, see Friedel

Freyer, see Freier

Freyermuth, Freymuth, Freymuht (free spirit) 115

Freyhofer (free court) 84

Freyling (free man) 109

Freyman (free man) 109

Freymeyer (free farmer) 93

Freysinger (fr Freising) 122

Freytag, see Freitag

Freyvogel (free bird, outlaw) 109

Frez, see Fritz

Friand 159, see Freund

Friauf 159, see Fruehauf

Fric 159, see Frick

Frichi 159, see Fritschi

Frick 53, Fricke, Frickel 55 < Friedrich)

Frickenhaus (house on the Frick) 83, 65

Frickenstein (mountain near the Frick) 83, 73

Fricker, Frickert 74 (dweller on the Frick) 83

Frickinger (fr Fricking 122, belonging to Friedrich) 59, 123

Frickmann (dweller on the Frick) 83, 94

Frickmann (follower of Friedrich) 94

Fridag, Fridy 159, Friday 153, see Freitag

Fridel, see Friedel

Fridley 159, see Friedlich

Frideric, Friderick, Friderich, Fridrich, see Friedrich

Friebach (public brook) 77, see Friedbach

Friebe (fr Slavic *vrba*, willow tree) 89, 146

Frieberger, see Freiberger

Fried, Friede, Frieds 164 (peace), also < Friedrich

Friedbach (foamy brook) 77

Friedbald, Friebald (peace + bold) 47, 46

Friedberg, Friedberger (fr Friedberg 122, peace mountain) 47, 68

Friedburg (peace castle, walled castle) 47, 73, 122

Friedel 55, Friedle 159, Friedl (friend, sweetheart)

Friedemann, see Friedmann

Friedenberg, see Friedberg

Friedenheim, see Friedhaim

Friedensthal (peace valley) 76

Friedenwald (peace forest) 47, 72

Friederic, see Friedrich

Friedgen 53, 55 < Friedrich)

Friedhaber (peacemaker) 138

Friedhagen (walled enclosure) 47, 123

Friedhaim (fr Friedheim 122, peace hamlet, walled hamlet) 47, 123

Friedhof, Friedhoffer (cemetery) 47, 92

Friedke 53, 55 > Friedrich

Friedland, Friedlaender (fr Friedland) 121

Friedle 159, Friedly 159, Friedler, see Friedel

Friedlein 55, Friedline 159 < Friedrich

Friedlich (peaceful) 115

Friedman, Friedmann (peace
man) 115, also < Friedrich
Friedrich, Friederich, Friedrichs
164, Friederick, Friedericks,
(peace + ruler) 47, 46
Friedrichsson (son of Friedrich)
59
Frieling 159, see Fruehling
Friemann, see Freimann
Friend 153, Friendlich, see
Freund, Freunlich
Friermood 159, see Freyermuth
Fries, Friess, Friese, Frieser,
Friesche, Friesner (Frisian,
often a false plural of Frey)
121
Frieschknecht (Friesian servant)
Friesenhahn (fr Friesenhagen
122, Frisian hamlet 121)
Frietag 159, see Freitag
Friethrick 159, see Friedrich
Frietsch 53 < Friedrich
Frigh 159, see Frey
Frik, Frike, see Frick, Fricke
Friley 159, see Freilich
Frind 159, see Freund
Fring, Fringe, Frings 164 < St.
Severin 131
Frisch, Frische (fresh, lively 115),
also < Friedrich
Frischkorn, Frishkorn 159 (fresh
grain) 106
Frischman, Frischmann, see
Frisch
Frischmut (fresh courage) 115
Frischolz (wood cutter) 95
Frishcorn 159, see Frischkorn
Frist (period, time limit)
Fritchi 53, Fritsch, Fritschi,
Fritsche, Fritscher, Fritschel
55, Fritschler, Fritschner,
Fritzsch < Friedrich
Fritz, Fritts 159, Fritze, Fritzel,
Fritzges, Fritzsche, Frizzel,
Fritzius < Friderizius, Latin
for Friedrich 141

Fritzmann 94, Fritzner < Fried-
rich
Fritzweiler (Friedrich's villa,
peace village) 123
Froberg, see Frohberg
Frock 159, see Frack
Froeb, Froeber (willow, fr Slavic:
*vrba*) 89, 146
Froebel (undaunted) 115
Froehlich, Froehlicher, Froehlig,
Froelig, Froeli, Froehly 159
(joyful) 115
Froehling, see Fruehling
Froehlke, see Froehlich
Froembdling, see Fremdling
Froeschle 55 (little frog) 115
Froese, see Fries
Froh (merry) 115
Frohbart (merry beard) 112, 115
Frohberg (merry mountain) 68
Frohboese (quick to anger) 115
Frohlich, Frolic, Frolick, Frohligh
159, see Froehlich
Frohling (merry person) 115
Frohman, Frohmann (merry man)
115, 94
Frohn, Frohne, Frohner, Frohnert
74 (court messenger, corvée
payer) 139
Frohnder, see Frohn
Frohnmayer (overseer of corvée
service) 93
Frohsinn (merry disposition) 115
Frohwein (merry friend) 115
Frolich, Frohligh 159, see Froeh-
lich
From, Frome, see Fromm
Froman, see Frohmann
Fromberg 122, see Frommberg
Fromknecht (faithful servant) 139
Fromm, Fromme, Frommer
(useful, pious) 138
Frommberg (swamp mountain)
80, 68
Frommeyer (industrious farmer)
138, 93

Frommholt (pious dear) 138, 48
Fronacker (lord's field, corvée
field) 139
Froneberger (corvée mountain)
139, 68
Froner, see Frohn
Fronfelder, Fronfelter (corvée
field) 139, 84
Fronheuser, Fronhyser (corvée
houses) 137, 65, 66
Frosch, Frosh 159 (frog, house
name) 62
Froschauer (fr Froschau 122, frog
meadow) 84
Frost, Frostz 164 (frost)
Frostdorf, Frostdorp (frost village)
123
Frowenfelder 159, see Frauen-
felder
Frucht (crop, fruit) 106
Fruchtbaum (fruit tree) 89
Fruchtel 55, Fruchter, Frucht-
mann, Fruchterman (fruit
dealer) 106
Fruden 159, see Freuden
Fruechte (crops, fruit dealer) 106
Frueh (early riser) 115, see also
Frey
Fruehan (early cockcrow) 143
Fruehauf (early riser) 115
Fruehauf (child sired before
marriage) 119
Fruehling (spring) 143
Fruehsang, Fruesang (early song)
Fruehstueck (breakfast)
Fruehwein (early wine) 106
Fruendt, see Freund
Fruetag (morning, Friday) 143
Fruetrank (early drink)
Fruh, Fruhling, see Frueh,
Fruehling
Fruhwirth (early host) 96
Fruke, see Frauke
Frum, see Fromm
Fruman (worthy man) 138, 94
Fry, Frye, Freyer, see Frey

Fryberger, see Freiberger
Frydag, see Freitag
Frydman 159, see Friedmann
Frydryck 159, see Friedrich
Fryer, see Freier
Freyermouth 159, see Freyer-
muth
Fryfogel, see Freivogel
Fryling, see Freiling
Frymyer 159, see Freymeyer
Fuchs (fox, furrier, house name)
106
Fuchsberger (fr Fuchsberg 122,
fox mountain) 68
Fuchsmann (furrier) 96
Fuchsschwanz (fox tail, furrier)
96
Fuechtner, see Fichtner
Fuegel, Fuegli, Fueglin (skilful)
115
Fuehrer (leader, carter) 96
Fuellen (foals) 91
Fuellenweide (foals' meadow) 84
Fueller (glutton) 115
Fuellgrabe (Fill-the-grave!, grave
digger) 116
Fuenfrock (five cloaks) 112, 117
Fuenkelstein, see Finkelstein
Fuerchtegott (Fear God!) 116, 140
Fuerst (prince) 109
Fuerstein 159, see Feuerstein
Fuerstenberg (prince's mountain)
68, 122
Fuerstler, see Foerstler
Fuerstmann (prince's follower)
109, 94, see Forst
Fuerstner, see Foerstner
Fues, Fuess, Fuos, see Fuss
Fuesser (pedestrian, infantryman)
107
Fuessler (one who works for the
*Barfuessler*, Barefoot Friars)
110
Fuetter (fodder) 105
Fuetze (pond, puddle, fr Latin
*puteus*) 80

Fug, Fuege (pleasant) 115
Fuge, Fuger, Fugman (overseer) 96
Fugler, see Vogler
Fuhlroth (rotted clearing, swampy clearing) 80, 126
Fuhr 159, Fuhrer, see Fuehrer
Fuhrman, Fuhrmann, Furman (carter) 96
Fuhrmanneck (carter's place) 96, 85
Fuks 159, see Fuchs
Fuksman 159, Fuksmann, see Fuchsman
Fulbright 159, 162, see Volkbrecht
Fulcher, Fulker, see Volker
Fulda (name of city) 122
Fuldner (fr Fulda) 122
Fulenbacher (swamp brook) 80, 77
Fulenwider 159 (foal's meadow) 84
Fulenwider 159 (swamp meadow) 80, 84
Fulger, see Folger
Fulk, Fulker, see Volker
Fullbrake 159, see Vollbrecht
Fullenkam, Fullenkamp (foal's field) 84
Fuller (fuller, fr Latin *fullare*) 96
Fulle, see Fuellen
Fullewiler (foals' hamlet) 123
Fullmer, Fulmer, see Volkmar
Fults 159, Fultz, Fultze, see Voltz
Funderburk < von der Burg (from the castle) 69, 73
Funk, Funck, Funke (spark, unstable person) 115
Funkel (spark, smith) 106
Funkenstein (spark mountain) 73
Funkhauser, Funkhouser 159 (fr Funkhaus 122, spark house) 65
Furch (furrow)
Furcht (fear) 115
Furchtgott, see Fuerchtegott

Furman (ferryman) 96, see also Fuhrmann
Furrenbauer (furrow farmer, plowman) 91
Furst 159, see Fuerst
Furstenberg, see Fuerstenberg
Furstmeyer, Furstmeier (manager of prince's farm) 93
Furth (ford, suburb of Nuernberg) 122
Furthemeyer (ford farmer) 78, 93
Furtmiller (ford miller) 78, 103
Furtwanger (sloping meadow at the ford) 78, 71
Fusel (bad liquor, taverner) 96
Fuselbach (bad liquor creek) 77
Fuss, Fuess (foot, leg, foot of mountain, see also Fuchs)
Fusselbaugh 159, see Fuselbach
Futerer, Futter, Futterer, Futerman 96 (feeder, fodder dealer) 106
Fux, Fuxe, see Fuchs
Fuxmann, see Fuchsmann
Fyfer, see Pfeiffer

## G

Gaas, Gaass, see Gas
Gabble 159, see Gabel
Gabe (gift)
Gabel 122, Gabell, Gabler, Gabeler, Gabelmann (fork, fork maker) 106
Gabel, Gabell, Gabler, Gabelmann 94, (dweller at a road fork) 65
Gabelsberg (fork mountain) 68
Gaberle 55 < St. Gabriel 136
Gabhart 159, see Gebhard
Gable 159, Gabler, see Gabel, Gebel
Gabriel, Gabriels 164 (an archangel) 136
Gach (quick, turbulent) 115
Gack (silly, foolish) 115

Gackenbach (swamp stream) 80, 77, 122

Gackenback (shepherd's hut) 77

Gade, Gaden (chamber, room)

Gade 53 < Gottfried, Gottschalk, etc.

Gade (miner) 96

Gadermann (dweller by the village gate) 65

Gadjohann (handsome John) 115

Gaeb (pleasant, welcome) 115

Gaebel (skull) 114

Gaebler, see Gabel, Gabler

Gaedeke, Gaedtke, see Goedeke

Gaehring, see Goering

Gaengel (leadstring, horse trainer), see Gangel

Gaensebein (fenced yard for geese) 84

Gaensebein (goose leg) 114

Gaenshirt (goose herder) 95

Gaenslein 55, Gaensle, Gennsli (gosling) 91

Gaensler (goose raiser) 95, 91

Gaerber, see Gerber

Gaerstener, see Gerstner

Gaertel 55 (little garden, gardner) 84, 98

Gaertner, Gaertener (gardner, fr Garden or Garten) 84, 98

Gaes, Gaesser, see Gaessner

Gaestel 55 (little stranger, little guest) 120

Gaetge 55, see Goetz

Gaetz, see Goetz

Gafke 55 (little gift)

Gager (fr Gagen) 122

Gahl, Gahler (fr Gahlen) 122

Gahr, Gahre, Garht 74 < Garmann, speer man) 46, 94, 53, see Gart

Gahraus, see Garaus

Gahs, see Gas

Gaier, see Geier

Gaiger, Gaigler, see Geiger

Gail, Gailing, see Geil

Gainer, see Gehner

Gais (goat) 91

Gaisel, Gaiselmann, see Geisel, Geiselmann

Gaiser, see Geiser

Gaister, see Geister

Galander (lark) 115

Galgenschwank (gallows bird, initiation name) 117

Gall, Galle, Gallen < St. Gallus 131, fr St. Gall 122, 139

Galler, Gallner (servant at St. Gall) 139

Gallinger (fr Galling) 122

Gallman, Gallmann (servant of St. Gall) 139, 94

Gallmeyer (bailiff at St. Gall) 93, 139

Gallster (incantation, warlock) 96

Gallus (St. Gall) 131

Galm (noise) 115

Galster, see Gallster

Gambach, see Gandbach

Gambel, Gamble 159, see Gamber

Gamber, Gambert 74, Gampert (acrobat, entertainer) 96

Gambler, Gambolt 159, see Gambel

Gamerman, see Kammerman

Gamertsfelder (field on a ridge) 84

Gamp, see Kamp

Gamper, Gampffer, Gampert 74, see Gamber, Kaempfer

Gams, Gamse (chamois, chamois hunter) 91

Gamstetter (fr Gamsstaedt, chamois place) 122

Gand, Gandel, Gandelman 94 (pebble field) 71, 84

Gandbach (swamp brook) 80, 77

Gandenberg (stony mountain) 71, 68

Gander, Gandermann (swamp dweller) 80

Gang, Gange, Ganger, Gangl

Gangler (stream) 77
Gangel (huckster) 105
Gangenmeyer (farmer on a
stream) 93
Gangloff, Ganglof (gait + wolf, cf.
Wolfgang) 48
Gangmueller (miller on a stream)
77, 103
Ganke 55, Gankel 55 < Janke
(Johann) 134
Gann (magic, magician) 96
Gans, Ganss, Gansman (goose,
goose herder) 91, 115
Gansberg, Ganzberger (goose
mountain) 68, 122
Gansburg (goose castle) 73, 122
Gansel 55, Gaensel (little goose)
91, 115
Ganser, Gansler, Gansner, Gan-
sert 74 (goose raiser) 91, 115
Ganten, Gantner (goose raiser)
91, 115
Ganter, Ganther (auctioneer) 96,
also see Guenther
Ganz, Gantz, Gantze, Gantzer,
Ganzert 74 (whole, complete),
see Ganser
Ganzemueller, Gantzenmueller
(goose miller) 91, 103
Gaphard 159, Gapehard, Gape-
hart, see Gebhard
Gapp, see Gabe
Gar (spear) 46
Garaus (Bottoms up!) 117
Garbe, Garben, Garbes 164
(sheaf)
Garber < Garbrecht, see also
Gaerber
Garbrecht (spear + brilliant) 46,
47
Gardenhour 159 (fr Gartenau,
garden meadow) 84, 84, 151
Gardenhour 159 (garden digger)
84, 151
Gardner 159, see Gaertner
Garecht, see Garrecht

Garfinkel, Garfinkle 159, Gar-
fuenkel (carbuncle, fr Latin
*carbunculus*)
Garg, see Karg
Garhard, Garheart 159, see
Gerhard
Garinther, see Kaerntner
Garke 53, 55, Garken < Gerhard
Garlach, see Gerlach
Garling, see Gerling
Garman, Garmann (spear + man)
46, 94
Garmes 53, 164, Garms < Gar-
mann
Garmhausen (Garmann's houses)
65, 122
Garn (yarn, snare, fish or fowl
netter) 106, 91
Garner (snarer, fish netter) 91, 96
Garrecht (Quite right!) 117
Garreis, see Garaus
Garrel 53, Garrels 164, Garrelt
74, Garrelmann 94 < Gerhold
(spear + loyal) 46, 48, 53
Garrel (place name, swamp) 80,
122
Garst, Garster, see Karst
Garstener, see Gerstner
Gart, Garth, see Geert, Garthe
Gartelmann (gardener) 84, 94
Gartenhaus (gardenhouse) 84, 65
Gartenhoff, Garthoff (garden
yard) 84, 92
Gartmann (gardener) 84
Gartner, see Gaertner
Garver, see Gerber
Garz, see Geert
Gasel 159, see Gesell
Gasner, see Gass
Gaspar, Gaspars 164, see Caspar
Gass 122, Gasser, Gassert 74,
Gassner, Gasmann, Gassmann
(dweller on a street, shortened
form) 65
Gassenheimer (hamlet on a road)
65, 123

Gassinger (dweller on a road) 65

Gassel, see Kassel

Gassel, Gassler, see Gass

Gassmann, see Gass

Gassmeyer (farmer on the road)
65, 93

Gassner, see Gass

Gast, Gastmann (stranger, guest)
120

Gasteier, Gasteiger (dweller on a
steep mountain path) 71

Gastmeyer (newly arrived farmer)
120, 93

Gastorf (village on the high land)
123, 122

Gastreich, Gastrich (hospitable)
115

Gattermann, Gattener (dweller by
a rail fence) 84

Gattling, Gatling (kinsman,
comrade) 119, 151

Gatz, Gatzke 55 (fr Gatzen 122),
see Katz

Gau (district, countryman)

Gaubatz (Slavic place name) 146

Gauch (cuckoo, fool) 115

Gauchenauer (fools' meadow) 84

Gauckler, Gaukler (juggler) 96

Gaudenberger (one who has seen
the *Mons Gaudium*), see
Freudenberger

Gauer (countryman)

Gauf, see Kauf

Gaug, Gauger (gadabout) 115

Gaugle 159, Gaugler, see Gauckler

Gaugh 159, see Gauch

Gaughund (stray dog) 115

Gaul, Gauler (horse, carter) 96

Gaum (gum) 114

Gaum (man)

Gaumer (overseer) 96

Gaus, Gause, Gauss, Gausman
94, Gauslin, Gaussmann, see
Gans

Gausebeck (goose creek) 77

Gausepohl (goose pond) 80

Gautz, see Kautz

Gaver 159, see Geber

Gawff 159, see Kauf

Gayer, see Geier

Gayger, see Geiger

Gayheart 159, Gayhardt, see
Gerhard

Gayle, Gayler, see Geil, Geiler

Gayring 159, see Goering

Gazell 159, see Gesell

Gearheart 159, see Gerhard 151

Geartner 159, see Gaertner

Geating 159, Geeting, Geedig, see
Gueting

Gebaur, Gebauer (peasant) 91

Gebbe 53, Gebberd < Gebhard

Gebeke 53, 55 < Gebhard

Gebel 53, 55 Gebele, Gebelein 55
< Gottfried 53

Gebel 159, see Giebel

Geber, Gebers 164, Gebert 74,
Geeber (giver)

Geber 53, Gebers 164, Gebert 74
< Godebrecht or Gottfried 53

Gebhard, Gephardt, Gebhart (gift
+ strong) 46

Gebhauer 159, see Gebauer

Geble 159, see Gebel 151

Gebrecht (gift + bright) 47

Gecht, Gechter (impetuous person) 115

Geck, Gecke, Geckel 55, Geckler,
Geckeler (fop, dandy) 115

Gedance 159 (fr Danzig) 122

Geddoecke 53, 55 < Gottfried

Gedion (OT Gideon) 135

Gedult (patience) 115, 139

Geebel 159, see Gebel

Geeber, see Geber

Geehreng, see Gehring

Geel Haar, Geelhaar (yellow
haired) 112

Geer, Geers 164, see Gehr

Geerdes 164, Geerdert 74, see
Geert

Geerdsen, see Geert

Geerke 53, 55, Geerken (little Gerhard)

Geerling 53, 55 < Gerhard

Geert, Geerts 164, Geertsen 59, Geertke 55 < Gerhard

Gees, Geesman 94, Geesmann, Geesaman 159, see Gieseke

Geesler 159, see Giessler

Geest (dweller on high dry ground) 68

Gefeller (dweller by a waterfall) 77

Geffert < Gebhard

Geffinger < Gebhard

Geffken 53, 55, Gefken < Gebhard

Gegenwart (presence)

Geger, Gegner (opponent, dweller outside of village or across the street)

Gehau (forest) 72

Gehauf (Go up!) 116

Gehaut (Go out!) 116

Gehl, Gehle, Gehler, Gehlert 74, Gehlmann 94 (yellow haired) 112

Gehlbach (swamp brook) 80, 77

Gehman 94, Gehmann, Gehner (dweller on a slope) 71

Gehr, Gehres 164, Gehret 74 < Gerhard, Gerwin, Gerbert

Gehrhard, Gehrhardt, see Gerhard

Gehrich 53, Gehrig, Gerick < Gerhard, Gerbrecht, etc.

Gehring, Gehringer, see Goering, Goeringer

Gehrke 53, 55, Gehrken, Gehrlein < Gerhard, Gerbrecht, etc.

Gehrman, Gehrmann, Geermann (spear + man) 46, 94

Gehrt, see Geert

Gehse (speer) 46

Geib, Geibe, Geibig (filth) 115

Geidel (braggart, spendthrift) 115

Geidt (greed, desire) 115

Geier (gerfalcon, vulture) 115, see Allgeier

Geierman (falconer) 91, 94

Geiersbach (vulture brook) 77

Geiersbuhler (vulture hill) 67

Geiershofer (vulture farm) 92

Geifuss, see Geilfuss

Geigel, Geiglein 55 (little fiddle, little fiddler) 96

Geigenbach (fiddle brook) 96, 77

Geigenberger (fr Geigelberg 122, fiddle mountain) 96, 68

Geigenmeyer (occupant of the Geigenhof, or farmer on the Geigenbach) 96, 73, 77, 94

Geigenmueller (miller on the Geigenbach) 96, 103, 83

Geiger, Geigert 74 (fiddler) 96

Geigerheim (fiddlers' hamlet) 96, 123

Geigermann (fiddler) 96, 94

Geigmueller, see Geigenmueller

Geil, Geils 164, Geiler, Geilert 74 (lively, wanton) 115

Geil (swamp) 80

Geilenkirchen (swamp church) 80, 122

Geilfuss, Geilfuess (lively foot, lively person) 115

Geilhaar (yellow haired) 112

Geimer (spearpoint + famous) 46, 47

Geis, Geise, Geiss (goat, goatherd) 91

Geisbert (noble scion + brilliant) 47, 47

Geisdoerfer (fr Geisdorf 122, goat village) 123

Geisel, Geisler, Geissler, Geisselmann 94 (hostage)

Geisel, Geisler (whip, flagellant)

Geisemeyer (goat farmer) 91, 93

Geisenheimer (fr Geisenheim 122, goat hamlet) 123

Geisenrotter (goat clearing) 126

Geisenstein (goat mountain) 73

Geiser (goatherd) 91
Geisfel (goat skin) 106
Geishirt, Geissert (goat herder)
 91, 95
Geising, Geisinger (fr Geising)
 122
Geisler (spear + army) 46, 46
Geisler (goat raiser) 91
Geismann (goat man) 91
Geismar (swamp pond) 80, 122
Geisreiter (goat clearing) 126
Geisreiter (goat rider, nickname
 for tailor) 104, 117
Geiss, see Geis
Geissberg (goat mountain) 68
Geissblatt (honeysuckle) 89
Geissbuehl (goat hill) 68
Geissel, Geissler, see Geisel,
 Geisler
Geissendorfer (goat village) 123
Geissheimer (fr Geissheim 122,
 goat hamlet) 123
Geissinger (fr Geissing) 122
Geissler (flagellant) 110, 122
Geist (spirit) 122, see Geest
Geist (dregs, sediment)
Geister (spirits)
Geisthardt (spirit + strong) 46
Geistlich (spiritual, clerical)
Geisweiler (goat hamlet) 127
Geiswinckler (goat forest) 69
Geisz, see Geis
Geit, Geite, Geithe (greed) 115
Geitdorfer (fr Geitdorf 122, goose
 village) 123
Geitz, Geiz, Geize, Geitzer (greed)
 115
Geitzmann (greedy man) 115
Gelb, Gelber (yellow, blond) 112
Gelbach (swamp brook) 80, 77,
 122
Gelbart (yellow beard) 112
Gelbaugh, see Gelbach
Gelbert, Gelberdt, see Gilbert
Gelbke 55 (little blond) 112
Gelblum (yellow flower) 89

Geldemeister (guild master)
Gelder, Geldern, Geldermann 94,
 Gelderlaender (fr Geldern in
 the Netherlands) 121
Geldhaeuser (money exchanger)
 65, 96
Geldmacher (goldmaker, alche-
 mist, minter) 96
Geldman, Geldmann (money
 man) 96, 94
Geldreich, Geldrich (money rich)
Gelerter (scholar, savant) 96
Gelfert < Gelfrat (merry + coun-
 sel) 47
Gelhaus (yellow house) 65, see
 Gellhaus
Gelinek, see Jellinek
Gelke 53, 55 < Gelmar (wanton,
 cocky) 115
Geller (sacrifice + army) 46
Geller (town crier) 109
Geller, Gellert 74, Gellermann 94,
 (yellow haired) 112
Gellermann, see Geldermann
Gellhaus, Gellhausen (guild
 house) 65
Gellinger (fr Gelling) 122
Gellmann, Gelman, see Geldmann
Gellner, Gelner (goldsmith) 96
Gellwasser (marsh water) 80
Gelpke 55 (marsh brook) 80
Gelriche, see Geldreich
Geltman, see Geldman
Geltner (goldsmith) 96
Gembler, see Gamber
Gemeinbauer (farmer on the
 common) 91
Gemeiner (private soldier) 107
Gemp, Gempp, Gemper, see
 Gamper
Gemuendt (mouth of stream) 79
Gems (chamois, chamois hunter)
 91
Genau (exact) 115, 117
Gencel 159, see Gaensel
Gender (auctioneer) 96

Gerrard 159, see Gerhard

Gerrecht, see Gerecht, Garrecht

Gerring, Gerringer, see Gehring

Gerrsmann (Gerhard's follower) 94

Gersbach (Gerhard's brook) 77, 122

Gersch, Gersh 159, Gerschmann (barley farmer) 91

Gerschberg, see Gerstenberg

Gershengorn 159, see Gerstenkorn

Gershman 159, see Gerstman

Gerstbrein (barley porridge) 112

Gerstman (barley dealer, raiser) 106, 91

Gerschheimer (barley hamlet) 123

Gerschwiller (barley village) 127

Gersdorf (barley village) 123

Gersh 159, Gershman, see Gersch

Gerst, Gersten (barley) 91, 106

Gerstacker, Gerstaecker (barley field) 84

Gerstel 55, Gerstle 159, Gerstler, Gerstner (barley dealer) 106

Gerstemeyer, Gerstenmeier, Gerstemeir, Gerstenmeyer (barley farmer) 93, 91

Gerstenberg, Gerstenberger (fr Gerstenberg 122, barley mountain) 68

Gerstenblith (barley blossom) 89

Gerstendoerfer (barley village) 123

Gerstenfeld, Gerstenfield 153 (barley field) 84

Gerstenhaber (barley farmer) 92, 91

Gerstenkorn (barley grain) 91, 106

Gerstenschlaeger (barley thresher) 96

Gerstman, Gerstmann (barley dealer) 106, 94

Gerstmeyer, Gerstmyer 159, see Gerstemeyer

Gerstner (barley dealer or raiser) 106, 91

Gerteisen (goad) 106

Gertelmann, see Gartelmann

Gert 53, Gerth, Gerthe, Gertz 164 < Gerhard

Gerthner, Gertner, see Gaertner

Gertler 159, see Guertel

Gertz 53, 164, Gertzmann 94 < Gerhard

Gerung 53, 55 < Gerold

Gervinus (Latin for Gerwin) 141

Gerver, see Gerber

Gerwig (spear + battle) 46, 46

Gerwin (spear + friend) 46, 48

Geschke 55 (clever, cunning) 115

Geschwind, Geschwinds 164, Geshwend (swift) 115

Gesell, Gesele, Geseller (companion)

Gesinder (following)

Gess, Gesser, Gessler, Gessner, Gessel, see Gasner

Gestl 55, see Gast

Getrost (confident, optimistic) 115

Gettel, Gettle 159, Gettleman (kinsman, peasant youth) 119

Gettenberg (swamp mountain) 80, 68

Gettenmueller (miller near the swamp) 80, 103

Getter, Getner, Gettermann (caster, founder) 96

Gettman, Gettmann (caster, founder) 96

Getts 159, Getz, Getze, see Goetz

Getzandanner, see Giessendanner

Getzenberg (foundry mountain) 68

Geuter, Geutert 74, see Geit

Gevantmann (mercer) 96

Gewinner (winner)

Gewirtz (spice dealer) 106

Gex 164, see Geck

Geyer, see Geier

Geyger, see Geiger

Gitting, Gittings 164, Gittinger (fr
  Gitting) 122
Glaas, see Glas
Glaatz, see Glatz
Gladbach (swampy brook) 80, 77,
  122
Glade, Gladen (shining) 115
Glade (swamp) 80
Gladfelder, see Glatfelder
Glaenzer (shining) 115
Glaeser, Glaesener, Glaesmann,
  Glasman, see Glas
Glahn (dweller on the Glan) 83
Glaiber 159, see Kleber
Glance 159, see Glantz
Glantz, Glanz (brilliance) 115
Glarner (fr Glarus in Switzer-
  land) 121
Glas, Glaser, Glaeser (glazier) 96,
  106
Glaskopf (glass cup, maker of
  glass cups) 96, 106
Glass, Glasser, Glassler, Glassner
  (glazier) 96, 106
Glassbrenner, Glassmann (glass
  maker) 96
Glassmeyer, Glasmeier, Glasmyer
  159 (manager of the glass
  factory) 96, 93
Glatfelder, Glattfelter, Gladfelder
  (smooth field) 84
Glatfelder (swampy field) 80, 84
Glatt (smooth) 115
Glatthaar (smooth hair) 112
Glatz, Glaz, Glatzer (bald man)
  112
Glaub (faith)
Glauber (believer, creditor) 115
Glaubitz (Slavic place name) 146
Glauch, Glaucher (fr Glaucha)
  122
Glauer (clever) 115
Glauner (cross-eyed) 113
Glaus, Glauser, see Klaus, Klau-
  ser
Glaz, Glazer, see Glatz, Glatzer

Gleim (swamp) 80
Gleisbach (shiny brook) 77
Gleissner (hypocrite) 115
Gleit, Gleitsman 94, Gleitsmann,
  Gleitzmann (mounted guard)
  107
Glendemann, Glindemann (fr
  Glinde 122, swamp) 80
Gleser, see Glaser
Glessner (glazier) 96
Glick, see Glueck
Glicksman, Glicksmann (lucky
  man) 115, 94
Glickstern, see Glueckstern
Glimph (sport, fun) 115
Glind (fenced area) 84
Glindeman (dweller in a fenced
  area) 84, 94
Glindeman (swamp dweller) 80,
  see Glendemann
Glitman, see Gleit
Glitsch (spear) 46
Glock, Glocke, Glocker, Glockner
  (bell ringer) 109
Glockengeter (bell caster) 96
Glockmann (bell ringer) 109, 94
Gloecker, Gloeckner, Gloekler, see
  Glock
Glor < St. Hilarius 131
Gloster, see Kloster
Glotz, Gloetzel 55, see Klotz
Gluckstern (lucky star) 117
Glueck, Gluck (luck, fortune) 117
Glueckauf (miner's greeting) 116
Glueckselig (blissful) 115
Glug, see Klug 115
Glut, Gluth (fire)
Gmeiner (commoner, community
  leader, private soldier) 107
Gmeinwieser (user of common
  pasture) 84
Gnade (mercy, grace) 138, 116
Gnaedig (gracious) 115, 138
Gnann, Knann (cousin, name-
  sake) 119
Gnau, see Genau

Gob 53 < Jacob 135
Gobel, Gobbel, see Goebel
Gobrecht < Godebrecht (god +
   bright) 47
Gochenauer, Gochenour 159,
   Gochnauer (fools' meadow) 84
Gockeler, see Gauchler
God, Godt, see Gott
Gode, Goday 159 (good) 115, 43,
   157
Godebrecht (god + bright) 47
Godfried, Godfrey 153, see
   Gottfried
Godlove 153, see Gottlieb
Godman 153, see Gottmann,
   Gutmann
Godschalk, Godschalks 164, see
   Gottschalk
Godt, see Gott
Goebel 53, 55, Goebbel, Goebels
   164, Goebeler, Goebling 55 <
   Godebrecht
Goecke 53, 55, Goeckeler <
   Gottfried
Goedeke 53, 55, Goedike <
   Gottfried
Goegel, Goegell (juggler, jokester)
   96
Goehke 53, 55 < Gerhard
Goehl, Goehler, Goehlert 74
   (swamp dweller) 80
Goehmann (dweller on the Goe)
   83
Goehre (swamp dweller) 80, see
   also Goehring
Goehring 53, 55, Goehringer <
   Gerhard
Goeldener, Goeller, Goellner,
   Goellman (gold miner) 96
Goeller, Goellner, see Gellner
Goellnitz (Slavic place name 122)
   146
Goeltner, see Goldener
Goeltz (animal castrator) 96
Goenner, Goeners 164 (patron)
Goepel, Goepell, see Goebel

Goepfert < see Gebhard
Goeppner (jacket maker) 96
Goerg, Goergen, Goerges, see
   Georg
Goering 53, 55 < Gerhard
Goerner, see Gerner
Goerres < St. Gregorius 131
Goertler, see Guertler
Goertz 53, 164 < Gerhard
Goertzhain (Gerhard's grove) 72
Goessling (gosling) 91, 115
Goessling (fr Goesslingen) 122
Goetche (barrel maker) 96
Goetel, Goethals 164, 159, see
   Goettel
Goethe < godfather 119
Goetsch 53, Goetsche < Gottfried
Goetschalk, see Gottschalk
Goette (baptized child) 119
Goettel 53, 55, Goettig, Goetting,
   Goettling 55 < Gottfried,
   Gotthard
Goetz 53, Goetze < Gottfried, etc.
Goetzel 53, 55, Goetzelman,
   Goetzelmann < Gottfried
Goetzendorf (Gottfried's village)
   123, 122
Goetzinger (fr Goetzing) 122
Goetzke 53, 55 < Gottfried
Gogel (relaxed, merry) 115
Gohde 53 < Gottfried
Gohl (Slavic for bald), 146, see
   also Kohl
Gohn, see Kohn
Gohr, Gohrmann 94 (fr Gohr)
   122, see Gormann
Gohring, see Goering
Gohs, Gohse, Gohsman 94, see
   Gans
Gold, Golde, Golden (gold, gold-
   smith) 96
Goldacker (gold field) 84
Goldbach, Goldbeck (fr Goldbach
   122, gold brook) 77
Goldband (gold band) 106
Goldbaum (gold tree) 89, 148

Goldberg 122, Goldenberg, Goldbergh, Goldberger, Goldeberger (gold mountain) 148

Goldblatt (gold leaf, goldsmith) 96

Goldblum, Goldbloom (gold flower) 89, 148

Goldcamp (gold field) 84

Goldeisen (gold iron) 148

Goldenbaum, see Goldbaum

Goldenberg, see Goldberg

Goldenblum, see Goldblum

Goldencrown 153, see Goldenkron

Golder, Golderman 94 (goldsmith) 96

Goldfarb (gold color) 148

Goldfeder, Goldfedder (gold feather) 148

Goldfine 159, (gold fine) 148, 159

Goldfinger (gold finger, ring maker) 96

Goldfuss (gold foot) 148, 117

Goldgeier (golden vulture, house name) 62, 149

Goldhaber (gold possessor)

Goldhammer (gold hammer, house name) 62, 149

Goldhammer (yellow hammer) 115

Goldhar (golden hair) 112

Goldhirsch (golden stag, housename) 62, 149

Goldhofer (proprietor of the Goldhof, gold farm) 92

Goldhorn (gold horn, house name) 62

Goldklang (sound of money) 117

Goldman, Goldmann (gold man, goldsmith) 96, 94

Goldmeyer, Goldmeier (occupant of the Goldhof) 93, 94

Goldner (gold worker) 96

Goldreich, Goldrich (rich in gold)

Goldschmidt, Goldschmitt (goldsmith) 96

Goldstad (gold city)

Goldstein (gold stone, topas, jeweler) 73, 122

Goldstern (gold star, house name) 62, 149

Goldstick (gold piece) 159

Goldstrom (gold stream) 77

Goldvogel (golden bird) 62

Goldwasser, Goldwater 153 (Danzig cognac) 106

Goldwein, Goldwine 159, Goldwyn (gold friend) 48

Goll (bullfinch, fool) 115

Goller (collar) 106

Gollmenz (fr *Kalmincz*, Slavic place name) 146

Gollnitz (fr Golnitza 122, Slavic place name) 146

Gollner, see Goeller

Gollstadt, see Goldstad

Golltermann (quilt maker) 96, 94

Gollermann (fr Goltern) 122, 94

Golt, see Gold

Goltze, Golz (fr Goltzen 122, Slavic place name) 146

Gombert, see Gumbert

Gommel 53, 55 < Gumbert

Gompf, see Kampf, also Gump

Gompertz 164, Gomprecht, see Gundbrecht

Gonce 159, see Gans

Gonder 159, Gonderman, see Guenther, Guenthermann

Gonder, see Gander

Gondorf (pre-Germanic place name) 122

Gongloff 159, see Gangloff

Gonnerman 159, see Guenther mann

Gonsman 159, see Gans, Gansman

Gonter 159, Gontert, see Gunther

Gontrum 159, see Guntram

Good ..., see Gut...

Goodbrood 153 (good bread, baker) 96

Goodhard 153, see Gotthard

Goodknecht 153, see Gutknecht
Goodman 153, see Gutmann
Goodmuth 153, see Guthmuth
Goodnight 153, see Gutnacht
Goodyear 153, 162, see Gutjahr
Goontz 159, see Kuntz
Gorenberg (bog mountain) 80
Goring 159, see Goering
Gorman, Gormann (dweller near
    a bog) 80
Gorn 159, see Korn
Gorr 53 < Gregorius 131
Gorth, see Gurth
Gortler, see Guertel
Goos (goose) 91
Goschen (OT Goshen) 135
Gosdorfer (fr Gosdorf, goose
    village) 123, 122
Gosdorfer (fr village on the Gose)
    83
Gosmann, see Goss
Gosner (goose raiser or dealer) 91,
    106
Goss, Gossmann (Goth) 120
Gosse, Gossen, Gosser (drainage
    ditch) 81
Gossler, Gosseler (fr Goslar, dirty
    water) 122
Got ..., see Gott
Gotcher 159, see Goettcher
Gotfried, see Gottfried
Gothe, Gothen (place name) 122
Gotlib 159, see Gottlieb
Gotschall, Gotshall 159, see
    Gottschalk
Gott, Gotte (God, usually fr
    Gottfried, etc., or actor in
    miracle play) 111
Gottbehuet (God forbid!) 117
Gottberg (swamp mountain) 68,
    80, 122
Gottdiener (God's servant) 140
Gottemoeller (monastery miller)
    139
Gotter 53 < Gottfried

Gottesfeld, Gottfeld (God's field,
    glebe land) 84, 139
Gottesman (convent or monastery
    worker) 139, 94
Gottfried (God + peace) 138, 140
Gotthard (god + strong) 46, 46
Gottheimer (God hamlet) 123
Gotthelf, Godhelf (God + help)
    140
Gotthold (dear to God, god + rule)
    140
Gottleben (life in God) 140
Gottleben (swamp village) 80, 127
Gottlieb, Gottliebs 164, Gottleib
    159 (God + love) 140
Gottmann (man of God, monas-
    tery worker) 139, 140, 94
Gottschalck, Gottschalk, Gott-
    schall, Gottsalk 159 (God +
    servant) 140
Gottsegen, Gottsagen 159 (divine
    blessing) 140
Gottskind (child of God) 140
Gottsmann, Gottesmann (God's
    man, vassal or employee of a
    monastery) 140, 139, 94
Gottwald, Gottwalt, Gotwalt,
    Gottwalts 164, Gottwals (God +
    rule) 140
Gotz 53, Gotze, Gotzen < Gott-
    fried
Gouchenauer, Gouchenour 159,
    Gouchnour (fools' meadow) 84
Goucher 159 (dweller on a mea-
    dow) 84
Goucker 159, see Gauger
Goughenour 159, see Gauche-
    nauer
Gouldman 159, see Goldmann
Graaf, see Graf
Graas, see Grass
Grab, Grabe, Grabs 164, Graben
    (grave, grave digger) 96
Grabau (grave meadow) 84, 122
Grabbe, Grabbe (grabber, seizer),
    see Grab

Grabel (rivulet) 79
Grabeman (grave digger) 96
Graben (ravine) 76
Grabenheimer (ravine hamlet)
123
Grabenkamp (grave yard) 84
Grabenstein (gravestone) 73, see
Graffenstein
Graber (engraver) 96
Graber, see Graeber
Grabill 159, see Kraehbuehl
Grable 159, see Grabel
Grabner (dweller near a ditch)
Graebe, Graeber, Graebner,
Graebener (grave digger) 96
Graef, Graefe, Graeff, Graeffe, see
Graf
Graefinstern 159 (the count's
star)
Graeser, see Graser
Graeul, Grauel (atrocity) 115
Graf, Graff, Graffe, Graef, Grave,
Groff (count) 109
Graffenperger (fr Grafenberg,
count's mountain) 68, 122
Graffenried (count's marsh) 81,
122
Graffenstein (count's mountain)
73
Graffmann (count's man) 94, 109
Grafstein, see Graffenstein,
Grabstein
Graft, see Kraft
Grahl, Grahls 164 (chalice) 106
Grahn, Grahne, see Kran
Graim, see Greim
Grall, see Grahl
Gram, Gramm, Gramer, Gram-
mer, see Kraemer
Gramberg (fr Grambergen, mud-
dywater mountain) 68, 122
Gramm, Grams 164 (angry), see
Gram
Gramueller (grey miller) 103
Grandadam (big Adam) 113, 135

Grander, Grandner, Grandfield
153, see Grantner, Grantfeld
Grandt (trough) 122, see Grant
Graniwette, Granwetter (juniper
tree) 89
Grannemann (dweller near the
junipers) 89, 94
Grant (gravel, pebbles)
Grantfeld (gravel field) 84
Grantmeyer, Grantmire 159,
Grantmyer 159 (fr the Grant-
hoff, pebble farm) 93
Grantner (dweller on gravel)
Grantzau (gravel meadow) 84
Granz, see Grant, Krantz
Grap, see Grab
Gras, see Grass
Grasberger (grass mountain) 68
Graser (official mower) 95, 109
Grashof (grass farm) 92
Grasmeher (grass mower) 95
Grasmick, Grasmueck (hedge
sparrow) 115, 117
Grass, Grasse, Grasser, Grass-
mann (grass, meadow guard)
96
Grassau (grass meadow, meadow
guard) 84, 122
Grassman, see Grass
Grassmick, see Grasmick
Grat (ridge) 68
Gratz, Gratze (fr Graetz, Slavic
for castle) 122, 146
Gratz 53 < Pacratius 131
Grau, Graue, Grauer, Graumann
94 (graybeard) 112
Grauel, Graull 159, see Graeul
Graulich, Grauling (dreadful) 115
Graumann, see Grau
Graus (grey) 112, see also Kraus
Grausam (cruel) 115
Graustein (greystone) 73
Grave, 159, Graves, 164, see Graf
Graybill 159, Graybeal 159, see
Kraehbuehl
Grayligh 159, see Greulich

Griebler, see Gruebler
Grief, Griefe, see Greif
Grieg, Grieger, see Krieger, also <
  Gregorius
Griem, Grieme (fr Griemen) 122,
  108
Griem (mask, helmet) 46, 108
Griener 159, see Greiner
Griep, see Greif
Griepenkerl (Grab the rascal!)
  116, 117
Griepentrog (Grab the trough!)
  116, 117
Gries (gravel)
Griesacker (gravel field) 84
Griesammer, Griesamer, Griese-
  mer, Grieshammer (fr Gries-
  heim 122, gravel hamlet) 123
Griesbach (gravel brook) 77, 122
Griesbaum (gravel tree) 89
Griesbeck (gravel brook) 77
Griese, see Greis
Grieshaber (rough-ground oats)
  112
Griesheim (gravel hamlet) 123,
  122
Grieshoff (gravel farm) 92, 122
Griesing, Griesinger (fr Griesin-
  gen) 122
Griesmar (gravel swamp) 80
Griesmeyer, Griesmyer 159 (fr
  the Grieshof, gravel farm) 93
Griess, Griesse, Griessler, Gries-
  smer (dweller on sandy soil)
Griessmann, see Griesmeyer
Grievogel (griffin) 62
Griffe (marsh ditch) 122
Gril, Grill (cricket, whimsical
  person) 115
Grillenberg 122, Grillenberger
  (cricket mountain) 68
Grim, Grimm, Grimme (grim) 115
Grimbacher 122, see Grumbacher
Grime 159, see Greim, Grimm
Grimké 55 (little Grimm) 157

Grimm, Grimmer (grim, un-
  friendly) 115
Grimmel, see Krimmel
Grimmelman (crooked man) 113
Grimmiger (fierce) 115
Grinberg 159, Grinblatt, see
  Gruenberg, Gruenblatt
Grindel 122, Grindler, Grind-
  linger (swamp dweller) 80
Grindelwald (forest in Switzer-
  land) 72
Grindle 159, see Grindel
Griner 159, see Greiner
Grinspun 159, see Gruenspan
Gripinkerl, see Griepenkerl
Gripp, see Griepp
Grisbach, see Griesbach
Grise 159, see Greis
Grist, see Christ
Gritz, Gritzner (grist maker) 96
Grob, Grobb, Grobe (crude) 115
Grob, Grober (swamp dweller) 80
Grobbacher, Grobbaker (swamp
  brook) 80, 77
Grobleben (swampwater settle-
  ment) 80, 122
Groegger 53 < Gregorius 131
Groen, Groene, Groener, Groenest
  (green)
Groenewald, see Gruenewald
Groenheim (green hamlet) 123
Groenig, Groening, Groeninger (fr
  Groeningen) 122
Groening (yellow hammer) 115
Groenthal (green valley) 76
Groenwood 153, see Gruenewald
Groeschel (small silver coin) 117
Groesser (larger) 113
Groessinger (fr Grossingen) 122
Groethausen, see Grosshaus
Groff, Groffe (crude, rough) 115,
  see also Graf
Groh, Grohe (gray) 112
Grohmann (graybeard) 112
Grohn (green) 112
Grohskopf, see Grosskopf

Groll, Grollman 94 (grassy marsh) 80
Groll, Grolle (grudge)
Groller (sulker) 115
Gromann (graybeard) 112, 94
Grombein 159, see Krummbein
Gronau, Gronaw 159 (green meadow) 84, 122
Grondt, see Grund
Gronberg, see Gruenberg
Grone, see Krone
Groneck, see Kroneck, Grueneck
Gronemeyer (dweller on the Gronhoff) 93
Gronewold (green wood) 72
Gronhoff (green farm) 92, 122
Gronholz (green wood) 72
Groninger (yellow hammer) 115
Grooman, see Grohman
Groon (swamp) 80, see Gruen
Groos, see Gross
Groote 39, see Gross
Groover 159, see Gruber
Gropp, Groppe, see Grob
Grosch, Groschel (penny) 117
Groscup 159, see Grosskopf
Grosfeld, Grosfield, see Grossfeld, Grossfield
Grosh 159, see Grosch
Grosholtz (big forest) 72
Grosnickle 159, see Grossnickel
Gross, Grosse, Gros, Grose, Grosz, Groos (large) 113
Grossarth (grandeur) 115
Grossbach (large brook) 77
Grossbart (big beard) 112
Grossberg (big mountain) 68
Grossblat, Grossblatt (large leaf) 89
Grosscup 159, see Grosskopf
Grossenaker (large field) 84
Grossfeld, Grossfield 153 (large field)
Grossgebauer (big farmer) 91
Grosshandler (wholesaler) 105
Grosshans (Big Johnny) 113

Grosshart, Grosshard (large forest) 72
Grosshaupt (bighead) 114
Grosshaus, Grosshauser (fr Grosshausen 122, large house) 65
Grosskopf (bighead) 114
Grosslicht (big light, big clearing) 126
Grossman, Grossman (big + man) 113, 94
Grossnickel, Grossnickle 159 (Big Nicholas, Nicholas the elder) 113
Grossweiler, Grosswiler (fr Grossweil 122, large hamlet) 127
Grosz, see Gross
Grote, Groth, Grothe, Grotte, see Gross
Grotegut (large estate) 92
Grotendick, Grotendiek (big dike) 82
Groteyahn 159, see Grotjan
Grothaus, Grothhaus, Grothusen (large house) 65
Grotheim (large hamlet) 123
Grothof (large farm) 92
Grothman, see Grossman
Grotjan (Big John, John the elder) 113
Grousaam 159, see Grausam
Grovenstein 159, see Graffenstein
Grover 159, Groover, see Gruber
Grub, Grube (hollow, pit, mountain cove) 76
Grubel, see Gruebel
Grubenhoff (farm in a hollow) 76, 92
Grube (pitfall, bear trap) 91
Gruber, Grubert 74 (dweller in a *Grube* or hollow) 76
Grubmeyer (farmer in the dell) 76, 93
Grueber, Gruebel, Grueblel (brooder) 115, see Gruber
Gruel 159, see Greul

Gruen, Gruene, Gruener (green)
112
Gruenast (green branch) 89
Gruenau (green meadow) 84
Gruenbaum (green tree) 89
Gruenbacker 159 (green brook) 77
Gruenbeck (green brook) 77
Gruenberg, Gruenberger (green
mountain) 68, 112
Gruenblatt, Greenblat (green
blade, leaf) 89
Gruenburg (green castle) 73
Gruendel, Gruendl (swamp) 80
Gruendelberger (swamp moun-
tain) 80, 68
Gruender (founder), see Grund
Gruender, Gruendler (valley
dweller) 76
Gruene, Gruener, Gruenert 74
(green) 112
Grueneck (greenfield) 84
Gruenewald 122, Gruenwalt
(green forest) 72
Gruener, see Grueninger
Gruenfeld (green field) 84, 122
Gruenholt (green wood) 72
Gruenhut (green hat, housename)
112, 62
Grueninger (yellow hammer) 115
Grueninger (fr Grueningen) 122
Gruenspan (green chip, verdigris)
Gruenstein (green mountain) 73,
122
Gruenthal (green valley) 76, 122
Gruenwald 122, see Gruenewald
Gruesser (greeter, blower of
hunting horn) 91
Gruenzweig (green + twig, host's
sign) 63
Gruess (greetings) 116
Gruetter (fr Gruett) 122
Gruhl (place name) 122
Grumbach 122, Grumbacher
(swamp brook) 84, 77, see
Krumbach

Grumbein, Grumbine 159
(crooked leg) 114
Grumm, see Krumm
Grunau (green meadow) 84, 122
Grunbaum 159, see Gruenbaum
Grunberg 159 (green mountain)
68
Grund, Grunder (bottom, valley)
76
Grundlach (valley lake) 76, 80
Grundman, Grundmann (valley
dweller) 76
Grundmueller (valley miller) 76,
103
Grundner, see Grundmann
Gruner, Grunert 74, see Gruener,
Gruenert
Grunewald 122, Grunwald, see
Gruenewald
Grunsfeld, see Gruenfeld
Gruntman, see Grundman
Grupe, Grupp (grouper fisher-
man) 115
Grupenhoff, see Grubenhoff
Gruse 159, see Krause
Gruss, Grusz, see Gruesse
Gruve, Gruver, see Grube,
Groover
Gruylich 159, see Greulich
Gryder 159, see Kreider
Gryner 159, see Greiner
Grys, see Greis
Gschwandel, Gschwantner
(dweller in a clearing) 126
Gschwind (quick) 115
Gsell, see Gesell
Guckel (rooster) 115, 91
Guckenberger, Guckelsberger
(rooster mountain) 68
Gucker, Guckert 74 (lookout)
Gude (swamp) 80, see Gut
Gudekunst, see Gutkunst
Gudeman, see Gutman
Guderian, Guder Jan (Good John)
144
Gudikunst, see Gutkunst

Gudermuth, see Gutermuth
Guedemann, Guedermann, see
    Gutmann
Guelberth, see Gilbert
Gueldner (gilder)
Guelich (Juelich, principality on
    the Rhine) 121
Guempel, see Gimpel
Guendelach, see Gundlach
Guender, see Guenther
Guenst (favor) 117
Guenter, Guentert 74, see
    Guenther
Guenterberg (Guenther's moun-
    tain) 68
Guenther (battle + army) 46, 46
Guentherman (follower of Gunt-
    her) 94
Guenz 53, Guentzer, Guntzel 55,
    Guenzler, see Guenther
Guenzburg (Guenther's castle) 73
Guering, see Goering
Guertel, Guertler (belt maker)
    106
Guess 159, see Gess
Guetemann, see Gutmann
Gueth, Guethe, Guether, see Gut
Gueting (man of substance,
    dweller on an estate) 92
Gugel, Gugle 159 (cowl wearer or
    maker) 112, 96, 106, see Kugel
Guggenbuehler (fr Guggenbuehl
    122, swamp hill or cuckoo hill)
    67
Guggenheim (swamp hamlet or
    cuckoo hamlet) 123
Gugler (cowl maker or wearer, fr
    Latin *cuculla*) 96, 110, 112, see
    Kogler
Guhl, Guhler (fr Guhlen) 122, see
    Kuhl
Guinter 159, Guinther, see
    Guenther
Gulde, Gulden (guilder) 117
Guldenfuss, see Goldfuss
Gulich, Gulick, see Guelich

Gull (swamp dweller) 80
Gullberg (swamp mountain) 80,
    68
Gumbert, see Gundbrecht
Gumpel < Gundbold (battle +
    brave) 46, 46
Gumpelman (acrobat) 96
Gumpert, see Gumbert
Gundacker < Gundwaker (battle
    + brave) 46
Gundbrecht (battle + bright) 46,
    47
Gundel 53, 55 < Gundolf, Gund-
    rum, etc.
Gundelach, see Gundlach
Gundelfinger (fr Gundelfingen)
    122, or < Gundolf
Gunder, see Gunther
Gunderberger (Gunther's moun-
    tain) 68
Gunderdorf, Gundersdorf, Gun-
    derstorff (Gunther's village)
    123
Gunderman, see Guentherman
Gundersheimer (Gunther's
    hamlet) 123
Gundlach (battle + play) 46
Gundlach (stagnant pond) 80
Gundolf (battle + wolf) 46, 48
Gundrum, see Guntram
Gunkel, Gunkelmann, see Kunkel
Gunn 159, see Kuhn
Gunselman 159, see Kuntzelman
Gunst (favor)
Gunter, see Guenther
Guntermann (follower of Guent-
    her) 94
Gunteroth (Gunther's clearing)
    126
Gunther (battle + army) 46, 46,
    49
Guntram (battle + raven) 46, 48
Guntrum, see Guntram
Guntzel 53, 55 < Gunther
Guntzenhauser (fr Gunzenhausen
    122, Guenther's houses) 65

Gunzelman, see Kuntzelman
Gunzenheimer (fr Gunzenheim
122, Guenther's hamlet) 123
Gurth (girth, girdel) 106
Gurtner (girth maker) 96
Gurts, see Kurtz
Guss, Gusman 94, Gussmann
(founder, caster) 96
Gusstein (sink) 73
Gust, Gustl 55 < Augustus 141
Gustav < Swedish, Gustaf (for
Gustavus Adolphus)
Gut, Guth, Gute (good, property,
estate) 92
Gutekunst (good skill) 115
Gutenberg (good mountain) 68
Gutenbrunner (fr Gutenbrunnen
122, good fountain) 79
Gutenschwager (good in-law, good
kinsman) 119
Gutensohn (Guda's son) 60
Gutermann (good man) 115, 94
Gutermuth (good disposition) 115
Gutfleisch (good meat, butcher)
96
Gutfreund (good friend) 115
Gutgesell (good fellow) 155
Guth, see Gut
Guthaber (estate owner) 92
Gutheim (estate hamlet) 92, 123
Guthhard (good + strong) 46
Guthman, see Gutmann
Gutjahr (New Year's Day) 143
Gutke 55 (small estate) 92
Gutknecht (worker on an estate)
92
Gutkunst, Gutekunst (good skill)
117
Gutmann, Guthman, Gutman,
Gutzler (good man, man own-
ing an estate) 92, 138
Gutschall, see Gottschalk
Guttenberger, see Gutenberg
Guttmann, see Gutmann
Gutwald, see Gottwald
Gutwillig (affable) 115

Gutzel, see Gut
Guyer, see Geier
Gwinner (winner)
Gwirtzman, see Gewirtz
Gyger, see Geiger

# H

Haacke, see Hacke
Haacker (retailer) 105
Haaf, see Haff
Haag, Haage, Haager, see Hag,
Hager
Haak, Haake, Haackel (fr Haak
122, hook) 106
Haan, see Hahn
Haanecam (cock's comb) 84
Haar, Haare, Haars 164 (hair)
112
Haar (flax) 91, 106
Haarbleicher (flax bleacher) 96
Haardt, see Hardt
Haarhaus (fr Haarhausen 122,
marsh house) 80, 65
Haarmann (marsh dweller 80),
see also Hermann
Haarmeyer (marsh farmer) 80, 93
Haart, see Hart
Haartz, see Hartz
Haas, Haase (fr Haas 122), see
Hase
Haaseler, see Hassler
Haasmann, see Hasmann
Hab (possessions)
Habacher, Habacker (fr Halbach)
122
Habbeck, Habbecker (hawker) 91
Habbecker (fr Habbecke, swamp)
122
Habben < Hadebert (battle +
bright) 53, 46, 47
Habberle (oat grower) 91
Habecker, Habegger, see Habbeck
Habel (Slavic for St. Gall) 146
Habenicht (Have not! 116, or I
have not 117)

Haber, Habers 164, Habert 74
(oats, oat dealer) 106
Haberacker (oatfield) 84
Haberbosch (oat bush) 72
Habercam, see Haberkam
Haberecht (Be right!, Know-it-all)
116
Haberer (oat dealer) 106
Habergans (oat goose) 115
Haberger (fr Haberg) 122
Haberkam, Haberkamp (oat field)
84
Haberkorn (oat grain) 106
Haberl, Haberle, Haberly 159 (oat
farmer) 91
Haberland, Haberlander (oatland)
122
Haberling 122, see Haberl
Haberloh (oat forest) 72
Habermaas (oat measure) 106
Habermann (oat dealer) 106
Habermehl (oat meal) 106, 112
Habersack (oat sack)
Habersat (newly sowed oatfield)
84
Habersieck (oat fen) 80
Haberstad (oat landing)
Haberstamm (oat stalk)
Haberstich (oat - steep slope)
Haberstock (oat stalk)
Haberstroh (oat straw) 106
Habich, Habicht, Hebicht (hawk,
hawker) 115, 91, 96
Habighurst (hawk hurst) 72
Habight 159, see Habich
Habluetzel (Have little!, or I have
little) 116, 117
Habmann, see Habermann
Hach, Hache, Hachen (youth) 112
Hachelbach (muddy brook) 77
Hachenberg (hawk mountain) 68,
122
Hachenburger (fr Hachenburg,
hawk castle) 73
Hacher (flax hackler) 95
Hachlage (swamp water - lair) 80

Hachmann (dweller by swamp
water) 80, 94
Hachstein (swamp mountain) 80,
73
Hacht, Hachtmann 94, see
Habich
Hachthal (swamp valley) 80, 76
Hack, Hacke (rake) 106, see also
Hag
Hackbart (rake beard) 112
Hackenberg (swamp mountain)
80, 68, 122
Hackendorf (swamp village) 80,
123
Hackenmueller (swamp water -
miller) 80, 103
Hackenschmied (rake smithy) 96
Hackenshmit 159 (rake smith) 96
Hacker, Hackert 74 (raker) 96,
see also Haacker
Hackermann, Hackler (huckster,
retailer) 105
Hacklander (swamp land) 80
Hackmann, see Hagmann,
Hackermann, Hakenschmied
Hackmeister (master of the
enclosure) 123
Hackstiel (rake handle) 106
Hadamar (battle + famous) 46,
47, 122
Hadamar (swamp marsh) 80
Hadd 53 < Hadeward (battle +
guard) 46, 47
Hadel, Hadeler (bog dweller) 80
Hadepohl (swampy pond) 80, 80
Hader, Haderman 94, Haderle 55,
Hadler, Hadner (quarreler)
115, 122
Hadwig (battle + battle) 46, 46
Haeberle 55, Haebbeler, Hae-
berling (young goat) 91
Haebler (yeast dealer) 106
Haech (pot hook, cook) 96
Haechel (hook, hook maker, cook)
96, 106
Haechler (flax hackler) 96

Haeckler (vineyard worker) 96

Haefell, Haefele, Haeffele, Haffeli, Hefley 159, Haeffler, see Hafner

Haefer, Haefner, Haeffner, see Hafner

Haeg 122, Haege, see Hag

Haeger, Haegler, Haegele, Haegmann 94 (dweller in an enclosure) 123

Haehl, Haehle (swamp) 80

Haehler (fence for stolen goods) 96

Haehn 122, Haehner, Haehnert 74 < Haginher (master of the enclosure) 123

Haehnel 55, Haehnle, Haehnlein (little rooster) 115

Haekel, see Haechel

Haelblein (ha'penney) 117

Haell, see Haehl

Haemel (sheep castrator) 95

Haemmer, see Hammer

Haemmerer, Haemmerle 55 (hammerer, smith) 96

Haen, Haenes 164, Haenle 55, see Haehn

Haendel, Haendler (trade) 105

Haendel (fight)

Haener, see Haehn

Haenle 55, see Haehnel

Haensel 55 (little John)

Haentschel 55, see Hensch

Haerdel 55, see Hert

Haering, see Hering

Haertel 55, Haertele, see Hert

Haerter, Haertter (communal herdsman, communal shepherd) 95

Haertz, see Hertz

Haesle, Haesler, Haeseler, Haessler, see Hasel

Haesemeyer, see Hasemeyer

Haeubt, see Haupt

Haeuser, Heuser, see Haeusler

Haeusler, Haeussler (householder, cotter) 65

Haeussli 55 (little house) 65

Haf, Haff (harbor, bay)

Haf, Haff, Haffen (oats) 91, 106

Hafele 55, see Hafner

Hafemeyer, Hafemaier (farm overseer) 93

Hafemeyer (oat farmer) 93

Hafen, Haffen, Hafenmeister (harbor master) 109

Hafer, Haffer, Hafers 164, Hafert 74 (oats, oat dealer) 91, 106

Haferkamm, Haferkamp (oat field) 84

Haferkorn (oat grain, oat seller) 106

Hafermann (oat dealer) 106

Haff, Haffen, see Haf

Haffentraeger (oat carrier) 96

Hafferstock (oat stalk)

Haffmann, see Hoffmann

Hafner, Haffer, Haffner, Haeffner (potter) 96

Hafstaetter, see Hofstetter

Haft (custody, bailiff) 109

Hag, Hage, Hagen (fr Hag 122, enclosure, hedge) 123

Hagbereg, see Hackenberg

Hagebaeke (hedge stream) 123, 77

Hageboek (hedge beech) 123, 89

Hagebom (thornbush) 123, 89

Hagedorn (hawthorn) 123, 89, 122

Hagel, Hagle 159, Hagler, Hagele (fr Hagel 122, hail)

Hagelauer (hail meadow) 84

Hagelberg (hail mountain) 68, 122

Hagelgans (snow goose) 115

Hagelmaier (enclosure farmer) 93

Hagelstein (hailstone, a name for the devil) 122, 131

Hagemann (enclosure dweller) 123, 94

Hagemeier, Hagemeyer, Hagmaier (manager of the enclosure) 123, 93

Hagemueller (miller by the enclosure) 123, 103

Hagen, Hagens 164 (fr Hagen 122, enclosure, hedge) 123

Hagenauer (enclosed meadow) 123, 84

Hagenbach, Hagenbeck (hedge brook) 123, 77

Hagenbach (swamp brook) 80, 77, 122

Hagenberg (enclosure mountain) 123, 68, 122

Hagenbruch (enclosure quarry) 123, 80

Hagenbuch, Hagenbucher, Hagenbucker 159 (hornbeam) 89

Hagendorf (enclosed village 123, 123, village on the Hagen 83)

Hagendorn, Hagedorn (hawthorn) 89, 123

Hagenhoff, Hagenhoffer (enclosed farm) 124, 92

Hagenkamp (enclosed field) 123, 84

Hagenkotter (cotter in an enclosure) 123

Hagenkotter (cotter on the Hagen) 83

Hagenleite (enclosed slope) 123, 71

Hagenmeyer, Hagenmayer, Hagmaier (enclosure farmer) 123, 93

Hagemeyer (farmer on the Hagen) 123, 93

Hagenmueller (miller at the enclosure 123, 103

Hagenmueller (miller on the Hagen) 83, 103

Hager, Hagers 164, Hagert 74, Hagermann 94 (dweller in an enclosure) 123

Hagerskamp (field belonging to a *Hager*) 123, 84

Hagius (latinized form of Hage) 141

Hagmann (dweller in an enclosure) 123, 94

Hagmauer (enclosure wall) 123, 100

Hagner, see Hager

Hahn, Hahne, Haan (rooster, house name) 115, 62

Hahnberger (rooster mountain) 68

Hahnberger (swamp mountain) 80, 68

Hahner (swamp dweller) 80

Hahnfeld (swamp field) 80, 84

Hahnstein (rooster mountain) 73

Hahnstein (swamp mountain) 80, 73

Hahr, see Haar

Hahrtman, see Hartmann

Haibler (hood maker) 96

Haid, Haidt, Haide, see Heid, Heide

Haidbrueck (heath bridge) 81, 71

Haight 159, see Heid, Heide

Haigler, see Hegel

Hail, Hailer, Hailler, Hailmann, see Heil, Heiler, Heilmann

Hailfinger (fr Heilfingen) 122

Hailgen, see Heiligen

Haimbaugh, see Heimbach

Hain (grove), see also Hagen

Hainemueller (miller at the grove) 103, 72

Hainle 55, see Heinle

Hains, Hainz, Haintz, see Heinz, Heintz

Haiser, see Heiser

Haisler, see Heussler

Haiter (swamp) 80, see Heiter

Haitz 164, see Heid

Hake, see Haak

Hakenkamp (swamp field) 80, 84

Haker, see Hoeker and Hacker

Halbach (swamp brook) 80, 77, 122

Halbauer (half-owner of a farm, sharecropper) 91

Halber (ha'penny) 117

Halbright 159, see Albrecht

Halberstadt (German city) 122

Halbfass (half barrel, tenant farmer) 91

Halbfoerster (half-owner of forest rights)

Halbgewachs, Halbgwachs (half grown) 113

Halbmeyer (half-owner of a farm) 93

Halbritter (half-knight) 107

Halbrunner (swamp spring) 79

Haldemann (dweller on a slope) 71

Halden (slopes) 71, 122

Halder, Halderman 122, see Haldemann

Halfacre 159, see Huffacker

Halfadel (half-noble) 46

Halfmann (share cropper) 91, 94

Halikman 159, see Heiligmann

Hall (Swiss town) 122

Hallbauer, see Halbbauer

Halle (hall, German city) 122

Hallebach, Hallenbeck (brook along a slope) 71, 77

Halleman (swamp dweller) 80, 94

Hallenbach (swamp brook) 80, 77

Hallenberger (fr Hallenberg 122, swamp mountain) 81

Hallenburg (swamp castle) 81, 73, 122

Hallendorf, Hallendorff (swamp village) 80, 123

Haller (fr Hall or Halle 122), see also Heller

Hallfrisch 159, see Helfrich

Hallick, see Heilig

Hallmann, see Hellmann, Heilmann

Halls, see Hals

Hallwachs, see Halbgewachs

Halm (blade, stalk) 89

Halman, see Hallmann

Halper, Halpert, see Alper, Alpert

Hals (throat) 114

Hals (mountain pass) 68

Halt (halt) 116

Haltdichwohl (Keep well!) 116, 117

Haltemann, see Haldemann

Haltenberg (steep mountain) 68

Haltenhof (slope farm) 71, 84

Haltenmeyr (slope farmer) 71, 93

Halter, Haltermann 94 (owner, proprietor)

Halter, Haltmann, see Haldemann

Haltwanger, Haltiwange (sloping field) 71, 84

Halverstadt (city name) 122

Halwig, see Helwig

Hamacher, Hamacker, see Hammacher

Hamann, Hamannt 74 < Johann

Hambach, Hambacher (fr Hambach 122), reed brook 81, 77, see also Hagenbeck

Hamberg, Hamberger (fr Hamberg 122, reed mountain) 81, 68, see also Hagenberg

Hambrecht (body + bright) 124, 47

Hambright 159, see Hambrecht

Hambruck (reed bridge) 71

Hamburg, Hamburger (fr Hamburg 122, reed brook castle) 81, 73

Hamel, Hamelmann 94 (fr Hameln, Hamlin, swamp) 122

Hamer, see Hammer

Hamermann, see Hammermann

Hamlin (fr Hameln) 122

Hamm, Hamms 164 (horse collar) 106

Hammacher (horse collar maker) 96

Hammann 53 < Johann
Hammecker, see Hammacher
Hammel, Hammel (wether) 91,
  see Hamel
Hammelgarn (fish net) 106, 91
Hammelmann, fr Hamlin (Ham-
  eln) 122, 94
Hammer 122, Hammers 164,
  Hammermann 94, 94, Ham-
  merer (hammer, hammer
  maker, smith, carpenter) 96,
  106
Hammer, Hammermann 94,
  Hammerer (maker of horse
  collars) 96, 106
Hammer < Hadumar (battle +
  famous) 46, 47
Hammerbacher, Hammerbacker
  159 (hammer brook) 77
Hammerbauer (fr the Hammer-
  hoff, hammer farm) 91
Hammerberg (hammer mountain)
  68
Hammerlein 55 < Hammer
Hammerschlag (hammer blow,
  smith) 96
Hammerschmidt, Hammersmith
  152 (hammer smith) 96
Hammerstedt (hammer city) 122
Hammerstein (hammer stone,
  mountain) 73, 122
Hammeyer, see Halbmeyer
Hammler, see Hamelmann
Hammon, Hamon (OT name) 135
Hampe, Hampel 55 < Hagen-
  brecht (enclosure + bright) 123,
  46
Hampf, see Hanf
Hampfling (hemp grower or
  dealer) 91, 106
Haendler (merchant, huckster)
  105
Han (reeds or swamp) 81, also see
  Hahn
Hanauer, Hannauer (fr Hanau,
  marsh meadow) 122

Hanawalt (marsh wood) 80, 72
Hanback, Hanbeck (marsh creek)
  80, 77
Hance 159, see Heintz
Hand (hand) 114
Handel, Handle 159, Handler,
  Handelsman 94, Handelman
  (trade, trader) 105
Handschuh, Handshu 159 (glove,
  glover) 112, 106
Handschumacher (glover) 96
Handtke 55 (little hand) 114
Handwerk, Handwercker, Hand-
  werger (craft, craftsman) 96
Hanengrath (chicken bone) 117
Hanf (hemp) 91, 106
Hanfeld (marsh field) 80, 84
Hanfling (hemp grower or dealer)
  91, 106
Hang, Hange, Hangg, Hanger
  (slope dweller) 71
Hangarter (slope orchard) 71, 84
Hangleiter, Hangleitner (dweller
  on a steep slope) 71, see
  Hagenleitner
Hangner (fr Hangen 122, slope
  dweller) 71
Hangsleben (slope property) 71,
  127
Hangstorfer (slope village) 71, 123
Hanitsch 53 < Johannes
Hank 53, Hanke, Hankel 55 <
  Johannes
Hanmann, Hannemann, see
  Hahnmann, Hahnemann <
  Johann
Hann, see Hahn
Hanna 53, Hannah < Johann
Hannauer, see Hanauer
Hanneman, Hannemann (follower
  of Hanna) 94
Hanner, see Haener
Hannes 53, Hanns < Johannes
Hannibal (Carthaginian general)

Hans, Hansi, Haensel 55, Hans-
elmann 94, Hansemann <
Johann
Hansa (Hansa)
Hansberger, Hansberry 159
(Hans' mountain) 68
Hanschel 53, 55 < Johannes
Hanschildt, see Hanschel
Hansel 53, 55, Hansele, Hansell,
Hanzel (little John)
Hanselmann (brownie) 134, see
Heinzelmann
Hansen (son of Johann) 59, 134
Hanser, Hanssener, Hansser,
Hanssers 164 (member of
Hanseatic league)
Hansing 53, 55 < Johannes
Hansle 55, see Hansel
Hansman (follower of Hans) 94
Hanson (son of Hans) 59
Hanstein, see Hahnstein
Hantske 53, 55 (Little John)
Hanz, Hanzel, see Hans, Hansel
Hanzer, see Hanser
Hapacher (fr Happach 122,
enclosure brook) 123, 77
Hapelbach (nightshade + brook)
89, 77
Hapelfeld (nightshade + field) 89,
84
Happel, Happolt < Hadebold
(battle + brave) 46, 46
Harbach, Harback, Harbeck,
Herbach (fr Harbach 122,
swamp brook) 81, 77
Harbarth, Harbert, Harbertz 164,
see Herbert
Harbaugh 159, see Harbach
Harbers 164, Harbert, Harberts
164, Harbrecht, see Herbert
Harbold < Haribald (army + bold)
46, 46
Harbst, see Herbst
Harburger (fr Harburg, army
castle) 46, 73, 122
Harcke (rake) 106

Hard, Hardt, Hart, Harth (strong)
46
Hardekop, Hardekopf (hardhead)
115
Harden 53, Hardelen < Hartwig
Hardenberg (wooded mountain)
72, 68
Hardenstein (forest mountain) 72,
73
Harder, Harders 164 (forester) 96
Hardeward (strong + guard) 46,
47
Hardewig, see Hartwig
Hardmann, see Hartmann
Hardner, see Hartner
Hardrich, Hardrick < Hartrich
(strong + rule) 66, 66
Hardt (forest) 72, 122
Hardt, Hardtke 55, see Hirsch
Hardtmann, see Hartmann,
Hirschmann
Harebeck (swamp creek) 80, 77
Haren (swamp) 80, 122
Harenberg (swamp mountain) 80,
68
Harenmann (swamp dweller) 80,
94
Harf (harp, harpist) 96, 106
Harf (man fr Harff in the
Rhineland) 122
Harfner (harpist) 96
Haring (herring, herring dealer)
115, 106
Harje 55, Harjes 164, Harjis <
Hermann, Herwig, etc.
Harkabus (harquebusier) 107, 108
Harke, Harkmann 94 (rake,
raker, rake maker) 96, 106
Harkel 55 (little rake) 106
Harkelroad 159 (little rake
clearing) 126
Harm, Harms 164 (weasel) 115
Harm 53 < Hermann
Harman, see Hermann
Harmar (army + famous) 46; 47

Harmening 53, Harming < Hermann
Harmsdorff 122, see Hermsdorf
Harmsen, son of Harm 59
Harnisch, Harnish 159 (armor, harness) 108
Harnischfeger (armor burnisher) 108
Harniss (armor, harness) 108
Harpe (harp, harpist) 96, 106
Harpst, see Herbst
Harr, see Haar
Harre 53 < Hermann, Herwig, etc.
Harsch (military troop) 107
Harschberger, see Hirschberger
Hart, Hardt, Harth (fr Hart 122, wooded mountain) 72
Hart, Harte, Harter, Hartel 55, Hartsel 94, Hartzel, Hartzell, Hartzel, Hartzler (strong 46), also short for names beginning in Hart.
Hart (stag) 62
Hartel, Hartle 159, see Hart
Hartenbach (muddy brook) 80, 77
Hartenberg (wooded mountain) 68
Hartenstein, Hartstine 159 (wooded mountain) 73, 122
Hartfeld, Hartfelder (fr Hartfeld 122, stag field) 84, see Hirschfeld
Hartge 55 (little stag) 62
Harth 122, see Hart
Harthause, Harthousen 159 (stag house) 62
Harthkopf, see Hartkopf
Hartig, see Hartwig
Harting 53, 55, Hartting, see Hartwig
Harting, Hartinger (place name) 122
Hartje 53, 55, Hartjen, see Hartwig
Hartkopf (hard head) 115

Hartkopf (stag head, house name) 62
Hartlager (fr Hartlage) 122
Hartlaub (forest foliage) 72
Hartleb (forest property) 72, 127
Hartlein 55, Hartline 159 (little stag)
Hartlieb (strong + dear) 46
Hartlieb, see Hartleb
Hartmann (dweller on a wooded mountain) 72, 94
Hartmann (strong + man) 46, 94
Hartmeyer (forest farmer) 72, 93
Hartmueller (forest miller) 72, 103
Hartmut, Hartmuth (strong + disposition) 46, 46
Hartnagel (nailsmith) 96
Hartner (forest dweller) 72
Hartog, see Herzog
Hartranft (hard crust, baker) 96
Hartsel 55, see Hart
Hartshorn (stag horn) 62, 106
Hartsock 159, Hartsook, see Herzog
Hartstein (wooded peak) 72, 73
Hartstein (hard stone) 73
Hartsuck 159, see Herzog
Hartung (strong man) 46
Hartway 159, see Hartweg
Hartweg (path through forest) 72
Hartwig, Hartwigsen 59 (strong + battle) 46, 46
Hartz, Hartze (fr the Harz Mountains), see also Hart
Hartzel 55, see Hart
Hartzfeld (field in the Hartz) 84, see also Hirschfeld
Hartzog, Hartzok, see Herzog
Harwig (army + battle) 46, 46
Harz, see Hartz
Hasch, Hasche (Slavic for Johannes) 134
Hascher, Haschert 74 (policeman) 109
Hase, Has (hare) 5, 115

Hasekamp, Hasenkamp (hare field) 115, 84

Hasel, Hasele (hazel) 89

Haselbach (hazel brook) 89, 77, 122

Haselberger (hazel mountain) 89, 68

Haselbrug (hazel bridge) 89, 71

Haselhorst (hazel hurst) 89, 72, 122

Haselkorn (hazel nut) 89

Haselman, Haselmann (dweller in the hazel) 89

Haselmeyer (farmer in the hazel trees) 89, 93

Haselwander (hazel slope) 89, 71

Hasemann (hare man) 115, 94

Hasemeyer (occupant of the Hasehoff, hare farm) 115, 93

Hasenau, Hasenauer (hare meadow) 115, 84

Hasenbein (hare leg) 114

Hasenberg (hare mountain) 68, 112

Hasenclever (fr Hasenclev, rabbit clover) 122

Hasenei (rabbit egg) 118

Hasenfeld (hare field) 84, 122

Hasenfus (hare leg) 114

Hasenjaeger (hare hunter) 5, 91

Hasenkamp (hare field) 84

Hasenlauer (hare catcher) 91

Hasenpflug (Hate the plow!, guild name) 116

Hasener (hare raiser or catcher) 91, 96

Hasenzahl (rabbit's tail) 115

Hashaar (rabbit hair) 115

Hashagen (hare hedge) 5, 123

Haskamp, see Hasenkamp

Haslack (hare lake) 80

Haslbeck, see Haselbach

Hasler, Hassler (dweller among the hazels) 89

Hasli 55 (little hare)

Haslinger, Hasslinger (fr Hasling) 122

Hasman (hare + man) 94

Haspel (yarn reel, windlas) 106

Haspelhorn (turnstile arm, toll collector) 109

Hasper, Haspert 74 (swamp water) 80

Hass, Hasse (hare, hate) 5

Hassel (fr Hassel 122, swamp) 80, see also Hasel

Hasselbach, Hasselbacher, Hasselbaecher (fr Hasselbach 122, brook running through hazel trees, swampy brook) 89, 80, 77

Hasselhoff (hazel farm) 89, 92

Hasselmann, see Haselman

Hasselmeyer, see Haselmeyer

Hasselwanger (hazel slope) 89, 71

Hassenau, see Hasenau

Hassenpflug, see Hasenpflug

Hassinger (fr Hassingen) 122

Hassler (dweller among the hazel trees) 89

Hasslinger (fr Hasslingen) 122

Hassmann, see Hasmann

Hassner, see Hasmann

Hasso 53 < Hartmann

Hatman, Hatmann, Hattsmann (dweller in the fen) 81, 94

Hatt (fen, bog) 81

Hatto 53 < Haduwulf (battle + wolf) 46, 48

Hattenberger (hill in a fen) 81, 68

Hatz, see Hetz

Haub, Haube (cap, hood, helmet) 106, 108

Haubeil (hewing axe, woodsman) 91, 106

Haubensack (clothing quartermaster) 107, see Hobensack

Hauber, Haubert 74 (cap or hood maker) 96

Hauberger (deforested mountain) 68, see Heuberg

Hauch (breath, hunting cry) 91, also < Hugo
Hauck 53, Haucke < Hugo
Haudt, see Haut
Haueisen (mattock) 106
Hauenstein (Hew the stone!) 116, 122, cf. Steinhauer
Hauer, Hauers 164, Hauert 74 (hewer, chopper) 95
Hauer (wild boar tusk, hunter) 91
Hauf, Hauff, Haufmann (heap, military detachment) 107
Hauf, Hauff (place names) 122
Haufler (trooper) 107
Haug, Hauge, Haugg, Haugk, Haugs 164, Hauk, Hauke < Hugo
Hauhn, see Huhn
Haukamp (deforested field) 84
Haumann (hay dealer) 106, 94
Haumeister (hay ward) 109
Haumesser (hackknife) 8, 106
Haunschild (Hack the shield!, mercenary) 116
Haupt, Haubt (head) 114
Hauptman, Hauptmann (captain) 107
Haus, Hauss, Hausz, Hause, Haussen (house, usually a shortened form) 65
Hausberger (fr Hausberg 122, house mountain) 65, 68
Hauschild, see Haunschild
Hausdorf (house village) 65, 123
Hausemann, Hausener, see Hausmann
Hausen (houses, probably shortened fr some name like Hagenhausen) 65, 122
Hausenbeck (brook amoung the houses) 65, 77
Hausenflug, see Hasenpflug
Hauser, Hausermann 94 (householder) 65
Haushalter (householder) 65

Haushauer (house builder) 65, 100
Hausknecht (domestic servant) 96
Hausleiter (house leader) 65
Hausler, see Haeusler
Hausman, Haussmann (house owner, farmer) 65, 94
Hausner (house owner) 65
Hausrat, Haussrad (household belongings) 65
Hausser, Haussner, see Hauser, Hausner
Hauswald (house forest) 65, 72
Hauswart, Hauswarth (house guardian) 65, 47
Hauswirt, Hauswirth (master of the house) 65
Haut, Hauth, Hautz 164 (skin, hide, skinner) 96, 106
Haut, Hauth, see Hut, Huth
Hauver 159, see Huber
Havel, Havelmann 94 (dweller along the Havel, marsh) 80, 83
Havener, Havenner, see Hafner
Haver (oats) 91, 106
Haverkamp, see Haberkamp
Haverland, see Haberland
Haverle, see Haberle
Havermehle, see Hafermehl
Haverstein (oat mountain) 68
Havervass (oat barrel) 106
Hawffman 159, see Hoffmann
Hayd, Hayde, Hayden, see Heidt, Heide, Heiden
Hayduck, see Heiduk
Hayl, see Heil
Hayler, see Heiler
Hayn, Hayns 164, see Hain
Hayner, see Heiner
Hayser, see Haeuser, Heiser
Hax, see Hack
Heaberlin 55, 159, see Haeberle
Headrich 159, Headrik, see Heidrich
Heagler 159, see Huegler
Heald 159, see Held

Healer 152, see Heiler
Hearl 159, Hearle, see Hoerl
Heartman 159, see Hartmann
Heatterich 159, see Heidrich
Heavener 159, Heavner, see
  Hafner
Heaver 159, see Hueber
Hebenstreit, Hebstreit (Start the
  fight!) 116
Hebbel, see Hebel
Hebeisen (crowbar) 106
Hebel, Hebeler (lever) 106
Hebel (sourdough, baker) 106, 96,
  122
Heber 122, Heberer, Hebeler,
  Hebert 74, Hebermann 94, see
  Hafer, Hafermann
Heber, Heberer (loader, carrier)
  96
Hebermehl, see Hafermehl
Hebigt, see Habicht
Hebner 159, see Huebner
Hech, Hechler (flax hackler) 95
Hechelberger (hackle mountain)
  68
Hecht (pickerel) 115, 106
Heck, Hecke (hedge) 123, 122
Heckel, Heckle 159, Heckler
  (vineyard worker) 96
Heckel, see Hech
Heckenberg (hedge mountain)
  123, 68
Heckendorf (hedge village) 123,
  123
Heckendorn, Heckedorn, Hecke-
  thorn 153 (hedge thorn) 123,
  72
Heckenlaub (hedge leaves) 123,
  89
Hecker, Heckert 74, Heckler,
  Heckner, Heckener, Heckmann
  94 (enclosure dweller) 123
Heckrote, Heckerotte (hedge
  clearing) 123, 126
Hedrich, Hederich, Hedrick,
  Hedricke, see Heidrich

Heckscheer, Heckscher (hedge
  shears) 106
Heckwolt 159 (hedge wood) 123,
  72
Hedwig, see Hadwig
Heer (army) 46 or < Hermann
Heerdt, see Herd
Heeter 159, see Hueter
Hefer, Hefler, Hefner, Heffer,
  Heffler, Heffner, Hefermann 94
  (yeast dealer) 106
Heffner, see Haefner
Heflebower 159 (yeast farmer) 91
Hefright 159, see Hilfreich
Heft, Hefter (clasp maker, buckle
  maker) 96, 106
Hegberg (hedge mountain) 123,
  68
Hege, Hegeman, Heggeman, see
  Hag, Hageman
Hegel, Hegl, Hegeler, Hegler
  (enclosure dweller) 123
Hegen (see Hecke)
Hegenauer, see Hagenauer
Hegendorn, see Heckendorn
Hegelmaier, Hegemeyer (pro-
  prietor of an enclosed farm) 93
Heger, Hegner, Heggler, Heg-
  mann, see Heckmann
Heger (gamekeeper, forester) 109
Hehl, Hehle, Hehler (concealer,
  fence) 96
Hehr (sublime), see also Heer
Hehr (jay) 115
Hehring, see Hering
Hehrmann, see Hermann
Heibel 159, see Huebel
Heiberger, see Heuberger
Heibly 159, see Hueble
Heicher, see Heucher
Heichler (hypocrite) 115
Heickel (fastidious, critical) 115
Heid, Heide, Heidt (heath, hea-
  then) 81
Heidecker, Heideke < Heidenreich
Heidegger, see Heidecker

Heidel (blueberry) 89
Heidelbach (blueberry brook) 89, 77
Heidenman (heath dweller) 81
Heidelbauer (blueberry farmer) 89, 91
Heidemeier, Heidemeyer, Heidmayer (dweller at the Heidehof, heath farm) 81, 93
Heidenberger (heath mountain, heathens' mountain) 81, 68
Heidenman, see Heideman
Heidenreich, Heiderich, Heidrich (heathen?, heath? + rule) 81, 46
Heidt, Heidts 164, see Heid
Heidtman, see Heideman
Heiduk (Magyar infantryman) 107
Heier, Heiert 74, see Heger, Hauer
Heierman, see Heuerman
Heiger (heron) 115
Height 159, 162, see Heid
Heikel, see Heickel
Heil, Heill (fortune, prosperity, blessing) 138
Heiland (the Savior) 140
Heilbrunn, Heilbrun, Heilborn, Heilbronn 122, Heilbronner, Heilbrunner (holy + spring, healing spring) 138, 79, 122
Heilemann (healer) 96, 138
Heiler (healer) 96, 138
Heilig (holy) 138
Heiligenberg (saints' mountain) 138, 68
Heiligendorf (saints' village) 138, 123
Heiligentag (All Saint's Day) 143
Heiligenthal (saints' valley) 138, 76
Heiliger (saint) 131
Heiligmann (holy man) 138
Heilmann, see Heilemann

Heim, Heimer, Heimert 74 (home, hamlet, a shortened form) 123
Heimbach (hamlet + brook) 123, 77, 122
Heimbaugh 159, see Heimbach
Heimberger (fr Heimberg 122, hamlet mountain) 123, 68
Heimbert (home + bright) 123, 47
Heimburg (home castle) 123, 73, 122
Heimgarten (home garden) 123, 84
Heimlich (furtive, secretive) 115
Hein 53, Heine < Heinrich
Heinbaugh 159, see Hagenbach
Heinberg, see Hagenberg
Heinbuch, Heinbuck 159, see Hagenbuch
Heindorf, see Hagendorf
Heinefeld, Heinefield 153, see Hagenfeld
Heineke 53, 55, Heinecke, Heinecken < Heinrich
Heineman 53, 94, Heinemann < Heinrich
Heiner 53, Heinert 74 < Heinrich
Heinfelder, see Heinefeld
Heinhauser (fr Heinhaus 122, grove house) 72, 65
Heinickel 53, 55, Heinkel < Heinrich
Heining 55, 123, Heininger < Heinrich
Heinke 53, 55 < Heinrich
Heinle 53, 55, Heinlein < Heinrich
Heinmann, see Heinemann
Heinmeyer (farmer in the grove) 72, 93, see Hagenmeyer
Heinmueller (miller at the grove) 72, 103
Heinolt, Heinoldt < Heinholt (home + loyal) 47, 48
Heinrich, Heinrichs 164, Heinrick (home + master) 47, 46

Heinritz < Henricius, Latin for
Heinrich 141
Heins, Heinsmann, see Heintz
Heintz, Heintze, Heintzen, Heinz,
Heinze, Heintzler (diminutive
of Latin *Henrizius*, for
Heinrich)
Heintzel, Heintzler, Heintzel-
mann, < Heinrich
Heinzer (follower of Heinz)
Heinzeroth (Heinz's clearing) 126
Heinzmann 94 < Heinrich
Heis, Heiss 122, Heise (hot), see
also Heidenreich
Heisch (hellish) 131, 131
Heischman (devil) 131
Heisel, see Haeusel
Heisemann, Heissmann, see
Hausmann
Heisenberg (scrub forest moun-
tain) 68, 122
Heisenbuettel (scrub forest house)
65
Heisenstein (scrub forest moun-
tain) 73, 122
Heiser (hoarse) 114, see also
Haeuser
Heiser 53 < Heidenrich
Heisler, see Haeusler
Heisner, Heisman, see Hausner,
Hausman
Heiss, Heisse, Heisser (hot) 115
Heissler, see Haeusler
Heist, Heister (young beech tree)
89, 122
Heisterhagen (beech enclosure)
89, 123
Heisterman (dweller among the
beeches) 89
Heit, Heith, Heitz 164, see Heidt
Heitecke (heath field) 81, 84
Heitkamp (heath field) 81, 84,
122
Heitmann, Heitzmann (heath
man) 81, 94
Heitmeyer, see Heidemeyer

Heitz, Heitzler (stoker, fireman)
96
Heizer (stoker) 96, see Haeuser
Hejne, see Heine
Hejduk, see Heiduk
Hejl, see Heil
Hejn, see Hain, Hein, Heine
Hekenturm (tower surrounded by
hedge, *turm* from Latin *turris*)
123
Helbert, see Elbers
Helbig, Helbing, Helbling
(ha'penny) 117
Helbrand, see Hildebrant
Held, Heldt (hero) 46
Heler, see Hehler
Helf, see Helfer
Helfenstein (Stone of Help) 140,
122
Helfer, Helfert 74 (helper)
Helfrich, Hilfreich (helpful) 138
Helge (healthy, fortunate) 155
Hell, Helle (brilliant, bright) 115
Hellauer (bright meadow) 84
Hellbach (bright brook) 77
Helldorfer (bright village) 123
Hellebrand, see Hildebrand
Helleman, Hellemanns 164, see
Heilmann, Helman
Heller, Hellert 74 (small coin fr
Hall) 117
Hellerbran (hell's fire) 131
Helling, Hellinger (fr Helling 122,
see Helbling
Hellinghausen (place name) 122
Hellmann (dweller on a steep
slope) 71, see Heilmann
Hellmer, Hellmers 164 (dweller
on a steep slope) 71, see Hel-
mer, Helmers
Hellstern (bright star)
Hellstrom (bright stream) 77
Hellwage (hell's chariot, the
Great Bear, the Big Dipper)
Hellwege (army road, *strata
publica*) 65, 122

Hellwig, see Helwig
Helm (helmet) 108
Helman, see Heilmann
Helman (devil) 131
Helmbacher (fr Helmbach 122,
    helmet brook) 46, 77
Helmbarth (helmet + battle axe)
    46, 46
Helmbold, Helmboldt (helmet +
    brave) 46, 47
Helmbrandt (helmet + sword) 46,
    46
Helmbrecht, Helmbright 159
    (helmet + brilliant) 46, 47
Helmeister (the devil) 131
Helmer, Helmers 164, Helmert 74
    (helmet maker) 46, 108
Helmer < Hildemar (battle +
    famous) 46, 47
Helmholtz (shaft wood, for spears,
    etc.) 46, 96, 108
Helmke 55, Helmken (little
    helmet) 46, 108
Helmle 55, Helmy 159 (helmet,
    helmet maker) 108
Helmrath (helmet + counsel) 46,
    46
Helmreich, Helmrich (helmet +
    rule) 46, 46, see Himmelreich
Helmstaetter (fr Helmstadt) 122
Helmuth (helmet + disposition)
    46, 46, 49
Helpenstine 159, see Helfenstein
Helschein, Helshine 159 (bright
    sheen)
Helsel 55 (little throat) 114
Helser (lover)
Helt, see Held
Heltzel (forest dweller, woodman)
    96
Heltz, Heltzel 55 (hilt, hilt maker)
    108
Helvenston 159, Helvenstone 153,
    see Helfenstein
Helveti (Helvetian, Swiss) 121,
    141

Helwig, Helwick, Helvig < Hil-
    tiwic (battle + battle) 46, 46
Helzer 159, see Helser
Hembrick 159, see Hambrecht
Hemd, Hembt (shirt) 106
Hemelright 159, see Himmelreich
Hemerich, see Emerich
Hemerlein 55 (little hammer), see
    Hammer
Hemler, see Himmler
Hemmenger (fr Hemmingen) 122
Hemmer (swamp dweller) 80
Hemmerle 55, see Hemerlein
Hemmerichs 164, see Himmel-
    reich
Hemming, see Hambrecht
Hemminghaus (Hemming's house)
    65
Hemmingway < Hemmingweg
    (Hemming's path) 65
Hemmler, see Himmler
Hempel, Hempele, Hemple 159,
    Hempelmann < Hambrecht
Hempel, Hempfling (hemp grower
    or dealer) 91, 106
Hench 53, Henchell < Johann
Hencke 53, 55 < Heinrich
Henckel 53, 55, Henkel, Henkle
    159, Henckels 164, Henckler,
    Hinkel < Heinrich
Henckeljohann (Henry John)
Henckelman 53, 94, Henckel-
    mann < Heinrich
Hendel, see Haendel
Henderer, see Hinderer
Hendler, see Haendler
Hendrichs 164, Henricksmann 94
    < Heinrich
Hendrick, Hendricks 164, Hend-
    riks, Hendrikse < Heinrich
Heneger, see Heinecke
Henel 53, 55 < Heinrich
Hengel, Hengler, see Henkel
Hengst (stallion) 91, 106
Hengstebeck (stallion brook) 77

Hengstenberg (stallion mountain)
68, 122
Henig 53, 55 Hening, Heninger <
Johannes
Henke 53, 55 (little Henry)
Henkel, Henkle 159, Henkels 164,
Hinkel, Henkelman 94,
Henkelmann (handle, see
Henckel)
Henn, Henne, Henny 159 (hen),
or < Heinrich
Henne (place name) 122
Henneberger (fr Henneberg 122,
chicken mountain, Johann's
mountain) 134, 68
Hennecke, Henneckes 164,
Henneken, see Heinecke
Hennel, see Henel
Hennemann, see Heinemann
Hennes 53 < Johannes
Hennig 53, 55, Henniger, Hen-
nick, Henning, Hennings 164,
Henninger < Johann
Hennighausen (John's house) 65
Hennlein 55 (little John)
Henrech, see Heinrich
Henrich, Henrichs 164, Henrick,
Henricks, Henricksen 59, see
Heinrich
Henritz, Henrici (son of Hen-
ricius, Latin for Heinrich) 141
Henry 153, see Heinrich
Hensch, Henschel 55, Henschen,
Henschle 159, Henshel 159, see
Hentsch
Hensel 53, 55, Hensler, Henseler
< Johannes
Henss 53, Henssel 55, Henssler,
Henssmann < Johannes
Hentsch, Hentscher, Hentzschel,
Hentscher (glove maker) 96,
106
Hentz, Henz, Henze, Henzel 55,
Henzell, Hentzel, Henzler <
Johannes

Hepel, Heppler (pruning knife)
106
Herald, see Herold
Herb, Herber (bitter), see Herbert
Herbach (swamp brook) 80, 77,
122
Herberg, Herberger (army +
shelter) 46, 47
Herbert, Herberts 164, Herberth
(army + bright) 46, 47
Herbig, see Herwig
Herbold, Herbolt (army + bold)
46, 46
Herboldtsheimer (Herbold's
hamlet) 123
Herbrand, Herbrandt (army +
sword) 46, 46
Herbrecht (army + bright) 46, 47
Herbst (harvest, autumn) 143
Herd, Herde, Herdt, Herdte
(herd) 95
Herder (herder) 95
Herford 122, Herfurth (army
crossing) 46, 78
Hergenrother (fr Hergenroth) 122
Herger, Hergert 74 (army +
spear) 46, 46
Herget, see Herrgott
Hergott, see Herrgott
Herguth (army + wealth) 46, or
see Herrgott
Herholt (swamp forest) 80, 72, see
Herold
Herich, Herig, see Hering
Hering (herring, seller of her-
rings) 115, 106
Herl 53, 122, Herle, Herlein 55 <
Hermann
Herliberg (glorious mountain) 46
Herling 53, Herlinger < Hermann
Herman, Hermann, Hermans 164,
Hermanus 141 (army + man)
46, 94
Hermsdorf, Hermannsdorfer
(Hermann's village) 122
Hermsen (son of Hermann) 59

Hernberger (the Lord's mountain)
139, 122
Herold 122, Heroldt (army + ruler
46, 46, herold in miracle play
111)
Herr, Herre, Herrn (hoary, senior,
master) 113
Herrdegen (army + thane) 46
Herrenbauer (the Lord's peasant,
monastery servant) 139
Herrgott (Lord God) 117
Herrimann, Herrmann, see
Hermann
Herring, Herrink, see Hering
Herrisperger, see Hirschberger
Herrlich (Splendid!) 117
Herrnknecht (the Lord's servant,
monastery worker) 139
Herrman, Herrmann, see Herman
Herrold, see Herold
Hersberger, see Hirschberger
Hersch, see Hirsch
Herschbach, see Hirschbach
Herschberger (fr Herschberg 122),
see Hirschberg
Herschbrunner (stag fountain) 79
Herschel 55, Herschell (little stag)
Herschfeld, Herschfield 153 (stag
field) 122, see Hirschfeld
Herschfenger (deer catcher) 91
Herschman, see Hirschman
Hersen (millet) 91, 106
Hersh 159, see Hirsch
Hershy 159, see Hirschi
Hert, Herte, Hertel 55, Herthel,
Hertlein, Hertle 159 < various
names beginning in hart)
Hertsch, see Hirsch
Hertter 53, Hertler < Hartwig,
Hartlieb, etc.
Hertwig, see Hartwig
Hertz (heart)
Hertzbach, see Hirschbach
Hertzberg (rosin mountain) 68,
see Hirschberg

Hertzel, Herzels 164 (little heart),
see also Hert
Hertzfeld (fr Herzfeld 122, stag
field) 84, see Hirschfeld
Hertzstein (heart mountain) 68
Hertzstein (stag mountain) 73
Herwagen (army wagon) 46
Herwig, Herweck (army + battle)
46, 46
Herz, see Hertz, Hirsch
Herzag, see Herzog
Herzberg, Hertzberger (fr Herz-
berg 122, heart mountain) 68,
see also Hirschberg
Herzel, see Hertzel
Herzer (resin gatherer) 95
Herzfeld 122, see Hertzfeld
Herzig (sweet, charming) 115
Herzog, Hertzog (duke, army
leader) 46, 109
Herzogin (duchess, man in
duchess's employ) 109
Herzstein (rosin mountain) 73
Heselbach, see Haselbach
Hesler, see Hassler
Heslin 55 (little hare)
Hess, Hesse, Hessen (Hessian)
121, also < Hermann
Hesselbach 122, Hesselbacher,
see Haselbach
Hesselberg (hasel mountain) 89,
68, 122
Hesselgesser (dweller on the
hazel road) 89, 65
Hessler, see Hassler
Hessling, Hesslinger (fr Hesslin-
gen) 122
Hessenauer, see Hasenauer
Hetler, Hettler (goatherd) 91, 95
Hetman, Hettmann (Polish,
captain, fr Hauptmann) 107,
146
Hetrich, Hettrich, Hetterrich, see
Heidrich
Hettel, Hettler, Hettelman (goat,
goatherd) 91

Hettich < Hadebert, battle +
bright 46, 47
Hettinger, Hettner (fr Hettingen)
122
Hetz, Hetzel, Hetzler, Hetzner
(beater on hunt) 91
Hetz 53 < Hermann
Heu (hay) 106
Heubaum (hay tree) 89
Heubeck (hay brook) 77
Heuberger (fr Heuberg 122, hay
mountain) 68
Heubusch (hay bush) 89
Heucher (dweller on a fen) 80
Heuer (this year's wine, vintner)
96, fr Heue 122
Heuermann (vintner) 96
Heugele, see Huegel
Heule (howl)
Heuman, Heumann (hay dealer)
106, 94
Heuse, Heuser, Heuss, see Haus,
Haeuser
Heusler, Heussli 55, Haeussler,
see Haeusler
Heusman, see Hausman
Heusser, see Hauser
Heuwarth (hay ward) 96, 109
Hevener, Hevner, see Hafner
Hever, see Hefer
Heyd, Heyde, Heydt, Heyden, see
Heid
Heydel, see Heidel
Heydeman, see Heideman
Heydrick, Heydricks 164, see
Heidrich
Heyduk, see Heiduk
Heyer, Heyerman 94, see Heuer,
Heuerman
Heyl, Heyler, see Heil, Heiler
Heyland, see Heiland
Heyliger, see Heiliger
Heylmann, Heylemann, see
Heilmann
Heyman, Heymann, see Heine-
mann

Heyn, see Hain, Hein, Heine
Heynemann, see Heinemann
Heys, see Heiss
Heyser, see Heiser
Hibler 159, Hible, Hiblein 55,
Hibbler, see Huebler
Hibscher, Hibschman, see Hueb-
scher, Huebschman
Hice 159, see Heiss
Hickelmann, see Huck
Hickman, see Heckmann
Hide 159, Hides 164, see Heidt
Hiebel, Hiebler, see Huebler
Hieber, Hiebert, see Hueber,
Huebert
Hiebner, see Huebner
Hiegel, see Huegel
Hienreik 159, see Heinrich
Hiepler, see Huebler
Hierl (sword) 46
Hierl 53 < Hermann
Hieronymus, Hieronimus (St.
Jerome) 131
Hiersfeld, see Hirschfeld
Highberger 153, see Heuberger
Highfield 153, see Heufeld
Highler 159, see Heiler
Hight 159, see Heid
Hilberg, Hilberger (hill in swamp)
80, 72
Hilbers 164, Hilbert, Hilbricht,
see Hildebrecht
Hilboldt, Hilbolt (battle + bold)
46, 46
Hilbrand, see Hildebrand
Hild 53, Hildt, see Hildebrand
Hildebrand, Hildebrant, Hilden-
brandt, Hiltenbrandt (battle +
sword) 4, 46, 46, 49
Hildebrecht (battle + bright) 46,
47
Hildeger (battle + spear) 46, 46
Hildemar (battle + famous) 46, 47
Hildemut (battle + disposition)
46, 47

Hildesheimer, Hiltzheimer (fr Hildesheim 122, marsh hamlet) 80, 123
Hildihart (battle + strong) 46, 46
Hildner (swamp dweller) 80
Hildrich, Hildrick (battle + rule) 46, 47
Hildt, see Held
Hildwein (battle + friend) 46, 48
Hile 159, Hiler 159, Hilmann 159, see Heile, Heiler, Heilmann
Hilfrich (helpful) 138
Hilgartner (swamp garden) 80, 98
Hilgenberger, see Heiligenberg
Hilger 122, Hilgers 164, Hilgert 74 < Hildeger
Hill, Hille, Hiller < Hildebrand, Hildeger, etc.
Hillebrand, Hillenbrandt, see Hildebrand
Hillegas, Hillegass (swamp road) 80
Hillen (swamp) 80
Hillenbrand, see Hildebrand
Hillenburg (castle in swamp) 80, 73
Hillferding (fr Hilferding) 122
Hillgard, Hillgartner, see Hilgartner
Hilliger, see Heiliger
Hillikman, see Heiligmann
Hillmann 53, 94, Hillikman < Hildebrand, Hildebert, etc.
Hillmer, 53, Hillmar, see Hildemar
Hillmuth, see Helmuth
Hillsee (holly lake, swamp lake) 89, 81
Hillsinger (fr Hillsing) 122
Hillstrom (swamp stream) 80, 77
Hilmer, see Hildemar
Hilnbrand, see Hildebrand
Hilpert < Hildebrecht (battle + bright) 46, 47
Hilscher (swamp dweller) 80

Hilse (dweller near the holly trees, or near the swamp) 89, 80
Hilseberg (holly mountain) 89, 68
Hilsenbeck (holly brook, swamp stream) 89, 77
Hilsenrad, Hilsenrath (holly clearing) 89, 126
Hiltner (attic)
Hiltz (swamp) 80, 122
Hiltzheimer (swamp hamlet) 80, 123, see also Hildesheimer
Himebaugh 159, Himebook 159, see Heimbach
Himel 159, see Himmel
Himelfarb 159, see Himmelfarb
Himelmann 159, see Himmelmann
Himelsbach 159, see Himmelsbach
Himelright 159, see Himmelreich
Himler 159, see Himmler
Himmel (heaven, sky, probably a house name) 62, 122
Himmelberger (fr Himmelberg 122, heaven mountain) 68
Himmelfarb (sky color) 148
Himmelmann, see Himmler
Himmelreich, Himmelrich (kingdom of heaven) 140
Himmelsbach, Himmelsbacher (swamp brook) 80, 77
Himmelserb (inheritor of the kingdom of heaven) 140
Himmelwright 159, see Himmelreich
Himmer 159, see Hubmeier
Himmler (occupant of Haus zum Himmel) 61
Himpel, Himple 159, Himpler, see Hempel
Hinaman 159, see Heinemann
Hince 159, see Heintz
Hinck, Hincke, Hinckel 55 (limper) 113
Hinck 53 < Heinrich

Hinckel, Hinkelmann 94 (baby
chick) 115, 91
Hinde, Hinda (hind)
Hindeleuthner (fr the backslope)
69, 71
Hinderberger, see Hinterberger
Hinderer, Hindermann 94
(dweller behind the village) 69
Hinderhoffer (occupant of the
Hinderhoff, farm out back) 69,
84
Hindriks, see Hendriks
Hine 159, Hinelein 55, see Hein,
Heinlein
Hinebaugh 159, see Heimbach
Hineman 159, see Heinemann
Hines 159, see Heinz
Hinkel, Hinkle 159, Hinkelmann
94, see Hinckel
Hinnen (dweller "back there") 69
Hinrich, Hinrichs 164, see
Heinrich
Hinsch 53, Hinsche < Heinrich
Hintenach (in pursuit) 69
Hinterberger (fr Hinterberg 122,
fr behind the mountain) 69, 68
Hintz 53, Hintze, Hintzel 55,
Hinz, Hintzman 94, Hintz-
mann, Hinzman < Heinrich
Hiob (OT Job) 135
Hipner, see Huebner
Hipp, Hippe, Hippmann 94
(pruning knife) 106
Hipp 53 < Hildebert 46, 47
Hippel, Hipple 159, Hippler,
Hippelmann (waffel seller) 106
Hippenstiel (pruning knife han-
dle) 106
Hippert 53, see Hildebrecht
Hipsch, Hipscher, see Huebsch,
Huebscher
Hipskind 159 (well-mannered
child) 115
Hirnschal (skull) 114
Hirsch, Hirsche (stag, hart) 48,
62, 63, 149

Hirschbach (stag brook) 77
Hirschbein (deer bone) 48, 106
Hirschberg, Hirschberger (fr
Hirschberg 122, stag mountain)
48, 68
Hirschbiehl, Hirschbuhl, Hirsch-
buehler (stag hill) 48, 67
Hirschblond (stag blond) 112
Hirschburg (stag castle) 48, 73
Hirschenfang (stag catch) 91
Hirschfeld, Hirschfield 153 (stag
field) 48, 84, 122
Hirschhausen (stag house) 48, 65,
122
Hirschheimer (stag hamlet) 48,
123
Hirschhizer 66, see Hirschhausen
Hirschhorn (antlers, deer horn)
48, 62, 106
Hirschi, Hirschy 159 (little stag)
48
Hirschkind (little stag) 48
Hirschle 55 (little stag) 48
Hirschler, Hirschner (stag hunt-
er) 48, 91
Hirschman 94, Hirschmann (stag
man) 48
Hirschstein (stag mountain) 73
Hirse (millet) 91, 106
Hirsh 159, see Hirsch
Hirshauer 159 (fr Hirschau 122,
stag meadow) 48, 84
Hirshbein 159, see Hirschbein
Hirshberg 159, Hirshfeld, see
Hirschberg, Hirschfeld
Hirshi, Hirshy, see Hirschi
Hirshizer 159, see Hirschhizer
Hirt 122, Hirth, Hirtz 164 (shep-
herd, herdsman) 95
Hirtzel 159, Hirzel, see Hirsch
Hiser 159, see Heiser, Haueser
Hisle 159, Hisler, see Haeusle,
Haeusler
Hiss 159, Hisser, see Heis and
Heuss
Hite 159, see Heidt

Hiter 159, see Heiter, Hueter
Hitner, see Huettner
Hitter, see Huetter
Hitz (heat)
Hitz (goat) 91
Hitzelberger (fr Hitzelberg) 122
Hitzler, see Hutzler
Hixenbaugh 159 (Hick's brook)
Hizer 159, 66, see Haeuser
Hobach, Hobeck (high brook) 77
Hobell, Hobelmann 94 (carpent-
er's plane, carpenter) 98, 106
Hobensack (hops sack, hops
dealer) 106
Hober, Hobert 74, Hobart, Hob-
erman 94 < Hadebracht (battle
+ bright) 46, 47
Hoberg, see Hochberg
Hobler (planer, carpenter) 98
Hoblitz, Hoblitzell (Plane little!,
cabinet maker) 116, 96
Hobman, Hobmann, Hobner, see
Hoffmann
Hobt, see Haupt
Hoburg (fr Hochburg 122, high
castle) 73
Hoch (high, tall man) 113
Hochberg (high mountain) 68
Hochbrueckner (fr Hochbruck
122, dweller by the high
bridge) 71
Hochfelden, Hochfellner (fr
Hochfeld 122, high fields) 84
Hochgenug (High enough!) 117
Hochhalter (dweller on a high
slope) 71
Hochhaus (tall house) 65, 122
Hochheim, Hochheimer (high +
hamlet, a city and famous
wine) 123, 122
Hochheiser, Hochhiser 159
(dweller in a high house) 66
Hochhut (high hat) 112
Hochkeppel (high cap) 122
Hochlander (highlander)

Hochman, Hochmann, see Ho-
mann
Hochmut (high spirits, arrogance)
115
Hochnadel (high needle)
Hochrein (high path) 65
Hochreuter (fr Hochreute 122,
high clearing) 126
Hochschild (high shield) 62
Hochstadt, Hochstaedtler (fr
Hochstadt 122, high city, high
shore) 71
Hochstein (high crag) 73, 122
Hochstetter, Hochstettler, see
Hochstadt
Hochwald (high forest) 72, 122
Hochwart (high lookout) 122
Hock, Hocke, Hocken (retailer,
huckster) 105
Hockenbrock (fr Hockenbroich)
122
Hockhaus 159, see Hochhaus
Hockstein 159, see Hochstein
Hodel (wagon cover, huckster
with wagon) 105
Hodler (huckster, ragman) 105
Hoebecke (from Hoebeck) 122
Hoebener, see Huebner
Hoeblich, see Hoeflich
Hoebling (courtier) 92
Hoechst (high place, ridge, name
of city) 122
Hoeck, Hoeckel 55 (huckster) 105
Hoecker, Hoeckert 74 (seller of
foodstuffs) 105
Hoef... , Hoeff.... , see Hof, Hoff
Hoefle 159 (small court, small
farm) 92
Hoefler, Hoeffler, Hoefner (far-
mer) 92
Hoeflich (courtly, courteous) 115
Hoefnagel, see Hufnagel
Hoefner, see Haffner
Hoeh, Hoehn, Hoehne, Hoehner
(heights)

Hoehenholtz (forest on the heights) 72

Hoehl (cave)

Hoehler (dweller near a cave)

Hoehn, see Hoeh

Hoehn (scorn) 115

Hoelle (hell) 131

Hoelscher (maker of wooden shoes) 96

Hoeltz, Hoeltzer, Hoelter, Hoeltzel, Hoeltzle, Hoelzl, see Holtz

Hoener (scorner) 115

Hoenig, see Honig

Hoenstein, see Hohenstein

Hoeper, see Hoepfner

Hoepfel, Hoepflinger (hops dealer) 106

Hoepfner (hops dealer) 106

Hoeppel, Hoeppner, see Hoepfner

Hoerauf (army + wolf) 46, 48, folketymology: "Stop it!" 116

Hoerder, see Herder

Hoerger, Hoeriger (serf) 109

Hoerger (fr Hoergen) 122

Hoering (place name 122), see Hering

Hoerl 53, Hoerle 55, Hoerli, Hoerlein < Hermann

Hoermann, see Hermann

Hoerner (horn maker) 96

Hoernle 55, Hoernlein (little horn)

Hoerich, Hoericks 164, see Herich

Hoersch, see Hirsch

Hoerst (place name) 122, see Horst

Hoertz (place name) 122, see Herz

Hoesler, see Hessler

Hoetz (place name) 122, see Hetz

Hof, Hofe, Hoff (yard, court) 92, 122

Hofacker, Hoffacker, Hoffecker (fr Hofacker 122, field belonging to farm or court) 92, 84

Hofer, Hoffer (farmer) 92

Hofer (fr Hof) 122

Hoffart, Hoffarth (pride, arrogance) 115

Hoffart, Hoffwart (keeper of the court) 109

Hoffbauer (peasant working for court) 92, 91

Hoffberg, Hoffberger, Hoffenberg (court mountain) 92, 68, 122

Hoffecker, see Hofacker

Hoffeiser 159 (farm houses) 92, 65, 66

Hoffeld (court field or high field) 92, 84, 122

Hoffer, Hoffert 74, Hofferth, Hoffhers 164 (manager of a cloister farm 92, fr Hofe 122)

Hoffheintz, Hoffheins (hired hand) 95

Hoffheiser (occupant of the Hoffhaus, farm house) 92, 65, 66

Hoffherr (gentleman of the court) 92

Hoffman, Hofmann, Hoffmanns 164 (courtier, manager of a cloister farm) 92

Hoffmantel (court cloak) 112

Hoffmaster 153, Hoffmeister, see Hofmeister

Hoffmeyer (court farmer, estate manager) 92, 93

Hoffnar, see Hofnar, Hofer

Hoffnagel, see Huffnagel

Hoffner, see Hofer

Hoffpauir, see Hoffbauer

Hoffstadel (farm stable, court stable) 92

Hoffstatt, Hoffstaetter, Hoffstetter, Hoffstaedler (fr Hoffstadt, court city) 122

Hofius, Hoffius (latinized Hoff) 141

Hoflich 159, see Hoeflich

Hofmann, see Hoffmann

Hofmeister (manger of cloister) 92

Hofmeyer, see Hoffmeyer

Hofmiester 159, see Hofmeister
Hofnagel, see Hufnagel
Hofnar (jester, court fool) 96
Hofner, see Hoffer
Hofrichter (court judge) 109
Hofstadter, Hofstetter (fr Hofstadt 122, farmstead) 92
Hofweil, Hofwyl (fr Hofweiler, farm belonging to court) 92, 127
Hogedorn, see Hagedorn
Hogendorf, see Hagendorf
Hogenkamp, see Hagenkamp
Hogel, see Hagel
Hohemeyer (farmer on the heights) 93
Hohenberger (high mountain) 68, 122
Hohenbrink (high hill) 74
Hohenhaus (high house) 65
Hohenholtz (high forest) 72, 122
Hohenloh (high forest) 72, 122
Hohenschilt, see Hochschild
Hohenstein (high crag) 73, 122
Hohenthal (high valley) 76
Hohl, Hohler, Hohlmann (fr Hohl 122, hollow), see Hollmann
Hohlbein, see Holbein
Hohlsteiner (fr Holstein) 121
Hohlweg (sunken way) 65
Hohman 94, Hohmann (tall man, prominent man) 113, 115 see Hofmann
Hohmeyer, see Hoffmeyer
Hohn, Hohne (contempt) 115
Hohn (heights) 122
Hohnholz (high forest) 72
Hohr (place name 122), see Haar
Hoit, see Heid
Holand, Holland, Hollander (Holander) 121
Holbach, Holback 159 (swamp brook) 80, 77, 122, see also Hollebach
Holbein (bowlegged) 114

Holbrunner (elder tree spring) 89, 79
Hold, Holdt, Holt, Holder (loyal, beholden, dear) 48
Holderbaum (elder tree) 89
Holdermann, see Hollmann
Holdorf (elder village) 89, 123, 122
Holemann 159, see Hollmann
Holfeld, Holfelder (swamp field) 80, 84
Holl, Holle (elder tree) 89, 122
Holland, Hollandt, Hollander, see Holand
Hollebach, Hollenbach (swamp tree brook) 80, 77, 122
Holleman, Holliman 159, see Hollman
Hollenbaugh 159, Hollabaugh, Hollobaugh, see Hollenbach
Hollenbach, Hollenback 159, Hollenbeck (swamp brook) 80, 77, 122
Hollender, see Hollander
Hollenschade (elder shade) 89
Hollenschein (elder sheen) 89
Hollenstein (elder mountain) 89, 68
Holler 159, see Haller
Hollerbach (elder brook) 89, 77
Hollinger (fr Hollingen) 122
Hollinger (swamp dweller) 80
Hollkamp (sunken field) 84
Hollman, Hollemann, Holloman, Hollomann (swamp dweller) 80, 94
Hollman (dweller among the elders) 89
Hollstein 122, see Holstein
Holm (crossbeam)
Holm (island) 122
Holmann, see Hollman
Holschuh, Holsche, see Holtzschuh
Holser, see Holtzer
Holsinger, see Holtzinger

Holst, Holste (forest dweller) 72

Holst (fr Holstein) 121

Holstein, Holsteiner, Hollstein, Holsten (fr Holstein) 121

Holster 159, see Holtzer, Holtser

Holston, see Holstein

Holt, Holte, Holth, Holtzer (forest) 72, 122

Holt, Holter, see Hold

Holtgreve (forest warden) 72, 109

Holthaus, Holthausen (forest house) 72, 65, 122

Holthoff (forest farm) 72, 92

Holthus, Holthusen (forest house) 40, 72, 65

Holtkamp (forest field) 72, 84, 122

Holtman, Holtmann (woodman) 72, 94

Holtmeyer (occupant of the Holthoff) 72, 93, 94

Holtscher (wood dealer) 106

Holtschneider (wood carver) 92

Holtschulte (forest magistrate) 109

Holtspan (wood chip, woodcutter) 96

Holtstein, see Holstein

HoltStone 159, see Holtstein

Holtz 122, Holts 159, Holtze, Holtzer (wood, wood dealer) 106

Holtzapfel, Holtzappel (crabapple) 89, 122

Holtzbender (barrel stave maker) 96

Holtzendorf (forest village) 72, 123, 122

Holtzer, Holtser 159, Holtzner (woodman) 72

Holtzhacker (wood cutter) 95

Holtzhauer (wood cutter, woodpecker) 95, 115, 100

Holtzhauser (house in forest) 72, 65, 122

Holtzinger (fr Holtzing 122, belonging to the forest) 72, 59

Holtzman, Holtzmann (woodman) 72, 95, 94

Holtzschuh, Holtzshoe 153 (wooden shoe) 96, 106

Holtzwarth (forest keeper) 72, 109

Holtzworth (wooded river island) 72, 79

Holweg, Holweck, see Hohlweg

Holz ..., see Holtz ....

Holzapfel, see Holtzapfel

Holzbauer (forest farmer) 72, 91

Holzberg 122, Holzberger (forest mountain) 72, 68

Holzborn (forest spring) 72, 79

Holzer, see Holtzer

Holzermann, see Holtzmann

Holzgang (fetching wood) 96

Holzhammer (wooden hammer) 106

Holzhausen 122, Holzhauser, see Holtzhauser

Holzheid (wooded heath) 72, 81

Holzhueter (forest guard) 109

Holzknecht (lumberman) 95

Holzli 55 (little forest) 72

Holzman, Holzmann, see Holtzmann

Holzmueller (sawmiller) 96

Holzopfel 159, see Holzapfel

Holzschmidt (forest smith) 72, 96

Holzschneider (sawyer) 104

Holzschuh, Holzschu, see Holtzschuh

Holzworth, see Holtzworth

Homan, Homann, Homanns 164, see Hohmann

Homberg, Homberger (fr Homberg) 122

Homburg (fr Homburg) 122

Homeister, see Hoffmeister

Homeyer, Homeier, see Hoffmeyer

Hommel 159, see Huml

Homrighausen (town in Wittgenstein) 122

Honacker, see Hohenecker

Honecke, see Hunecker

Honeyman 153, see Honig
Hong 159, see Hang
Honig, Honigs 164, Hoenig, Honik, Hoenik (honey, bee-keeper) 95
Honigsberg, Honikberg (honey mountain) 68
Honnold, see Hunold
Hons 159, Honts, see Hans
Honsa 159, see Hansa
Honstein, see Hohenstein
Hoobler 159, see Huebler
Hooch, see Hoch
Hoof, Hoofman, see Hoff, Hoffmann
Hoofnagel, Hoofenagel, see Hufnagel
Hoogstraten (high street) 65
Hook (point)
Hookheim 159, see Hochheim
Hoop, Hoope, Hoopen, see Hoff, Hauf, Hopf
Hoopengardner, see Hopfengaertner
Hooper 159, Hoopert 74, see Huber
Hooser 159, see Hauser (Huser)
Hoover 159, see Huber
Hoovler 159, see Huebler
Hopack, Hoppacher (hops brook) 77
Hopf, Hopfe (hops) 91, 106
Hopfensack (hops sack) 106
Hopfgaertner (hop grower) 91, 98
Hopfgarten, Hopfengaertner (hops garden) 98, 122
Hoppenfeld (hops field) 84
Hoppenstein (hops mountain) 73
Hoppler, Hoppner, Hoppmann (hops dealer) 106
Hora (Slavic: forest) 146
Horath (place name) 122
Horbach, Herbach (swamp creek) 80, 77, 122
Horberg (swamp mountain, wooded mountain) 80, 68

Horcher (listener, hearer) 115
Hord, Horde (treasure)
Horein (high path) 65
Horenberg (swamp mountain) 80, 68
Horenkamp (swamp field) 80, 84
Horenstein (swamp mountain) 80, 73, see also Hornstein
Horger, see Hoerger
Horich, Horichs 164, see Hoerger
Horlacher (fr Horlach 122, swamp pond) 80
Horlander (swamp land) 81
Horn, Hoerner (fr Horn) 122
Horn (horn, mountain peak, promontory) 68
Horn (wedge of field projecting into forest) 84
Hornbach, Hornbacher, Hornback 159, Hornbake 159, Hornbeck, Hornbecker (brook near peak, swamp brook) 80, 68, 77, 122
Hornberg, Horenberg, Hornberger (fr Hornberg 122, peaked mountain) 68, 68
Horner, Hoerner, Hornemann (horn blower) 96
Horner (dweller near mountain peak) 68
Horner (at end of field) 84
Hornig, Horniger, Hornick, Horning 55 (probably fr Slavic hora, mountain) 68, 146
Hornisch 159, see Harnisch
Hornle 55, Hornlein (little horn) 68
Hornsperger (peak mountain) 68, 68
Hornstein (peak mountain) 68, 73, 122
Hornung (frost, February) 143
Hornung (bastard) 119
Horst (hurst) 72, 122
Horstkamp (hurst field) 72, 84
Horstman, Horstmann (dweller in a hurst) 72, 94

Horstmeyer (farmer at a hurst)
72, 93
Horter, Hortmann, Hortel (trea-
sure keeper) 109
Hose (chainmail leggings, hose)
108
Hospelhorn 159, see Haspelhorn
Hoss, Hosse, Hossen, see Hess
Hossbach, Hossbeck (Hessian
brook) 121, 77
Hosselrode (hazel clearing) 89,
126
Hossler, see Hassler
Hostetter, Hostetler, see Hoff-
stetter
Hoth, Hotter, Hotler, Hottmann
94 (milliner, hat maker) 96
Hotop, Hotopf (Hat off!) 116
Hottenbach, Hottenbacher
(swamp brook) 80, 77, 122
Hottendorf (swamp village) 80,
123
Hottenstein (swamp mountain)
80, 73
Hotzinger (fr Hottzingen) 122
Houch 159, see Hauch
Houck 159, Houk, see Hauk
Houderscheldt 159, see Haun-
schild
Houer 159, see Hauer
Houf 159, Houff, see Hauf
Hough 159, see Hauch
Houpt 159, see Haupt
House 153, see Haus, Hauss
Householder 152, see Haushalter
Houseknecht 153 (domestic
servant)
Housely 159, see Haeusle
Houseman 153, see Hausmann
Housen 159, see Hausen
Houser 159, see Hauser
Housewart 159, see Hauswart
Housewird 159, see Hauswirth
Housewright 159, Houseright, see
Hauswirth

Housman 159, Housmann, see
Hausmann
Houtman 159, see Hauptmann
Houts 159, see Haut
Hovere 159, see Huber
Howarth, see Heuwarth
Hower 159, see Hauer
Howse 159, Howser, Howze,
Howzer, see Haus, Hauser
Hoy 159, see Heu
Hoyden, see Heid
Hoyer (guard, watchman) 96
Hoylmann 159, see Heilmann
Hoyt, see Heid
Hub, Hube, Huben (fr Hub 122,
hide of land) 91
Hubbach, Hubacher (farm brook)
91, 77
Hubbe 53 < Hubert
Hubbel, Hubel (hill) 72
Huber, Hubers 164, Huberd 74,
Hubbert 74, Hueber (cultivator
of one hide of land) 91
Hubert, Huberts < St. Hubertus
(mind + bright) 47, 131, 137
Hubmeier, see Huber
Hubner, see Huber
Hubsch, Hubscher, Hubschman,
see Huebsch, Huebschmann
Hubschmidt, Hubsmith 153
(smith owning one hide of land)
91, 95
Huch 53 < Hugo
Hucht (thicket) 72
Huck, Huckel, Hucker (marsh
dweller) 80
Huckestein (marsh mountain) 80,
73
Hudepohl (hut pond) 81
Hudt, see Hut
Huebel, Huebler (hill) 67
Huebenthal (Hueben Valley 76,
Hueben 122, prehistoric name
of brook) 83
Hueber, Huebner, see Huber

Huebsch, Huebscher, Huebschert 74 (courtly, handsome) 115
Huebschmann (courtier) 92
Huegel, Huegler, Huegeler (hill) 67, 122, see Hugo
Huegelmeier, Huegelmeyer (hill farmer) 67, 93
Huelle (swamp) 80, 122
Huelskamp (marsh field) 80, 84
Huelskamp (holly field) 89, 84
Huelsmann (swamp dweller) 80, 94
Huelsmann (dweller among the hollies) 89, 94
Huemmelmann, see Himmelmann
Huemmer, see Hubmeier
Huene (giant) 62
Huenecke (descendant of the giants)
Huenemeyer (farmer near a cairn) 93
Huepner, see Huber
Huerde (fence gate) 84
Huesmann, see Hausmann
Huessler, see Heussler
Hueter, Huether (keeper, guardian) 96
Huette, Huetter, Huettner (hut, workplace) 65
Huettig (fr Huttingen) 122
Huff (hoof, probably short for Huffschmidt) 96
Huff, see Hoff
Huffaker (small farm) 84
Huffbauer (farmer owning a hide of land) 91
Huffer, Huffert 74 (blacksmith) 96, see Hofer
Huffines, see Hoffheintz
Huffman, Huffmann, see Huber, Hoffmann
Huffschmid, Huffschmidt, Huffschmit (blacksmith) 96
Hufmeister, see Hoffmeister
Hufnagel, Hufnail 153 (horseshoe nail, blacksmith) 96

Hufschmidt, see Huffschmidt
Hug 53, Hugi < Hugo
Hugel, Hugele, Hugeles 164, see Huegel
Hugelsheim (hill hamlet) 67, 123
Hugo (thought, mind) 47
Huhn, Huhner (chicken, poultry dealer) 91, 106
Huhnebein (chicken leg, chicken bone) 114
Huismann, see Hausman
Hullstein, see Holstein
Huls, Hulls, Hulst 74 (marsh, holly) 89, 80
Hulsemann, Hulsmann (marsh dweller, dweller in the holly) 80, 89
Hulsheyser (swamp houses, holly houses) 80, 89, 65, 66
Hulshoff (marsh farm) 80, 92
Hulshoff (holly farm) 89, 92
Hulslander (marsh land) 80
Hults 159, Hultz, see Holtz
Humbert (bear cub + bright) 48, 47
Humboldt (bear cub + loyal) 48, 48
Humburg (bear cub + castle) 48, 73
Huml, Hummel, Hummell (bumblebee, restless person) 115, 122
Hummelbaugh 159 (bumblebee brook) 77
Hummer (lobster) 106
Humpe 53 < Humbert
Humperding < Humbert, follower or descendant of Humbert 123
Humple, see Huml, Hummel
Hunbach (swamp brook) 80, 77
Hund, Hunds 164, Hundt (dog, keeper of the hounds)
Hundert (hundred)
Hundertmark (hundred marks) 117

Hundertpunt (hundred pounds)
114, 117
Hunecker (chicken yard) 85
Hunger (hunger)
Hunger, see Huenecke
Hungerbiehler, Hungerbuehler,
Hungerpiller (hunger hill,
sterile hill) 67
Hungerbrunnen (intermittent
spring) 79
Hunold (young bear + loyal) 48,
48
Hunsberger, see Huntsberger
Hunt, see Hund
Hunt, Hunting (fr the Hunt
River) 83
Huntman, Huntmann, Hunte-
mann (keeper of the hounds)
91
Huntsberger (fr Huntsberg 122,
mountain on the Hunt) 68, 83
Hupf, Hupfl (hops) 91, 106
Hupfauf (Jump up!) 116
Hupfeld, Hupsfeld, Hupfield 153
(hop field) 84
Hupfer (hop dealer) 106
Hupfenstiel (hops pole)
Hupman, Huppman (hops dealer)
106
Huppert, see Hubert
Hursh 159, Hurshman, see
Hirsch, Hirschman
Hurst (thicket 122), also see
Horst
Hurt (hurdle, woven fence) 84,
106, 122
Hurter, Hurther (wattle weaver)
96
Hurtig (swift, brisk) 115
Husch (mine goblin, gremlin)
Husemann, see Hausmann
Husen 122, see Hausen
Husener, see Hausner
Husenfeld (house field) 65, 84
Hushagen (house enclosure) 65,
123

Huskamp (house field) 65, 84
Husmann, Hussmann, see
Hausmann
Huss (Czech: goose) 146
Husselbaugh 159, see Haselbach
Husserle, see Haeusler
Hussmann, see Hausmann
Hut, Huth (hat, hatter) 106
Hut, Huth (herdsman) 95
Huter, Hutmann 94 (guard) 96
Hutmacher (milliner, hat maker)
96
Huttelmeyer (owner of irregularly
shaped farm) 93
Hutter, Huetter (cotter)
Hutter (milliner) 96
Huttner, Huettner (cotter, metal
worker) 96
Hutz, Hutzell, Hutzler (seller of
dried fruit) 106
Huver 159, see Huber
Huyser, see Haeuser
Hybler 159, see Huebler
Hyde 159, Hydes 164, see Heid
Hydrick 159, see Heidrich
Hyer 159, Heyers 164, see Heuer
Hysenhhood 159, see Eisenhut
Hyl 159, Hylman, see Heil,
Heilmann
Hynes 159, see Heinz
Hyser 159, 66 see Haeuser,
Heiser
Hyx 159

# I

Iager, see Jaeger
Ibach (brook, with prehistoric
name *iba* meaning brook or
water) 77, 122
Ibe 159, see Eib
Iberg (water mountain) 68, 122
Ice 159, see Eis
Icenroad 159, Icenrode, see
Eisenrode
Ichinger (fr Ichingen) 122

Ickel, Ickels 164 (fr *ik* meaning water)
Ickle 159, see Eickel
Idleman 159, see Edelmann, Eitel
Iermbruster 159, see Armbruster
Igel (hedgehog) 48
Igelhart (hedgehog + strong) 48, 56
Igelsbach (hedgehog brook) 48, 77, 122
Iglhaut (hedgehog skin, thick skinned) 115
Ihl, Ihle, Ihler (dweller by the Ihle) 83
Ihrich, Ihrig, see Erich
Ihrlick 159, see Ehrlich
Ikeler 159, see Eichler
Ikels 159, see Eichels, Eichholtz
Iler 159, see Eiler
Ilg, Ilgen (St. Aegidius or St. Kilian) 131, 122
Ilgenfritz (Fritz fr Ilgen)
Ilger (fr Ilgen) 122
Illich, Illig, see Ilg
Ilmen (dweller by the Ilm) 79, 83
Ilmenau (meadow on the Ilm) 83, 84
Iln (name of river) 83, 84
Ilnau (meadow along the Iln) 79, 84
Ilrich, see Ulrich
Imbach (in the brook) 69, 77, 122
Imboden (in the valley) 69, 96
Imbs (beeswarm) 91, 95, 122
Imbsweiller (beeswarm village) 123
Im Busch (in the brush) 69, 72, 122
Imdahl (in the valley) 69, 76, 122
Imdorf (in the village) 69, 123
Imel 159, see Immel
Imgarten (in the garden) 69, 84
Imhof, Imhoff (in the farmyard) 69, 92
Imke 55 < Irmin (powerful, pagan god)

Immel 53 < Emmerich
Immenhauser (fr Immenhausen 122, bee house) 65
Immer (river name) 83
Immermann (dweller on the Immer) 83
Immergut (always good) 115, 139
Imthurn (in the tower, *thurn*, fr Latin *turris*) 69
Imwald, Imwold (in the forest) 69, 71
Inderfurt, Inderfurth (in the ford) 69, 78
Indergand (in the rubble field) 69, 84
Inderly 159, see Enderle
Indermuhle (in the mill) 69, 103
Inderwiess (in the meadow) 69, 84
Indorf (in the village) 69, 123, 122
Ingber (spice dealer) 106
Ingel, Ingels 164 (swamp) 80, see Engel, Engels
Ingelhof (swamp farm) 80, 92, see Engelhoff
Ingelmann, see Engelmann
Ingelhard, see Engelhart
Inhalter (proprietor)
Inhoff (in the court yard) 69, 92
Insel 122, Insul (island, fr Latin *insula*)
Inselmann (island man) 94
Interlaken (between the lakes, place in Switzerland, fr Latin *interlacus*) 122
Irlbacher 159 (swamp brook) 80, 77, see Erlebach
Isaac, Isaacs 164 (OT name) 135
Isberg 159, see Eisberg
Ischler (fr Ischel 122, or dweller by the Ische) 83
Ise 159, see Eise
Isemann 159, see Eisemann
Isenberg 159, Isenberger, see Eisenberg, Eisenberger
Isengard 159, see Eisengard

Isenhard 159, see Eisenhard
Isenhour 159, see Eisenhauer
Isenhut 159, see Eisenhut
Isenminger 159, see Eisenmenger
Isenring 159, see Eisenring
Isenschmidt 159, see Eisenschmid
Isensee 159 (iron lake) 82
Isenstadt 159, see Eisenstadt
Iser 159, see Eiser
Iser (dweller near the Iser) 79
Isermann 159, see Eisermann
Isler 159, see Eisler
Isner 159, see Eisner
Israel (OT name) 135
Issel, Isselmann 94 (fr Issel) 122
Ittenbach (place name) 122, 77
Itzig 53 < Isaac
Iunge, see Junge
Izeley 159, see Eise, Eisele
Izlar 159, see Eisler

**J**

Jaac 53, 135, Jaaks 164 < Jacob
Jack 53, 135 Jacke < Jacob
Jackel 55, see Jaeck
Jacker, Jackert 74 (jacket maker) 96
Jackle 55, see Jaeck
Jackman (follower of Jack) 94
Jacob, Jacobs 164, Jacobes, Jacobus 141 (OT name) 135
Jacobi, Jacoby (son of Jacob) 142
Jacobsen, Jacobson, Jacobsohn (son of Jacob) 59
Jaeck, Jaecks 164, Jaeckel 55, Jaekel, Jaeckle, Jaeckli, Jaecklein, Jaegli (little Jacob)
Jaegemeyer (farmer with hunting rights) 91, 93
Jaeger, Jaegger, Jaegerl 55, Jaegermann (hunter) 91
Jaegerschmidt (smith with hunting rights) 91, 96
Jaeggli 55, see Jaeck
Jaekel 55, see Jaek

Jaeschke 55 < Johannes
Jaffé (OT Japhet) 135
Jag (hunt, hunter) 91
Jagdhuber (farmer with hunting rights) 91, 92
Jagdman (hunter) 91
Jager, Jagerman 94, Jagmann, Jagler, see Jaeger
Jahn, Jahns 164 < Johann
Jahnke, Jahncke (little John) 55
Jahr, Jahren (year)
Jahrhaus < Gareis (wrought iron, smith) 96
Jakob, see Jacob
Jakobi, see Jacoby
Jan, Jans 164 < Johann
Jandorf (John's village) 123
Janing 55, Janning, Jannings 164 < Johann
Jans, see Gans
Janse, Jansen, Janssen, Janssens 164, Janson (son of John) 59
Jantz, Jantzen, Janz (son of John) 59
Jauch (liquid manure, peasant) 112
Jauchler (spreader of manure) 96
Jaul, see Gaul
Jauss < Josef, Jost
Jedermann (Everyman, in miracle plays) 111, 94
Jeeter 159, see Jeter
Jegelhardt 159, see Igelhard
Jeger, see Jaeger
Jehle 53 < Ulrich
Jehrling (yearling, annual)
Jelling (Slavic: stag, elk) 146
Jenner (January) 143
Jenning 53, 55, Jennings 164 < Johann
Jensch 53, Jentzsch, Jentz < Johann
Jensel 53, 55, Jensen < Johann, see also Gensel 134
Jentsch < Johann
Jergen 159, see Juergen

Jeschke 53, 55 < Johannes
Jeter, Jeters 164, Jetter (weeder,
  gatherer) 95
Jingling 159, see Juengling
Jmhof, see Imhof
Joachim, Jochem, Johen (OT
  name) 135
Job 153, see Hiob
Jobst 164, 74 < OT Hiob (Job) 135
Joch (yoke, mountain pass) 68
Joder (Theodor) 131
Joel, Joell (OT name) 135
Joellenbeck (dirty brook) 77, 122
Joerg, Joerge, Joerger, Joergens
  59, Joerk, Joerke ( St. George)
  135
Johan, Johann, Johannes (John)
  135
Johanknecht (servant John) 139
Johansen, Johannssen (son of
  John) 59
John 53 < Johann
Johnsen, Johnson (son of Johan)
  59
Johst, see Jost
Jonas (OT Jonah) 135
Jonck, see Jung
Joncker, see Junker
Jong, see Jung
Jonger, see Junger
Jontz, Jontzen < Johannes
Joost, see Jost
Jordan (OT name) 135, 122
Jorge, Jorgen, Jorgens 164, see
  Joerg
Joseph, Josef (NT name) 131
Jost (St. Jodocus) 131
Jucker (swamp dweller) 80, see
  Junker
Jud, Jude, Judd, Judmann 94
  (Jew) 121
Judenburg (Jew castle) 73
Judi 159, see Tschudi
Juengling (youth) 113
Juengst (youngest) 113
Juergen, Juergens 164 < Georg

Juergensen, son of Juergen 59
Juhl, Jule, Jul (Yule) 143
Juker, see Junker
Julig (fr Juelich) 121
Julius (Latin name) 141
July (July) 143
Juncker (young lord, squire) 109
Jung, Junge (young) 113
Jungandreas (young Andrew) 113
Jungblud, Jungblut (young
  blossom) 89
Junge, Junges 164 (youth) 113
Junger, Jungers 164, Jungert 74
  (youth, disciple) 113
Jungfermann (convent servant)
  139
Junggust (Young Augustus) 113
Junghahn, Junghane (young
  rooster) 91
Junghans (John the younger) 113
Junghaus (young house) 65
Junginger (young man) 113
Jungk, see Jung
Jungling, see Juengling
Jungman, Jungmann (young
  man) 113
Jungreis (new branch)
Jungst (youngest) 113
Junk, see Jung
Junker, Junkermann 94, see
  Juncker
Jupp < Joseph 131
Jurgen, Jurgens 164, Juergensen
  59, see Juergen
Juss 53, Jusse < Justus, Jodocus
Just, Justus (Latin name, "just")
  141, see also Jost
Justice 159, see Justus

### K

Kaal, see Kahl
Kaatz, see Katz
Kabel (cable, lot for drawing,
  river name) 83, 122, see also
  Gabel

Kachel, Kachele (tile, tile maker) 96, 106

Kachler, Kachner (tile maker, potter) 96

Kade (swamp) 122

Kaefer (beetle, perseverant person) 115

Kaeferstein (beetle mountain) 73

Kaegel, see Kegel

Kaehle, Kaehler, see Kehle, Kehler, Koehler

Kaelber, see Kalb

Kaemerlin 55, Kaemerling (court servant)

Kaemmel (occupant of house *zum Kaembel*, "to the Camel") 62

Kaemmerer (chamberlain, treasurer) 109

Kaes, Kaess, Kaese (cheese, fr Latin *caseus*) 105, 106, 112

Kaesemeyer (cheese farmer) 93

Kaessler, see Kessler

Kaestner (chest maker) 98

Kaestner (manager of the granary) 109

Kaeufer (purchaser), see also Kofler

Kafer 159, see Kaefer

Kafka (Czech: jackdaw) 115, 143

Kagle 159, see Kegel

Kahl, Kahle, Kahler, Kahlert 74 (bald, fr Latin *calvus*) 114

Kahlbach (muddy brook) 80, 77, see Kaltenbach

Kahlbaugh 159, see Kahlbach

Kahlberg, Kahlenberg (bald mountain) 68, 122

Kahler, see Kohler

Kahm, see Kamm

Kahn, Kahns 164 (rowboat)

Kahn, see Cohn

Kahnbach (rowboat brook) 77

Kaigler 159, see Kegler

Kail, Kailer, see Keil, Keiler

Kaiser, Kaisser (emperor, fr Latin *caesar*)

Kalb, Kalbe (calf) 91

Kalbaugh 159, see Kahlbach

Kalberer (calf raiser or dealer) 91, 106

Kalbfleish (calf meat, veal, butcher) 96

Kalbfuss (calf foot, butcher) 96

Kalbskopf (calf's head) 114, 62

Kalcher (chalk maker, fr Latin *calcarius*) 96

Kalckbrenner, see Kalkbrenner

Kaldenbach, see Kaltbach

Kaler, see Kahler

Kalichmann (chalice maker, fr Latin *calix*) 96

Kalkbrenner (lime burner) 96

Kalkbrunn (chalk spring) 79

Kalk, Kalker, Kalkmann 94, Kalkus 141 (lime maker, fr Latin *calx*) 96

Kall, Kaller, Kallert 74, Kallner, Kallman 94 (dweller by a stream) 77

Kallemeyer, Kallmeyer, Kallmyer 159 (farmer on a stream) 77, 93

Kallenbach 122, see Kaltenbach

Kallenberg, Kallenberger (stream mountain) 77, 68

Kallenstein (stream mountain) 77, 73

Kalman, see Kall

Kalmbach, Kalmbeck, see Kaltenbach

Kalteisen (cold iron, smith) 96, 122

Kaltenbach, Kaltbacher, Kaltenbacher, Kaltenbacker, Kalterbach (cold brook) 77, 122

Kaltenbaugh 159, see Kaltenbach

Kaltenborn (cold spring) 79, 122

Kalp, see Kalb

Kalthof (cold farm) 92, 122

Kaltreider, Kaltrider 159 (cold clearing) 126

Kaltschmidt (coppersmith, kettle smith) 96

Kaltwasser (cold water)
Kalwe (bald, fr Latin *calvus*) 114
Kamber (comb maker) 96
Kamerer, see Kammerer
Kamm (ridge of mountain) 68
Kamm (comb, combmaker) 96, 106
Kamman (comb maker) 96, 106
Kammer (chamber, fr Latin *camera*) 122
Kammerad (comrad)
Kammerdiener (valet) 109
Kammerer, Kammerle, see Kaemmerer
Kammermann (chamberlain, administrative official) 109
Kammermann (dweller on a ridge) 68, 94
Kammeyer (farmer on a ridge) 68, 103
Kamner (comb maker) 96
Kamp, Kampe, Kamps (field, fr Latin *campus*) 84, 122
Kampenmueller, Kampfmueller (miller with a cogwheel) 84, 103
Kamper, Kampmann 94 (champion, fr Latin *campus*) 84
Kampf, Kampfer (struggle, struggler, fr Latin, *campus)*
Kamphaus (field house) 84, 65, 122
Kamphoefner (fr the Kamphoff, field farm) 84, 92
Kampmayer, Kampmeyer (field farmer) 84, 93
Kamrath (ridge clearing) 68, 126
Kamrath (cogwheel) 96
Kandel, Kandell, Kandelin 55 (pitcher) 106, 122
Kandlbinder (pitcher maker) 96
Kangiesser, see Kannengiesser
Kann, Kanne (can, pitcher, fr Latin *canna*) 106
Kannenberg (pitcher mountain) 68, 122

Kannengiesser, Kannengieser, Kannengieszer (pewterer) 96
Kant, see Gand
Kantor, see Cantor
Kantzler (chancelor, fr Latin *cancellarius*) 109
Kapfer (gazer)
Kapfer (dweller at a mountain peak) 68
Kaplan, Kaplon 159 (chaplain) 110
Kapp, Kappe, Kapps 164, Kappenmann 94 (cowl maker, Capuchin monk) 96, 106, 110
Kappe (hill) 68
Kappel (chapel, place in Switzerland) 122
Kappeler, Kappelmann (cap maker) 96
Kappler (monk, occupant of a chapel) 110
Kappus (cabbage farmer, fr Latin *caput*) 91
Kaps, see Kappus
Karch, Karcher, Karchner (carter, fr Latin *carruca*) 96, see also Karg
Karg, Karger (clever, stingy) 115
Karinther (Carinthian) 121
Karl, Karle (man, Charles, cloister servant) 139
Karlbach (Charles' brook) 77
Karli (son of Karl) 142
Karmann (basket maker) 96, 94
Karp 53 < St. Polycarp 131
Karp (carp) 115
Karsch (lively, merry) 115
Karseboom, see Kirschbaum
Karsner, see Kirschner
Karst, Karsten, Karstner, Karstmann 94 (mattock) 106
Karst (bare alpine land)
Karst (Christian) 131
Kas, Kase, Kass, see Kaes, Kaese, Kaess

Kaschenbach (cherry brook) 89,
77
Kasekamp (cheese field) 84
Kasemann (cheese dealer) 106
Kasemeyer (folk-etymology fr
Casimir), see Kaesemeyer
Kasmann, see Kasemann, Gass-
mann
Kaspar, see Caspar
Kassebaum (chestnut tree) 89
Kassel, Kassler, Kasselmann (fr
Kassel) 121, 122
Kastendiek, Kastendyk (chestnut
dike) 89, 81
Kastner, see Kaestner
Kastor (Latin *castor*, beaver,
Bieber) 141, 122
Kat, Katt, Katte, Kattner, Kath-
mann 94 (cotter)
Katterfeld (fenced field) 84
Kattermann, see Gattermann
Katz, Katzen (cat) 115
Katz (fr Hebrew *Kahanzedek*
priest) 110, 147
Katzenbach, Katzenbacher
(swamp brook) 80, 77, 122
Katzenberg, Katzenberger (cat
mountain) 68, 122
Katzenelnbogen (cat's elbow,
probably folk-etymolgy fr
Celtic) 3, 4, 122
Katzenmayer, Katzenmeyer,
Katzmeier (fr the Katzenhof,
swamp farm) 93
Katzenstein, Katzenstine 159 (cat
mountain) 73, 122
Kaub 122, Kaube, Kaubes 164
(bullrushes) 81
Kauder, Kauders 164 (fr Chur in
Switzerland) 122
Kauf, Kauff, Kauffer (purchase,
merchant, fr Latin *caupo*) 105
Kaufler, Kauffler (inhabitant of a
*Kofel*) 67
Kaufmann, Kauffman (merchant)
105

Kaul (swamp) 80
Kaulbach (swamp brook) 80, 77,
122
Kaulfuss (clubfoot) 114
Kaup, Kaupp (merchant) 105
Kautz (screech owl) 115, 122
Kayler 159, see Kehler, Koehler
Kayser, see Kaiser
Kazmier 159, see Kaesemeyer
Keabler 159, see Kuebler
Keagle 159, see Kegel
Keane 159, see Kuehn
Keasel 159, Keasler, see Kiesel,
Kiessler
Keating 159, see Gueting
Keaver 159, see Geber, Kieffer
Keber, see Geber
Kebhart 159, see Gebhard
Keck (lively) 115
Keebler 159, see Kuebler
Keefer 159, see Kieffer
Keefover 159, Kefauver, see
Kiefhofer
Keehn 159, Keehner, see Kuehn,
Kuehner
Keel 159, Keeler, see Kuehl,
Kuehler
Keen 159, Keene, Keener, see
Kuehn, Kuehne, Kuehner
Keenaple 159 < Kienappel (pine
cone)
Kees, Keesen < Cornelius
Keesler 159, see Kiessler
Keeting 159, see Gueting
Kegel, Kegelmann (illegitimate
child) 119
Kegler (ten-pin player)
Kehl, Kehle (throat) 114, also <
Wolfskehl 122
Kehl (narrow gorge) 76
Kehler (fr Kehl, swamp) 122, see
also Koehler
Kehr, Kehrs 164, Kehrer, Kehr-
mann 94 (dweller on the Kere)
83, 122
Kehs, see Kaes

Keibler 159, see Kuebler
Keichenmeister 159, see Kuech-
enmeister
Keicher (gasper, wheezer) 114
Keidel (course or misshapen
person) 115
Keifer 159, see Kieffer
Keil (wedge, woodchopper) 95
Keiler (wild boar) 115, 91
Keilhauer (boar tusk) 91
Keilhauer (woodcutter) 95
Keilholtz (wedge for splitting
wood, wood chopper) 95
Keillor 159, see Keiler
Keim (germ, sprout)
Keim 53 < Joachim 135
Keiper, Keipert 74 (fish netter) 91
Keiser, Keisser, see Kaiser
Keisersmith 159 (imperial smith)
110
Keisler, see Kessler
Keiss 159, see Kies
Kelbaugh 159 (swamp brook) 80,
77
Kelberman (calf dealer) 91, 106
Kelch, Kelchner (chalice, calice
maker, fr Latin *calix*) 96
Kell, Kelle (ladle, trowel, mason)
106, 122
Kelle (swamp) 81
Kellenberger (fr Kellenberg,
swamp mountain) 81, 68, 122
Keller, Kellers 164, Kellner
(cellar, cellar master, fr Latin
*cellenarium*) 102, 122
Kellerhouse 153 (cellar house) 65
Kellermann, Kellermeyer (butler,
keeper of the cellar) 102, 94, 93
Kellner, Kelner, see Keller
Kelly 159, see Kell
Kelnoffer (swamp farmer) 81, 92
Kelsch, Koelsch (from Cologne)
122
Kelteisen, see Kalteisen
Kelter, Keltner (winepress,
vintner, fr Latin *calcatura*) 96

Kem, Kemler, Kemmler, Kemmer,
Kemner, Kemmacher (comb
maker) 96, 106
Kemerer, see Kaemmerer
Kemmel (resident on a ridge) 68
Kemmel, see Kam
Kemp, Kempe, Kempel, Kempf,
Kempfer, Kemper, Kemperle,
Kemphfer 159, Kemperly 159
(champion) 84
Kempt, Kempter (fr Kempten)
122
Kendel, Kendal 159 (fr Kenel) 122
Kenimer 159, Kenimar, see
Genheimer
Kenner (connoisseur) 115
Kenpf, see Kemp
Kensler 159 < Kentzler (chance-
lor)
Kentner (Slavic: stand for beer
and wine barrels) 146
Kentner (fr Kenten) 122
Kentzel 159 (raised ground) 68,
see Kuentzel
Kephart 159, see Gebhard
Keplinger, see Kepplinger
Keppel, Kepple 159, Keppler,
Kepler, Kepner (cap maker, fr
Kappel) 96, 106, 122
Keppelhoff (chapel court) 156
Kepplinger (fr Kepplingen)
Kerbe (notch, score, taverner) 96
Kerber (basket maker) 96
Kerch ..., Kerck, see Kirch ...
Kerchner, see Kirchner
Kerg, Kerge, Kerger, see Karg
Kerhart 159, see Gerhard
Kerker (prison, fr Latin *carcer*)
Kerkhof 92, 122, see Kirchhoff
Kerkhuis (church house) 65
Kerkner, see Kirchner
Kerl (fellow, rascal) 115
Kermes, Kermisch (kermess,
church festival) 143
Kern (kernel)
Kern (handmill) 103, 122

Kernberg, Kernberger (mill
  mountain) 103, 68, 122
Kernebeck (swamp stream) 80, 77
Kernenbeck (miller of coarse
  grain) 103
Kerner (carter) 96, see also
  Koerner
Kersch 122, Kerschner, Kersch-
  man, see Kirsch, Kirschner,
  Kirschman
Kerschbaum (cherry tree) 89, 122
Kerschensteiner (cherry stone)
  89, 73
Kerschner, see Kuerschner
Kerse, Kerser (Christian) 140
Kershbaum 159, see Kirschbaum
Kerst, Kersten (Christian) 139,
  see also Gerst
Kerzner (candle maker) 96
Kesbauer, Kesemeyer (swamp
  farmer) 80, 91
Kese, see Kaese
Keslar, Kesler, see Kessler
Kessel, Kessell, Kessels 164
  (kettle, kettle maker or bur-
  nisher, fr Latin *cattilus*) 101
Kesselring (kettle hook, cook) 106
Kessler (kettle maker, tinker) 96
Kestenbaum (chestnut tree) 89
Kestenberg (chestnut mountain)
  89, 68
Kestenholtz (chestnut wood,
  cabinet maker) 89
Kester, Kesster, Kestner, Kestler,
  Kestermann, see Kaester
Ketchindaner 159, see Getzend-
  anner
Ketelhut (kettle lid) 96, 106
Kettelberger (kettle mountain) 68
Kettenring (chain mail) 108
Ketter, Ketterer, Kettler, Kettner
  (chain maker, fr Latin *catena*)
  96
Ketzer (heretic, fr Latin *Cathari*)
Keuler (mallet maker) 96
Keusch (pure, virgin) 115

Keyl, see Keil
Keyser, Keysers 164, see Kaiser
Kibler 159, Kiebler, see Kuebler
Kiefer, Kiefere, Kieffer, Kjefner,
  Kieffner, Kiefert 74 (cooper, fr
  Latin *cuparius*) 96, 101
Kiefhofer (fr the Kiefhof, pine
  farm) 89, 92
Kieger 159, see Geiger
Kiehl, Kuehl (cool)
Kiehn, Kiehner, see Kuehn
Kiehnle 55, Kienke 55 (little pine)
  89
Kienast (pine branch) 89
Kienholdt (pine forest) 89, 72
Kienz, Kientz 159, see Kuentz
Kies, Kiess (pebbles)
Kiesel, Kiessel, Kieseler, Kiesling,
  Kiessling (pebbles)
Kieselhorst (pebble hurst) 72, 122
Kieser, Kiesler (beverage taster,
  weight tester) 109
Kiesewetter ("Check the weath-
  er!") 116
Kiesselbach (pebble brook) 77,
  122
Kiessling (dweller in the pebbles
  or gravel) 122
Kifer 159, Kiffer, see Kieffer
Kihl 159, see Kuehl
Kihn 159, see Kuehn
Kilberg, see Kilchberg
Kilchberg (church mountain) 68,
  122
Kilchenstein (church mountain)
  73
Kilcher (chief cleric in a church)
  110
Kile 159, Kiler, see Keil, Keiler
Kilgen, Kilian, Killian (St. Kilian,
  Irish monk) 131
Kimmel, Kimmell, Kimmelman
  94, see Kuemmel
Kimmerle 55, see Kuemmerle
Kimpel 159, see Guempel
Kince 159, see Kuentz

Kind, Kindt, Kindl 55, Kindle 55,
Kindlein 55, Kinder (child)
Kindermann (schoolmaster) 96,
94
Kindsvater, Kindervater (baptismal sponsor) 119
Kinn, Kinlein 55 (chin) 114
Kinsberger 159, see Guenzberg
Kinsbrunner 159 (Guenther's
well) 79
Kinsel 159, see Kuenzel
Kinnss 159, see Kuentz
Kinstler 159, see Kuenstler
Kintz 159, Kintzel, Kintzer, see
Kuentz, Kuentzel, Kuentzler
Kinzinger (fr Kinzingen) 122
Kipp, Kippe, Kipper, Kippers 164
(dweller on the Kippe) 83
Kippenberg (marsh mountain) 80,
68
Kippenberg (mountain on the
Kipper) 84, 68
Kippenbrock (brake on the Kippe)
83, 80
Kirbach, see Kirchbach
Kirberger, see Kirchberg
Kirch (church, dweller near the
church) 71
Kirchbach (church brook) 77, 122
Kirchberg, Kirchberger (church
mountain) 68, 122
Kirchenbauer (church builder) 96
Kirchbauer (peasant on glebe
land) 139, 91
Kircher, see Kirchner
Kirchgaessner, Kirchgesser,
Kirchgessner (dweller on
church alley) 65
Kirchhausen (church houses) 65,
122
Kirchhof, Kirchhoff, Kirkhof,
Kirchhoffer (church yard,
cemetery) 8, 71, 92, 122
Kirchman (sexton) 110
Kirchmeier (glebe farmer) 139, 93

Kirchner (employee of church,
dweller near church) 71, 110
Kirchoff, see Kirchhoff
Kirck, Kircke, Kirckner, Kirkner,
see Kirch, Kirche, Kirchner
Kirk... , see Kirch
Kirn, Kirner (swamp) 80, see
Kern, Kerner, Koerner
Kirsch (cherry, fr Latin *ceresia*)
89
Kirschbaum, Kirschenbaum
(cherry tree) 89, 122
Kirschenhofer (fr the Kirschhof,
cherry farm) 89, 92
Kirschensteiner (cherry stone) 89,
73
Kirscher, Kirschner, see
Kuerschner
Kirschermann, Kirschenmann,
Kirschman (cherry grower or
dealer) 89, 106
Kirschner, see Kuerschner
Kirschstein (cherry stone) 89, 73
Kirsh ...159, see Kirsch ...
Kirsh 159, Kirshman, Kirsher,
etc., see Kirsch etc.
Kirst, Kirsten (Christian) 131
Kirts 159, Kirtz, see Kuertz
Kiselburgh 159 (gravel castle) 73
Kiser 159, see Kaiser
Kisner 159, Kissner, see Kistner
Kissinger (fr Kissing or Kissingen, swamp area) 80, 122
Kist, see Christian
Kister, see Kuester
Kister, Kistner, Kistler, Kistenmacher (chest maker, fr Latin
*cista*) 96
Kitsintander 159, see Getzendanner
Kittel, Kittle, Kittelmann, Kittleman 159 (smock, baker,
miller, etc.) 112, 106
Kittner, Kittler (monk, smock
wearer, smock maker) 112, 96,
110

Kitz, Kitzer, Kitzmann 94 (kid,
goatherd) 91, 95
Kitzbiehl, Kitzbuel (goat hill) 67
Kitzing, Kitzinger (fr Kitzing) 122
Kitzmiller (kid miller) 103
Kitzover (kid farm) 92
Klaas 53 < Nikolaus
Klaff (gossip) 115
Klaeger (public prosecutor) 109
Klaffenbach (resounding brook)
77, 122
Klag, Klage, Klager (complaint,
complainant) 115
Klamm, Klamman 94 (dweller in
a gorge) 76
Klang (sound)
Klapf (cliff) 68
Klapp (shutter, trapdoor)
Klapp, Klapper, Klappert 74
(gossip) 115
Klappauf (Open up!) 116
Klapproth (clearing in the Hartz
Mountains) 126
Klar, Klaar, Klarr, Klahr (clear)
115
Klarmann (man of rectitude) 115,
138, 94
Klas 53, Klaas, Klass, Klassen,
Klaus < Nikolaus
Klatthaar, see Glatthaar
Klatzkopf (bald head) 114
Klaucke (wise man) 115
Klaue (claw, cloven hoof) 114
Klauenberg, Klaunberg (claw
mountain) 68, 122
Klaus 53, Klauss < Nikolaus 122
Klause, Klausen 122, Klauser,
Klausener, Klausmann,
Klaussner, Klausler (hermit's
cell, hermit, fr Latin *clausum*)
110
Klause (gap) 68
Klausmeyer, Klausmayer, Klau-
smeier (farmer near hermit's
cell, in a gap) 103
Klausmier 159, see Klausmeyer

Kleamann 159, see Klehmann
Kleb, Klebe, Klebes 164, Kleber,
Klebert 74 (dweller in a damp
place) 80
Kleber, Klebert 74 (plasterer) 96
Klee 53 < Nikolaus
Klee (clover) 89
Kleebach (clover brook) 89, 77
Kleebauer (clover farmer) 89, 91
Kleeberg (clover mountain) 89,
68, 122
Kleefeld (clover field) 89, 84, 122
Kleefisch (fr Cleves) 121
Kleepuhl (clover pond) 89, 80
Klees 53 < Nicklas
Klef (cliff) 122
Kleger, Klegermann, see Klaeger
Klehmann (plasterer) 96, 94
Kleiber (clay plasterer) 96
Kleid, Kleidlein 55, Kleiderlein
(clothing, clothier) 96, 106
Klein, Kleine, Kleiner, Kleines
164, Kleinert 74, Kleinle 55,
Kleinlein, Kleinmann 94,
Kleinmeyer 103 (small, little)
113
Kleinbach (small brook) 77
Kleinbaum (small tree) 89
Kleinberg (small mountain) 68,
122
Kleindienst (corvée service) 139
Kleinfeld, Kleinfield 153, Klein-
feldt, Kleinfelder, Kleinfelter
(small field) 84, 122
Kleinhammer (small hammer,
carpenter) 96, 122
Kleinhans (Little John, John the
younger) 113
Kleinhauf (small heap, small
troop) 107
Kleinhaus (fr Kleinhausen 122,
small houses) 65
Kleinheinz (little Henry) 113
Kleinhenn (small hen) 115
Kleinjohann (small John, John
the younger) 113

Kleinknecht (secondary hired hand) 95

Kleinkopf (small head) 114

Kleinman (small man) 113

Kleinmichel (little Michael, Michael the younger) 113

Kleinpeter (little Peter, Peter the younger) 113

Kleinschmidt, Kleinsmith (locksmith) 96

Kleinschrot (small grain, groats, miller) 103

Kleinsteuber (fine dust)

Kleis 53, Kleiss < Nikolaus

Kleist, Kleistner (paster) 96

Klem 53, Klemm, Klement, Klementz < St. Clementius 131, 94 (name of pope)

Klemann, Kleemann, Klehmann < St. Clementius 131

Klemm, Klemme, Klemmer (penurious, stingy) 115, see Klempner

Klemmich, see Kleinmichel

Klempner (tinsmith) 96

Klenck, Klenk, Klencker, Klenkel 55 (dweller by a marsh pool) 80

Klepp, Klepper, Kleppner, Kleppert 74 (gossip, calumniator) 115

Klepper (nag, jade; tenant who pays in horses) 91

Klette (bur)

Kletter (hanger-on) 115

Kliebenstein (Split the stone!, quarryman) 116

Klimper, see Klempner

Klinbach 159, see Kleinbach

Klinck, Klincken (dweller by a marsh pool) 80

Kline 159, see Klein

Klinedienst 159, Klinedinst, see Kleindienst

Klinefelter 159, see Kleinfeld

Klinejohn 153, see Kleinjohann

Kling, Klinge, Klinges 164 (deep gorge with noisy stream) 76, 122

Klingebuhl, Klingebuehl, Klingebiel (gorge hill) 76, 84

Klingehoffer, Klingenhoffer, Klingenhofer, Klingelhofer, Klingelhoefer, Klingelover (fr the Klingehoff, gorge farm) 76, 92

Klingel, Klinkel (small bell) 106

Klingelhofer, see Klingehoffer

Klingelschmidt (bell smith) 96

Klingemann (dweller in a gorge) 76, 94

Klingemeyer, Klingenmeier (gorge farmer) 76, 93

Klingenbach (resounding stream) 76, 77

Klingenberg (resounding mountain) 68, 122

Klingenbuehl (resounding hill) 67

Klingenhagen (gorge enclosure) 76, 123, 122

Klingenhofer (fr Klingenhof 122), see Klingehoffer

Klingenschmidt, Klingensmith 153, (sword smith, cuttler) 96

Klingenstein (gorge mountain) 76, 73, 122

Klinger, Klingermann 94, Klingmann (swordsmith) 96, 108

Klinger (gorge dweller) 76

Klinghoffer fr Klinghof 122), see Klingehoffer

Klingler (public crier) 109

Klingmann 94, Klingmeyer 93 (occupant of a gorge) 76, 94, 93

Klink, Klinke (latch, locksmith) 96

Klinkhamer, Klinkhammer (latch hammer, locksmith) 96

Klinsmith 153, see Kleinschmidt

Klippenstein (craggy mountain, cliff) 73

Klob (plump coarse person) 114, 115

Klobenholtz (split fire wood, wood cutter) 96

Klock, Klocke, Klocker, see Glock, Glocke, Glocker

Klockmann (wise man) 115

Kloekner, Klocker (bell ringer) 96

Kloepfer, Kloeper, Kloepper (knocker)

Kloes, Kloese (dumpling, cook) 112, 96

Kloetzel 55, Kloetzli, see Klott

Kloosterhuis (cloister house) 65

Klopfenstein (Strike the stone!, quarryman) 116

Klopfer (mallet) 106

Klopfinstern ("Beat your fore-head" in remorse) 116

Klopp (flax swingle) 106, 112

Kloppenstein (stone for sharp-ening scythes, see Dengler) 73

Kloppmann (flax swingler) 95

Klosmann 53, 94, Klossmann, Klossner < Nikolaus

Kloss, Klosse (lump, clump)

Kloss 53 < Nikolaus

Kloster, Klostermann 94 (cloister, monk, fr Latin *claustrum*) 110, 122

Klotfelder (log-strewn field) 84

Klott, Klotz (block, log, clumsy person) 115

Klotzbach (stream full of logs) 77

Klouser 159, see Klause

Klueg, Klug, Kluge, Kluger, Klugmann 94 (clever) 115

Klung, Klunck, Klunk (tassel maker) 96

Knabe, Knapp, Knapp (boy) 113

Knabschneider (boy's tailor) 96

Knann, see Gnann

Knapp, Knappe (page, boy, miner) 113, 96

Knauer (course person) 115

Knauf, Knauff (nob, stub)

Knaus (niggardly) 115

Knebel (crossbar) 106

Knecht (servant, hired hand) 96

Knechtel 55, Knechtle (little servant) 97

Kneemoeller 159, see Niemoeller

Kneip (knife, shoemaker) 106, 96

Kneip, Kneipe, Kneiper (taverner) 96

Kneiss (gneiss)

Knell, Kneller (noisy person) 115

Knepper (button maker) 96

Knie (knee) 114

Knieper (users of pincers, such as cobblers and leather workers) 96

Knieriemen, Knierim 159 (knee strap, leather worker) 106

Knipe 159, Kniper, see Kneip, Kneiper

Knittel, Knittle 159 (cudgel, crude person) 115

Knobel, Knoble 159 (round ele-vation) 74, 122

Knoblauch, Knobeloch (garlic seller) 106, 122

Knochen (bones) 113, 122

Knochenhauer (butcher) 96

Knode, Knodt (knot)

Knoechel, Knochel (knuckle) 113

Knoedler (dumpling maker) 96

Knoepfel, Knoepfler, Knoepf-macher (button maker, button seller) 96, 106

Knoll, Knolle (hill, mountain top) 67, 68, 122

Knopf, Knopfle, Knopfler, Knoe-pler (button, button maker) 106

Knopp 122, see Knapp, Knopf

Knor, Knorr (nob, knot, hunch-back) 113

Knor (hill) 68

Knous 159, see Knaus

Knur, see Knor, Knauer

Kobel, Kobler (fr Kobel, swamp) 122

Knobel (little shelter, birdcage)
Koben (hut, pig pen, pig raiser)
91
Kobenhof, Kobenhoeffer (pig
farm) 92
Kobenhof (Jacob's farm) 134, 92
Kober (basket, back pack, fish
trap, huckster) 96, 106
Koblentz, Koblenz (Koblenz, a
city) 122, 130
Kobler (back pack carrier, cotter)
105
Kobold (gremlin)
Koch, Koche (cook, fr Latin
*coquus*) 96, 102
Kochenauer (meadow on the
Koche) 83, 84
Kochenburger (fr Kochenburg,
castle on the Koche) 83, 73
Kochenderfer 159, see Kochendorf
Kochendorf, Kochendorfer (village
on the Kocher) 83, 123, 122
Kochenreiter (clearing on the
Kocher) 83, 126
Kocher 122, Kochert 74 (cook,
dweller on the Kocher) 93, 83
Kocher, Kochert 74, see Koecher
Kocherthal (Kocher valley) 83, 76,
122
Kochheiser (occupant of a cook
house) 65, 66
Kochmann (cook) 102, 94
Kock 39, Kocks 164, see Koch
Koder, see Koeder
Koeb 53, 134, Koebel 55, Koebelin
55 < Jacob
Koecher (quiver, quiver maker)
96
Koechli 55 (little cook) 96
Koeder (bait)
Koefler (dweller on a Kofel) 67
Koefler (trunk maker) 96
Koegel, see Kegel
Koegler (juggler) 96
Koegler (dweller on mountain top)
68

Koehl, Koehle, Koehler, see Kehl,
Kehler
Koehler, Koeller, Koehleret 74
(collier, charcoal burner) 95,
122
Koehlerschmidt (charcoal smith)
96
Koehn 122, Koehne, Koehne-
mann, see Kuehn, Kuehne,
Kuehnemann
Koehten (fr Coethen, East Ger-
man city) 122
Koelbel, Koelbl, Koelble 159,
Koelber (battle club)
Koell, Koelle, see Kell, Kelle
Koellner, see Kellner
Koenemann, see Kuehnemann
Koenig (king) 41, 109
Koenigsbauer (royal farmer) 91
Koenigsberg, Konigsberg (Prus-
sian city) 122
Koenigsburg (royal castle) 73
Koenigsfeld (king's field) 84, 122
Koenigsmark (royal boundary)
122
Koepfgen 55 (little head) 114
Koepke 53, 55, 134 < Jacob
Koeppel, see Keppel 122
Koerber (basket maker) 96
Koerner (user of handmill) 103,
122
Koerner (granary supervisor) 109
Koerper, Koerpert 74 (body, fr
Latin *corpus*)
Koerschner, see Kuerschner
Koestel, Koestle 159, Koestler
(boarder)
Koester, see Kuester
Koestner, see Kestner
Koetter (cotter)
Kofel, Koffel, Kofler, Koffler,
Kofer (projection on slope of
mountain, see Unterkofler) 67
Kofer, see Kofel

Koffer (trunk, fr Latin *cophinus*, but often corruption of *kofler*) 96

Kofman 159, Koffman, Koffmann, see Kaufmann

Kogel, Kogler (cowl, monk, hood maker, fr Latin *cuculla*) 106, 122

Kogel, see Kugel

Kohde, see Gode

Kohl, Kohle (cabbage, cabbage dealer, fr Latin *caulis*) 106

Kohlbauer (cabbage planter) 91

Kohlbecker (swamp brook) 80, 77

Kohlbecker (cabbage brook) 80, 77

Kohlberg, Kohlenberg, Kohlenstein (coal mountain) 68, 73, 122

Kohlberg (cabbage mountain) 68, 73, 122

Kohlenbrenner (charcoal burner, collier) 95

Kohleisen (collier's poker, collier) 95

Kohler, Kohlerman 94 (collier, charcoal burner) 95

Kohlfelt (cabbage field) 84

Kohlhammer, see Kohlheim

Kohlhas 53, Kohlhaas < Nikolaus

Kohlhas (cabbage hare, nickname for peasant) 112

Kohlhauer (coal digger) 95

Kohlhaus, see Kohlhas 122

Kohlhaver 159, see Kohlhof

Kohlheim (cabbage hamlet, coal hamlet) 123

Kohlhof, Kohlhoff (cabbage farm) 92, 122

Kohlman, Kohlmann (collier) 95, 94

Kohlmeyer (fr the Kohlhoff, cabbage farm) 93

Kohn, Kohne, Kohner, see Kuhn, Cohen

Kohnke 55, Kohnle (little Kuhn)

Kolb, see Kalb

Kol, Kole, Koler, see Kohl, Kohler

Kolbach (cabbage brook) 77

Kolbacher, see Kohlbecker

Kolbe, Kolby 159, Kolben (club) 122

Kolker, see Kalk, Kalker

Kollenborn 159, see Kaltenborn

Kollenbach 159, see Kaltenbach

Koller (cape) 112, 106

Koller (giddiness, frenzy) 115

Kollman, Kollmann, Kollner, Kolman, see Kohlmann

Kolpach, see Kolbach

Kolter (plowshare, fr Latin *culter*) 106

Konder 159, see Gunther

Kone, see Kohn

Konig 159, Konik, see Koenig

Konigsberg, see Koenigsberg

Konigsdorffer (king's village) 123

Konkel, Konkle 159, see Kunckel

Konrad, see Conrad

Konradi, son of Konrad 142

Konts 159, Konz, see Kuntz

Konzelman 159, see Kuenzelmann

Koobler 159, see Kuebler

Koog (polder) 84

Koogel 159, Koogle, Koogler, see Kugel

Kool 159, Kooler, see Kuhl, Kuhler, Kohler

Koolhoff 159, see Kuhlhoff

Koon 159, Koons 164, see Kuhn, Kunz

Koonce 159, Koons, see Kunz

Koontz 159, see Kuntz

Koop, Koopman, Koopmann, see Kauf, Kaufmann

Kopald (cobalt)

Kopf (head, cup, fr Latin *cuppa*) 114

Kopp 53, 134 < Jacob, see also Kapp, Kopf

Koppel 53, 55, 134 < Jacob

Koppel (common pasture) 122

Koppel (leash, leash of hounds, hunter) 91
Koppelberger (mountain with common pasture) 68
Koppenhafer, Koppenhaver, Koppenhofer, Koppenhoffer, Koppenhoefer (fr Koppenhoefen 122, Jacob's farm) 92
Koppelmann (farmer with rights to common pasture) 94
Koppenhoffer (farmer who pays rent in capons) 92
Kopper (bloodletter) 96, see Kupfer
Koppman, see Kaufmann
Korb (basket, fr Latin *corbis*, basket maker 106, child found in a basket, fr the Korb 83)
Korbach 122, Korbeck (swampy brook) 80, 77
Korber (basket maker) 96
Kordes 53 < Conrad
Korenberg, see Kornberg
Korenblit, see Kornblit
Korff, Korfes 164, Korfmann 94 (basket, basket maker) 96, 106
Korn (grain, wheat, grain dealer) 91, 106
Kornblatt (corn blade)
Kornblit (grain blossom) 89
Kornblum (cornflower) 89
Korner, see Koerner
Kornfeld (grain field) 84
Kornguth (grain farm) 92
Kornhaus (granary) 65
Kornhauser (granary manager) 109
Kornhizer 159, 66, see Kornhauser
Kornman, Kornmann 94 (grain raiser, grain dealer) 91, 106
Kornmesser (official grain measurer) 109
Kornmeyer, Kornmayer (grain farmer) 93
Kornreich (rich in grain)

Kornscheuer (grain barn, granary) 65
Kornstein (grain mountain) 68
Korper 159, see Koerper
Korpman, see Korber
Kort, Korte, Korten, Korter, Korth, Kortte, Kortz, see Kurtz
Korthals (short neck) 114
Kortjohann (short John) 113
Kortkamp (short field) 84
Kortschenkel (short legs) 114
Korz, see Kurtz
Kost, Koster, Kostermann 94 (taster), see Kuester
Kotch 159, see Koch
Kotchenreuter 159, Kotchenreuther, see Kochenreiter
Koth, Kothe (mud, filth)
Kotmair (mud farmer) 93
Kotsch 159, see Koch
Kotschenreuther 159, see Kochenreiter
Kottenbach (granary creek) 77
Koubek 159, Koubik, see Kuhbach
Koufman 159, see Kaufmann
Kougl 159, see Kugel
Kouns 159, Kountz, see Kuntz
Kouperstein 159, see Kupferstein
Koutz 159, see Kautz
Kowellentenz 159, see Coblentz
Kraatz, see Kratz
Krabacher (crow brook) 77
Krabbe (crab, active person) 115
Krach (noise) 115
Krack, Kracke (crow) 115
Krack (underbrush) 72
Krabacher (crow brook) 77
Kraeber, see Graeber
Kraehbuehl (crow hill) 67
Kraehe (crow) 115
Kraeher (crow catcher) 96
Kraemer, Kraehmer (shopkeeper, retailer) 105
Kraenckel, Kraenkel (sickly) 115
Kraetzer, see Kratzer

Kraeuter, Kraeuther (herbs, herb seller) 106
Kraff, see Graf
Kraft, Krafte, Krafft (strength) 115
Kraft (river name) 83
Krager 159, see Krueger
Krahe 159, see Kraehe
Krahenbuhl 159, see Kraehbuehl
Krahling 159 (little crow)
Krahmer, see Kraemer
Krahn, see Kran
Kral, Krall, Kralle (claw) 114
Kral (Czech: king, fr Carl) 146
Krallmann (fr Krall) 122, 94
Kram (retail trade, huckster's pack, huckster) 105, 122
Kramer, Kramers 164, see Kraemer
Kramp, Krampf (cramp)
Kran, Krane (crane) 115
Kranck (sick) 115
Kranefeld (crowfield) 84
Kranick, Kranich (crane) 115
Kranitzfeld (border field, fr Slavic) 84, 146
Krankheit (sickness)
Krannewetter, Krannebitter (juniper forest) 89
Krantz, Kranz, Krans 159 (wreath, rosary) 106
Kranwinckel (crow woods, crane woods) 72
Krapf, Krapfer (fritter) 106, 112
Krapf (hooked nose, hunched back) 114
Krass (crass, gross) 115
Kratz 53 < St. Pancratius 131
Kratz, Kratzer, Kratzler, Krazer (scraper, wool comber) 96
Kraus, Krauss, Krause, Krauser, Krausman 94 (curly haired) 112
Krausam, see Grausam
Kraushaar (curlyhead) 112, 159

Krauskob, Krauskopf (curly headed) 112
Kraut, Krauth (greens, herbs) 106
Krauter, Krautler, Krauthman 94, Krautz, Krautze, see Kraeuter
Krauthammer (fr Krautheim, herb hamlet) 123, 122
Kraybil 159, Kraybill, Kraybell, see Kraehbuehl
Kreager 159, see Krueger
Kreamer 159, see Kraemer
Kreatchman 159, Kreatchmann, see Kretschmann
Krebs (crab, crab catcher, sign of zodiac) 96, 143
Kreczner, see Kretsch
Kreek 159, see Krueg
Krefeld (swampy field) 80, 84
Kreft, see Kraft
Kreger 159, Kregar, Kreeger, see Krueger
Kreh (crow) 115
Krehbiehl 159, see Kraebuehl
Krehmeyer (fr the Kraehoff, crow farm) 93
Krehnbrink (crow hill) 74
Kreider, Kreidler (chalk maker or seller, fr Latin *creda*) 96, 106
Kreideweiss (chalk white) 112
Kreig 159, Kreigh, Kreiger, see Krueg, Krueger
Kreiner 159, see Greiner
Kreis, Kreiss, Kreise (circle, district), see Greis
Kreisberg (district mountain) 68, see Kreutzberg
Kreischer (screamer) 115
Kreisel, Kreisler (spinning top)
Kreiter (quarreler) 115, see Kraeuter
Kreitz (cleared land 126, 122), also see Kreutz
Kreitzberg (cleared mountain), see Kreutzberg
Kreitzer, Kreitzner, see Kreutzer

Krell, Kreller (cross-patch) 115
Krell, see Grell
Kremer, see Kraemer
Kremeyer (fr the Krehhof, crow
 farm) 93
Kremp, Krempf (hat with turned
 up brim) 112
Krempe (swamp) 80
Krempel (wool carder) 96
Krenkel, see Kraenkel
Krentz, Krenzmann 94, see
 Grentzel
Kreps, Krepps, see Krebs
Krepp, Krepner (dweller on a
 sunken path) 65
Kress (cress, fr Latin *cresso*) 89
Kressmann (Christian) 131, 94
Kretsch, Kretschmer, Kretsch-
 mar, Kretchmer, Kretschmann
 94 (tavern keeper, fr Slavic) 9,
 96, 146
Kretz, Kretzer, Kretzel, Kretzler
 (collector of fines) 109, 122
Kreuder, see Kreider, Kraeuter
Kreuger 159, see Krueger
Kreul, see Greul
Kreuscher, see Kreischer
Kreuth, see Gereuth, Kraeuter
Kreutz, Kreuz, Kreutziger,
 Kreutzinger (crusader, dweller
 on a cross road) 122
Kreutzburg (cross castle) 73
Kreutzer (a coin) 117
Kreuzberger (fr Kreuzberg 122,
 cross mountain) 68, 122
Krey, Kreye, Kreyer (crow)
Kreyder, see Kreider
Kreymer 159, see Kraemer
Kreyss, see Kreis
Krick 159, see Krueck
Krickstein (crutch mountain) 73
Kridel 159, Kridler, Krideler, see
 Kreidler
Krieder 159, Kriedler, see Kreider
Krieg (war), see Krug
Krieger, see Krueger

Kriegmann, Kriegsman, see
 Kruegmann
Kriegsmann (soldier) 107
Krieter (querulous person) 115
Kriger 159, Krigger, Krigman, see
 Kruegman
Krimm 122, see Grimm
Krimmel, Krimmell (crooked) 114,
 122
Krimmelbein (crooked leg) 114
Kriner 159, see Greiner
Krings 53 < St. Quirinus 131
Krise 159, see Kreis
Krisfeller, Christfelder (Christ's
 field) 140
Krisler 159, see Kreisler
Krisman, Krissman, see Kress-
 mann
Krist, Kristian, see Christ, Chri-
 stian
Kritz 159, Kritzer, see Kreutzer
Kroat (Croat, Croatian merce-
 nary) 121, 107
Krob, Krobs 164, Krober, see
 Grob
Krock, Krocker (fr Crock or
 Cracow) 122
Kroder, Kroeder, Kroeter (toad)
 113
Kroeger, see Krueger
Kroeher, see Kraeher
Kroemer, see Kraemer
Krog, Kroger, Krogh, Krogman 94
 (fr Krog 122), see Krug,
 Krueger, Kruegman
Krohn, see Kron
Krol, Kroll, Krall (Slavic for king
 [Carl]) 146
Kroll (curly) 112
Kromer, see Kraemer
Kromholz, Krompholtz, see
 Krumbholz
Kromm, see Krumm
Kron, Krone, Kroner, Krohne
 (crown)
Kronau, see Gronau

Kronawetter 159, see Kranne-
wetter
Kronberg, Kronberger, Kronen-
berg, Kronenberger, Krone-
berger (crown mountain) 68,
122
Kronburger (fr Kronburg 122,
crown castle) 73
Kroneck (crown field) 85
Kronenschild (crown shield)
Kronewetter 159, see Kranne-
wetter
Kronfeldt (crown field) 84
Kronforst (crown forest) 72
Kronhoff (crown farm) 92
Kronk 159, see Krank
Kronmaier, Kronmeyer (crown
farmer) 93
Kronmueller (crown miller) 103
Kronsbehn (crane leg) 114
Kronstadt (crown city) 122
Kroon, see Kron
Kropf, Kropp (crop, goiter) 114
Krouse 159, Krouss, see Kraus,
Krause
Kroushaar, Kroushour 159, see
Kraushaar
Krout 159, see Kraut
Krueck (crutch) 114
Krueckeberg, Kruckeberg (fr
Krueckenberg 122, crutch
mountain) 68
Krueger (tavern keeper) 63, 96
Kruegmann (tavern keeper) 63,
96, 94
Kruelle (curly) 112
Kruesy, see Kraus
Kruetzer 159, see Kreutz
Krug, Krugs 164, Krug (pitcher,
tavern, taverner) 63, 96, see
Krueger
Kruger, Krugman, see Krueger,
Kruegmann
Kruise 159, see Kraus
Krull (curly) 112
Krum 159, see Krumm

Krumbach (crooked brook) 77
Krumbein, Krumblebeim 159
(crooked leg) 114
Krumbholz, Krumholtz,
Krummholtz (bent wood for
wheel, wheelwright) 96
Krumenacker (crooked field) 84
Krumhus (crooked house) 65
Krumlauf (crooked course) 77
Krumm (crooked) 114
Krummeck (crooked field) 85
Krumpholz, see Krumbholz
Krup, Krupp (croup, crupper)
Krus, Kruse, Krusen, Kruser, see
Kraus
Kruth, see Kraut
Krutmann, Krautmann (spice
dealer) 106, 94
Kruttschmer, see Kretschmer
Kryder 159, see Kreider
Kryger 159, see Krueger
Krygsman 159, see Kriegsmann
Kubach, Kubeck, see Kuhbach
122
Kubel 159, Kubler, see Kuebel,
Kuebler
Kubel, Kubler (mountain ridge)
68
Kuche, see Kueche
Kuchenbeisser (cookie biter) 112
Kuchenmeister (chief cook) 96,
102
Kuckuck (cuckoo) 115
Kuebel, Kuebele, Kuebler, Kue-
beller 159 (tub, bucket maker)
96
Kuefer, Kuefner, see Kieffer
Kuefus, see Kuhfuss
Kuegler, see Kugel
Kuehl, Kuehler, Kuehling,
Kuehlman 94 (dweller near a
pit or mine)
Kuehlwein (cool wine, tavern) 63,
102
Kuehn, Kuehne, Kuehner,
Kuehnert 74 (brave man) 115

Kuehnemann (brave man) 115, 94
Kuemmel, Kuemmelmann 94
(carraway seed, fr Latin
*cuminum*) 106
Kuemmerle 55 (miserable crea-
ture) 115
Kuempel, see Kump
Kuenlin 55, see Kuhn
Kuenst, Kuenstler (artist, artisan)
96
Kuentzel, Kuenzel, see Kuntz
Kuenz, see Kuntz
Kuerschner (furrier) 96
Kuessnacht (city in Switzerland)
122
Kuessner (bolster maker) 96
Kuester, Kuesterle 55 (sexton, fr
Latin *custos*) 110
Kuettner (cowl wearer, cowl
maker, monk) 96, 112, 110
Kufel, Kufler, see Kieffer
Kuffner, see Kiefer
Kugel, Kugel, Kugler (cowl, cowl
maker, fr Latin *cuculla*) 96,
106, 41
Kugel, Kugelberg (round topped
mountain) 68
Kuhaar (cow hair)
Kuhbach (cow brook) 77, 122
Kuhfuss (cow foot, club foot) 114
Kuhhirt (cowherd) 95
Kuhl, Kuhle, Kuhler, Kuhlert 74,
Kool 159 (pond, pit) 81
Kuhlenberg (cool mountain) 68
Kuhlmann, Kuhlman, Kuhle-
mann, Kuehlemann (dweller
on a pond) 81
Kuhlmeyer (farmer at the pond)
81, 93
Kuhltau (cool dew)
Kuhlwetter (cool weather)
Kuhmann (cow man) 91, 94
Kuhn, Kuhne, Kuhnen, Kuhns
164, Kuhner, Kuhnert 74,
Kuhnke (brave) 115, also <
Konrad

Kullenberg, Kullberg, see Kuhl-
enberg
Kullenthal (cool valley, pond
valley) 81, 76
Kulm (peak) 68
Kulman, Kullmann, see Kuhl-
mann
Kulp (carp) 115
Kumeler, see Kuemmeler
Kumet, Kummet, Kumeth, Ku-
mith 159 (horse collar) 106
Kummel, Kummell, Kummel-
mann 94, see Kuemmel
Kummer (sorrow) 122
Kummerbach (sorrow brook) 77
Kummerling 55, Kummerle 55
(stunted tree) 89
Kump, Kumpel, Kumper, Kumpf,
Kumps 164, Kumpermann
(barrel maker) 96, 106, 122
Kumpfmiller (miller with over-
shot wheel) 103
Kumpost (kind of sourkraut,
peasant food) 112
Kuncel 159, see Kuentzel
Kunckel, Kunkel, Kunkele (dis-
taff, fr Latin *conucula* 106,
relative on distaff side 119)
Kunert, see Kuehnert
Kung, Kunig, see Koenig
Kunisch 53 < Conrad
Kunkel, Kunkl, Kunkle 159,
Kunkler, Kunkelmann 94 <
Conrad, see Kunckel
Kunnert, see Kuehnert
Kuno, see Kuhn, Conrad
Kunolt, Kunoldt (brave + rule) 46,
48
Kunrad, see Conrad
Kunsman 159, see Kunstmann
Kunst (art, skill) 96, also< Con-
stantius
Kunstler, see Kuenstler
Kunstmann, Kuntzler, Kuntz-
man, Kuntzmann, Kuntzel-

mann, Kunzelman (artisan) 96,
94
Kuntsman 159, see Kunstmann
Kuntz, Kuntze, Kunz, Kunze,
Kundtz, Kunzle 55, Kuhns 164
< Conrad
Kuper, Kuperman, see Kupfer,
Kupfermann
Kuperberg, see Kupferberg
Kuperstein, see Kupferstein
Kupfer, Kupfermann 94 (copper
dealer, fr Latin *cuprum*) 106
Kupferberg (copper mountain) 68
Kupferschmid (coppersmith) 96
Kupferstein (copper ore) 73
Kupp, Kupper, Kuppert 74
(dweller on a mountain peak)
68
Kuppenheim (town in Baden) 122
Kupperman, see Kupfer, Kup-
ferman
Kur (fr Chur in Switzerland)
Kuradi, Kunradi (son of Kurad)
142
Kurad, Kurath < Conrad
Kurcfeld 159 (short field) 84
Kurcz, see Kurtz
Kurland, Kurlander (territory on
the Baltic) 121
Kursner 159, Kurstner, see
Kuerschner
Kurt 53, Kurth, Kurtz 164,
Kurtze, Kurz, Kurts 164, 159 <
Conrad
Kurtenbach (short brook) 77
Kurtz (short) 113
Kurtzendorf (short village) 123
Kurtzman 94, Kurtzman, Kurtz-
meyer 93 (short man) 113
Kurtzweil (pastime, leisure) 115
Kurzman, see Kurtzman
Kuss (kiss), or < Dominicus 1
Kussmaul, Kusmaul, Kuszmaul
(not "kiss mouth" but Czech for
"tousel-haired") 112, 146
Kuster, see Kuester

Kutler, Kuttler (maker or wearer
of cowls 106, or fr Kutten 122)
Kutscher, Kutcher 159, Kut-
chermann 94 (coachman, fr
Hungarian) 96
Kutner 159, see Kuettner
Kyle 159, Kyler, see Keil, Keiler
Kyser 159, see Kaiser
Kyssel, see Kiesel
Kyseler, see Kieseler

## L

Laage, see Lage
Lach, Lack (laugh) 115
Lach (blaze on a tree)
Lach, Lache (puddle, lake) 80, 82,
122
Lachberg (boundary mountain) 68
Lachenicht (Don't laugh!) 116
Lachenmann, see Lachman
Lacher, see Lachner
Lacher (incanter, see Lachmann)
Lachman, Lachmann (leech,
incanter) 96
Lachmann (dweller at a pond) 81
Lachner (dweller on a boundary
or on a pond) 81
Lachter (laughter) 115
Lack, Lacker (laquer, laquerer)
96, 106, 122
Lacke, see Lach
Lackmann, see Lachmann
Lackner (meat pickler) 96
Lackner (dweller by a pond) 81
Lademacher (chest maker) 94, 98
Laden (window, store) 105
Lader, Ladner (loader) 96
Laderer 159, see Lederer
Laechler, Laechner (laugher) 115
Laechner, see Lachner
Laemmer (lambs) 91
Laendler (countryman)
Laerch (lark) 115
Laessig (easy-going) 115
Laeuenstein (lion mountain) 73

Langenthal (long valley) 76, 122
Langenwalter (fr Langenwald
122, long forest) 71
Langer (tall mann) 113
Langereis (long journey)
Langfeldt 122, see Langenfeldt
Langfield 153, see Langenfeldt
Langguth, Languth (long estate)
92
Langhaar (long hair) 112
Langhage (long enclosure) 123,
122
Langhals (long neck) 114
Langhans (tall Johnny) 113
Langhaus (long house) 65, 122
Langheim (long hamlet) 123, 122
Langheinrich (tall Henry) 113
Langhirt (tall herdsman) 113, 95
Langhoff, Langhoffer, Langen-
hoffer (long farm) 92
Langhorn, Langhorne (long horn)
Langhorst (long hurst) 72, 122
Langhutte (long hut) 65
Langkammerer (tall chamberlain)
109
Langloh (long forest) 72
Langman, Langmann (tall man)
113, 94
Langmichel (tall Michael) 113
Langnau, Langenau, Lankenau
(long meadow) 84
Langohr (long ear) 114
Langrock (long gown) 112, 147
Langsam (slow) 115
Langschmidt (tall smith) 96, 113
Lanhart, see Lahner
Lannert, see Lahner
Lansman, see Landsman
Lantz, Lants, Lans, Lantz 122
(spear, lance, fr Latin *lancea*)
107, 108
Lantzer (pikeman) 107
Lapp (rag, fool) 115
Lappersdorf (Luitfried's village)
123
Lass (serf, bondsman) 109

Lasser 53 < Lazarus 131
Laster (vice) 115
Laster (packman) 96
Lastfogel, Lastvogel (load carri-
er?) 96
Lastinger (prunella weaver) 96
Lastner (burden carrier) 96
Latz (codpiece) 112, 106
Lau, Laue (thin forest) 72
Laub, Laube, Lauber, Laubner
(leaf, foliage, arbor) 89
Laubach (forest brook) 77, 122
Laubenstein (lion mountain) 73
Laubheim, Laubheimer (swamp
hamlet) 80, 123
Lauch, see Lau
Lauch, Laucher, Lauchner (leek,
leek seller) 89, 106
Lauck, Laucks (St. Luke) 131
Laudenslager 159, Laudenslayer
159, Laudenschlaeger, see
Lautenschlaeger
Laue, see Lau
Lauenroth (lion clearing) 126
Lauenstein (lion mountain) 73,
122, see Loewenstein 122
Lauer, Laur, Laurer, Lauerman
94 (tanner) 96
Lauerenroth (tanner's red,
tanner) 96, 106
Lauf, Laufe (course, track of
game, hunter) 91, 122
Laufenberger, Lauffenburger 159
(waterfall mountain) 68
Laufenburgen, Laufenburger,
Lauffenburger (waterfall castle)
73, 122
Laufer, Lauffer, Laufert 74
(runner) 96
Laufer (fr Lauffen) 122
Lauffen (waterfall, places in
Switzerland and Wurttemberg)
122
Laug, Lauge (lye) 106
Laughner 159, see Lochner

Lauman, Laumann (forest dweller) 72

Laumann, see Lauer

Laun (mood, disposition) 115

Laupheim 122, see Laubheim

Laur, see Lauer

Lauritzen, see Lorentz

Laus 53 < Nikolaus

Lausch (listen, hearken)

Lauss (boundary)

Laut, Lauth (loud) 115

Laut, Lauth (lute) 106

Lautenbach (swamp brook) 80,
77, 122

Lautenbach (town in Prussia,
loud mountain) 122

Lautenschlaeger, Lauteschlager
159 (lute player) 96

Lauter (swamp) 80

Lauterbach (swampy brook) 80,
77, 122

Lautermilch (pure milk)

Lauterwasser (pure water)

Lauterwasser (swamp water) 80

Lauth, see Laut

Lauthans (noisy Johnny) 115

Lautman, Lauthman (lute player)
96

Lautringer (fr Kaiserslautern)
122

Lax (salmon) 115

Layman 159, see Lehman

Lazarus (NT name) 131

Leab 159, see Lieb

Leabhart 159, Leapheart, see
Lepbhard

Leaderer 159, see Lederer

Leaderman 159, see Ledermann

Leahman 159, see Lehman

Leap 159, see Lieb

Leapart 159, Leaphart, see
Lepard

Leatherman 159, see Ledermann

Lebegut (Live well!) 116, 117

Leber (liver)

Leber (river name) 83

Leberecht (Live right!) 116, 139

Leberknight 159, see Lieberknecht

Lebermann (dweller on the Leber)
83, also see Liebermann

Lebherz 159 (dear heart)

Lebkucher (cookie baker) 96

Lebolt, see Leopold

Lech, Lechert 74, Lechmann 94
(dweller on the River Lech,
swamp) 80, 83

Lech, Lechner, Lechnir 159,
Lechman, see Lehner

Lechleiter, Lechliter 159, see
Lichleiter

Leckner, see Lech

Leder, Lederer (leather, leather
worker) 96, 106

Lederhos (leather breeches,
peasant) 112, 122

Lederkremer, Lederkraemer
(leather merchant) 106

Ledermann (leather worker) 96,
106, 94

Ledig (single, free) 115

Leeb 159, Leeby, see Lieb, Liebe

Leebmann 159, see Liebmann

Leer (empty)

Leffel, Lefler, Leffler, see Loeffler

Lehder, see Leder

Lehfeld (tenant field) 84

Lehm, Lehmer (clay, ceramics
worker) 96, 106

Lehman, Lehmann (tenant), see
Lohmann

Lehmbeck (clay brook) 77, 122

Lehmkuhl (clay pond) 81, 122

Lemberg (clay mountain) 68, 122

Lehn, Lehen (fief) 122

Lehne (steep slope) 71

Lehner, Lehnerd 74, Lehnert 74,
Lehnerts 164, Lenerz,
Lehninger (tenant) 109, 122

Lehnhoff (rented farm) 84

Lehnwald (forested fief) 71

Lehr (teaching, teacher) 96

Lehr (swamp) 80, 122
Lehrer, Lehrman 94, Lehrmann
(teacher, minister) 96, 109
Lehrkind (pupil, apprentice)
Lehrmann (swamp dweller) 80, 94
Leib, Leiber, Leibert 74 (body)
Leibenguth (life and property, a
serf) 109
Leibheim (fr Leipheim) 122
Leibknecht (body servant) 96, see
Liebknecht 159
Leibnitz (Slavic place name) 122
Leibrock (body gown) 112
Leichnam, Leichtnam (corpse)
Leicht (light) 113, 115
Leider (sufferer, patient)
Leidhauser, see Leithauser
Leidhauser (taverner) 65
Leidig, see Ledig
Leidner, see Leitner
Leihkauf (loan purchase, drink
sealing a bargain)
Leihofer, Leihoffer (tenant) 92
Leim (clay)
Leimbach, Leimback (clay brook,
swamp brook) 80, 77, 122
Leimberg, Leimberger (clay
mountain) 68
Leimkuhler (clay pond) 80
Leinauer (clay meadow) 84
Leinbach, Leinbacher, Leine-
bacher (clay brook) 77, 122
Leinberger, Leineberger, Lein-
berry 159 (fr Leinberg 122,
clay mountain) 68
Leine (leash)
Leineweber, Leinweber (linen
weaver) 96
Leinhardt, see Leonhard
Leinwand (cloth, mercer) 106
Leip, Leipp (fr Leipe 122), see
Leib
Leipold, Leippold, see Leopold
Leis, Leiss, Leise, Leiser (soft,
softly) 115
Leisler, Leissler (wainwright) 96

Leist (last, schoemaker) 104, 106,
122
Leite, Leitner (dweller on a slope)
71
Leitenberger (slope mountain) 71,
68, 122
Leiter (ladder) 106
Leiter (leader)
Leithausen, Leithaeuser, Leit-
hauser, Leitheuser (occupant of
house on slope) 71, 65
Leitheimer (fr Leitheim, hamlet
on a slope) 71, 123, 122
Leither, Leitmann 94, Leitzmann
(guide)
Leithiser 159, 66, Leithizer, see
Leithausen
Leitinger, see Leite
Leitner, see Leite
Lembach, Lembeck (swamp
brook) 80, 77, 122
Lemberg, Lemberger (swamp
mountain) 80, 68
Lembchen 55, Lembke, Lembcke,
Lemke, Lembeke (little lamb)
91
Lemer, see Laemmer
Lemke, see Lembchen, also <
Lamprecht
Lemmenhoffer (lamb farm) 91, 92
Lemmer, see Laemmer
Lemmer, Lemmert 74, Lemmer-
man 94 (shepherd) 95
Lemmlein 55 (little lamb) 91
Lempke 55, see Lembchen
Lenard 159, Lennert, see Leon-
hard
Lence 159, Lencz, see Lentz
Lendel, see Laendler
Lendeman 94, Lendemann,
Lendermann, see Laendler
Lendler, see Laendler
Lener, see Lehner
Lenert, Lennert, see Lehnert
Lengfelder, Lengenfelder (fr
Lengfeld 122), see Langenfelder

Lenhard, Lenhardt, Lenhart, see
Leonhard, Lehner
Lenhof, Lenhoff, Lennhof, see
Lehnhoff
Lenker (steerer, driver)
Lennerd 159, Lennert, Lennard,
see Lenhard, Lehner
Lents 159, Lentz 122, Lenz,
Lenzer, Lentzer (spring 143) or
< Lorentz, St. Laurentius 131
Leonberger (lion mountain) 48, 68
Leonhard, Leonhardt, Leonhart,
Leonheart 159, Leonard 159
(lion + strong) 46, 49
Leonhardi (son of Leonhard) 142
Leonhauser (lion house) 48, 65
Leopold, Lepold (folk + brave) 46,
46
Lepart, Lepert, Lepperet, Lep-
hardt (leopard, or lion +
strong) 48, 46
Lepetit (French, little one) 144
Lepper, Leppert 74 (shoe repair-
er, clothes patcher) 96
Lerch, Lerche, Lercher, Lerge,
Lerich, Lerik (lark, joyful
person) 115, 122
Lerner (learner, pupil)
Lesch, Lesch, Lescher, Leschert
74, Leschner (one who lives on
the Lesch) 83
Leschke (Slavic, "forest dweller")
146
Leser, Lesemann (reader) 96
Lesser, Lessner (bloodletter) 96
Lessing, Lessig (Slavic for forest
dweller) 146, 122
Letsch, Letscher (weak-kneed)
115
Lettermann 159, see Ledermann
Leu (lion)
Leubecker (fr Leubeck 122, lion
brook) 77
Leubolt, Leuphold, see Leopold
Leucht, Leuchter (light)

Leuenberg (lion mountain) 68
Leuew (lion) 48
Leuffer, Laeufer (runner, deer's
leg) 96
Leupold, see Leopold
Leutbrand (volk + sword) 46, 46
Leuthaeuser, see Leithaeuser
Leuthold (folk + dear) 46, 48
Leutner, Leuthner, see Leitner
Levering 159 < Liebering 55 (dear
one)
Leverknight 159, see Lieber-
knecht
Lewald (lion forest) 48, 71, see
also Lehwald
Lewenberg, Lewenberger (lion
mountain) 48, 68
Lexer 53 < St. Alexius 131
Leybold, see Leopold
Leydeman, see Luedemann
Leydiker, see Luedeker
Leyer, Leier (lyre) 96, 106
Leypold, Leypoldt, see Leopold
Libendraut 159 (dearly beloved)
Liber 159, Liberman, see Lieber,
Lieberman
Libert, Libhart, Lebhart (leopard,
lion + strong) 48, 46
Lichliege (swamp marsh) 80
Lichliter, Lichtliter, see Licht-
leiter
Licht, Lichte 122, Lichter (light,
clearing) 126
Lichtblau (light blue) 112
Lichtenauer (cleared meadow)
126, 84
Lichtenberg, Lichtenberger
(clearing + mountain) 126, 68,
122
Lichtenfeld, Lichtenfeldt (cleared
field) 126, 84, 122
Lichtenfels (treeless cliffs) 68, 122
Lichtenstaig, Lichtenstaiger (fr
Lichtenstaig) in the Thurgau)
122

Lichtenstein, Liechtenstein
(European principality 121 and
various cities 122)
Lichtenthal (cleared valley) 126,
76
Lichtenwald, Lichtenwalner
(cleared forest) 126, 71, 122
Lichtfuss (light foot) 115
Lichtleiter, Lickliter 159, Lick-
lighter (cleared slope) 126, 71
Lidke 53, 55, Lidtke < Ludolf
Lieb, Liebe, Liebel 55, Lieber,
Liebert 74 (dear one) 115
Liebegott (Love God!) 116, 117,
139
Liebele 55, Libley 159 (dear one)
Liebemann, Liebman, Liebmann
(dear man) 115
Liebendorf (inherited village) 127,
123
Liebengut, Liebenguth, see
Leibenguth
Liebenthal (inherited valley) 127,
76
Lieber, Liebert 74 (inheritence +
army) 127, 46
Liebergott (dear God) 117
Liebering 55 (dear one) 115
Lieberknecht (dear servant) 139
Liebermann (dear man) 115, 94
Liebeskind (love child, illegiti-
mate child) 119
Liebesmann (dear man) 115, 94
Liebfeld (inherited field) 127, 84
Liebgott, see Liebegott
Liebhold (dear, fond) 115
Liebknecht (dear servant) 139
Liebrecht (Love right!) 116, 139,
see also Leberecht
Lied (damp region) 80
Liederbach (salmon stream) 77,
122
Liedtke 53, 55, Liedtzke < Ludolf
Lienenberger 159, see Luene-
berger

Lienhard, Lienhardt, see Leon-
hard
Liepmann, see Liebemann
Liepold, see Leopold
Light 153, see Licht
Light 159, see Leite
Lightenberger 159, see Lichten-
berger
Lighthizer 159, 66, Lighthiser,
see Leithaeuser
Lightfoot, see Lichtfuss
Lightner 159, see Leitner
Lilienfeld (lily field) 89, 84
Lilienkamp (lily field) 89, 84
Lilienthal, Lillienthal, Lilenthal
(lily valley) 89, 76, 122
Limbach, Limbaugh, Limbacker
159 (swampy brook [fr *lint*]) 80,
or see Leinbach
Limberger (fr Limberg 122, linden
mountain) 89, 68, see
Leimberger
Lime 159, see Leim
Limmat (Swiss river) 83
Limpert, see Lambert
Linaweaver 159, see Leineweber
Linck, Linke, Linker, Linkert 74
(left, left-handed) 114
Lind, Lindt, Linde, Linder,
Linders 164, Lindler, Lindner
(dweller near the linden trees)
89
Lindauer (fr Lindau, swampy
meadow) 80, 84, 122
Lindbeck (linden brook) 89, 77
Lindbeck (swampy brook) 80, 77
Lindberg (linden mountain) 89,
68
Lindblat (linden leaf) 89
Linddorf, Lindorf (linden village)
89, 123, 122
Lindeman 94, Lindemann,
Lindemeyer 93, Lindemyer
(dweller near the lindens) 89
Lindemann (dweller near the
swamp) 80, 94

Lindenauer (linden meadow) 89,
   84
Lindenauer (swamp meadow) 89,
   84
Lindenbaum (linden tree) 89
Lindenberg, Lindenberger (linden
   mountain) 89, 68, 122
Lindencamp (linden field) 89, 84
Lindenfeld, Lindenfelder (linden
   field) 89, 84, 122
Lindenmeyer (farmer by the
   swamp) 80, 93
Lindenmuth, Lindemuth (gentle
   disposition) 115
Lindenschmidt, Lindenschmid
   (smith under the linden trees)
   89, 96
Lindenstrutt, Lindenstruth (fr
   Lindenstruth 122, linden
   swamp) 89, 80
Linder, Lindner, Lindener, Lin-
   deman 94 (dweller near linden)
   89
Linderborn (linden spring) 89, 77
Lindhorst, Lindhurst, Linhorst
   (linden hurst) 89, 72, 122
Lindler, Lindner, Lindt, see
   Lindeman
Lindmeyer (farmer by the linden)
   89, 93
Lindmood 159, see Lindemuth
Lindober, see Lindauer
Lindorf (swampy village) 80, 123
Lindrud (linden clearing) 89, 126
Linebarger 159, see Leinberger
Linebaugh 159, see Leinebach
Lineweaver 159, see Leineweber
Lingelbach, Lingelback (mud
   brook) 77, 122
Lingenberg (muddy mountain) 68
Lingenfeld, Lingenfelder, Ling-
   enfelter, Lingerfelt (swampy
   field) 84
Lingert, see Linhard
Linger, Lingner, Lingerman
   (dweller near the swamp) 80

Linhard 159, Linhardt, Linhart,
   see Leonhard
Link, Linker, see Linck, Lincker
Linnbaum, see Lindenbaum
Linneman, see Lindeman
Linnenkamp, see Lindencamp
Linnestruth, see Lindenstrutt
Lins, Linse, Linsen (lentil) 91,
   106
Linsenmeyer, Linsenmyer (lentil
   farmer) 93
Lintner, see Lindeman
Lintz, Linz (fr Linz) 122
Lion, Lyons (fr French *lion*) 144
Lipmann 53, Lipp, Lippmann 94
   < Philipp
Lippelt, Lippolt < Leopold
Lippersdorf (Leutbrand's village)
   46, 46, 123
Lippert, Lipphart, see Lebhart
Lisch 122, Lischer, see Lescher
List (intelligence, cunning, skill)
   115, 122
Litfass (wine barrel) 96
Litinger (dweller on a slope), see
   Leitner
Little 153, see Luetzel
Litz, Litze (lace) 96, 106, 112
Litzeldorf (little village) 123
Litzen 53, Litzmann 94 < Ludwig
Liveright 153, see Leberecht
Livingood 159, see Leibenguth
Loan 159, see Lohn
Lob, Lobe, Lober (praise, praiser)
Lobach, Lobeck (forest brook) 71,
   77, 122
Lobauer (forest peasant) 71, 91
Lobaugh 159, see Lobach 77, 151
Loberger (forest mountain) 72, 68
Lobmueller (forest miller) 72, 103
Loch (hole, ravine) 76, 122
Lochbaum (hollow tree, boundary
   tree) 89
Lochner (dweller by a pond) 80
Lochstampfer, Lochstamphor 159
   (hole stamper)

Lock (pond) 80
Lock (lure, trapper) 91, 96
Lockermann (dweller by a
swamp) 80
Lockhoff (pond farm) 80, 92
Lockner, see Lochner
Loden (shag, course woolen cloth)
96, 106, 112
Lodenkemper (shag field) 84
Lodwig, see Ludwig
Loeb, Loeber, Loebl 55, Loeblein
55 (lion)
Loeb (fr Loebau) 122, see also
Loew
Loechel 55 (little hole)
Loeff, see Loeb
Loeffel, Loeffler (spoon, spoon
maker) 96, 106
Loesch (extinguish), see Lesch
Loescher, Loeschner, Loeschke 55
(stevedore)
Loesser, see Lesser, Leser
Loew, Loewe, Loewen (lion) 48,
62, 63
Loewenberg (lion mountain) 48,
68, 122
Loewenstein, Leuwenstein (lion
mountain) 48, 73, 122
Loewenstern (lion star) 48, 148
Loewenthal, Lowenthal (lion
valley) 48, 76, 122
Löffler 159, see Loeffler
Lofink (wood finch) 115
Loh (flame)
Loh 122 (forest 71, swampy area
80), see Hohenloh
Lohaus (forest house) 71, 65, 122
Lohaus (tanner's shop) 65, 122
Loher, Lohgerber (tanner) 96
Lohoeffer (forest farm) 72, 92
Lohman, Lomann (forest man,
tanner) 72, 96, 94
Lohoefer (fr the Lohoff, forest
farm) 92, 122
Lohmeyer (forest farmer) 72, 93
Lohmuller (forest miller) 72, 103

Lohn, Lohner, Lohnes 164, Loner,
Lohnert 74 (reward, rewarder)
Lohn, Lohner (dweller on the
Lahn) 83, 122
Lohr, Lohre, Lohrman 94, Lohr-
mann, Lorman (fr Lohr 122,
dweller on the Lohr 83)
Lombart, Lombarth, see Lampart
Loman, see Lohman
Longacker 159 (long field) 84
Longanecker 159, Longenecker,
see Langenecker
Longbrake 159, see Lamprecht
Longnecker 159, see Langenecker
Longhoffer 159, see Langhoffer
Longschade 159 (long shadow)
Longnacker 159, see Langenacker
Loos, Loose (lot, fate) 122
Loos 53, Loose, Looser < Ludwig
53
Lor, see Lohr
Lorbach (laurel brook) 89, 77, 122
Lorch, Lorche (place name) 122
Lorentz, Lorenz, Lorentzen,
Lorincz (St. Lawrence) 131
Lortz 53, Lorz, see Lorentz
Losacker (field drawn by lot) 84
Losch, Losche, Loscher, Loschert
74 (costly leather, leather
worker) 96
Lothringer (fr Lorraine) 121
Lotz, Lots, Lotse (pilot) 96
Lotze 53 < Ludwig
Loub 159, see Laub
Louk 159, see Lauck
Loudenschlager 159, Louden-
slager, see Lautenschlaeger
Louderback 159, see Lauterbach
Loudermilk 159, Loudmilk
Loudermil, see Lautermilch
Loudiwick 159, see Ludwig
Louge 159, see Laug ·
Loughman 159, see Lachman
Loughner 159, see Lachner
Loun 159, see Laun
Lovenstein 159, see Loewenstein

Luthardt (loud + strong)
Luther (loud + army) 47, 46, 49
Luthold, Ludholtz (retinue +
loyal) 46, 48
Lutjen 53, 55 < Ludolf, Luther,
etc.
Lutman, see Lauthman, Ludman
Luts 159, see Lutz
Lutter 53 < Ludwig
Lutterbeck 122, see Lauterbach
Luttig 53 < Ludolf
Luttich (fr Liege 122)
Luttman, see Lutman
Luttrodt (Ludwig's clearing) 126
Lutwycke, see Ludowice
Lutz 53, Lutze, Lutzel, Lutzens
164 < Ludwig
Lutzel (little) 113
Lux (lynx) 115
Lux (Latin, light)
Luxemburg, Luxenburg, Luxen-
berg 159 (a principality, little
castle) 121
Luz, see Lutz

# M

Maack, Maak, Maag (kinsman)
119
Maas, Mass (Meuse) 83, 122
Maasch (marsh)
Macher 159, see Metzger
Mass (ThoMAS) 131
Machler, see Mackler
Macht (power) 46
Mack 53, Mag, Mak, Makh <
Markward
Mackel, see Makel
Mackler (broker) 96
Mader, Maeder, Maehder (mower)
95
Mader (dyer, dye seller) 96, 106
Madreiter (meadow clearing) 125
Maehler, see Mehler
Maenhart, see Meinhart
Maerker (observer, umpire)

Maerten, Maertens 74, see Martin
Maertz, Maerz, Mertzke 55
(March) 143
Maessner, see Mesner
Mag, Magen (kinsman) 119
Magaziner (keeper of the maga-
zine) 109
Magdeburger (fr Magdeburg 122,
the Virgin's city) 122
Magenheim, Magenheimer (fr
Magenheim 122, kinsmen
hamlet) 123
Magenhoffer (fr Magenhof 122,
kinsman farm) 92
Mager, Magers 164 (thin) 114
Magerfield 153 (infertile field) 84
Magnus (Latin, great) 141
Maher 159 (mower) 95
Mahl, Mahle (meal, time)
Mahler (miller) 103
Mahler (painter) 96
Mahlstedt (parliament place) 122
Mahn (admonition), see Mohn
Mahnke 53, 55 < Mangold
Mahr, Mahrer (swamp) 80
Mahrenholtz (swamp forest) 80,
72, 122
Maiden, see Meiden
Maienshein 159, see Mayenschein
Maier, see Meyer
Mailender (fr Milan) 122
Mainfort (Main ford) 78, 122
Mainhard, Mainhardt, see Mein-
hard
Maintzer, Mainzer (fr Mainz 122)
129
Mair, Maiers, see Meyer, Meyers
Maisel, Maizel 159, see Meisel
Maisner, see Meissner
Maijer, see Meyer
Makel, Makell (stain, spot, Latin
*macula*)
Makler (broker) 96
Mal (boundary)
Malchior, Malcher, see Melchior
Maler (painter) 96

Maltz, Maltzer, Malz, Maltzman 94 (malt, brewer) 96, 106, 122
Mance 159, see Mantz
Mandel, Mandell, Manndel (almond) 158, see Mantel
Mandelbaum (almond tree) 89
Mandelberg (almond mountain) 89, 68
Mandelblat (almond leaf) 89
Manfred, Manfretz 164 (man + peace or protection) 94, 47
Mangel (lack)
Mangold < Managwalt, great + power) 46
Manhim 159, see Mannheim
Manlich (manly) 115
Mann, Manne, Manns 164 (man, vassal) 94, or < Hermann
Mannalther (adult) 113
Mannbar (marriageable) 113
Mannheit (manhood)
Mannhardt, see Meinhard
Mannheim, Mannheimer (fr Mannheim, swamp hamlet) 122
Mannherz (man heart) 115
Mannlein (little man) 94
Mansfeld (fr Mansfeld) 122
Mansfield 153, Mansfeild, see Mansfeld
Mantel, Mantell (coat, fr Latin *mantellum*) 112, 106
Mantel, Mantell (fir tree) 89, 122
Mantler (coat dealer) 106
Mantz, Manz < St. Manitius) 131, see Mangold
Mar, Marr (swamp) 80
Marbach, Marbaker 159 (swamp brook) 80, 77, 122, see Markbach
Marburger (fr Marburg 122, swamp castle) 80, 73
Marckel 53, 55 < Markwart
Marcksteiner (boundary stone) 73
Marcus (St. Mark) 131

Marder, Marders 164 (marten) 115
Marenburg, see Marburg
Margenthaler, see Mergenthaler, Morgenthaler
Margot (famous + god) 47, 131
Margraf (margrave) 109
Marienborn (Mary's sprint) 50
Marius (Roman name) 141
Mark, Marck, Marks, Marcks, Marx, Marcus (St. Mark, name of a pope) 134
Markbach (boundary brook) 77
Markel 53, 55, Markels 164, see Markwart
Markhart (boundary + strong) 46
Markstein (boundary stone) 73
Markus (St. Mark) 131
Markwart, Markward, Markword, Markwordt, Marckwart, Markwardt (guardian of the boundary) 47
Markwitz (boundary village, march village) 123
Marner (mariner) 96
Marold (famous + loyal) 47, 48
Marquard, Marquart, Marquardt, see Markwart
Marsch, Marscher, Marschke 55 (marsh) 80
Marschall, Marschalk (horse + servant, marshall) 107
Marscheck (marsh field) 80, 84
Marschuetz (horse guard) 107
Marstaller, Marsteller (horse + stall, equerry) 107
Mart, Martel 55, Marten, Martens, Martenz, see Martin
Marti 53 < Martin
Martin, Martins, Marthin (St. Martin, name of pope) 134
Martinus (St. Martin) 141
Martini (son of Martinus) 142
Martinssen (son of Martin) 59
Martz, Marz, see Maertz
Marx, see Mark

Masbach, see Mosbach
Maschauer (swampy meadow) 80, 84
Maschbaum (swamp tree) 80, 89
Mass (measure, see Thomas) 1
Masse (quantity, mass)
Mathaus, see Matthaeus
Matheis, Mathai, see Matthias
Matt, Matz, see Matthaeus
Matt (sloping meadow) 71
Matthaeus (St. Matthew) 131
Matthias, Mattheiss, Matteis, Mattis, Mattice 159 (St. Matthew) 131
Matthiesen, Matthyssen (son of Matthias) 59
Mattmueller (miller on the sloping meadow) 71, 84
Mattmueller (miller on the Matte) 83
Matz 53, Matzen < Matthaeus or Mattias)
Matzdorf (Matthew's village) 123
Matzger 159, see Metzger
Matzke 53, 55 (little Matz) 113
Mauer 122, see Maurer
Mauershagen (walled enclosure) 123
Maul, Maule (mouth, probably large or deformed) 114
Maul, Mauler (mule) 91
Maultasch (distorted face) 114
Maurer, Mauer, Mauerer (mason, fr Latin *murus*) 100
Mauritz, Maurits 159, Mauriz, see Moritz
Maus, Mause, Mauss (mouse) 115
Mauser, Mausser (mouser)
Maut, Mauth, Mauthe, Maute, Mautz 164, Mauter, Mautner (toll collector) 109
Max 53 < St. Maximilian 131
May (May) 143
Maydag, see Maytag
Mayenbaum (may tree, maypole) 89

Mayenschein (as bright as May) 115
Mayer, Mayers 164, see Meyer
Mayerhafer 159, Mayerhaver, see Mayerhoff
Mayerhoff, Mayerhoffer (fr Mayerhoff 122), see Meyerhoffer
Mayhler 159, see Mehler
Maykranz (May wreath)
Maynard 159, Maynerd, see Meinhard
Mayr, see Meyer
Mayerhofer, see Meyerhoffer
Mayse (titmouse) 115
Maytag (Mayday) 143
Mealy 159, see Muehle
Mearkle 159, see Merkel
Mease 159, see Mies
Mechelke 55 (little Michael) 113
Mechler, see Mackler
Meckel, Mechtel < Mechthild (power + battle) 46, 46, 53, 54, 122
Mecklenburg (German province) 121
Meder, see Mader
Medicus (Latin, doctor) 141
Meece 159, see Mies
Meer (sea, swamp) 80, 122
Meerholtz (swamp forest) 80, 72
Meerman (swamp dweller) 80
Mees, Meese, Meesen (swamp) 80
Meetze 159, see Muetze
Megenhardt (might + strong) 46, 46
Megenwart (might + guard) 46, 47
Meher (mower) 95
Mehl, Mehle, Mehler (meal, grist, miller) 106
Mehlman, Mehlmann (meal dealer) 106
Mehner, Mehnert 74, see Meinhard

Mehr 53, Mehren, Mehring <
  Merhold
Mehrenholtz (swamp forest) 80,
  72
Meichelsbeck < am Aichelsbeck
  (on the acorn brook) 70, 77
Meichelweg < am Aichelsweg (on
  the acorn path) 70, 65
Meichler (dweller near stagnant
  water) 79
Meiden (horses) 91
Meidenbauer (horse farmer) 91
Meier, Meiers 164, see Meyer,
  Meyers
Meierhenry 159 < Meyerhenrich
  (farmer Henry)
Meierhofer (fr Meierhof 122), see
  Meyerhofer
Meijer, see Meyer
Meil, Meile (mile, Latin, *mille
  passum)*
Meilchen 55 (short mile)
Meineke 53, 55, Meinecke <
  Meinhard
Meinhard, Meinhardt, Meinert,
  Meiner (might + strong) 46, 46
Meinhold (might + loyal) 46, 48
Meininger (fr Meiningen) 122
Meinke 53, 55, Meinken <
  Meinhard
Meinschein, see Meyenschein
Meinrad < Meginrat (power +
  counsel) 46 + 46
Meinstein (mountain on the
  Main) 83, 73
Meinster, see Muenster
Meintzer, Meinzer, Meinz (fr
  Mainz) 122
Meise (titmouse) 115
Meisel, Meisels 164 (mouse hawk)
  115
Meisenbacher (swamp water
  brook) 80, 77, 122
Meisenhalder, Meisenhelder,
  Meisenholder (songbird owner,
  songbird seller) 106

Meisenheim (swamp hamlet) 123,
  122
Meisner, Meissner (fr Meissen)
  122
Meissel (chisel) 106
Meissinger (fr Meissing) 122
Meister (master)
Meisterjan (Master John)
Meitzel (power)
Meixner, see Meisner
Mekeburg 159, see Mecklenburg
Melchior, Melcher, Melchers 164,
  Melchert 74, Melger, Melken
  (one of Three Kings) 111
Meltz, Meltzer, Melzer (malt
  maker, brewer) 96, 106
Memminger (fr Memming or
  Memmingen) 122
Mench 159, see Mensch
Mencken 55, Menke, Menken,
  Menkel 55 < Meinhard
Mendel 148, see Mandel
Mendelbaum, see Mandelbaum
Mendelsohn, Mendelssohn (son of
  Mendel) 59
Menge (multitude, retailer) 105
Mengel, Mengle 159, Mengele, see
  Mangel
Mengeldorff, see Mengersdorf
Menger, Mengers 164, Mengert
  74 (monger, fr Latin *mangari)*
  105
Mengersdorf (mongers' village)
  123, 122
Menges, Mengs, Mengen (fr
  Megingoz, might + Goth) 46,
  53, 54
Menhard, see Meinhard
Menke 53, 55, Mennecke, Menn-
  ing, see Meinhard
Menrad, see Meinrad
Mensch (human being)
Mensh 159, Mentch, see Mensch
Mentz, Menz, Mentze, Mentzer,
  Mentzel, Mentzell, Mentzel,
  Mentzl, Mentzer, see Maintzer

Merbach (swamp brook) 80, 77
Merck 53, Merckel 55, Merckle
159, Mercke, Merkle 159,
Merklin 55 < Markwart
Merfeld (marshy field) 80, 84, 122
Mergardt (swamp garden) 80, 84
Mergart (son of Merigarda) 60
Mergel, Mergl, Mergler (marl,
marl supplier, fr Latin *mar-
gila*) 106
Mergenthaler (marl valley) 76,
122
Merhold (famous + loyal) 47, 48
Merkel 53, 55, Merkle, see
Markwart
Merker, Merkertz 74, 164 (fr
Mark Brandenburg) 121
Mermelstein (marble) 73
Mersinger (fr Mersing) 122
Mertel 55, 53, see Marten
Merten, Mertens 164, Merthens,
see Martin
Merts, Mertz, Merz, see Maerz
Merwin (famous + friend) 47, 48
Mesman, see Messman
Mesmer, Mesner (sexton, fr Latin
*mansionarius)* 110
Mess (mass)
Messbach (swamp brook) 80, 77
Messenger, see Messing
Messer, Messerman, Messermann
(knife, knife grinder, cutler) 96,
106
Messer (official measurer) 109
Messerschmidt, Messerschmied,
Messersmith 153 (cutler, knife
maker) 96
Messing, Messinger, Mesinger
(brass, brass worker 96, 106),
or fr Messing 122
Messman, Messmann (attendant
at fair, at mass) 110
Messmer, Messmers, see Mesmer
Messner, see Mesmer
Meth, Methe (mead, taverner) 96
Methaus (tavern, taverner) 96

Metscher, see Metzger
Metschke 53, 55 < Matthaeus
Metter (mead maker) 96
Metz (inhabitant of Metz 122),
see Metzger, Matthias
Metzbower 159 (butcher farmer)
102, 91
Metzdorf (butchers' village) 102,
123, 122
Metzdorf (Mechthild's village) 123
Metzel, Metzler (butcher, fr Latin
*macellarius)* 102
Metzger (butcher, fr Latin *mat-
iarius)* 102
Meurer, see Maurer
Meusel (little mouse) 115
Mewes 53, Meves < Matthaeus
Mey, see May
Meyer (farmer, dairy farmer, fr
Latin *major domus, major
villae)* 93
Meyerhoffer, Mayerhofer (farm
managed by bailif) 93, 92
Meyers 164, Meyerson 59, see
Meyer
Meylaender, see Mailaender
Meyner < Meginher (might +
army) 46, 46
Meysel, see Meisel
Mezger, see Metzger
Michael, Michaels 164, Michaelis,
Michaeles, Michel, Michele (St.
Michael) 131
Michel, see Michael
Michel, Michels 164, Michler,
Michener, Michelman 94,
Michelman, Michelmann (large,
large fellow) 113
Michelbach (large brook) 77, 122
Michelbach (St. Michael's brook)
77, 122
Michelfelder (large fields) 84, 122
Michelfelder (St. Michael's fields)
84, 122
Michelsen (son of Michel) 59
Mick, Micks 164, see Mueck

Mickel, Mickle 159, see Michel
Middag, Middaugh 159, see
  Mittag
Middeldorp, Middendorf, see
  Mitterdorf
Middelkamp, Middelcamp (middle
  field) 84
Middelkauf (inbetween) 96
Middelman, see Mittelman
Middelstadt, Middelstaedt (mid-
  dle town)
Midnight 153, see Mitnacht
Miers 159, 164, see Meyer
Mies (marsh) 80
Miesbach (marsh brook) 80, 77,
  122
Mihle, see Muehle
Mil ..., mill ..., see Muehl
Milch (milk) 106
Milchberg (milk mountain) 68
Milcher, see Melchior
Milchsack (milk bag) 106
Mild (generous) 115
Milde (river name) 83
Mildenberg (gentle mountain) 68
Milhaus, see Muehlhaus
Milheim (mill hamlet) 123
Milhizer 159, 66, Milheisler, see
  Muehlhaus
Milhous 159, Milhouse 153,
  Milhouser, see Muehlhaus
Millberg, Millenberg, see Mueh-
  lenberg
Millen (place name) 122
Miller, see Mueller
Millhaus, Millhausen, Millhauser
  < Muehlhaus
Millhizer 159, 66, see Millhaus,
  Millhauser
Millhof (mill farm) 92, 122
Millhouse 153, Millhouser 159,
  see Muehlhaus 151
Millspaugh 159 (mill brook) 77
Millstein, Milstein (millstone) 73,
  see Muehlstein
Milner, see Muehlner

Milroth (mill clearing) 126
Miltonberger 159, see Milden-
  berger
Miltz (spleen)
Mince 159, see Muentz
Mincer 159, see Maintzer
Minch 159, Minnich, see Moench
Minchenberg, see Moenkeberg
Minchhoff (cloister farm) 92
Minck, see Mink
Minden (name of city) 122
Minderlein 55 (of low rank)
Minehart 159, see Meinhard
Mineweaser 159 < Mainwiese
  (meadow on the Main) 83, 84
Mingeldorf, see Mengersdorf
Minger, Mingers 164, see Menger
Mingersdorf, see Mengersdorf
Mink, Minke, Minken, Minkel 55
  (Wendish, miller) 146
Minne (love)
Minnegerode, Minnigerode
  (Minne's clearing) 126
Minnich, Minnick, Minnik, see
  Moench
Minster, see Muenster
Mintz, Mintze, Mintzes 164,
  Mintzer, see Muentz, Muentze,
  Muentze
Mire 159, see Meyer
Mischle 53, 55, Mischler, Mit-
  schler < Michael
Misel 159, see Meisel
Misener 159, Misner, see Meisner
Misslich (awkward, inconvenient)
  115
Mitnacht, Mittnacht, Mitternacht
  (midnight) 143
Missner 159, see Meisner
Mittag (midday) 143
Mittelberger, Mittenberger (mid-
  dle mountain) 68, fr Mittelberg
  122
Mitteldorf (middle village) 123
Mittelholz (middle forest) 72
Mittelkamp (middle field) 84

Mittelmann, Mittleman 159
(middle man, inbetween) 96
Mittelstadt, Mittelstaedt, Mittel-
stetter (middle city)
Mittenberger (fr Mittenberg) 68,
122
Mittendorf (in the middle of the
village) 123, 122
Mittenthal (in the middle of the
valley) 76
Mittermeier (middle farmer) 93
Mittersteiner (middle stone) 73
Mittnight 153 > Mitternacht
(midnight) 143
Mitz 159, see Muetz
Mix, see Mueck
Mizel 159, Mizell, see Meisel
Moan 159, see Mohn
Mock (female wild boar, see also
Mack)
Moeglich (possible) 117
Moehle, Moehler, see Muehle,
Muehler
Moelcher (milker, dairyman) 95
Moehm (aunt) 119
Moehlman, Moehlmann (miller)
103
Moeller, Moellers 164, Moell-
mann, Moelleken 55) 103, see
Mueller
Moench, Moenck (monk, fr Latin
*municus*) 110
Moenkeberg (monk mountain) 68,
122
Moennich, see Moench
Moersberger (marsh mountain)
80, 67
Moerschbacher (fr Moersbach
122, swamp brook) 80, 77
Moersdorf (swamp village) 80,
123, 122
Moeser, Moesinger (fr Moese 122,
marsh) 80
Moessbauer (marsh farmer) 80,
93
Moessinger, see Messing

Moessmer, see Messmer
Mohl, Mohle, Mohlberg, see
Muehle, Muehlenberg
Mohlberg, see Muehlenberg
Mohler, Mohlmann, see Mahler,
Mueller
Mohlhenry < Mohlheinrich
(Henry at the mill) 103
Mohn (poppy) 89
Monheim (poppy village) 123
Mohnkern (poppy seed) 89
Mohnberger (poppy mountain) 89,
68
Mohr, Mohrman, Mohrmann
(Moor, possibly actor in miracle
play) 111
Mohr (fen or bog) 80, 122
Mohrmann (dweller on a fen) 80
Molden, Molder, Moldenhauer,
Mollenhauer (trough maker)
96, 100, fr Moldau 122
Moler, see Mueller
Molk (milk, milk dealer) 106
Moll, Molle (heavy set) 114
Mollenhauer, Mollnauer, see
Molden
Moller, Mollere, see Mueller
Mollman, Mollman (miller) 103
Molnar, Molner, see Mueller
Moltke (Slavic: young) 113, 146
Moltmann (earthman, Adam)
Moltz, Moltz, Molz, Moltzer, see
Maltz, Maltzer
Momma, see Mumma
Monat, Monath, Monnat (month)
Monbauer (fr the Monhof, poppy
farm) 91
Monch 159, see Moench
Mondorf (moon village, poppy
village) 123
Mondschein (moonlight) 148
Monheit, see Mannheit
Monich, Monick, Monk, see
Moench
Montag (Monday) 143
Moon, see Mohn

Moor 122, Moore, see Mohr
Moos (fen, bog) 80, 122
Moosbrugge (bridge on the fen) 80
Moosmann (dweller on a fen) 80
Morast (marsh, morass) 80
Morganstein 159, Morganstern,
   Morganthal, see Morgenstein,
   Morgenstern, Morgenthal
Morgedaller, see Morgenthaler
Morgen (morning) 122, 143
Morgenroth (morning red) 148,
   122
Morgenstein (morning stone) 73,
   148
Morgenstern (morning star, mace)
   107, 108, 148, 122
Morgenthal, Morgenthaler
   (morning valley) 76, 148, 122
Morgenthau (morning dew) 148
Morgott, see Margot
Morheim (fen hamlet) 80, 123
Moritz (St. Mauritius) 131, 122
Morman, Mormann (dweller on
   the fen) 80
Morningstar 153, see Morgen-
   stern
Morris 159, 148, see Moritz
Morsberger, Morstein (swamp
   mountain) 80, 81, 68, 73
Morsch (rotten, decayed)
Morschhauser (decayed houses)
   65
Morschheimer (fr Morschheim,
   rotten + hamlet) 81, 123, 122
Morstadt, Morstaedter (fen city)
   80
Morstorff (fen village) 80, 123
Mosbach, Mosbacker (marshy
   brook) 80, 77, 122
Mosberg (marsh mountain) 80,
   68, 122
Mosburg (marsh castle) 80, 73
Mosel (fr the Moselle) 83, 122
Moser, Moseman, Mosemann
   (dweller on a marsh) 80
Moser (place name) 122

Moses, Mose (OT name) 135
Mosmiller (marsh miller) 80, 103
Mosner (marsh dweller) 80
Moss, see Moos
Mossbach, Mossbacher, see
   Mosbach 122
Mosser, see Moser
Mosshamer (bog hamlet) 80, 123
Mossmann (dweller on a marsh)
   80
Most (grapejuice, fr Latin must-
   um) 96, 112
Mott, Motte (moth)
Motz, see Matz
Moul 159, see Maul
Mous 159, Mouser, see Maus,
   Mauser
Mowl 159, see Maul
Mowrer 159, see Maurer
Much (marshy stream) 81, 122
Mueck, Muecke, Muck, Mick,
   Micks 164, Mix (midge, gnat,
   restless person) 115, 122
Mueckenberg (gnat mountain) 68,
   122
Mueckenfuss (gnat leg) 114
Muegge, see Muecke
Mueh (trouble, effort)
Muehl (mill) 103
Muehlebach (mill brook) 103, 77
Muehleisen, Muehlseisen (mill
   axeliron)
Muehlenberg (mill mountain) 68
Muehlenstein (millstone) 73
Muehler, see Mueller
Muehlhaus, Muehlhause,
   Muehlhausen, Muehlhauser
   (mill house) 65
Muehlheim (mill hamlet) 123
Muehlhoff (mill farm) 92
Muehlke 55 (little mill) 103
Muehlman (mill man, miller) 103
Muehsam (toilsome, tedious) 115
Mueller (miller, fr Latin molina-
   rius) 103
Muench, see Moench

Muencheberg (monk mountain) 110, 68

Muendel 55, Muendlein 55 (little ward)

Muenster (minster, fr Latin *monasterium*) 122

Muensterman (worker for, or dweller near a minster) 139

Muentz, Muentze, Muenz, Muenzen (coin, minter, fr Latin *moneta*) 106

Muessig (vacnt, leisurely)

Muetz (cap, cap maker) 96, 106

Muetzenberg (cap mountain) 68

Mugg, see Mueck

Muhl 159, Muhly, Muhler, see Muehle, Muehler

Muhlbach 159, see Muehlbach

Muhlbauer 159 (farmer at the mill) 91

Muhldorf 159 (mill village) 123

Muhleisen 159, see Muehleisen

Muhlenbruch 159 (quarry at the mill) 80

Muhlhaus 159, Muhlhausen, see Muehlhaus, Muhlhausen

Mulhauser 159, see Muehlhaus

Muhlmeister 159 (master miller) 103

Mulinari (miller, fr Latin *molinarius*) 142

Mullendorf 159 (mill village) 123

Muller 159, see Mueller

Mullhausen 159, see Muehlhaus

Mumma, Mumme (masquerader)

Munch, see Moench

Mund, Mundt, Mundth (guardian) 47, see Siegmund

Mundel 55, Mundelein 55, see Muendel, Muendlein

Munich, see Moench

Munk, Munck, Munke, see Moench

Munkshower 159, Munschauer, Munshower (monk's meadow) 84

Munster 159, Munsterman, see Muenster, Muensterman

Munter (lively, merry) 115

Muntz 159, Munz, Muntzer, Munzer, Munzert 74, see Muentz

Munzenmayer 159 (foreman at the mint) 96

Murach (swamp river) 80, 79

Murbach (swamp brook) 80, 77, 122

Murdorf (swamp village) 80, 123

Murgenstern 159, see Morgenstern

Murlach (swamp pond) 80, 81

Murnau, Murner (swamp meadow) 80, 84, 122

Muschel (mussel)

Musiker (musician) 96

Musculus (Latin, muscle) 141

Muss < Dominicus, Hieronymus 131

Musse (leisure) 115

Musselman, Mussellmann (Moslem, one who has fought the Moslems)

Must, see Most

Muth, Muthe (courage, disposition, mood) 46

Muth 53 < Helmuth

Muthart (courage + strong) 46, 46

Mutscher, Mutschler, Mutschke 55 (baker of long loaves) 96

Mutter (official measurer) 109

Myer 159, Myers 164, see Meyer

Mynhard 159, see Meinhard

Myrs 159, Myers 164, see Meyer

Myster 159, see Meister

# N

Naab (river name) 83

Naas, Nass (wet), see Nase

Nachbar, Nachbahr (neighbor)

Nachlas (legacy)

Nacht (night) 143

Nachtigal, Nachtigall (nightin-
gale) 115
Nack 122, Nacke (nape of neck)
114
Nack (ridge) 68
Nader (sewer)
Nadler, Nadeler, Nadelmann
(needle maker) 96, 106, 148
Naegele, Naegeli (little nail,
clove) 106
Naff, see Neffe
Nafzger, Naffzer, Naftziger
(sleepy person) 115
Nagel, Nagell, Nagele, Nagl,
Nagle 159, Nagler (nail, nail
smith) 96, 98, 106
Nagengast (stingy host) 96, 115
Nahrgan, Nahrgang (earning of
nourishment, livlihood)
Nahm, Name (name)
Nanamacher 159, see Nonnen-
macher
Nangesser 159 (probably fr
Nongazzer)
Napfel, Nappel (an apple) 89
Nase, Nasemann (nose, prom-
ontory) 114, 74
Nass (wet), see Nase
Nassau, Nassauer (fr Nassau,
swamp meadow) 80, 121
Nast (fr Ast, branch cutter) 95
Nastvogel (nest bird) 115
Nathan (OT name) 135
Natter (adder) 115
Nau, Nauer, Nauert 74, Nauerz
74, 164 (dweller near the
Naue) 83
Nauman, Naumann (new man),
see Neumann 34
Naumburg (new castle) 34, 73,
122
Neander (Greek for Newmann)
143
Nease 159, see Nies
Nebel (fog)

Nebeling (fr land of fogs, cf.
Nibelungen)
Needleman 153, see Nadelmann
Neef, Neefer, see Neff
Neesemann (son of Agnes) 60
Neff, Neffe (nephew) 119
Nefzger, see Nafzger
Negele, Negle, see Naegele
Neher (ferryman) 96
Nehring (nutrition, subsistence),
fr Nehring or Nehringen 122
Nehrkorn (fattening corn)
Neibauer, Neibuhr, see Neubauer
34
Neibling, Neiblinger, Nuebling,
see Nebeling
Neibrand (new clearing) 34, 126
Neid, Neider, Neidert 74 (envy,
hater) 46, see also Neidhard
Neidenbach (stream brook) 83, 77
Neidenberg (place name) 68
Neidhard, Neidhart, Neidhardt
(hate + strong) 46, 46
Neidig (envious) 115
Neidlinger (fr Neidling or Neid-
lingen) 122
Neifeld (new field) 34, 84
Neighoff 159, see Neuhoff 151
Neihart, see Neidhart
Neihoff 34, see Neuhoff
Neikirk 34, see Neukirk
Neimann 34, see Neumann,
Niemann
Neimiller 34 (new miller) 103
Neischwanger 34, see Neusch-
wander
Neisser (dweller near the Neisse
River) 83
Neiswander, Neiswender, Neis-
wenter, Neiswinter 159, see
Neuschwander
Neithard, see Neidhard
Nelde 53 < Arnold
Nembhard (one who likes to take)
115
Nemeyer 169, see Niemeyer

Nemth, Nemetz, Nemitz, see
   Nimmitz
Ness (fr Nessen) 122
Nessel (nettle) 89, 72
Nesselroth (nettle clearing) 89,
   72, 126
Nessler (dweller in the nettles)
   89, 72
Nester (Greek, Nestor) 143
Neter (sewer) 96
Nett, Netter, Nettman (dweller on
   the Nette) 83
Nettelbladt (nettle leaf) 89
Netz (net, netz fisherman) 91, 106
Neu (new, new settler)
Neubach, Neubacher, Neubeck,
   Neubecker (new brook) 77
Neubauer, Neubaier (newly
   arrived farmer, fr the Neuhof,
   new farm) 91
Neuber, Neubert 74, Neuberth,
   see Neubauer
Neuberger (fr Neuberg 122, new
   mountain) 68
Neuburger (fr Neuburg 122, new
   castle) 73
Neudorff 122, Neuendorff (new
   village) 123
Neuenschwander, Neuenschwand
   122, see Neuschwander
Neufeld, Neufeldt (new field) 84,
   122
Neugart, Neugarth, Neugarten
   (new garden) 84, 122
Neugebauer, see Neubauer
Neuhart, Neuharth, see Neidhart
Neuhaus, Neuhausen, Neuhauser
   (new house) 65, 122
Neuhof, Neuhoff (new farm) 92,
   122
Neukamp (new field) 84, 122
Neukirch (new church) 122
Neuland, Neulander (newly
   cleared land) 125, 122
Neuman, Neumann (fr the Neu-
   hoff, new farm)

Neumark (new boundary marker)
   122
Neumarkt (new market) 122
Neumauer (new wall) 100
Neumayer, Neumeier, Neumeyer
   (new farmer), or fr the Neuhof
   (new farm) 93
Neumeister (new master)
Neumyer 159, see Neumayer
Neun, Neuner (nine, ninth) 143
Neunuebel (nine evils)
Neupert, see Neubauer
Neuremberg, see Nuernberg
Neureuther (new clearing) 126
Neuschaefer, Neuschafer (new
   shepherd) 95
Neuschwander, Neuschwender
   (new clearing) 126
Neuschwanger, see Neusch-
   wander
Neustadt, Neustater, Neustadt 55
   (new city) 122
Neuwirth (new host) 96
Newbauer 153, see Neubauer
Newberger 153, see Neuberger
Newfeld 153, see Neufeld
Newhagen 153 (new enclosure)
Newhart 153, see Neidhart
Newhiser 153, 66, see Neuhaus
Newhof 153, see Neuhof
Newman 153, see Neumann
Newmeyer 153, see Neumeyer
Newmister 153, see Neumeister
Newschwanger, see
   Neuschwander
Newstead 153, see Neustadt
Newwirth 153 (new host)
Ney 34, see Neu
Neymeyer 34, see Neumeyer
Neys, see Neiss
Nibling, see Nebling
Nice 159, see Neiss
Nicewonder 159, Nicewander, see
   Neuschwander
Nicholas, see Nikolaus
Nicht, Nichter (not, naught)

Nick 53 < Nikolaus
Nicklaus, see Nikolaus
Nickel, Nickels (nickel), or <
Nikolaus
Nickel (decoy owl) 115
Nickelmann (water sprite)
Nicodemus (St. Nicodemus) 131
Nicolai, Nicolay < Nikolaus
Nicolas, Nicolaus, see Nikolaus
Nider ..., see Nieder
Nidorf, see Neudorf
Niebe (merry, lively) 115
Niebel, see Nebel
Nieber 34, see Neubauer
Niebuhr 34, Niebur, see Neu-
bauer
Nied, Niede (nailsmith) 96, 106
Niedenthal, Niedentohl 159 (low
valley) 76
Nieder (low)
Niederauer (fr Niederau 122, low
meadow) 84
Niederhaus, Niederhausen,
Niederhauser (fr Niederhausen
122, low house) 65
Niederhof, Niederhoff, Nieder-
huber (low farm) 92, 122
Niedermayer, Niedermeyer (fr the
Niederhof, lower farm) 93
Niederman, see Niedermayer
Niedhart 159, see Neidhart
Niehaus 34, see Neuhaus
Niehof 34, see Neuhof
Niel, Nielmann (swamp, swamp
dweller) 80
Nieman, Niemann, Niman, see
Neumann
Niemand, Niemandt (no one)
Niemeier 34, Niemeyer, see
Neumayer
Niemiller 34, see Neumiller
Niemitz, see Nimitz
Niemyer 34, 159, see Neumayer
Niemoeller 34 (proprietor of the
new mill) 103

Nierendorf (lower village) 123,
122
Nierhaus (lower house) 65
Nierman, see Niederman
Niermeyer, Niermyer, see Nied-
ermayer
Nies, Niese, Nieser, Niess, Nies-
sler, Niessmann (usufruct, also
< Dionysius and Ananies)
Nighswander 159, see Neusch-
wander
Nighthart 159, see Neidhart
Niklas, Niklaus, see Nikolaus
Nikolai, see Nikolaus
Nikolaus, Nikolas (St. Nicholas,
name of a pope) 134
Nimann, see Nieman
Nimitz, Nimetz, Nimtz (Slavic:
"the dumb one," German) 122
Nipp, Nipper, Nippert 74 (dweller
near water) 81
Nissen (lice, lice eggs)
Niswander 159, see Neu-
schwander
Niswonger 159, see Neu-
schwanger
Nitchmann 159, see Nitsch
Nitsch 53, Nitszche, Nitschmann
94 < Nikolaus
Nitze 53 < Nikolaus
Niwenhous 159, see Neuhaus
Nobel (noble, name of lion in
Renard cycle)
Noble 159, see Nobel
Nodhart, see Nothart
Noes (place name) 122
Nofziger, see Nafziger
Nohrnberg 159, see Nuernberg
Nolder 53 < Arnold
Noll, Nolls 164, Noller, Nollmann
(heavy, simple person) 115
Noll, Knolls 164 (hill) 68
Nollendorf (hill village) 68, 123
Nolt 53, Nolte, Nolting 55,
Noelting < Arnold
Noman, see Naumann

Nonemacher, see Nonnemacher

Nongazzer (resident on nun alley) 65

Nonnenmacher, Nonemaker (pig castrator) 95

Noppenberger (woolnap mountain) 68, 122

Norbeck (northern brook) 85, 77

Norberg, see Nordberg

Nord, Nordt, North (north) 85

Nordahl (north valley) 85, 76

Nordberg (northern mountain) 85, 68, 122

Nordbrook, Nordbruch (northern brake) 85, 80, 122

Nordbruck (northern bridge) 85

Nordhaus, Nordhauser (fr Nordhausen 122, north house) 85, 65

Nordheimer, Northeimer (north hamlet) 85, 123

Nordhoff (northern farm) 85, 92

Nordhus, see Nordhaus

Nordlingen, Nordlinger (fr Nordlingen) 122

Nordman, Nordmann (northerner, Northman) 85

Nordorf (north village) 85, 123, 122

Nordstrand (north beach) 85, 122

Nordstrom (north stream) 85, 77

North (north) 85

Notenbom, see Nottebom

Notestein 159, Notstein (battle mountain) 46, 68

Noth (plight, battle)

Nothard (battle + strong) 46, 46

Notte (nut) 89

Nottebom, Nottebohm, see Nussbaum

Nowack, Nowak (Slavic: new man) 146

Nuechterlein 55 (moderate drinker) 115

Nuernber, Nuernberger (fr Nuremberg) 122

Nueschler (buckle maker) 96

Nuess, Nuessli 55, Nueslein, Nuesslein (little nut) 89

Numeyer 159, see Neumeyer

Nummer (number)

Nunamacher, Nunnamacher, see Nonnenmacher

Nungesser, see Nongazzer

Nurenberg, see Nuernber

Nushagen (nut hedge) 123

Nusholtz (nut wood) 89

Nuss, Nusse (nut) 89, 106

Nussbauer, Nusbauer, Nuszbaurn (nut farmer) 91

Nussbaum, Nusbaum, Nussbaumer (nut tree) 89, 62

Nusterer (maker of rosaries) 96

Nuswanger 159, see Neuschwanger

Nyenhuis, see Neuhaus

Nymann, see Neumann

## O

Oakes 159, see Ochs

Oben (up above)

Obenauer (upper meadow, beyond the meadow) 84

Obendorf, see Oberdorf

Obenheim (water hamlet) 80, 123 see Oberheim

Obenheyser 66 (upper houses, beyond the houses) 65

Ober (boss, superior)

Oberbeck (upper creek, across the creek) 77

Oberberger (fr Oberberg 122, upper mountain, beyond the mountain) 68

Oberdahlhof (upper valley farm) 76, 92

Oberdorf, Oberdoerfer (fr Oberdorf 122, upper village, beyond the village) 123

Oberfehl, Oberfell (beyond the swamp) 80

Oberfeld, Oberfeldt, Oberfelder
(upper field, beyond the field)
84, 122

Oberheim (upper hamlet) 123

Oberheuser (upper houses) 65

Oberholtz, Oberholtzer (beyond
the forest) 72, 122

Oberkirch, Oberkirche (upper
church) 122

Oberkofler (upper monticule) 67

Oberkuhn (temerarious) 115

Oberlaender, Oberlander (highlander, fr Oberland 122)

Oberle 55, Oberlin 55 < Albrecht

Oberman, Obermann (boss,
superior)

Obermayer, Obermeyer, Ober-
meier (chief bailiff) 93

Obermiller, Obermueller, Ober-
muller 159 (chief miller) 103

Oberndorf 122, see Oberdorf

Oberscheimer, Obersheimer
(upper hamlet) 123

Oberst (colonel) 107

Oberthaler (fr Oberthal, upper
valley) 76, 122

Obitz, see Opitz

Obman, Obmann (steward) 96

Obrist, see Oberst

Obser, Obster (fruit grower or
dealer) 89, 106, 143

Ochs (ox) 91, 149

Ochsenbacher (fr Ochsenbach
122, ox brook) 77

Ochsenberger (fr Ochsenberg 122,
ox mountain) 68

Ochsenfuss (ox foot) 114

Ochsenhirt (ox herder) 95

Ochsenreiter (ox clearing) 126

Ochsenreiter (ox rider) 117

Ochsenschwantz (ox tail) 112

Ochsner (ox raiser or seller) 91,
96

Odenwald, Odewalt, Odewaelder
(swamp mountains, mountain
range along Rhine) 121

Oechsele 55, Oechsle, Oechslein,
Oechslin, Oechselin, Oexli
(little ox) 149

Oechsener, see Ochsner

Oechsler, see Ochsner

Oechsli 55 (see Oechsele)

Oefner, Oeffner (oven tender,
oven maker) 96

Oehl (oil, oil dealer, fr Latin
*oleum)* 106, 122

Oehler, Oehlers 164, Oehlert 74,
Oehleret, see Ulrich, Eyler

Oehli (OT Eli) 135

Oehlstrom (eel stream) 77

Oelberg (Mount of Olives) 122

Oelhaf, Oelhafer (oil pitcher, oil
dealer) 106

Oelken, Oelker (oil dealer) 106

Oellen, Oeller, Oelmann, Oellen-
schlaeger (oil maker) 96

Oertel 53, Oertli 55 < Ortulf
(point of sword + wolf) 46, 48

Oesch 122, Oescheler, Oeshler,
see Esch, Eschelmann

Oesler (fr Oesel) 122

Oeste, Oester 122, Oesterle 55,
Oesterlein 55, Oesterlin,
Oesterling, Oestermann (east-
erly, man fr the east) 85, see
Oster

Oestreich, Oestreicher, Oester-
reicher (Austrian) 121

Oetken 55 (little otter)

Oetting, Oettinger (fr Oettingen,
122

Oexler, see Ochsner

Ofenstein (oven stone) 73

Offenbach, Offenbacker 159
(swamp brook) 80, 77, 122

Offenhauser (fr Offenhaus 122,
swamp house) 80, 65

Offenstein (open stone) 73

Offer, Offerman, Offermann, see
Opfermann

Offner, Ofner, see Oefner

Oheim (uncle) 119

Ohl 122, Ohle < Odal (inherited property 47), see also Ahl
Ohl, see Oehl
Ohlbach 122, see Ahlbach
Ohlendorf, see Altdorf
Ohlenschlaeger, Ollenschlager (oil maker) 96
Ohler (oil dealer) 106
Ohlhausen (old houses) 65
Ohlhausen (swamp houses) 80, 65
Ohlhaver (last year's oats)
Ohli, Ohliger, Ohlinger (oil dealer) 106
Ohlhoff (old farm) 92
Ohlhausen (old houses) 65
Ohlmacher (oil maker) 96
Ohlmann (old man) 113
Ohlmeyer (proprietor of the Ohlhoff) 93
Ohlschlaeger, see Ohlenschlaeger
Ohlweiler (old village) 123, 122
Ohlwein (old friend) 48, see Alwin
Ohm, Oheim, Ohms 164 (mother's brother) 119
Ohm (river name) 83
Ohne (without, see Ahn) 122
Ohnemann (without a husband)
Ohnesorg, Ohnisorg 159 (without worry) 115
Ohnfeld (without a field) 84
Ohnhaus (without a house) 65
Ohnschild (without a shield)
Ohr (ear) 114
Ohrbach, see Auerbach
Ohrenschall (ear deafening noise)
Ohrle 55 (little ear) 114
Ohrndorf, Orendorf (village on the Oren) 83, 123
Okner 153, see Eichner
Oldekamp (old field) 84
Oldenburg (old castle, German province) 73, 121, 122
Oldendorf, Ollendorf (old village) 123, 122
Oldhouse 153, see Althaus

Oldhuis, see Althaus
Olenschlaeger, see Ohlenschlaeger
Olinger, Ollinger (fr Ollingen) 122
Ollrich, Olrick, see Ulrich
Olm, Olmert 74, see Ulm
Olthof, see Althoff
Onangst, Ohnangst (without fear) 115
Opdebeek (on the brook) 69, 77
Openbrink (on the hill) 69, 74
Opfer, Opher (sacrifice, fr Latin *operari*)
Opfermann (sexton) 110
Opfertuch (sacrificial cloth)
Opitz 53 < Albrecht
Oppenheim, Oppenheims 164, Oppenheimer (open hamlet) 123, 122
Oppermann, see Opfermann
Oppert 53 < Albrecht
Oppitz, see Opitz
Oppmann, see Obmann
Ordemann, see Ortmann
Ordner, see Ortmann
Orebaugh 159, see Auerbach
Orendorf, Orndorf (village on the Oren) 83
Orendorf (swamp village) 80, 123
Orff 53 < Ordolf (sword point + wolf) 46, 48
Orgelfinger (organ finger, organist) 96
Orgelmann (organ player) 96
Orndorf, see Arndorf
Ornhold, see Arnold
Ornstein, Orenstein, see Arnstein
Ort, Orth, Ord, Oertli 55 (place) 122
Ort, Orth (point of sword or spear 46, point of land)
Ortel 53, 55, Ortell < Ortlieb, Ortwin, etc.
Ortlieb (point of sword + dear) 46, 48

Ortman, Ortmann, Orthmann, Ortmeyer (dweller at the end of the village) 94, 93

Ortner, see Ortmann

Ortwein (sword point + friend) 46, 48

Ortwig, Orwig (point of sword + battle) 46, 46

Osmann, see Ostmann

Ossenecker (ox field) 84, 85

Ossenfort (ox ford) 78

Ost (east) 85

Ostberg (east mountain) 85, 68, 122

Ostendorf (east village) 85, 123, 122

Oster (easter, easterner) 143

Osterberg, Osterberger (east mountain) 85, 68, 122

Osterhaus, Osterhouse 153 (eastern house) 85, 65

Ostericher (Austrian) 121

Osterle, see Oesterle

Osterling (easterner) 85

Osterloh (eastern forest) 85, 72

Osterloh (Easter fire) 122

Osterman, Ostermann, see Ostmann

Ostermayer, Ostermeier, Ostermeyer (eastern farmer) 85, 93

Ostermueller (eastern miller) 85, 103

Ostertag (Easter) 143

Osthaus (eastern house) 85, 65

Ostheim (easterm hamlet) 85, 123

Ostmann (eastern man) 85

Ostreicher (Austrian) 121

Oswald, Ostwalt, Osswald (god + rule, English saint) 47, 71, 131, 137

Otfried (treasure + protection) 47, 47

Otmar (treasure + famous) 47, 48

Ott, Otte, Odt, Utt (treasure) 47

Otten, Ottens 164 < Otto 122

Ottenbach (Otto's brook) 77

Ottendorf, Ottendorfer (Otto's village) 123, 122

Ottenheim, Ottenheimer (Otto's hamlet) 123

Otter (otter, otter hunter) 91, 122

Otterbach (swamp brook) 80, 77, 122

Otterbein (otter bone, otter leg)

Ottersheim (otter hamlet) 123

Overholser 159, see Oberholtzer

## P

Paasch, see Pasch

Pabst (pope, fr Latin *papa*) 110, 134, 143

Pabstmann (member of papal party) 110, 94

Pachmann, Pachmeyer (tenant farmer) 93

Pacht, Pachter, Paechter (tenant) 109

Packer, Packert 74, Packard 74, see Bacher

Packer (wholesaler) 105

Packheiser 66 (bake houses) 65

Paebke 55 (little priest) 110

Paetz 122, see Betz

Paetzsch 53, Paetsch < Petrus

Paff, see Pfaff

Paffenbach (priest's brook) 110, 77

Paffenroth (priest's clearing) 110, 126

Pagel, Pagels < Paulus

Pahnke 55 (Slavic, young lord) 146

Painter (dweller in a fenced inclosure) 84

Palmer (palmer) 110

Palzgraf, see Pfalzgraf

Palsgrove 159, see Palzgraf

Pamberg, see Bamberg

Pancer 159, see Pantzer

Panebaker 159, Pannabaker, Pannabecker, see Pfannenbecker

Pantel, see Bandel

Pantzer, Panzer (breastplate, fr Latin *pantex*) 108

Pape (priest, Latin *papa*) 110

Papel (poplar) 89

Papelbaum (poplar tree) 89

Papenberg, see Pappenberg

Papendorp (priest's village) 110, 123

Papp, Pappe, see Pape

Pappenberger (priests' mountain, swamp mountain) 80, 110, 68

Pappenheim (swamp hamlet) 80, 122, 123

Pappenheimer (priests' hamlet) 110, 123

Pappler (dweller by the poplars) 89

Papst, see Pabst

Paris, Pariser (Parisian, journeyman who trained in Paris) 122

Parkent, Parmenter (fustian dealer) 106

Parr (pair, couple)

Parris, see Paris

Part, Parth, Partz 164, see Bart

Pasch 122, Pasche (Easter 143), also fr French dice game

Paschke 53, 55 < Paulus

Passaw, Passauer (fr Passau, Latin *castra batava*) 122

Passmann (dweller in a pass) 68

Pastorius (Latin for Schaefer) 141

Pate, Path, Pathe (godfather, fr Latin *pater*) 119

Patz 53, Patzer < Balthasar

Pauck, Paucker, Pauckner (drummer) 96

Paul, Pauls, Paulus (St. Paul, name of pope) 134

Pauli, Pauly (son of Paulus) 142

Paulig, Pauling 53, 55, Paulinger, Paulmann < Paulus

Paulitsch 53 < Paulus

Paulus (St. Paul) 134

Pausch, see Baus

Pause (pause)

Paynter 159, see Painter

Peagler, see Buegler

Peal 159, Pealer, see Buehl, Buehler

Pech 122, Peche (pitch, tar maker) 96; see also Beck

Pechmann (tar maker) 95

Pechtle, see Bechtle

Peck, see Beck

Peel 159, Peeler, see Buehl, Buehler

Peffer, Peffers 164, see Pfeffer

Peifer, Peiffer, see Pfeiffer

Peightel 159, see Bechtel

Peil, see Pfeil

Peiper, see Pfeiffer

Pelgrim, Pelegrim, Pellegrin, see Pilgrim

Pelican (pelican, house name) 62, 148

Peltz, Pelz, Peltzer, Peldner, Peldtmann (pelt, hide worker, fr Latin *pelis*) 96

Pennecker (little bear) 48

Penner (salt maker) 96

Pennypacker, Pennybaker, see Pfannenbecker

Pentz, see Bentz

Pepper, Peppermann, see Pfeffer, Pfeffermann

Perger, see Berger

Perle (pearl)

Perlman (pearl dealer, possibly Ashkenazic metronym for "Pearl's husband")

Perlmutter (mother of pearl) 106

Perlroth (pearl red) 148

Pershing 159, Persing, Persinger, see Pfirsich

Peter, Peters 164, Peterlein 55,
Peterke 55, Petrus (St. Peter)
131, 135
Peterly (son of Peter) 59, 142
Petersen, Peterson (son of Peter)
59
Petri, Petry (son of Peter) 142
Petsch 53 < Peter
Petz, Petts 159 (bear) 48, also <
Peter)
Petzold 53 < Peter
Peukert (drummer, person fr
Peuker in Silesia) 96, 122
Peyer, see Bayer
Pfaar 122, see Pfarr
Pfadenhauer (thread maker) 100
Pfaeffer (priest) 110
Pfaeffikon (priest village) 110,
127
Pfaff, Pfaffe (priest, fr Latin
*papa*) 110
Pfaffenbach (priests' brook) 110,
77
Pfaffenberger (fr Pfaffenberg 122,
priests' mountain) 110, 68
Pfaffmann (priest's man) 94
Pfahl (stake, fr Latin *palus*)
Pfaltz, Pfaltzer (Rhenish Pala-
tinate, from Latin *palatium*)
121
Pfalzgraf (palgrave, fr Latin
*palatium* + *graf*) 109
Pfanne, Pfanner (pan, pan maker,
fr Latin *panna*) 106
Pfannebecker (cake baker) 96
Pfannenstiel, Pfanstiel (pan
handle)
Pfanner (pan maker) 96
Pfannkuchen (pancake, baker) 96
Pfannstiel, see Pfannenstiel
Pfarr (pastorate, fr Latin *parro-
chia*) 122
Pfarrer (pastor) 110
Pfau (peacock) 115

Pfeffer, Pfeffermann (pepper,
seller of pepper, fr Latin *piper*)
106
Pfefferkorn (pepper corn, spice
dealer) 106
Pfeifenberger, Pfeiffenberger (pipe
mountain) 68
Pfeifer, Pfeiffer, Pfeiffers 164,
Pfeifere (fifer, fr Latin *pipa*) 96
Pfeil, Pheil, Pheyl (arrow, fr Latin
*pilus*, a javelin) 108
Pfeiler (arrow maker, fletcher)
108
Pfennig, Pfenning (penney) 117
Pfingst, Pfingstag, Pfingsten
(Pentecost, Whitesuntide) 143
Pfirsich, Pfersich (peach, fr Latin
*malum persicum*) 89
Pfister, Pfistner, Pfisterer (baker,
fr Latin *pistor*) 102
Pfitz, Pfitze, Pfitzer, Pfitzel
(flagellant)
Pfitzner, see Pfuetzner
Pflanz, Pflantz (plant, fr Latin
*planta*) 89
Pflaum (plumb, fr Latin *pluma*)
89
Pflaumenbaum (plum tree) 89,
122
Pfleger (guardian, fosterer, judge)
Pflueger (plowman) 91, 46
Pflug (plow, plowman) 91
Pflug (a measure of plowland) 122
Pflugfelder (arable field) 84
Pfoersching, see Pfirsich
Pfoertner, Pfortner (gate keeper,
fr Latin *porta*) 96
Pfriendtner, Pruendner (pre-
bendary) 110
Pfontz, see Puntzius
Pfortzheim (town in Baden) 122
Pfuetzner, Pfutzner (dweller by a
pond) 80
Pfuhl (puddle) 80, 122

Pfund (pound, fr Latin *pondus*)
Pfuntz, see Puntzius
Pfutzner, see Pfuetzner
Pfyfer, see Pfeiffer
Ph ..., look under Pf
Pheidler (shirt maker) 96
Pheifer, Phifer, Phieffer, see
   Pfeifer
Philip, Philips 74, Philipp (St.
   Philip) 131
Philipi (son of Philip) 142
Philips, Philipson (son of Philip)
   59
Phister, see Pfister
Phyffer, see Pfeifer
Pichler 41, see Buehler
Pickel, Pickelman (pick) 106, 122
Pickli (little pick) 106
Piefer, see Pfeiffer
Piehl, Piel, Pihl, see Buehl
Piehler, see Buehler
Pieper, see Pfeifer
Pieters 164, Pieterse, see Peter
Pilger, Pilgrim, Pilgram (pilgrim,
   fr Latin *peregrinus*)
Pilgrim < Biligrim (sword +
   helmet) 46, 46
Piller (sword + army) 46, 46
Piltz (mushroom, fr Latin *boleta*)
   106
Pinsel (artist's brush, fr Latin
   *penicillus*)
Piper, see Pfeifer
Pister, Pistor 159, see Pfister
Pitner, Pittner, see Buettner
Pitsenberger, Pitzenbarger
   (dweller near mountain peak)
   68
Plage (marshy grassland) 80
Planck (white) 112
Planckenhorn (white peak) 72
Platner, Plattner (sheet metal
   worker, armor maker) 108
Platte (small plateau) 68
Platz (place, village green, fr
   Latin *platea*)

Pless 53, Plesse, Plessi < St.
   Blasius 131
Plessing 53 < St. Blasius 131
Pletsch, Pletscher, see Platner
Plette, see Platner
Pletz (clothes patcher) 96
Plock, see Block
Poechler, see Beck, Bechler
Ploeg, see Pflug
Plug, see Pflug
Plum, see Blum, Pflaum
Plum 153, see Zwetschen
Plumenstein (flower stone) 73
Poehlman, Poehlmann, see Pohl-
   mann
Poehmer, see Boehmer
Poetzel 53, Poetzold, Poetsch <
   Peter
Poffenberger, see Pfaffenberger
Pogener, see Bogener
Pohl, Pohlner (Pole) 122
Pohl (pool, pond, swamp) 80, 122
Pohl 53, Pohle, Pohler, Pohling <
   Paulus
Pohl (stake, fr Latin *palus*)
Pohlhaus (fr Pohlhausen 122,
   pond houses) 80
Pohlman, Pohlmann (dweller near
   a pool) 80
Poland, Polander (fr Poland) 121
Poldermann (occupant of a
   polder)
Pollak (Pole) 120
Pollinger, see Bollinger
Polmann, Pollmann, Pollner,
   Polner, see Pohlmann
Polther 53, Poltermann < St.
   Hippolytus 131
Pommer (Pomeranian) 121
Pommer (place name) 122
Pool 159, Poole, see Puhl
Pope, see Pape
Popp, Popps 164, Poppe, see
   Papp, Pappe
Porcher, see Burckhard

Porkholder 159, 151 see Burg-
   halter 151
Portz (place name) 122
Posner (fr Posen) 122
Possart, Possert, see Bosshart
Posthumus (posthumous)
Pot 159, Pott, Potts 164, see Bote
Potasch (potash maker) 96
Poth, see Bote
Pothe, see Pot
Potsdammer (fr Potsdam) 122
Potter (potter) 96
Pottgiesser (potter) 96
Potthast (potroast, porridge) 112
Powledge 159, see Paulitsch
Pracht (splendor) 122
Praetorius (Latin for Schultheiss)
   9, 141
Praeuner, see Braeuner
Prag, Prager (fr Prague) 122
Prahl, Prall (splendor, luxury)
   115
Pramschufer, Pramschuefner
   (boat poler) 96
Prang, Prange (claw) 114
Pranger (pillory)
Praslaw (fr Breslau) 122
Prass, Prasse (glutton) 115
Praunmueller, see Braunmueller
Precht, see Brecht
Prechtel 53, 55 < Helmbrecht
Prediger (preacher, fr Latin
   *predicare*) 109
Preis, Preiss, Preise, Preisz
   (praise, price, prize, fr Latin
   *pretium*)
Preising, Preisinger (fr Preising-
   en) 122
Preissle, Preissmann (shoelace
   maker) 96
Preller (shouter) 115
Presser, Pressler (fr Breslau) 122
Presster, Prester, see Priester

Pretorius, see Praetorius
Pretzer, see Brett
Preusch, Preuscher, see Preuss
Preuss, Preussner (Prussian,
   North German) 120
Prevost, see Probst
Price 159, see Preiss, Preuss
Prieber, Pryber < Pribislav
   (Slavic) 146
Priest, Priester (priest, fr Latin
   *presbyter*) 110
Pright 159, see Brecht
Printz, Prinz (prince, fr Latin
   *princeps*) 109, 122
Probst, Propst (provost, fr Latin
   *praepositus*) 109
Prophet (prophet), fr Latin
   *propheta* 135
Prost (simple) 115, 122
Prost (Prosit, a Latin toast) 117
Pruder, see Bruder
Pruner, Prunner, see Brunner
Prysing 159, see Preising
Pryss 159, see Preis
Puehl (pillow, fr Latin *pulvinus*)
   106
Puetzbach (pond brook) 80, 77
Puhl (pool) 80
Puhlhoffer (farm by a pool) 80, 92
Pulgram, see Pilgrim
Pullmann, see Pulvermacher
Pulver (powder) 108
Pulvermacher (powder maker)
   108
Pundt, see Pfundt
Puntzius (Pontius Pilate, actor in
   morality play) 111
Pupper (doll maker) 96
Purpur (purple) 112
Putsch, Putscher, Putch (rioter)
   115
Putz (finery, cleaning) 115

## Q

Quade (wicked, dirty) 115
Qualbrink (agony hill) 74
Quandt, Quante (rascal) 115
Quandmeyer (rascal) 93
Quarengesser, Quarngesser (path
along the Quern) 83, 65
Quart (quart)
Quasebarth (glutton) 115
Quast (tassel, bather's whisk,
bath attendant) 96
Quell (spring) 79, 122
Quenzer (card player)
Querfurth (fr Querfurth, city on
the Querne) 83, 122
Querne (name of river) 83
Quetschenbach (plum brook) 89,
77
Quick (alive, lively) 115
Quirmbach (fr Quernbach) 122
Quitman (quince dealer) 89, 106

## R

Raab, Raabe, Raap, see Rab
Rabanus (Latin for Rabe) 141
Rab, Rabb, Rabe, Raben (raven)
115
Rab, see Rapp
Rabenau (raven meadow) 48, 84,
122
Rabenecke (raven field) 48, 85,
122
Rabenhorst (ravens' eyrie) 48, 72,
122
Rabenolt (raven + loyal) 48, 48
Rabenstein (raven crag) 48, 73,
122
Rach (vengeance) 115
Rachbach (muddy stream) 80, 77
Rackensperger (muddy mountain)
80, 68
Radabaugh 159, Radebaugh,
Radebach (marshy brook) 80,
77

Radebach 122, see Rautebach
Radecke (marshy field) 80, 84
Rademacher, Radermacher,
Radmacher (wheelright) 96
Rademan, Radman, Radmann
(marsh dweller) 80, see also
Rathmann
Rader, Radner, Raderman, see
Rademan
Radick 53, 55 < Radolf (counsel +
wolf) 47, 48
Radke 53, 55 Radtke < Conrad
Raeck, see Reck
Raeder, see Reeder
Raedermacher, see Rademacher
Raff, Raffer (scrawny person) 114
Raffensberger, Raffensbarger
(raven mountain) 48, 68
Raffschneider, see Reifschneider
Rafkamp (raven field) 48, 84
Ragle 159, see Regel
Rahder, see Rader
Rahl, see Rall
Rahm, Rahmm (cream) 122
Rahman, Rahmann (marsh
dweller) 80
Rahn (slender) 113
Rahn (brunet) 112
Rahnfelder, perhaps for Rhein-
felder
Raiber, see Reiber
Raibold < Raginbold (counsel +
bold) 46, 46
Raichert, see Reichert
Raiffschneider, see Reiffschneider
Rainard, see Reinhart
Rainer, see Reiner
Raisbeck, Raischbeck (rapid
stream) 77
Rall (water rail) 115
Rambach, Ramsbach (swamp
brook) 80, 77, 122
Ramberg, Ramberger, Ramsberg
(raven mountain) 68, 122
Rame, Rahme, Ramm, see Rahm

Ramelmeier (fr the Rammelhof,
    wether farm) 93
Ramer (creamer) 96
Ramhoff (wether farm) 92
Ramler, Rammler (wether, male
    hare) 115
Ramm (bear leek, *allium ur-
    sinum*) 89, 122
Rammelfanger (ram catcher) 117
Rammelkamp (wether field) 84
Rampmeyer, see Ramelmeier
Ramsau (meadow with bear leek,
    *allium ursinum)* 89, 84, 122
Ramsberg (raven mountain, or
    mountain with bear leek
    *allium ursinum*) 89, 68, 122
Ramsburg (raven castle) 48, 73
Ramsland (raven land) 48
Ramspacher, see Rambach
Ranck, see Ranke 122
Rand, Randt (edge of the shield,
    shield) 46
Randolf (shield + wolf) 46, 48
Ranft (bread crust, baker) 96
Rang, Rank (rank)
Ranke (tendril, climber, agile
    person) 115
Ranzenbach (rancid brook) 77
Rap, see Rapp
Raper, Rapert 74 < Ratbrecht
    (counsel + bright) 47, 47
Raphael (an archangel) 131
Rapp, Rappe (black horse) 91
Rappel, see Rappold
Rappolt < Ratbold (counsel +
    bold) 47, 46
Rasbach, Rashpacker 159, see
    Raschbacher
Rasch, Rasche (swift) 115
Raschbacher, Raschpacker (fr
    Raschbach 122, swift brook) 77
Rast (rest)
Rat, Rath (counsel) 47
Ratenmacher, see Rademacher
Rather, Ratherr (councilman) 109,
    159

Rathgeb, Rathgeber (advice giver)
Rathhauser (city hall) 65
Rathmacher, see Rademacher
Rathschild 159, see Rothschild
Ratmann, Rathmann, Rattmann
    (councilman) 109
Ratner, Rattner, see Radner
Ratschlag (advice)
Rattenauer (rat meadow) 84, see
    Reitenauer
Ratz, Ratze (rat) 115
Rau, Raue, Rauh, Rauher (rough,
    hairy) 115, 114
Raub, Rauber (robbery, robber)
Raubach 122, Raubaugh 159, see
    Rautebach, Rohbach
Raubenstine 159, see Rubenstein
Rauch (towsel haired) 112
Rauch (fish and meat smoker) 96,
    106
Rauchfass (incense burner) 106
Rauchhaus (smokehouse, meat or
    fish smoker) 96
Raudabaugh 159, see Rautebach
Raudenbach (Slavic river name)
    83
Raudenbusch (rue bush, fr Latin
    *ruta)* 89
Rauff (brawl) 115
Raugh 159, see Rau
Rauh, see Rau, Rauch
Raum (room, space) 122
Raun, Rauner (mystery, whis-
    perer) 122
Raup, Raupp, see Raub
Raup, Raupe (caterpillar)
Raupach, see Raubach
Rausbach, see Rauschbach
Rausch, Rauscher (rush, intoxi-
    cation) 122
Rauschbach, Rauschenbach (bull-
    rush stream) 81, 78
Rauschberg, Rauschenberg,
    Rausenberger (bullrush
    mountain) 81, 68

Rauscher, Rauschert 74 (illegit-
   imate child) 119
Rauschkorb (reed basket) 106
Rauth (rod)
Rayser, see Reiser
Raysinger, see Reisinger
Reach 159, see Reich
Read 159, see Ried
Reagle 159, see Riegel
Reahl 159, see Riehl
Ream 159, Reamer, see Riem,
   Riemer
Reaser 159, see Rieser
Reasoner 159, see Rieser
Reb, Reber, Rebert 74 (grapevine,
   vintner) 106
Reback 159, Rehbeck, see Reh-
   bock
Reberg (roe mountain) 68
Rebhahn, Rebhan, see Rebhuhn
Rebholtz (grapevine) 72, 122
Rebhoon 159, see Rebhuhn
Rebhuhn, grouse 115
Rebmann (vine dresser) 96
Rebsamen (grapeseed), see
   Ruebsamen
Rebstock (grapevine) 149
Rebuck, see Rehbock
Rechenberg (rake mountain,
   roebuck mountain) 68, see
   Reckenberger
Rechner (accountant) 169
Recht (Right!) 117
Rechter 159, Righter 159, see
   Richter
Rechthand (right hand)
Reck, Recke (hero) 42
Reckenberger (fr Reckenberg 122,
   marsh mountain) 80, 68
Reckenwald (marsh mountain)
   80, 71
Recker, Reckers 164, Reckert 74,
   Reckman (dweller by a marsh)
   80
Reckhaus (marsh house) 80, 65
Reckner, see Rechner

Rector (Latin, rector, headmaster)
   109, 141, see also Richter
Reddick, see Radick
Redeman, Redemann (swamp
   dweller) 80, see also Rademann
Redenbaugh 159 (swamp stream
   80, 77, 122), see also
   Reitenbach
Reder (councilman, see also
   Reeder) 109
Redmann, see Redemann
Ree ..., see Rie...
Reeb, see Reb
Reece 159, see Riess
Reed 159, see Riet
Reeder (ship owner) 96
Reem 159, Reemer, Reemsnyder
   159, see Riem, Riemer, Riem-
   enschneider
Reep, Reeper, Reepschlaeger
   (rope, rope maker) 106
Rees 159, Reese, see Ries
Reeser 159, Reezer, see Rieser
Reffner (censurer, rebuker) 115
Refsnyder 159, see Reifschneider
Regel (rule, fr Latin *regula*)
Regenhardt, see Reinhard
Regenhold, see Reinhold
Regensburg (castle on the River
   Regen) 83, 73, 122
Regenstein (rain mountain, rock
   on the Regen River) 83, 73, 122
Regenthal (Regen valley) 83, 76,
   122
Reger, Regert 74 (heron, thin
   person) 114, 115
Reger (restless person) 115
Regler (monk in orders) 110
Regner (dweller on the Regen) 83
Regters 159, 164, see Richter
Regul, see Regel
Reh (roe, roebuck) 115, 122
Rehbein (roe bone, roe leg)
Rehberg, Rehberger (fr Rehberg
   122, roebuck mountain, see
   Reberg) 68

Rehbock (roebuck) 115, 91
Rehder, see Reeder
Rehfeld (roe field) 84, 122
Rehfus, Rehfuss (roe foot) 114
Rehorn (roebuck horn)
Rehkemper (roebuck field) 84
Rehkopf (roebuck head) 114, 149
Rehling, Reehling, Reeling (rail-
ing) 122
Rehm, Rehmer 122, Rem (strap
cutter) 106, see also Reinmar
Rehman, Rehmann (marsh
dweller) 80, see Raimann
Rahmer, see Romer
Rehmeyer (marshland farmer) 80,
93
Rehmus (latinized Rehm) 141, see
Adoremus
Rehwalt (roebuck forest) 71
Rehweg (roebuck path) 65
Rehwinckel (roebuck forest) 72
Reiber, Reibert 74 (bath atten-
dant, masseur) 96
Reibetanz (dance leader) 96
Reich, Reiche (empire, of the
imperial party) 109, 122
Reich, Reicher, Reichert 74 (rich)
115
Reichard, Reichhardt, Reichart,
Reicharz 164 (rule + strong)
46, 46
Reichburg (imperial castle) 73
Reichel, Reichl, Reichle 159,
Reichelt 74, Reichler < Reich-
ard
Reichelderfer 159 (Reichel's
village)
Reichenbach, Reichenbacher
(swamp stream) 80, 77, 122
Reichenbaugh 159, see Reichen-
bach
Reichenberg (swamp mountain)
80, 68, 122
Reichenecker (fr Reicheneck,
swamp field) 80, 85, 122
Reichenfeld (swamp field) 80, 84

Reicher, Reichert 74, see Reich
Reichman, Reichmann (rich man,
imperial employee) 109
Reichter 159, see Richter
Reichwein (rule + friend) 46, 48
Reid 159, see Ried
Reidenauer 159, Reidnauer, see
Reitenauer
Reidenbaugh 159, see Reitenbach
Reider 159, Reiderman, see
Reiter, Reiterman
Reidheimer 159 (reed hamlet) 81,
123
Reidheimer (clearing hamlet) 126,
123
Reidnauer 159, see Reitenauer
Reif, Reiff (ripe, mature) 115
Reif (frost)
Reif (rope) 106
Reif, Reifen (ring, hoop, cooper)
106
Reiffschneider (rope maker) 96
Reifschnieder 159, see Reiff-
schneider
Reifsnider 159, Reifsnyder 159,
see Reiffschneider
Reigel 159, Reigle 159, see Riegel
Reiger (heron) 115
Reighard 159, Reighart see
Reichard
Reiger, Reigers 164, Reigert 74,
see Rieger
Reihart, see Reinhard
Reihl 159, see Riehl
Reihner, see Reiner
Reiland, see Rheinland
Reiman, Reimann (Rhinelander)
121, 151, 122
Reimar, Reimer, see Reinmar
Reimschneider, Reimsnyder 159,
Reimsnider 159, see Riemen-
schneider
Reimensnyder 159, Reimensnider
159, see Riemenschneider
Rein, Reine (clean) 115, see Rhein
Reinalt, see Reinhold

Reizer 159, see Reiser, Rieser
Rekenthaler (marsh valley) 80, 76
Rembold, see Reinbold
Remmensperger, see Riemen-
sperger
Remsber 159, Remsburg, see
Ramsberg, Ramsburg
Remshard (marsh forest) 80, 72,
122
Remsnyder 159, see Riem-
schneider
Renchler, see Rensch
Renck (vendace, a kind of fish)
115
Renecke, see Reinecke
Rennenkampf ("Run into battle!",
aggressive person) 115, 116
Renner, Rennert 74 (mounted
courier) 96
Renninger 53, 55, Reninger <
Reinhard
Renninger (place name) 122
Rennweg (path on mountain
ridge) 68, 65, 122
Renold, see Reinhold
Rensch 53, Renschler < Reinhard,
Lorentz
Rentner (pensioner)
Rentsch, Rentschler, see Rensch
Rentz, Rentzel, Renz, see Rensch
Rephann, see Rebhun
Repp, Reps 164, Reppe, Reppert
74 (marsh dweller), see Reb
Repphun, see Rebhuhn
Requardt < Rickward (rule +
guardian) 46, 47
Resch, Resh 159, Roesch, see
Rasch
Reser 159, see Rieser
Ress, Resse, Resse (swamp
dweller) 80
Ressmeyer (proprietor or occu-
pant of the Resshoff, swamp
farm) 93
Rester (fr Resten) 122
Restar 159, Resta, see Rester

Reth (rushes) 81
Rethman, Rettmann (dweller at
the rushes) 81
Rethmeyer, Rettenmeyer, Rett-
mayer (farmer in the marsh)
81, 93
Rettberg (marsh farmer) 81, 68
Rettenburg (castle on the rushes)
81, 73
Retter, Reter (saver)
Rettig (radish, fr Latin *radix*) 91,
106
Retz, Rez (dweller near swamp
water) 80
Reu (remorse) 115
Reucher, Reuchert 74 (meat or
fish smoker) 96
Reudenauer, see Reitenauer
Reus, Reuss, Reuse (eel trap) 106
Reusch, Reuschling (dweller in
the reeds) 81, 122
Reusenweber (eel trap maker) 96
Reuss (Swiss river) 83
Reuss (Russian) 121
Reutenbach, see Reitenbach
Reuter, Reuther (cavalryman) 107
Reuter, Reuther (dweller in a
clearing) 126
Reuthnauer, see Reitenauer
Reutlinger (fr Reutling) 122
Rewald, Rewold, see Rehwald
Rex (Latin for king) 109, 141
Rey ..., see Rei and Rhei
Reybold, see Reinbold
Reydenauer 159, Reydenhower
159, see Reitenauer
Reyder 159, see Reiter
Reylandt, Reylender, see Rhein-
land
Reymann, see Rheinmann
Reyngold, see Reingold
Reynhart, see Reinhard
Reynolds 164, 159, see Reinhold
Reys, see Reiss
Reyser, see Reiser
Reytenar 159, see Reitenauer

Reyter, see Reiter
Rezer 159, see Rieser
Rhein (Rhine) 83, 122
Rheinauer (meadow on Rhine) 83, 84
Rheinert, see Reinert
Rheinfeld (field on Rhine) 83, 84, 122
Rheinfels (Rhine cliffs) 83, 68
Rheingold (Rhine gold) 83
Rheinhard, Rheinhardt, see Reinhard
Rheinheim (hamlet on the Rhine) 83, 123
Rheinlaender, Rheinlender (Rhinelander) 121
Rheinstein (Rhine mountain, rhinestone) 83, 73, 122
Rheinstettler (fr Rheinstadt) 122
Rheinthal, Rheinthaler (Rhine valley) 83, 76, 122
Rheinwald (Rhine forest) 83, 71
Rhine 159, see Rhein
Rhinehart 159, see Reinhard
Rhinelander 159, see Rheinlander
Rhode 159, see Roth, Rode
Rhymer 159, see Reimer
Rhyner 159, see Reiner
Rhynhard 159, see Reinhard
Rice 159, see Reiss
Rich 159, see Reich
Richard 159, Richards 164, Richert, Richerdt, see Reichhard
Richburg 159, see Reichburg
Richman 159, see Reichmann
Richter, Richters 74 (judge) 109
Richtersweil (judge's village) 109, 123
Richwein, Richwin, Richwien 159, Richwiene (rule + friend) 46, 48
Rick 53, Ricke, Ricker, Rickerds 74, 164, Rickers, Rickert 74 < Richard, Henrik

Rickel 53, 55, Ricker, Rickert 74 < Reichhard
Rickenbacher, Rickenback 159, Reickenbaker (fr Rickenbach 122, swamp brook) 80, 77, 122, see Reichenbach
Rickhoff (ridge farm) 68, 84
Rickmann (ridge dweller) 68
Rickter 159, Ricktor, Rictor, see Richter
Ridder, see Ritter
Ridel 159, see Riedel
Ridelsberg 159, Riddleberger 159, Riddlespurger 159, see Riedelsperger
Ridenauer 159, Ridenhour, Ridener, see Reitenauer
Ridenbaugh 159, see Reitenbach
Rider 159, see Reiter
Rieb, Riebe, Riep 122, see Rueb
Riebau (turnip field) 84
Riebel, see Ruebel
Riebman (turnip man) 91, 105
Riebsame, see Ruebsamen
Riech 53, Riecher, Riechert 74, Riechner < Richard
Rieck 159, Riecke, Rieckert < Richard
Ried, Riedt, Riede, Reed 159 (reed, marshland) 81, 122
Riedel 53, Riedl, Riedal 159, Riedling 55, Ridelinger < Rudolf, Ruediger
Riedelsperger (Rudolf's mountain) 53, 68
Rieder, Riedner, Riedeman (marsh dweller) 81
Rieder (fr Rieden) 122
Riedheim (marsh hamlet) 81, 123
Riedheim (clearing hamlet) 125, 123
Riedmueller, see Riethmueller
Riegel, Riegle 159, Riegelmann (bolt, locksmith) 106
Riegel (ridge) 68

Rieger 122, Riegger, Riegert 74 (censurer), also < Ruediger

Riegler, Riegelman, Riegelmann (locksmith, night watchman) 96, 109

Riehl 53, Riel < Rudolf

Riehm, Riehme, see Riem, Riemen

Riem, Riemen (strap, strap cutter) 97, 106

Riemann (Rhinelander) 121

Riemenschneider, Riemenschnitter 159, Riemschneider (strap cutter) 97

Riemer (strap cutter) 97

Rienhard, see Reinhard

Rienhof (farm on the Rhine) 83, 92

Riepe, see Ruebe

Rieper, see Reeper

Ries, Riese (giant) 149

Ries, Riese, Riess (timber slide) 122

Riesberg (giant mountain) 68

Riesberg (timber slide mountain) 68

Riesch 53 < Rudolf

Riesenbeck (brook used for logging) 77, 122

Riesenfeld (logging field) 84

Riesenfeld (giants' field) 84

Rieser, Riesser, Reezer 159 (logger) 95

Riesinger 159, see Reisinger

Riet 122, Rieth 122, see Ried

Riethmueller (miller on the marsh) 81, 103

Rietweill (reed village, marsh village) 81, 127

Rietwiese (marshy meadow) 81, 84

Rietz 53, Rietze < St. Mauritius 131, 122

Right 159, see Recht

Righter 159, see Richter

Rightmeyer 159, see Reitmeyer

Rightnour 159, see Reitenauer

Rightor 159, see Richter

Rigler 159, see Riegler

Rimbach, Rimback (swamp water creek) 80, 122

Rimer 159, see Riemer

Rinde (bark, bark collector) 95

Rinder (cattle) 91

Rindfleisch (beef, butcher) 96

Rinfuss (cow foot, club foot) 114

Rindlaub (cattle foliage, probably house sign) 62, 149

Rindskopf (cow head) 114, 62, 149

Rine 159, see Rhein

Rinecker 159, see Reinecker

Rinehard 159, Rinehart, Rinehardt, Rineheart, see Reinhard

Rinehimer 159, see Rheinheimer

Rineholt 159, see Reinhold

Riner 159, see Reiner

Rinestein 159, see Rheinstein

Rinfret, see Reinfried

Ring, Ringe, Rings 164, Rinck, Rink (ring, city wall) 106

Ringel, Ringle 159, Ringeler, Rinkler (ring maker) 96

Ringelstein (place name) 122

Ringer, Ringers 164 (ring maker) 96

Ringgold, Ringold, see Rheingold

Ringold < Ringholdt (council + loyal) 47, 46

Rinman 159, see Rheinmann

Ringsdorf (circular village) 123

Ringwald (encircling forest) 72

Rink, Rinker, Rinkert 74, Rinkler (clasp maker) 106

Rink, Rinker, Rinkert 74 (round hill) 68

Ripke 53, 55, see Ruprecht

Ripley 53, 55, 159, Ripli < Ruprecht

Rippert, Rippart < Ruprecht

Rippe (rib) 114

Rippe (swamp grass) 81

Rippel 53, 55 < Ruprecht

Ripple 159, see Rippel
Risberg, see Riesberg
Risch (swamp) 80
Rischel (swamp dweller) 80
Rischenbeck (swampy brook) 80, 77
Rischhof (swamp farm) 80, 92
Rischstein (marsh stone) 80, 73
Riser 159, see Reiser, Rieser
Risinger 159, see Reisinger
Rismiller, Rissmiller (swamp miller) 80, 103
Riss, Risse (gap, gorge) 122
Riss (swamp) 80, 122
Risterholtz (bullrush forest) 81, 72
Ritenour 159 (fen swamp) 81, see Reitenauer
Riter 159, Rither, see Reiter, Ritter
Ritger, Ritgert 74, see Rutger
Ritmueller, Rittmiller (miller on the marsh) 80, 103
Ritschard (fr Old French Richard)
Rittenauer (reed meadow) 81, 84
Rittenbach (reed brook) 81, 77
Rittenhaus (reed house) 81, 65
Rittenhouse 153, see Rittenhaus
Rittenour 159, see Reitenauer
Ritter, Riter 159 (knight) 107
Ritterbusch (knight's crest)
Ritterbush 159, Ritterpush, see Ritterbusch
Ritterhoff (knight's court) 107, 92
Ritterhaus (knight's house, castle) 107, 65
Ritterman, Rittermann (trooper) 107
Rittmeister (cavalry captain) 107
Rittmeyer (reed farmer) 81, 93
Ritterscamp (knight's field) 107, 84
Ritz 53, Ritzel 55 (St. Euricius, St. Moritius, Henricius) 131
Ritzenberg (St. Moritz Mountain) 131, 68, 122

Ritzenthal (St. Moritz Valley) 131, 76
Ritzheim (St. Moritz hamlet) 131, 123
Ritzman, Ritzmann (servant of St. Moritz convent) 139
Rizer 159, see Reiser
Road 159, see Roth
Robacher, Robach, Robacker, see Rohback
Roberg, Roberge, see Rohberg
Robertus (Latin for Robert) 141
Robke 53, 55, Robken < Robert
Robling, see Roebling
Robrecht, see Ruprecht
Rock (gown) 112, 106
Rockefeller < Roggenfelder (rye fields) 84
Rockemann (rye dealer) 106
Rockenbach (rye brook) 77, 122
Rockenbauch (potbelly) 114
Rockenbaugh 159, see Rockenbach and Rockenbauch
Rockenbrod, see Roggenbrod
Rockenstihl (rye stalk, tall thin person) 114
Rockmueller (rye miller) 103
Rockstroh (rye straw) 106
Rodabaugh 159, Rodebaugh (clearing brook) 126, 77
Rodberg, Rodenberg (cleared mountain) 125, 68
Rode (clearing) 126
Rodefeld (cleared field) 126, 84
Rodeheaver 159, Rodehaver < Rodehoffer (clearing farmer) 126, 92
Rodel, see Rudel
Rodemann (forest clearer) 126
Rodemeier, Rodemeyer (clearing farmer) 126, 93
Roden (clearing) 125, 126
Rodenbach (clearing brook) 126, 77, 122
Rodenberg (cleared mountain) 126, 68, 122

Rous 159, Roush, see Rausch
Roushenbacht 159, see Rausch-
    enbach
Routh 159, see Rauthe
Rowe 159, see Rau
Rowland 159, see Roland
Royce 159, see Reuss
Rozen... 159, see Rosen
Rozencwaig 159, Rozencweig, see
    Rosenzweig
Rubenthal (turnip valley) 76
Rubert, see Ruprecht
Rubi, Ruby, Rubin, Rubins 164
    (ruby), see Rubinstein
Rubincam, Rubincamp (turnip
    field) 84
Rubinstein, Rubenstein (ruby) 73
Rubenstien 159, see Rubenstein
Rubrecht, see Ruprecht
Rubright 159, see Ruprecht
Ruch, see Rauch
Ruck, see Rueck
Rucker 53, Ruckert 74 < Ruediger
Rude 53 < Rudolf
Rudegaire 159, see Ruediger
Ruckstuhl (chair with back)
Rudel, Rudell (pack, herd)
Rudi 53, 55, Rudy < Rudolf,
    Ruediger
Rudiger, see Ruediger
Rudmann, Rudemann (leader of
    hounds, hunter) 91, or <
    Rudolf
Rudolf, Rudolph (illustrious +
    wolf) 47, 48
Rudolphi (son of Rudolf) 142
Rueb (turnip eater, turnip raiser
    or dealer) 112, 105
Ruebeck (turnip brook) 77
Ruebel (rape cultivator, fr Latin
    *rapum*) 91
Ruebenacker (turnip field) 84
Ruebenzahl (turnip tail, Silesian
    spook)
Ruebsamen (turnip seed)
Rueck (jerk)

Rueckdeschel (backpack, ruck-
    sack) 106
Rueckenbrot, see Roggenbrot
Ruecker, Rueckert 74 (dweller on
    ridge)
Rueckstuhl (back chair)
Ruede (large hound)
Ruediger (illustrious + spear) 47,
    46, 39
Rueg, Rueger (reproof) 115
Ruehl 53, Ruehle, Ruel < Rudolf
Ruemstall (Empty the stall!,
    horse thief) 116, 117
Rueppel 53, 55 < Ruprecht
Ruessel (trunk, snout) 114
Rueter (land clearer) 126, also
    error for Reuter
Ruetiger, Ruettiger, Ruettger, see
    Ruediger
Ruetsch (slide)
Ruf, Ruff, Roof 159 (call), or <
    Rudolf 53
Ruger, see Rueg
Ruh, Ruhe (rest) 115
Ruhl 53, Ruhle, Ruhling 55,
    Ruhlmeyer 103 < Rudolf
Ruhland, Ruland, see Roland
Ruhm (fame)
Ruhrwein (stir wine) 116
Ruhsam (restful) 115
Rukeyser (dweller in a ridge
    house) 67, 65
Rulmann 53, 94, Rullman <
    Rudolf
Rumbacker 159 (fr Rumbach 122)
    77
Rumbaugh 159, see Rambach
Rummel, Rummler (hurly-burly)
    115
Rump, Rumpf, Rumph (sieve in a
    gristmill) 106
Rumpf (torso) 114
Rumpel, Rumple 159 (noise
    maker) 115
Rund (round)
Rundberg (round mountain) 68

Rung, Runge (wainwright) 96, 106
Runkel, Runckels 164, Runckel (marsh root) 81, 122
Runkelstein (reed mountain) 81, 73
Runkhorst (swamp hurst) 81, 72
Ruoff, see Ruff
Rupert, Ruppert, Rupertus 141, see Ruprecht
Rupp 53, Ruppel 55 < Ruprecht
Ruppertsberger, Ruppersberger (Ruppert's mountain) 68, 122
Ruprecht, Rupprecht (famous + bright) 47, 47
Russ, Russe (rust), or < Rudolf 53
Russel, see Ruessel
Rust (reeds, rushes) 81, 122
Rust (rest, calm) 115
Rutger < Ruediger
Ruth, Rute (rod)
Ruth < Hrodomar (famous + famous) 47, 47
Rutmann, Ruttmann, see Rudmann
Rutsch 53 < Rudolf
Rutschild 159, see Rothschild
Rutschman 53, 94 < Rudolf
Ruttger, see Ruediger
Ruyter, see Reiter
Ryder 159, see Reiter
Ryecart, see Reichard
Ryland, Rylander, see Rheinlander
Rynhart, see Reinhart
Rynthal (Rhine valley) 83, 76
Ryser 159, see Reiser, Rieser
Rysling 159, see Reisling
Ryther 159, see Reither, Reuther
Rytter 159, see Ritter

## S

Saal (hall) 122
Saalig, see Selig
Saalwechter (hall waker) 96

Saar (fr the Saarland) 121
Saas (Saxon) 120
Saat (seed, newly planted grain field) 122
Saatfeld (newly planted grain field) 84
Saatkampt, see Saatfeld
Sabel, Sable 159 (saber) 108
Sabelhaus, Sablehaus (sable house, house name) 62
Sach (thing, cause)
Sachmann, see Sackmann
Sachs, Sachse (Saxon) 120
Sack (sack, trapper's net, Latin *saccus*) 122
Sackman, Sackmann (member of baggage train) 107
Sackreiter (clearing on a deadend road) 126
Sacks, see Sachs
Saddler, Sadtler, see Sattler
Saefried, see Siegfried
Saeger (sawyer) 96
Saegermueller (saw miller) 103
Saeli 53, 55 < Salomo
Saemann (sower) 95
Saemanshaus (sower's house) 65
Saemueller, see Seemueller, Saegemueller
Saenger (singer, cantor) 96
Saettler, see Settelman
Saeuberlich (clean) 115
Saffold, see Siegbald
Sager, Sageman, Sagenmann (minstrel) 96
Sagmiller 159, see Saegemueller
Sahl, see Saal
Sahli, see Sali
Sahn (cream) 106
Saidel, see Seidel
Saidemann, see Seideman
Sailer, see Seiler
Saks, see Sachs
Salbeck (swamp brook) 80, 77
Salberg (swamp mountain) 80, 68

Salinger 53, 55 < Salomo, also fr
Salingen 122
Salman, Salmann, Sallmann,
Sahlman (trustee, custodian)
Salmann (hall man)
Salmar, see Selmer
Salomo, Salomon, Salomon (OT
name) 135
Saltmann, see Salz
Saltner (forester, fr Latin *saltar-
ius*) 96
Salz, Saltzer, Salzer, Saltzman,
Saltzmann, Saltsman (salt
seller) 106, 122
Saltzberg, Salzberg (salt moun-
tain) 68, 122
Saltzgaver 159, Saltzgiver (salt
dealer) 106
Salzman, see Salz
Samann 159, see Saemann
Samenfink (seed finch) 115
Samet, Sameth, Sammet, Sam-
meth (velvet dealer, tailor) 106,
104
Samler, Sammler (collector)
Sammet, see Samet
Sampson (OT name) 135
Samstag (Saturday) 143
Samuel (OT name) 135
Sanbower 159, see Sandbauer
Sand, Sander, Sanders 164 <
Alexander, fr Sand 122
Sandbauer, Sandbower 159
(swamp peasant) 80, 91
Sandberg (swamp mountain) 80,
68, 122
Sanderson (son of Sanders) 59
Sandhaus (swamp house) 80, 65,
122
Sandhofer (fr Sandhof 122,
swamp farm) 80, 92
Sandkuhler (fr Sandkuhl 122,
swamp pool) 80, 80
Sandmann (swamp dweller) 80

Sandmeier, Sandmeyers 164,
Sandmyer 159 (fr the Sandhof,
swamp farm) 80, 93
Sanft (gentle) 115
Sanftleben (gentle life, bon
vivant) 115
Sanftmut (gentle disposition) 115,
139
Sanger, see Saenger
Sangmeister (choir leader) 96
Santen (fr Xanten) 122
Santer 53 < Alexander, or fr
Xanten
Santmeyer, Sandmeyers 164, see
Sandmeier
Sarazin (Saracen) 120
Sartor, Sartory, Sartorius (Latin
for tailor) 141
Sas, Sass, Sasse, Sassen, Sasser,
Sassman, Sassmann (Saxon)
120, 122
Sattel (saddle) 106, 122
Sattelthaler (saddle valley) 76
Sattler (saddler) 96, 98
Sattler (dweller on mountain
pass) 68
Sauber, Sauberlich (clean, fr
Latin *sobrius*) 115
Sauer, Saur, Sauers 164, Saure
(river name, spring, swamp)
80, 83
Sauerbach, Sauerborn (sour
brook, sour spring) 77, 79
Sauerbach, Sauerborn (southern
brook, southern spring) 85, 77,
79
Sauerbier (sour beer) 112
Sauerbrei, Sauerbrey (sour
pottage) 112
Sauerhammer (southern hamlet)
85, 123
Sauerhoff (southern farm) 85, 92
Sauerland ("southern land,"
mountain range in Westphalia)
121, 122
Sauermilch (sour milk) 112

Sauerwald (southern forest) 85,
72
Sauerwein, Saurwein (sour wine)
112
Saul (OT name) 135
Saulpaugh 159 (swamp brook, see
Salbeck)
Saum (hem, boundary) 106
Saum (load, pack animal, fr Latin
*suma*)
Saur, Saure, see Sauer
Saus, Sause (confusion, noise) 155
Sauter, Sautter, see Schuster
Sax, Saxen, see Sachs
Saxman, see Sackmann
Sayler, see Seiler
Scammele, see Schemel
Schaab, see Schabbe
Schaadt, see Schad
Schaaf, see Schaf
Schaal, see Schall
Schaar, see Schar
Schabbe (shabby, skinflint) 115
Schaber (scraper) 106
Schablein 55, see Schaeberle
Schach (checkmate, wooded area)
122
Schacht (mine shaft, gorge) 76,
122
Schacht, Schachtschneider (shaft
maker) 96
Schacht (reed-bank) 81
Schachtel (box, case) 106
Schachter, Schachtner, see
Schaechter
Schad, Schade, Schaden, Schadt
(swamp water) 80
Schad, Schaedlein 55 (loss,
damage)
Schadenfroh (full of malicious joy)
115
Schadel, Schadle 159, see
Schaedel
Schaeberle (scrapings)
Schaech, Schaecher (thief)
Schaechter (butcher) 96

Schaedel, Schadel 159 (skull) 114
Schaefer, Schaefers 164, Schaef-
fer (shepherd) 95
Schaeffler, see Scheffler
Schaeflein 55 (little sheep) 91
Schaefner, see Schaffner
Schaener 159, see Schoener
Schaenkel (leg) 114
Schaerer, see Scherer
Schaerf (sharp, sharpness) 115
Schaerzer, see Scherzer
Schaf, Schaff (sheep) 95
Schafer, Schafers 164, see
Schaefer
Schaffeld (sheep field) 84, 122
Schaffer, Schaffermann, see
Schaefer, Schaffner
Schaffhauser, Schaffhausen (fr
Schaffhausen, sheep fold) 65,
122
Schaffner, Schafner (steward,
manager) 169
Schaffroth (sheep clearing) 126
Schafstall (sheep fold)
Schaible, Schaibler, see Scheibel
Schaide, see Scheide
Schait (split log, wood chopper) 95
Schaler, see Schaller
Schalk, Schalck (servant) 96
Schall (loud sound)
Schallenberg 122, Schallenberger
(resounding mountain) 68
Schaller, Schallert 74 (noise
maker, public announcer) 109
Schalter (shutter, window, shop
keeper) 105
Schaltheis, see Schultheiss
Scham (shame, modesty) 115
Schambach (short brook) 77, 122,
see also Schaumbach
Schamberger (short mountain) 68,
see Schaumberg
Schamburg, see Schaumburg
Schamel, Schammel, see Schemel
Schamroth (red with embarrass-
ment) 115

Schanberger (reed mountain) 81,
see Schoenberger
Schanck, Schank, see Schenk
Schande (disgrace) 115
Schank, see Schenk
Schantz, Schantze, Schanz,
Schanze (redoubt, entrench-
ment) 107, 122
Schantzenbaecher, Schantzen-
becker (redoubt creek) 77
Schap, Schappes, see Schaf
Schaper (scoop, laddle) 96, 106
Schaper 39, Schapper, Schappert
74, see Schaeffer
Schar (crowd, troop) 107
Schard, Schardt, Schart (crack,
embrasure, shard)
Scharf, Scharfe, Scharff, Scharpf
(sharp, keen) 115
Scharfenberg, Scharfenberger
(sharp mountain) 68, 122
Scharffschmidt (knife grinder,
cutler) 96
Scharfstein (sharp stone) 73
Scharlach (scarlet, a fabric) 105,
106, 122
Scharman, see Scharrmann
Scharnagel (shingel nail) 106
Scharp, Scharpe, Scharpf,
Scharpp, see Scharf
Scharr (troop, band) 107
Scharrer (wool carder) 96
Scharrmann (trooper) 107
Schart, see Schard
Scharte (pass) 68
Schartner (dweller in a pass) 68
Schatt, see Schad
Schatz (treasure, dear one) 115,
122
Schatzle 53, 55, Schatzlein 55
(little treasure)
Schatzmann (treasurer) 96
Schau (view, sight)
Schaub, Schauber (sheaf, see
Schub)

Schaubach, Schaubacher, see
Schaumbach
Schauber, Schaubner (jacket
maker, thatcher) 96
Schauder (shudder) 115
Schauer, Schauerman, Schauer-
mann (shiver, shower)
Schauer (market inspector) 109
Schaufel, Schaufle 159, Schaufler,
Schaufele (shovel, shovel
maker) 96, 106
Schaufelberger (shovel mountain)
68
Schaum (scum, foam, skimmer)
96
Schaumbach (foam brook) 77
Schaumburg (lookout mountain)
68, 122
Schaumenkessel (cauldron for
skimming) 106
Schaumloeffel (skimming spoon)
106
Schazel 55 (little treasure)
Scheafer 159, see Schaefer,
Schiefer
Schechter, Schecter (Jiddish:
slaughterer) 96
Scheck (dappled horse)
Schedel, see Schaedel
Schedtlin, see Schaedel
Scheel 159, Scheele, Scheeler, see
Schiel, Schiele, Schieler
Scheeper, see Schaeffer
Scheer, Scheerer, Schehr, see
Scher, Scherer
Scheermann, see Schermann
Scheermesser (shearing knife)
106
Scheesler 159, see Schuessler
Scheetz 159, see Schuetz
Schef, Scheff, see Schief, Schiff
Scheffel (bushel) 106
Scheffel (*scabinus*) 109
Scheffer, Scheffers 164, see
Schaefer
Scheffler (barrel maker) 96

Scheffner, see Schaffner

Scheib, Scheibe, Scheibel 55 (disc, round pane) 106, 122

Scheid, Scheide, Scheidt (sheath) 106

Scheid (watershed, ridge, boundary) 68, 122

Scheidecke, Scheidekke, Scheidegger (dweller on a watershed or boundary) 122

Scheidel, Scheidler (arbitor)

Scheider, Scheidemann, Scheidmann (umpire)

Scheidt, see Scheit

Scheif, Scheiffler (crooked, askew) 114

Scheimer, Schaeumer (skimmer, cook) 96

Schein ..., see Schoen ...

Scheinberg 159, see Schoenberg

Scheinholtz 159, see Schoenholtz

Scheiss (feces), surely an American error for Schiess

Scheit, Scheidt, Scheiter, Scheitlein 55 (split log, woodcutter) 95

Scheitel, Scheitele (crown of the head)

Scheithauer (log splitter) 95

Scheldt (river name) 83

Scheler, Schelbert 74 (squinter) 114

Scheler (bark pealer) 95

Schell (bell, manacles) 106

Schellberg, Schellenberg, Schellenberger (swamp mountain) 80, 68, 122

Schellenschloeger, Schellenschlaeger (bell ringer) 96, 109

Scheller (bell ringer, see Schaller) 96

Schellhaas, Schellhas, Schelhase (flushed, startled hare) 114

Schellhammer (fr Schellheim, swamp hamlet) 80, 123, 122

Schellhaus, Schelhaus, Schelhause, Schelhouse 159 (swamp house) 65

Schellhorn (trumpet, trumpeter) 96, 122

Schelling, see Schilling

Schellkopf (noisy person) 115

Schellmann (bell maker) 96

Schemel, Schemmel (footstool, fr Latin *scamillus*) 106

Schene, see Schoen

Scheneberg (reed mountain) 81, 68, see Schoenberg

Schenefeldt (reed field) 81, 84, 122, see Schoenfeld

Scheneman, Schenemann, see Schoenemann

Schenfeld, see Schenefeldt

Schenk, Schenck, Schenke (cup bearer, innkeeper) 96

Schenkel, Schenckel (thigh) 114

Schenkemeyer (village taverner) 96, 93

Scheper, Schepers 164, Scheepers, see Schaeffer

Scheppler, see Scheffler

Scher, Scherr, Scherer, Scherrer, Sherer 159 (barber, shearer, warper) 106, 97

Scheraus (shearing house) 65

Scheretz, Scherretz, see Scherg

Scherf, Scherff, see Scharf, Scherflein 122

Scherflein 55 (widow's mite) 117

Scherg, Schergh, Scherge (beadle, hangman's helper) 109

Schermann (shearer) 96

Schermesser, Scheermesser (shearing knife, shearer) 106

Scherr, Scherrer, see Scher

Schertz, Schertze, Schertzer, Scherzer (jester, jokester) 96

Schetzel 55 (little treasure)

Scheu (shy) 115

Scheuch (frighten)

Scheuer (tithe barn) 122

Scheuermann (barn supervisor, barn builder) 96
Scheuermeyer (barn bailif) 93
Scheufler, Scheufeler (shovel maker) 96
Scheunemann (barn supervisor) 96
Scheunemann (manager of a tithe barn) 109
Scheuplein (little sheaf)
Scheurer, Scheuerman (scourer, occupant of a tithe barn)
Scheussler 159, see Schuessler
Schevaler (chevalier, cavalier) 107, 144
Schey, see Scheu
Scheydt, see Scheit
Scheyer, see Scheuer
Schick (skill, dexterity, well mannered) 115
Schicketanz (skillful dancer) 115
Schieber, Schiebert 74 (fr Schieben) 122
Schiedmann (arbiter)
Schief (crooked) 114
Schiefer, Schieffer (slater) 96
Schieferdecker (slater) 96
Schieffler (vacillator) 115
Schiel, Schiele (squinter) 114
Schiele 159, see Schule
Schierg, see Scherg
Schierman (marsh dweller 80, boundry dweller), see slso Schermann
Schiermeister (worker in charge of equipment) 96
Schiess (sharp gable)
Schiesser (baker's helper, dweller on a steep slope) 96, 71
Schiff, Schiffe (ship, boatman) 96, 62
Schiffbauer, Schiffhauer (ship builder) 96, 100
Schiffer, Schiffmann (boatman) 96
Schild, Schildt, Schiltz 164 (shield) 45, 108, 106, 62

Schilder (painter, shield decorator) 96, 108
Schildhauer (shield maker) 100, 108
Schildknecht, Schildtknecht (squire) 107
Schildkraut (thyssum) 89
Schildwachter, Schiltwaechter (sentry) 107
Schilf (bullrushes) 81
Schiller (redish wine) 96
Schiller (squinter) 114
Schilling (shilling) 117
Schilling (freedman) 109, 122
Schiltz, see Schultz
Schimel, Schimmel (white horse)
Schimmel (mildew)
Schimmelmann (greybeard) 112
Schimmelpfenig (miser) 115
Schimmelreiter (rider of a white horse)
Schimpf, Schimpff (play, amusement, entertainer) 96
Schinckel, see Schenkel
Schinkel (small tavern) 96
Schindel (shingle, Latin *scindula*) 96, 106, 122
Schindeldecker, Schindelmann (roof shingler) 96
Schindler (roofer) 96
Schine 159, see Schein
Schinkel 159, see Schenkel
Schipp (boat) 62
Schipper, Schippert 74, see Schiffer
Schirach (Wendish: George) 146
Schirm, Schirmer (protector) 169
Schirmacher (harness maker) 96
Schirra < Girard (French) < Gerhard (Germanic)
Schisler 159, Schissler, see Schuessler
Schlabach 159, see Schlebach
Schlachte (battle)
Schlachter, Schlacter 159 (slaughterer) 96

Schluecker, Schlucker (swallower, guzzler) 115
Schlueter, Schlueters 74 (locksmith, keeper of the keys)
Schlumberger (gorge mountain) 68
Schlund, Schlundt (gorge) 76
Schlusemeyer (sluice warden) 96
Schluter, see Schlueter
Schmach (disgrace)
Schmaehling (slender person) 113
Schmaek, see Schmeck
Schmeckefeffer (spice dealer) 106
Schmaeussner, see Schmeiser
Schmahl, Schmahle, see Schmal
Schmal, Schmale, Schmall (narrow) 114
Schmalbach (narrow stream) 77, 122
Schmaltz, Schmalz, Schmalz (lard, tallow, candler) 106
Schmaus (banquet)
Schmeck (gourmet, taster) 115
Schmeiser, Schmeissner (thrower, slinger)
Schmeltz, Schmelz (enamel 106, 122, fr Schmeltz 122), see Schmaltz
Schmeltz (iron foundry) 96
Schmeltzer (melter, smelter, enameler) 96, fr Schmeltz 122
Schmerbauch (lard belly) 114
Schmerz (pain)
Schmick 159, Schmicke, see Schmuek
Schmid, Schmide, Schmids 164, Schmidt, Schmidte, Schmidts 164, Schmidtt, Schmidtz, Schmit, Schmith 153, Schmitt, Schmitte, Schmitz (smith) 96
Schmidhauser (smithy) 65, 96
Schmidlein, see Schmittlein
Schmidtbauer, Schmidtmeyer (smith farmer) 96, 92
Schmidtknecht (smith's helper) 96
Schmied, Schmiedt (smithy)

Schmieg (cuddle)
Schmierer (laugher, smiler) 115
Schmiltz, see Schmeltz
Schmink (make-up, cosmetics) 106
Schmit, Schmitt, Schmitz, see Schmid
Schmittlein 55 (little smith) 96
Schmoke 159, see Schmueck
Schmoller (pouter, sulker) 115
Schmollinger (tar boiler) 95
Schmueck, Schmuck (adornament) 96, 106
Schmuecker (adorner) 96
Schmuecker (fr Schmueck, swamp) 122
Schmutz (dirt, filth) 115
Schnaack, Schnack (chitchat, nonsense) 115
Schnaack (deer fly) 115
Schnabel, Schnable 159 (snout, talkative person) 114, 115
Schnackenberg, Schnachenberg (deer fly mountain) 68
Schnader, see Schnatter
Schnaebele (little snout) 114
Schnaid (trail cut through woods) 122
Schnaider, see Schneider
Schnall, Schnalle (buckle) 106, 122
Schnap, Schnaps (brandy) 96, 106, 115
Schnatter (chatterer, gabbler) 115
Schnauber (snorter) 115
Schnauffer (snorter) 115
Schnautz (snout) 114
Schnebele, see Schnaebele
Schneberger (fr Schneeberg 68, 122), see Schneeberg
Schneck, Schnecke (snail, snake, slow poke) 115
Schneckenburg (snail castle) 73
Schnee (snow) 43
Schneebaum (snow tree) 89

Schneeberg, Schneeberger (fr
Schneeberg 122, snow moun-
tain) 68
Schneeganz (snow goose) 115
Schneehagen (snow enclosure)
123
Schneemann (snowman)
Schneeweiss (snow white) 112
Schneewind (snow wind)
Schneibly 159, see Schnaebele
Schneickburger, see Schnecken-
burg
Schneid, Schneiden (mountain
ridge, boundary) 68
Schneider (tailor) 104
Schneiderjohann (tailor John) 104
Schneidermann, see Schneider
Schnel, Schnell (swift, active) 115
Schnellbacher (fr Schnellbach
122, rapid brook) 77
Schnellenbach (rapid brook) 77,
122
Schnellewind (strong wind)
Schnellmann (fast man, active
man) 115
Schnepf, Schnepfe, Schnepp,
Schneppe (snipe, weakling) 115
Schneyder, see Schneider
Schnider 159, see Schneider
Schnierle, see Schnuerle
Schnitter (reaper) 95
Schnitzel (chip, wood carver) 106
Schnitzer, Schnitzler, Schnizler
(cutter, wood carver) 96, 122
Schnor, Schnorr (cadger, peddler)
105
Schnuck (small sheep) 91
Schnuerle (little string, heavy
raindrops)
Schnur (daughter-in-law) 119
Schnur, Schnurr, Schnurer,
Schnurman (string, string
maker) 96, 106
Schober, Schobert 74 (haystack)
122
Schoch (hay stack)

Schock, Schoek, Schockmann
(swamp) 80
Schoedel, see Schaedel
Schoeff (assessor) 109
Schoeffler, see Scheffler
Schoemaker 159, see Schumacher
Schoemburg (beautiful castle) 73
Schoen, Schoene, Schoener,
Schoenert 74 (beautiful,
handsome) 115, 122
Schoenau, Schoenauer (beautiful
meadow) 84, 122
Schoenbacher, Schoenback 159 (fr
Schoenbach 122, beautiful
brook) 77
Schoenbaum (beautiful tree) 89
Schoenberger (fr Schoenberg 122,
beautiful mountain, shiny
mountain) 68, 157
Schoenbild (beautiful picture)
Schoenblum (beautiful flower) 89
Schoenborn (beautiful spring) 79
Schoenbrot (beautiful bread,
baker) 96
Schoenbruck (beautiful bridge)
Schoendorf (beautiful village) 123,
122
Schoeneck, Schoeneker (beautiful
field) 85, 122
Schoenemann, Schoenmann
(beautiful man) 115
Schoener (fr Schoeningen 122),
see Schoen
Schoenfeld, Schoenfeldt, Schoen-
felder (beautiful field) 84, 122
Schoenfuhs (beautiful foot) 114,
117
Schoenhaar (beautiful hair) 112
Schoenhals (beautiful throat) 114
Schoenhardt (beautiful forest) 72,
122
Schoenherr (handsome gentle-
man), see Schoenhaar
Schoenhof (beautiful farm) 92,
122

Schoenholtz, Schoenholtzer (beautiful forest) 72, 122
Schoenhut (beautiful hat, miliner) 96, 106
Schoenkind (beautiful child)
Schoenknecht (beautiful servant)
Schoenleben (the good life, beautiful estate) 127
Schoenmann, see Schoenemann
Schoenmannsgruber (fr Schoenmann's valley) 76
Schoenthal (beautiful valley) 76, 122
Schoenwald, Schoenewalt (beautiful forest) 71
Schoenweiss (beautiful white) 112
Schoepf (scoop, place for drawing water)
Schofer, Schoffer, see Schaefer
Schoff (shed) 65
Schoffstal (sheep fold) 65
Schofner, see Schaffner
Schol, Scholl, Scholle, Schollen (soil, farmer, clodhopper) 91, 115
Scholler (farmer, clodhopper) 91, 115
Schollmeyer (dirt farmer) 93
Scholt, Scholten, Scholtz, see Schultz
Schomaker, Schomakers 164, see Schumacher
Schomann, Schooman 159, see Schumann
Schombach, see Schoenbach, Schaumbach
Schomberg (beautiful mountain) 68
Schomburg 122, Schomburger, see Schoemburg, Schaumburg
Schon 159, Schone, see Schoen
Schon ... , see under Schoen ...
Schonbach 159, see Schoenbach
Schonberg 159, see Schoenberg
Schonfeld (beautiful field) 84
Schonfield 153, see Schonfeld

Schopf (shock of hair) 112
Schopp 122, Schoppe (measure of wine) 106
Schorbach (dirty stream) 77, 122
Schornstein (chimney, chimney sweep) 96
Schorsch (fr French: Georges) 144
Schott, Schotte (curds) 112, 105
Schott (bulkhead) 122
Schott (Scot) 122
Schotter (gravel)
Schotthofer (dairy) 92
Schoultz 159, see Schultz
Schoumacker 159, see Schumacher
Schouster 159, see Schuster
Schoumburg 159, see Schaumburg
Schour 159, Schouwer, see Schauer
Schrader 159, Schraeder, see Schroeder
Schram, Schramm, Schramme (scratch, abraision, wound) 114
Schranck, Schrank (cupboard, wardrobe) 106
Schranne (crack in glacier)
Schrantz (split, sycophant) 115
Schraub (screw) 106
Schrecengost 159, Schreckengaust, Schrengost (Frighten the guest!) 116
Schreck (jump, fright) 122
Schreck (muddy ground) 80
Schreder, see Schroeder
Schreiber, Schreiver (scribe) 96
Schreibfeder (writing plume, scribe) 96
Schreier (town crier) 96, 109
Schrein, Schreiner (cabinet maker, fr Latin *scrinarius*) 99
Schrempff (cut, wound) 114
Schreter, see Schroeder
Schreyder (gristmiller) 96
Schreyer, see Schreier

Schriber 159, Schriver, see
Schreiber
Schroader 159, see Schroeder
Schrodt, Schroth, see Schrott
Schroeder, Schroeter, Schroter
159, Schroder (tailor) 104
Schroff (rugged) 115
Schroll (clod, clodopper) 91, 115
Schrott (bruised grain, groats)
106, 122
Schroyer, see Schreier
Schu (shoe, shoemaker) 96, 104
Schub (push, shove)
Schubdrein (Shove it in!) 116
Schubert, Schuberth (shoemaker)
104
Schuch, Schuchard, Schuchart,
Schuchardt (shoe, shoemaker)
96, 104
Schuchman, Schuchmann
(shoemaker) 104
Schuck, Schucks 74, Schucker,
Schuker, Schuckermann (shoe,
cobbler) 96, 104
Schude, Schuder, Schudt, Schudy,
see Schutt
Schuebel, Schueble 159 (bushel)
122
Schuele, Schuelle, see Schule
Schueler, Schuehler, Schueller,
see Schuler
Schuenemann, Schuenmann, see
Scheunemann
Schuerer, Schuermann (scourer)
96
Schuerholtz, Schuerholtz (fire-
wood) 106
Schuerholtz, Schuerholz (poker,
baker, etc.) 96
Schuessel, Schuessler (bowl,
bowlmaker, fr Latin *scutella)*
96, 106
Schuett, Schuette (rubble) 122,
see Schuetz
Schuetz (marksman) 107, 122
Schuh (shoe, shoemaker) 106, 104

Schuhl, see Schule
Schuhmacher (shoemaker) 104
Schuhmann, see Schumann
Schuhriem, Schuhriemen (shoe-
strap, shoe lace) 96, 106
Schuhwerk (footwear, cobbler)
104
Schuld, Schuldt (guilt, debt)
Schuldenfrei (debt free) 115
Schulder 159, see Schulter
Schuldheis, see Schultheiss
Schule, Schull (school, synagogue,
fr Latin *scola)*
Schulenberg (hidden mountain)
68, 122
Schulenburg (hidden castle) 73,
122
Schuler, Schuller (pupil)
Schulhoff (school yard) 92
Schulius (Latin for Schule) 141
Schulkind (school child)
Schullehrer (school teacher) 96
Schulmann, Schulmeister (tea-
cher, synagogue sexton) 96
Schult, see Schuld
Schult, Schulte, Schultes, see
Schultheis
Schulteis, see Schultheis
Schulter, Schulther, Schulters
164 (shoulder) 114
Schulter (debtor)
Schultheis, Schultheiss (village
magistrate) 109
Schultz, Schulz, Schulze, see
Schultheis
Schumacher, Schumaker, see
Schuhmacher
Schuman, Schumann, see
Schuhmacher
Schumer (skimmer of millk, etc.,
cheat) 96, 115
Schumm, see Schuhmacher
Schumpeter (Cobbler Peter) 104
Schunemann 159, see Scheune-
mann

Schunk, Schunke (shank, thigh) 114

Schupp (scale)

Schuppen (shed) 65

Schurman, Schurmann (dweller by a pond 80), see also Scheuermann

Schurtz, Schurz (apron, skirt, shirt, blacksmith, baker, etc.) 96, 106

Schuss, Schusz (shot)

Schuss (very steep slope) 71, 122

Schussele 55, see Schuessel

Schuster (shoemaker, fr Latin *sutor*) 104

Schut, Schutt, Schutte (rubbish, rubble)

Schutz, Schutze, Schutzman (watchman, guard) 109, see Schuetz

Schwaab, Schwab, Schwabe, Schwaber (Swabian) 120

Schwabeland, Schwabenland, Schwabland (Swabia) 120

Schwabline 55, 159 (little Swabian) 120

Schwach (weak) 114

Schwaeher (brother-in-law) 119

Schwager (brother-in-law) 119

Schwaiger, see Schweiger

Schwalb, Schwalbe (swallow) 115

Schwalb (dweller near the Schwalb, swamp) 83

Schwalbach (swamp brook) 80, 77, 122

Schwall, Schwalls 74 (swamp) 80, 122

Schwalm (name of river, swamp water) 80, 83

Schwamb, Schwamm, Schwam (sponge) 106

Schwan (swan) 48, 62

Schwander, Schwandner, Schwandter, Schwandtner, Schwaner (occupant of a clearing 126, fr Schwand 122)

Schwandt (clearing, see Schwander) 126, 122

Schwanebeck, Schwanenbeck (swan creek) 48, 77, 122

Schwanfelder (fr Schwanfeld 122, swan field) 48, 84

Schwanger (pregnant)

Schwank, Schwanke (swing, farce)

Schwantz (tail)

Schwarm (swamp) 80, 122

Schwarm (bee swarm, apiarist) 96

Schwart, see Schwarte, Schwartz

Schwarte (bristled hide, peasant's scalp) 114

Schwartz, Schwartze (black, brunet, blacksmith) 112, 96

Schwartzbach, Schwarzenbach (fr Schwartzbach 122, black brook) 77

Schwartzbart (black beard) 112

Schwartzberg (black mountain) 68

Schwartzenfeld (blackfield) 84, 122

Schwartzhaubt (black head) 112

Schwartzkopf (black head) 112, 122

Schwartzman (brunet) 112

Schwartzschild, Schwarzschild (black shield) 62, 149

Schwartzwelder 159, Schwarzwaelder (fr the black forest) 121

Schwarz, see Schwartz

Schwarzman, Schwarzmann, see Schwartzman

Schwarzschild, see Schwartzschild

Schwarzwalder 159, Schwarzwald, see Schwartzwelder

Schwatz (gossip, chatter) 115

Schwebel, Schwefel (sulphur) 106

Schwebel (little Swabian) 120

Schwegler (flutist, bagpiper) 96

Schweich (Be silent!)

Schweiger, Schweigert 74,
Schweigerts 74, 164, Schweig-
hart 74 (fr a cattle farm) 91,
92, 143
Schweighof (cattle farm) 91, 92,
122
Schweighoffer, Schweighoefer
(cattle famer) 91, 92
Schweighouser 159 (fr a
Schweighof)
Schweikert 74, Schweikhart,
Schweickhart < Schweiger
Schwein (swine, swineherd) 91
Schwein (swamp water) 80, 91,
115
Schweinfurt, Schweinfurth
(swamp water ford, a city) 80,
122
Schweinhart (wild boar + strong)
46, 46
Schweinsberg (boar mountain) 48,
68
Schweiss (sweat, blood)
Schweisshelm (blood + helmet) 46
Schweitz, Schweitzer, Schweizer,
Schweizzer (Swiss) 120
Schwemmer (rafter) 96
Schwenck, Schwenk, Schwenker
(brandisher)
Schwend, Schwender,
Schwendemann (dweller in a
clearing) 126
Schwenkel, Schwengel (swingbar,
clapper) 106
Schwentke 55, see Schwend
Schwentzel 55 (little tail)
Schwentzer (idler) 115
Schwer (heavy), see Schwaeher
Schwerd, Schwerdt, Schwert
(sword) 45, 108
Schwerdfeger, Schwerdtfeger
(sword burnisher) 108
Schwerdtner (sword maker) 108
Schwermann 119, see Schwaeher
Schwerdtle, Schwertlein 55 (little
sword) 96, 107, 108

Schwickert, see Schweiger
Schwieger, Schwiegert 74 (in-law,
mother-in-law) 119
Schwind, Schwindt (a clearing)
126, 122
Schwind, Schwindt (swift, tu-
multuous) 115
Schwindel, Schwindler (swindler)
115
Schwing (swamp) 80, 122
Schwingel (fescue grass) 89
Schwingschwert (Brandish the
sword!) 116
Schwitzer, see Schweitzer
Schwob, see Schwab
Schwoerer (swearer)
Schwol, see Schwall
Schwyzer, see Schweitzer
Schyre 159, see Scheuer
Scriber 159, see Schreiber
Scrivers 159, 164, see Schreiber
Seabald 159, Seabold, Seaboldt,
see Siegbald
Seacrist 159, see Sigrist
Seafred 159, Seafret, Seafrett, see
Siegfried
Seager 159, see Sieger
Seagle 159, see Siegel
Seaholz 159, Seaholz, see See-
holtz
Seaman 159, see Siemen, Sae-
mann
Sebald, see Siegbald
Sebastian (St. Sebastian) 131
Sebeniecher 159, see Sieben-
eichen
Sebert, see Siegbrecht
Sebold, Seboldt, see Siegbald
Sechrist 159, see Sigrist
Seckel 55 (satchel, satchel maker)
106
Seckel 53, 55 (little Isaac)
Seckinger (person fr Seckingen)
122
Secrest, Secrist, see Sigrist

Sedlmayer 159, see Sattelmeyer, 151
See (lake) 80, 122
Seebach, Seebacher (lake brook) 80, 77, 122
Seeberg, Seeberger (lake mountain) 80, 68, 122
Seebold 159, see Siegbald
Seeburg (lake castle) 80, 73
Seefeld, Seefeldt (lake field) 80, 84, 122
Seefret 159, see Siegfried
Seegel 159, Seegal, see Siegel
Seeger 159, Seegar, Seger, see Sieger
Seehausen (lake house) 80, 65
Seehaver 159, Seehofer (lake farm) 80, 92
Seehousz 159, see Seehausen
Seegmiller (sawmiller) 103, 151
Seegrist 159, see Sigrist
Seeholtz (lake forest) 80, 72
Seekamp (lake field) 80, 84, 122
Seel (soul)
Seel (swamp) 80, 122
Seelaender (fr Seeland, Zeeland) 121
Seelhorst (swamp hurst) 80, 72
Seelig, see Selig
Seelmann (swamp dweller) 80
Seemann (seaman) 96
Seemann (dweller on a lake) 80
Seemueller (miller on the lake) 80, 103
Seethaler (fr Seethal, lake valley) 122
Seets 159, see Seitz
Seewald (lake forest) 80, 71
Sefeldt, see Seefeld
Sefret, Seffret, see Siegfried
Sefues 53 < Josephus 135
Segbolt < Siegbald
Segel (sail) 106
Segel 159, Segal, Segall, see Siegel

Segeler, Segler (sailor, sail maker) 96
Segenreich (rich in blessing) 139, 148
Seger 159, Segers 164, see Sieger
Segfried 159 < Siegfried
Segmueller (sawmiller) 96, 103
Segrist, Segrest, see Sigrist
Sehl (swamp) 80, see also Seel
Sehlhorst (swamp hurst) 80, 72
Sehlmeyer (swamp farmer) 80, 93
Sehlsted (swamp place) 80
Sehr (scorch, burn)
Seib (sieve) 106
Seibald, see Siegbald
Seibel, see Siegbald
Seibert, Seipert < Siegbert
Seibold < Siegbald
Seibrandt < Siegbrand
Seidel, Seidl, Seidell (mug, pint) 106
Seideler, Seidler, Seidelmann (mug maker) 96
Seidemann, Seidenman, Seidman, Seidenspinner (silk worker) 96
Seidenberg (silk mountain) 68
Seidenfaden (silk thread, silk reeler, spinner) 96
Seidenschnur (silk thread) 106
Seidenstricker (silk knitter) 96
Seidner (silk worker) 96
Seif, Seifensieder (soap boiler) 106, 96
Seifert, Seiffert, Seifarth, Seifferth < Siegward, Seifried, Seifrit, see Siegfried
Seig 159, see Sieg
Seigel 159, see Siegel
Seigler 159, see Ziegler
Seil, Seile, Seiler (rope maker) 106
Seilback 159 (fr Seilbach 122, rope brook), see Selbach
Seiler (rope maker) 96
Seip 53, Seipel, Seipell, Seippel, Sippel, Seifold < Siegbald

Seippert < Siegbert
Seiss (sythe) 106
Seitz 53, Seiz, Seitzer < Siefried
Seivert, see Siegfried, Siegwart
Seivold, see Siegbald
Sekler (sack maker) 96
Selbach (swamp brook) 80, 77, 122
Selde (house, shelter) 65
Seldenreich (fortunate) 115, see Seltenreich
Selhorst (marsh hurst) 80, 72
Selig, Seliger (fortunate, blessed) 115, 139, 148
Seligman, Seligmann (blessed man) 115, 139, 148
Selkman 159, Selkmann, see Seligman
Sell, Selle 122, Seller, Sellner, Selman, Sellmann (marsh land) 80
Sellmayer, Sellmeyer (farmer on the marsh) 80, 93
Selmer < Salmar (hall + famous) 47
Selpert < Salbrecht (hall + bright) 47
Seltenreich (seldom rich) 115, see Seldenreich
Seltmann, see Selter
Selter, Seltz, Seltzer, Selzer, (salt merchant, meat and fish salter) 96, 106
Seman 159, Semans 164, see Saemann, Seemann, Sieman
Semmel, Semmler, Semler (blond) 112
Semmel, Semmler, Semler (white roll baker) 96
Senck, Senk, Senkler (inhabitant of a burned off clearing) 126
Sendeck (swamp field) 80, 84
Sendel, Senderling (swamp dweller) 80
Sender 53 < Alexander

Sender (dweller in a burned clearing) 126
Sendldorfer (swamp village) 80, 123
Senecker 159, Senneca, see Schoenacker
Senf (mustard) 106
Senfelder, Senffelder, Sennfelder (mustard field) 84
Senft (gentle) 115
Senftleber, see Sanftleben
Seng, Senge (burned off land) 84, 122
Sengebusch (burned shrubland) 72
Senger (singer) 96
Sengeysen (scorching iron) 106
Sengstake (Burn the poker!, stoker) 116, 96
Senkel (lace) 106
Senn (Swiss shepherd) 95
Sennhauser (occupant of shepherd's hut) 95, 65
Sens (reed grass) 81
Sensabaugh 159, Sensebaugh, Sensibaugh, Sensebach (reed brook) 81, 77
Sensenbrenner (reed burner) 96
Sensenmann (reaper) 95
Senstack, see Sengstake
Sentheim, see Sontheim
Sentz 53 <St. Vincent 131
Seohnlein 159, 55, see Soehnlein
Seppel 53, 55, Seppler, Seppi < Josef, Giuseppi
Sermatt 159 (fr Zermatt) 122
Sessler (chair maker) 96
Setmayer, see Sattelmeyer
Settelman, Settleman, Settle 159, Settler (dweller on a mountain saddle) 68
Settelmeyer, see Sattelmeyer
Setzer, Setzler, Setser (compositor) 96
Seuberlich, see Saeuberlich
Seubert, Seuberth < Siegbert

Seubold < Siegbald
Seuer, see Saeuer
Seuffert, Seufried < Siegfried
Seuter (shoemaker, fr Latin
    *sutor*) 104
Sevalt < Siegbald
Sevart, Severt, Sewert < Siegwart
Severin (St. Severin) 131, 122
Sewalt 159, see Seewald
Seybel < Siegbald
Seybert, Seybert < Siegbert
Seybold, Seybolds 164 < Siegbald
Seybrecht, see Siegbert
Seydel, Seydeler, see Seideler
Seydelmann, see Seideler
Seydelmann (silk worker) 96
Seydler, see Seydelmann
Seydt, see Seide
Seyfer, Seyfert, Seyvert, Seyferth,
    Seyfarth, Seyfardt < Siegwart
Seyfreet 159, see Siegfried
Seyfrid, Seyfrit, Seyfritz 164,
    Seyfried, Seyfriedt < Siegfried
Seyl, Sylar 159, see Seiler
Seyler, see Seiler
Seymond < Siegmund, Sigismund
Seyppel < Siegbalt
Sh ..., see under Sch ... (Only a
    small sample given here)
Shade 159, Shadlein 55, see
    Schad, Schadlein
Shach 159, see Schach
Shadle 159, see Schaedel
Shafer 159, Shaffer, Shaefer,
    Shaeffer, see Schaeffer
Shallenberg 159, see Schallen-
    berger
Shaller 159, see Schaller
Shambaugh 159, see Schaumbach
Shane 159, see Schoen
Shanebacker 159, see Schoen-
    backer
Shanefelter 159, see Schoenfelder
Shank 159, see Schenk
Shants 159, see Schantz
Sharp 159, see Scharf

Sharpstein 159, see Scharfstein
Shats 159, see Schatz
Shauder 159, see Schauder
Shauer 159, see Schauer
Shaumloffel 159, see Schaum-
    loeffel
Shaver 159, see Schaber
Sheaffer 159, see Schaeffer,
    Schiefer
Shealy 159, see Schiele
Shear 159, Shearman, see Scher,
    Schermann
Sheats 159, Sheets, Sheatsen, see
    Schuetz, Schuetzen
Sheeler 159, Sheely, see Schieler,
    Schiele
Sheib 159, see Scheib
Sheildknight 159, Scheldknight,
    see Schildknecht
Shellenberger 159, see Schel-
    lenberger
Shelley 159, see Schiele
Shendler 159, see Schindler
Shenk 159, see Schenk
Shepherd 153, Shepperd, see
    Schaefer
Sherman 159, see Schermann
Sherouse 159, see Scheraus
Shewmaker, see Schumacher
Shiller 159, Shilling, see Schiller,
    Schilling
Shilnite 159, see Schildknecht
Shimelman, see Schimmelmann
Shindle 159, see Schindel
Shine 159, see Schein, Schoen ...
Shinebach 159, see Schoenbach
Shirer 159, see Scheurer
Shissel 159, Shissler, Shislor, see
    Schuessel, Schuessler
Shmal 159, Shmall, see Schmal
Shnyder 159, see Schneider
Shoemaker 153, see Schumacher
Schoff 159, see Schaff
Sholl 159, see Scholl
Shonfeld 159, see Schoenfeld
Shonik 159, see Schoeneck

Shoney 159, see Schoene
Shonts 159, see Schantz
Shots 159, see Schatz
Shoup 159, see Schaub
Shrader 159, see Schroeder
Shriner 159, see Schreiner
Shriver 159, see Schreiber
Shroder 159, see Schroeder
Shrontz 159, see Schrantze
Shroyer 159, see Schreier
Shuler 159, see Schueler
Shults 159, see Schultz
Shuman 159, see Schumann
Shy 159, see Scheu
Sibert < Siegbert
Sible 159, see Seibel
Sibold < Siegbald
Sichel (sickle, fr Latin *sicilis*) 106
Sichelstiel (sickel handle) 106
Sicher (secure, fr Latin *securus*) 115
Sickafoos 159 < Ziegenfuss (goatfoot)
Sickler 159, see Ziegler, Sichel
Sidell, Sidle 159, see Seidel
Sides 159, see Seitz
Sidnor 159, see Seidner
Sieb, Siebe (sieve) 106, 122
Siebelt < Siegbald
Sieben (seven)
Siebeneichen (seven oaks) 89, 122
Siebenbuergen (place in Hungary, seven castles) 73
Siebenhaar (seven hairs) 112, 114
Siebenheller (seven pence) 117
Siebensohn (seven sons)
Sieber, Siebers 74 (strainer, siever) 106
Siebert < Siegbert
Siebold, Sieboldt < Siegbald
Sieck (sick) 114
Sieck (marsh) 80, 122
Sieckman (marsh dweller) 80
Siecrist 159, see Sigrist
Siedel, Siedler (settler)
Siedel, Siedler (boiler)

Siedentop (boiling pot) 106
Sieder (boiler) 96
Siefer, Sieffert, Siefferts 74, Sieverts, Sievers, Siewers, see Siegwart
Siefreit, see Siegfried
Sieg (victory) 47, 122
Sieg (river name, swamp) 80, 83
Siegbald (victory + bold) 47, 46
Siegbert, Siegbrecht (victory + bright) 47, 46
Siegbrand (victory + sword) 46, 46
Siegehrist 159, see Sigrist
Siegel, Siegal 159, Siegler, Siegle 159, Siegelman (seal, fr Latin *sigillum*) 106
Siegel 53, 55, Siegle 159 < Siegfried, Siegward, etc.
Siegenthaler, Siegenthahler (victory valley) 47, 76
Sieger, Siegert 74 (winner)
Siegfried, Siegfreit 159 (victory + protection) 47, 47
Sieghart (victory + strong) 47, 46
Siegler, see Siegel, Ziegler
Siegman, Siegmann (victor) 47
Siegmund, Sigismund (victory + guardian) 47, 47
Siegrist, see Sigrist
Siegwald (victory + rule) 47, 46
Siegwart, Siegworth 159 (victory + guardian) 47, 47
Siehdichum (Look around!) 116
Sieman, Siemann, Siemanns 74, see Siegman
Siemann (henpecked man, uxorious husband) 115
Siemer, Siemering 55 < Siegmar (victory + famous) 47, 47
Siemund, see Siegmund
Sieppert < Siegbert
Sievers 74, Sievert, Sieverts 74 < Siegwart
Sievold, see Siegbald
Sifert, see Siegfried

Sigafoose 159 < Ziegenfuss (goat foot)

Sigel 159, Sigal, Sigler, see Siegel, Siegler

Sigfried, Sigfritz < Siegfried

Sigman, Sigmon 159, see Siegman, Siegmund

Sigmund, see Siegmund

Sigrist (sexton, fr Latin *sacrum*) 110

Sigwalt, Siewald < Siegwald

Sigwart, see Siegwart

Silbaugh 159, see Selbach

Silber, Silbers 164, Silbert 74, Silver, Silvers 164 (silver, silver smith) 96, 106

Silberberg, Silverberg 153 (silver mountain) 68, 148, 122

Silbergeld (silver money)

Silberholz (silver forest) 72

Silberhorn (silver horn)

Silbermann, Silverman 153 (silver smith) 96

Silbernagel, Silvernail 153 (silver nail) 106

Silbersack (silver bag)

Silberstein, Sillverstein 159 (silver stone, silver mountain, litharge, silversmith) 73, 122

Silberzahn (silver tooth)

Siler 159, see Seiler

Silver ..., see Silber ...

Silvernail 153, see Silbernagel

Simeon (OT name) 135

Simmel (baker of white rolls) 106

Simmermann 159, see Zimmermann

Simon, Simons 164 (NT name) 131

Singer, Singert 74, see Saenger

Singhaus (concert house) 65

Singmaster 153, see Sangmeister

Singvogel (song bird) 115

Sinn (mind, idea)

Sinn (swamp water) 80

Sipart, see Siegbert

Sipe 159, Sipes 164, see Seib

Sipp, Sippen (kinsman) 119

Sippel, Sipple 159 < Siegbald

Sirach (OT name) 135

Sis, Siss, see Suess

Siskind, see Suesskind

Sites 159, see Seitz

Sitzer (sitter)

Sitzwohl (Sit well!) 116

Siverd, Sivert < Siegwart

Siwald 159, see Seewald, Siegbald

Sl ..., see under Schl ... Only a sample is given here.

Slabaugh 159, see Schlebach

Slagle 159, see Schlegel

Slater 159, see Schlatter

Slaubaugh 159 (meadow brook) 84, 77

Slauch 159, see Schlauch

Slaugenhoup 159 < Schlagdenhaupt (Hit the head!)

Slaughter 159, see Schlechter

Slaybaugh 159, Slayback, see Schlebach

Slaymaker 159, see Schleiermacher

Slechter 159, see Schlechter

Sleeman 159, see Schliemann

Slegel 159, see Schlegel

Sleifer 159, see Schleifer

Slemaker 159, see Schleirmacher

Slemmer 159, see Schlemmer

Slicher 159, see Schleicher

Slimm 159, see Schlimm

Slosser 159, see Schlosser

Slotman, see Schlosser

Slotter 159, see Schlatter

Slotterbach 159, Slotterback < Schlatterbach (marsh brook)

Slouk 159, Slough 159, see Schlauch

Slund 159, see Schlund

Sly 159, see Schley

Sm ..., see Schm ... Only a sample is given here.

Small 159, see Schmal

Smalts 159, see Schmaltz
Smelser 159, Smeltz, see
    Schmeltzer
Smick 159, see Schmueck
Smit 159, see Schmidt
Smith 153, see Schmidt
Smithmeyer 153, see Schmidt-
    bauer
Smithpeter 152 < Schmidtpeter
    (Peter the smith)
Smitsdorf < Schmidtsdorf (smith's
    village)
Smoke 159, see Schmuck, Rauch
Smouse 159, see Schmauss
Smucker 159, see Schmucker
Smyser 159, see Schmeisser
Sn ..., see under Schn ... Only a
    sample is given here.
Snavel 159, see Schnabel
Snavely 159, see Schnaebele
Snay 159, see Schnee
Sneckenberger 159, see
    Schneckenberger
Snee 159, see Schnee
Sneider 159, see Schneider
Snell 159, see Schnell
Snider 159, Sniders 164, see
    Schneider
Snively 159, see Schnaebele
Snowberger 153, see Schnee-
    berger
Snurr 159, see Schnur
Snyder 159, Snyders 164, see
    Schneider
Sockriter 159, see Sackreiter
Socks 159, see Sachs
Soeder, see Soeter
Soehnlein 55 (little son) 119
Soeldner, Soellner (mercenary, fr
    Latin *solidarius*) 107
Soeller (fr Soell) 122
Soeller (balcony, fr Latin *solar-
    ium*)
Soeter (shoemaker) 104
Sohn, Sohns 164 (son) 119
Sol, Soll (mud, bog) 80

Solberg (mud mountain) 68
Soldan, see Soltan
Soldier 153, see Soeldner
Soldner 159, see Soeldner
Solms (swamp water) 80, 122
Solomon 153, see Salomo
Soltan (sultan)
Solter, see Saltzer
Soltz, Soltmann, see Salz, also
    inhabitant of Solt 122
Sommer, Sommers 164, Somer,
    Somers 164 (summer)
Sommerfeld 122, Sommerfeldt,
    Sommerfelt (summer field) 84
Sommerfield 153, see Sommerfeld
Sommerkamp (summer field) 84
Sonderman, Sondermann (swamp
    dweller) 80
Sondheim (swamp hamlet) 80,
    123, 122, see Sontheim
Sonn, Sonne (sun)
Sonneborn (sun spring) 79
Sonnefeld, Sonnenfeld (sun field)
    84, 122
Sonnenberg (sun mountain) 68,
    122
Sonnenleiter, Sonnelitter 159 (fr
    Sonnenleite, sunny slope) 71
Sonnenschein (sunshine) 122
Sonnenthal (sun valley) 76
Sonntag (Sunday) 143
Sontheim (southern hamlet) 85,
    123, 122
Sooter 159, see Sutter
Sorber (Sorbian) 121
Sorg, Sorge, Sorgen (care, wor-
    rier) 115, 122
Sorgenfrei, Sorgenfrey (care free)
    115
Souter 159, see Suter
Sower 159, see Sauer
Sowerwine 159, see Sauerwein
Spaengler, see Spengler
Spaeth, Spaet, Spaete, Speth
    (late, tardy) 115
Spahn (swamp) 80

Spahr (sparrow) 115
Spaight 159, see Spaeth
Spainhour 159, Spainhower, see
  Spanhauer
Spalt (split)
Span (chip)
Spange (buckle, bracelet) 106
Spangenberg, Spangenberger
  (swamp mountain) 80, 68, 122
Spangenthal (swamp valley) 76
Spangler 159, see Spengler
Spanhauer (chip hewer) 95, 100
Spanier, Spanierman (Spaniard)
  121
Spann 122, see Span
Spar, see Spahr
Sparber, see Sperber
Sparenberg (sparrow mountain)
  68
Sparr (rafter) 122
Sparrenburg (sparrow castle) 73
Spath, see Spaeth
Spatz (sparrow, urchin) 115
Spealman 159, see Spielmann
Speas 159, see Spiess
Speece 159, Speas, see Spiess
Specht, Spaecht (woodpecker) 115
Speck (lard, pork seller) 106
Speck, Speckmann (raised path
  through a bog, corduroy road)
  65, 122
Speelmann, see Spielmann
Speer, Speers 74, Speert 74
  (spear) 107, 108
Speice 159, see Speiss
Speicher, Speichert 74 (granary,
  fr Latin *spicarium*) 122
Speidel (woodcutter's wedge) 95,
  106
Speier, see Speyer
Speigel 159, see Spiegel
Speight 159, Speights 74, see
  Spaeth
Speis, Speiss, Speise, Speiser
  (food, victualer) 106
Speishaendler (food handler) 106

Speismann (victualer) 96, 106
Speker 159, see Spieker
Spellerberg, see Spielberg
Spelmann, Spellmann, see
  Spielmann
Spener (needle maker) 96
Spengler, Spengel (tinsmith) 96
Sperber (sparrow hawk) 115
Sperl, Sperling 55, Sperlein 55
  (sparrow) 115
Sperlbaum (sparrow tree) 89
Sperre, Sperry 159 (baricade,
  closing) 122
Spessart, Spessard (mountain
  range, swamp forest) 80, 72,
  122
Speth 159, see Spaeth
Speydel, see Speidel
Speyer (city on Rhine) 122
Spice 159, Spicer, see Speiser
Spidel 159, Spidelle, see Speidel
Spiecher 159, see Speicher
Spiegel, Spiegler (mirror, fr Latin
  *speculum*) 106, 122
Spieker (large nail, spike) 106
Spieker (granary) 122
Spielacker (field drawn by lot) 84
Spielberg (lookout mountain, fr
  Latin *specula*) 68, 122
Spieler (player, gambler)
Spielmann, Spillman (minstrel)
  96
Spier, Spiers 74 (Speyer)
Spies, Spiess (spear, spit, spit-
  shaped field) 108, 106, 122
Spies (swamp) 80
Spiesman, Spiessman (pikeman)
  107
Spigel 159, Spigler, see Spiegel,
  Spiegler
Spigelmire 159 (fr the Spiegelhof,
  mirror farm) 93
Spiller, Spillman, see Spieler,
  Spielman
Spindel, Spindler (distaff, spin-
  ner, distaf maker) 106

Spingler 159, see Spengler
Spinnenweber, Spinneweber
(spinnerweaver) 96
Spinner, Spinnler (spinner) 96
Spittel, Spital (hospice) 122
Spittelmayer (hospice overseer)
93
Spittler, Spitler (worker in a
hospice) 96
Spitz, Spitzer, Spitzler, Spitzner
(point, dweller near a peak) 68,
122
Spitzberg (sharp peaked moun-
tain) 68
Spitznagel, Spitznagle 159 (sharp
nail) 106
Spitznas (pointed nose) 114
Spohn, see Span
Spohr (spur) 96, 106
Sponheimer (city name) 122
Spoon, see Span
Spoonhour 159, 100, see Span-
hauer
Spott, Spotz 74 (ridicule)
Sprecher (speaker) 115
Spreckels 164 (marsh dweller) 80
Sprengel (diocese) 122
Sprenkel, Sprenkle 159, see
Sprengel
Springel, see Sprengel
Springer, Sprenger, Springmann
(jumper, dancer 96, fr Springen
122)
Springfeld (spring field) 84
Sprinkel, Sprinkle 159 (freckles)
Spritz, Spritzer (spray, sprayer)
96
Spuecher, see Spiecher
Spuhler (spool maker) 96
Spund, Spunt (bung, taverner) 96
Spur (spoor)
Spyker, see Spieker
Staab, see Stabe
Staadt 122, see Stadt
Staal, see Stahl
Stabe (staff)

Stablein 159, 55 (little staff)
Stabler 159, see Staebler
Stack 53, Stach < St. Eustachius
131
Stackhouse 153, see Stockhaus
Stackman 159, Stackmann, see
Stockmann
Stadel, Stadeli (stable, barn) 122
Stadelman, Stadelmann (barn
supervisor) 96
Stadelmayer, Stadelmeier (barn
steward) 96, 93
Stader (dweller at a landing)
Stadfeld (field at the landing) 84
Stadler, Stadtler, Stattler (barn
supervisor) 96, 122
Stadt, Stadter, Stadtler, Staedt-
ler, Statler (townsman) 122
Staeblein 55 (little staff)
Staebler (staff-carrying official)
109
Staeheli, Staehle, Staehli, Staeh-
ler, Steheli, Steely 159, Stelly
159 (steel, blacksmith) 96
Staempfli 55, see Stempel
Staerk (strength) 115
Staetler (townsman)
Staffel (step, rung) 122
Stahl, Stahle, Stahler, Stahley
159, Stahlmann, see Staehli
Stahlschmit (steel smith) 96
Stahr (starling) 115
Staiger, see Steiger
Staigerwald (footpath forest) 65,
72
Stain, see Stein
Stainbach, see Steinbach
Stalden (steep path) 65
Staley 159, see Staeheli
Stall, Stallmann, Stalling 55,
Stallings 74 (stall, barn, sta-
bleman) 96, 122
Stallknecht (groom) 96
Stalmaster 153 < Stallmeister
(equerry)
Staltzfus 159, see Stoltzfus

Stambach, Stambaugh 159 (stump brook) 77, 122
Stamberg, Stammberger (stump mountain) 68, 122
Stambler, see Stammler
Stamgast (regular guest)
Stamitz, see Steinmetz
Stamm, Stam (stem, trunk)
Stammbach, see Steinbach
Stammler (stutterer) 114
Stampf, Stampfel, Stampfl (stamp, tamper) 106
Stampf (steep path) 65
Stanback, Stanbaugh 159, see Steinbach
Stance 159, see Stantze
Stand, Stand, Stant (condition)
Stang, Stange, Stanger (pole, stick, spear) 106
Stantze (stamp, die) 106
Stapf, Stapp (step)
Star, Stahr, Starr (starling) 115
Starck, Stark, Starke, Starker (strong) 115
Starkand (strong hand) 115
Startz 159, see Stortz
Stassen 53 < St. Anastasius 131
Stattler, see Stadtler
Staub, Staube, Stauber (dust)
Stauch (jolt)
Staud, Staude, Staut, Staudt, Stauder (shrubs, underbrush) 72
Staudehauer (brush clearer) 72, 100, 95
Staudemeyer, Staudenmaier (fr the Staudehoff) 72, 93
Stauffer (mug maker) 96
Stauffer (crag dweller) 68
Staup, see Staub
Stauss, see Steiss
Stautberg (brush mountain) 72, 68
Stayner, see Steiner
Steagall 159, see Stiegel
Stealy 159, see Staeheli 151

Stearn 159, Stearns 74, see Stern
Stebbins < St. Stephan 131
Stecher, Stechler (engraver) 96
Steckel, Stecker (swamp) 80
Stedler, Stedeler, see Stadtler
Steely 159, see Staeheli
Steenfeld, see Steinfeld
Steer 159, Steere, see Stier
Steermann 159 (cattle raiser) 91
Steffen, Steffel, Steffens, Steffy, see Stephan
Steg, Steger, Stegmann (footbridge, dweller by steep footpath) 71
Stegel 159, see Stiegel
Stegman (dweller by a footpath) 65
Stegmeyer, Stegmaier, Stegmeier (farmer by the footpath, or footbridge) 93
Stegmueller, Stegmiller (fr a mill with facilities for other activities) 103
Stehle, Stehli, Steheli, Stehlin, Stehll, see Staeheli
Stehr (grain measure) 96
Stehr (wether, ram) 91
Steidel (dweller in the brush) 72
Steier, see Steyer
Steif (stiff) 114
Steig, Steigler, Steigman (dweller by a footbridge, footpath) 65
Steiger, Steigler, Steigman (climber)
Steigerwald, Steigerwalt (footpath mountain) 65, 68
Steil, Steile (steep)
Steimetz, see Steinmetz
Stein (stone, stone worker) 73, 96
Steinach (stone terrain) 73, 79
Steinacker (stone field) 73, 84
Steinau, Steinauer (stone meadow) 73, 84, see also Steinhauer
Steinbach, Steinbacher, Steinback (stony brook) 73, 77

Steinbeck, Steinbecker (stony brook) 73, 77
Steinberg, Steinbergen, Steinberger (stone mountain) 73, 68
Steinbeisser (stone etcher, lithographer) 96
Steinbock, Steinboeck (ibex) 62
Steinborn, Steinbronn (stone spring) 73, 79
Steinbrech, Steinbrecher, Steinbrecker (stone crusher, quarryman) 96, 100
Steinbrenner (brickmaker) 100
Steinbrickner, Steinbrueckner (dweller by stone bridge)
Steinbrook 159, see Steinbrueck, Steinbruch
Steinbruch 122, Steinbruechel (quarry, quarryman) 73
Steinbrunner, Steinebrunner (fr Steinbrunn, stone spring) 79
Steinburg (stone castle) 73, 73, 122
Steiner, Steinert 74 (stone worker) 73, 143
Steinfeld, Steinfeldt, Steinfelder (stone field) 73, 84, 122
Steinfuhrer (stone hauler) 73, 96
Steingart (stone garden) 73, 84
Steingass (stone road, stone street) 73, 65, 122
Steingoetter (stone drains)
Steinhag (stone enclosure) 73, 123, 122
Steinhard, Steinhart (stone hard) 115
Steinhardt, Steinharter (fr Steinhardt, stone forest) 73, 72
Steinhauer (stone cutter) 73, 100
Steinhaus, Steinhauser, Steinhaeuser (fr Steinhaus 122, stone house) 73, 65
Steinheimer (fr Steinheim 122, stone hamlet) 73, 123
Steinheiser 66, see Steinhaus

Steinhice 159, Steinheiser, see Steinhauser
Steinhof, Steinhoff (stone farm) 73, 84, 122
Steinhorn (stone peak) 73, 68
Steinhorst (stone hurst) 73, 74
Steinhour 159, 66, Steinour, see Steinhauer
Steinhuebel (stone hill) 73, 67
Steiniger, Steinigger, Steininger (fr Steiningen) 122
Steiningen, see Steininger
Steinkamp (stone field) 73, 84, 122
Steinkirchner (fr Steinkirchen 122, stone church) 73, 71
Steinkoenig (wren) 115
Steinkopf (stone head) 115
Steinlein 55 (little stone) 73
Steinler (stony place) 73
Steinman, Steinmann (stone cutter) 96
Steinmaur (fr Steinmauren 122, stone wall, mason, dweller by a stone wall) 100
Steinmetz, Steinmets 169, 164 (stone cutter) 96, 100
Steinmeyer, Steinmeier (fr the Steinhoff) 93
Steinour 159, see Steinauer, Steinhauer
Steinrucken (stone ridge) 73, 68
Steinseiffer, Stainsayfer (stony brook) 73, 77
Steinthal (stone valley) 73, 76
Steinwald (stone forest) 73, 71
Steinwand, Steinwaender (stone wall) 73, 122
Steinway 159, see Steinweg
Steinwedel (stony ford) 73, 78, 122
Steinweg (stony path) 73, 65, 122
Steinwinder, see Steinwand
Steinwyk (stone village) 73, 123
Steiss (rump) 114
Steitz (fuller, cloth cleanser) 96

Steli 159, see Stelly
Stell (frame, holder)
Steller, Stellmach, Stellmacher, Stellman, Stellmann (wainwright, cartwright) 96
Stelling (marsh dweller 80, fr Stellingen 122)
Stellwagen, Stellvagen 159 (stage coach)
Stelly 159, Stelley, see Staeheli
Stelmach, Stelmack, see Steller
Steltz, Stels 159, Selzer, Stelzner (stilts, walker on stilts or crutches) 114, 106
Steltzfuss (wooden leg) 114
Stemm, Stemmer, Stembler, Stemler, Stemmler (marsh dweller) 80
Stempel, Stemple 159 (stamp) 106
Stenabaugh 159, Stenbaugh, see Steinbach
Stendal 122, see Steinthal
Stendorf (stone village) 73, 123
Stenert, see Steiner, Steinert
Stengel, Stengle 159, Stenglein 55 (stalk, thin person) 114
Stenhouse 153, Stenkamp, see Steinhaus, Steinkamp
Stentz 53, Stenzer < Polish: Stanislaw 146
Step, Stepf, see Stapp, Stapf
Stephan, Stephann, Stephans, Steffen, Steffe, Stephanus (St. Stephen, name of pope) 134
Stephani, Stephany, son of Stephan 142
Steppe (quilt) 106
Sterb (Die!) 116, 117
Sterchi, Sterki, Sterkee 159 (strength) 115, see Stuerki
Stern, Sterne (star) 62
Sternberg, Sternberger (swamp mountain) 73, 80, 68, 122
Sternburg (swamp castle) 73
Sterner (swamp dweller) 80

Sternfeld (swamp field) 80, 84, 122
Sternglass (telescope, astrologer) 96, 106
Sternheim, Sternheimer (swamp hamlet) 80, 123
Sternkamp (steer field) 84, 122
Sternschuss (comet)
Sternsdorf (swamp village) 80, 123
Sternthal (swamp valley) 80, 76, 122
Stettiner, Stettinius (fr Stettin) 9, 122, 142
Stettler, see Staedtler
Steubesand (fine sand)
Steuer (dowry, steering, tax, tax collector) 109
Steurer, Steuersman (steersman) 96
Steuernagel (tiller, helmsman) 96
Steyer, Steyert 74 (fr Styria, Steiermark) 121
Steyger, see Steiger
Stich (stitch, tailor) 104, 122
Stichel, Stichler (engraver, stylus) 106
Stichling (stickleback) 115
Stichter (founder) 96
Stick, Stickeler (embroiderer) 106, 122
Stickelbach (stickleback brook) 115, 77
Stiebel (dust)
Stief (steep)
Stiefel, Stieffel, Stieffler (boot, boot maker) 104, 106
Stieg (staircase) 122
Stiegel, Stiegler, Stiegman, Stiegmann (stile, dweller near a stile) 122
Stiel, Stiehl (handle, helve) 96, 106
Stier, Stierle (bull, steer) 91
Stierhoff (steer farm) 92

Stierlin 55, Stierlin (little steer) 91

Stiermann (keeper of breeding bulls) 91

Stiernkorb (beggar's basket)

Stiersdorfer (bull village) 123

Stiffler, Stifler, see Stiefel

Stigall 159, Stigler, see Stiegel

Stiger 159, see Steiger

Stile 159, Steiler, see Steil

Still, Stille, Stilling, Stillmann (tranquil person) 115

Stillwagon 159, Stillwagoner, see Stellwagen

Stimits 159, see Steinmmetz

Stimmel, Stimmell (stump of log, etc.)

Stine ..., see Stein ...

Stinebaugh 159, see Steinbach

Stindler (fisherman) 96

Stinefield 159, see Steinfeld

Stiner 159, see Steiner

Stinnes 53 < Augustinus 131

Stirn (forehead) 114

Stob, Stober (bath attendant) 96

Stock (stick, tree trunk) 122

Stockhausen (tree trunk hamlet) 65, 122

Stockmann, Stockmeister (jailor) 109

Stockmann, see Stuckmann

Stockschlaeger, Stockslager 159 (whipper)

Stockstill (stockstill, very quiet) 115

Stoehr, Stoer, Stoerr, Sterr 159 (sturgeon catcher 91 or dealer 105), see also Stehr

Stoekel 55, Stoeckl, Stoeckle, 159 Stoecklein, Stoeklin (little stick)

Stoff (stuff)

Stoffel 53, Stoffels 164 < Christoff

Stoffer 159, see Stauffer

Stolberg (mined mountain) 68

Stoll (mine gallery, miner) 96, see Stull, Stuhl

Stoll (loaf, slice, baker) 96, see Stull, Stuhll

Stoller, Stollman (miner) 96

Stolte (proud) 115

Stoltfus, Stoltzfuss (limper) 114

Stoltz, Stoltze, Stoltzer, Stolz (proud) 115

Stoltzenbach (proud brook) 77, 122

Stoltzenberg (proud mountain) 68

Stolz, see Stoltz

Stombaugh 159, see Stambach

Stombler 159, see Stammler

Stone 153, Stoner, see Stein, Steiner

Stonebach 153, see Steinbach

Stonebraker 153, see Steinbrecher

Stonecipher 159, Stonecypher, see Steinseiffer

Stonefield 153, see Steinfeld

Stoneking 153, see Steinkoenig

Stonesifer 153, see Steinseiffer

Stoots 159, see Stutz

Storch, Storich, Storck, Stork (stork) 114

Storm 153, see Sturm

Stortz (tumble, crash)

Stotler 159, see Statler

Stottlemeyer 159, Stottlemire 159, Stottlemyer 159, see Stadelmeyer

Stotz (log, clumsy person) 115

Stoudemeyer 159, Stoudemaier, see Staudemeyer

Stoudt 159, Stout, see Staude

Stouffer 159, Stoupher, see Stauffer

Stoup 159, see Staub

Straatmann, see Strattmann

Strabel, see Strobel

Strack (stiff, inflexible) 115

Strackbein (stiff leg) 114

Straecker, see Strecker

Strahl, Strahle 122, Strale (ray of light, arrow)

Straif, see Streif

Straight 159, see Streit

Strait 159, see Streit

Strand, Strant (beach)

Strang, Strange (leash, strip of land)

Strasberger, Strassberger (highway mountain) 65, 68, see Strassburger

Strasbaugh 159 (road brook) 65, 77

Strasburg, Strasburger, Strassburger (fr Strassburg) 122

Strass (road, highway, fr Latin *strata*) 122, see Strasser

Strasser, Strassler, Strassner, Strassman (dweller on a highway, fr Latin *strata*) 65

Strattmann, Stratmann, Strathmann (dweller on the street or road) 65

Stratemeyer, Stradtmeyer (farmer on the road, fr Latin *strata*) 65, 93

Straub, Straube, Strauber (towseled) 122

Strauch (bush, shrub, forest) 72, 122

Straup, see Straub

Straus, Strauss (bouquet)

Straus, Strauss (fight)

Straus, Strauss (ostrich, often a house name, fr Latin *struthio*) 62

Strausbaugh 159 (ostrich brook), see Strasbaugh

Strawsburg 159, see Strassburg

Streagle 159, see Striegel

Streber (striver) 115

Streck, Strecker (stretcher, stretch of land)

Strecker (torturer) 96

Streckfuss (Stretch a leg!) 116

Strehler (chaser)

Streif, Streiff (stripe, campaign)

Streif (mounted patrol) 107

Streigel 159, see Striegel

Streight 159, see Streit

Streisand, see Streusand

Streit 122, Streith, Streiter, Streitz 164, Streitman (struggle, struggler)

Streng, Strenger (strict) 115

Streusand (blotting sand, scribe) 96

Strick, Stricker, Strickert 74, Strickler, Strickman, Strickmann (knitter) 96

Strick (snare, trapper) 91

Stricker (poacher) 91

Strickler, see Stricker

Strider 159, see Streiter

Striegel, Strigel 159, Striegler (curry comb, fr Latin *strigilis*) 106

Strite 159, see Streit

Strobar, Strohbart (straw beard) 122

Strodtmann, see Stradtmann

Stroebel, Strobel, Stroble 159, Strobell, Stroblic (disheviled) 115

Stroessner, see Strassner

Stroh, Stro (straw) 122

Strohacker, Strohhecker (straw field) 84

Strohbach, Strohbaugh 159, Strohbeck (straw brook) 77

Strohbank (straw bench)

Strohkorb (straw basket, basket maker) 96

Strohmann, Stromann, Strohmayer 93, Strohmeyer, Stromier 159 (straw man, straw dealer) 106

Strohsacker (maker of straw sacks) 96

Strohschneider (straw cutter) 96

Strom, Strohm (stream, current, river) 79

Stromann, see Strohmann
Stromberg, Stromberger (stream mountain) 79, 68
Stromenger, Strominger (straw dealer) 106
Stromer, see Strohmann
Stromyer 159, see Strohmann
Strosnider 159, Stroosnyder, see Strohschneider
Strossner, see Strasser
Strotman, Strothmann, see Straatmann
Strouber 159, see Strub
Strough 159, see Strauch
Stroup 159, Stroupe, see Strub
Strouse 159, see Strauss
Strow 159, see Stroh
Strub 122, Strube, Strubel, Struble 159, Strubler (disheviled) 112
Strubhar (tousle haired) 112
Struck, Strucke, Struckmann (dweller in the bush) 72
Struckhoff (farm in the bush) 72, 92
Strueve, Struve, see Strub
Strumpf, Strumpfer, Strumpfler (stocking maker) 106
Strunck, Strunk (stalk, stump, stocky man) 114
Struss, see Strauss
Struth, Strutt (swamp) 80, 122
Struvel 159, Struwel, see Stroebel
Stube (heated room, bather) 96
Stubenrauch (room smoke)
Stuber (bath attendant) 96
Stuck, Stucke, Stucker, Stuckers 164, Stuckert 74 (dweller on stump-covered ground)
Stuckey 159, see Stucki
Stucki (tree stump)
Stude, see Staude
Studebecker, Studebaker, Stuttenbecker (shrub brook) 72, 77
Studenroth (brush clearing) 72, 126

Stuebe, see Stube
Stuehler (chair maker) 106
Stuerzebecker (tumbling stream) 77
Stuerzinbach (Jump in the brook!) 116
Stuhl, Stuhlmacher, Stuhlmann, Stuhlman, Stulman (chair, chair maker) 96, 106
Stuhldreher (chair maker) 96
Stull, see Stoll
Stultz, see Stoltz
Stum, Stumm, Stumli 55 (mute) 114
Stump, Stumpe, Stumpel, Stumpf, Stumpff, Stumpfel (blunt) 115
Stuntz, Stunz (stump, small barrel)
Stupp, Stupf (step, stoop)
Sturm, Sturms 164 (storm, violent person) 115
Sturman, see Steuermann
Sturmer (warrior) 107
Sturmfels, Sturmfelz (storm cliffs) 68
Sturtz (plunge, fall, steep slope) 71
Sturtzbach, Sturtzbecker (rapid stream) 77
Sturzenegger (field on a steep slope) 71, 84
Sturzinbach (Jump in the brook!) 116
Stutsman 159, see Stutzmann
Stutte (mare) 91
Stutts 159, see Stutz
Stutz (support)
Stutzmann (defender)
Stuver (heavy-set man) 114, see Stuber
Styer 159, Styers 164, see Steyer
Styger, Stygler, see Steig, Steiger
Styne 159, see Stein
Sucher, Suchman (searcher, hunting assistant) 91

Sudbrink (muddy hillock) 74
Sudbrok, Sudbrook (muddy
brake) 80
Sudeck, Sudek (south field) 85, 84
Suder, Sudermann (one dwelling
toward the south) 85, 94, or
name shortened fr one of the
following:
Suderode (south clearing) 85, 126,
122
Sudheim (south hamlet) 85, 123,
122
Sudhoff (south farm) 85, 92, 122
Sudler (slovenly worker) 115
Sudler (southerner) 85
Sudman, Sudmeyer (southerner)
85
Suehle (wild boar wallow)
Suehn (penitence, penance,
reconciliation) 138
Suender, Sunder (sinner) 138
Sues, Suess 122, Suesse (sweet)
115
Suesskind (sweet child) 115
Suessmann (sweet man) 115
Suessmuth (sweet disposition)
115
Suestrunk (sweet drink) 106
Suetterlin 55, see Suter
Sugarman 153, Sugerman, see
Zuckerman
Sulander, Sulender (southerner)
85
Sultan, see Soldan
Sultzbach, Sulzbacher, Sultz-
baugh 159, Sulsbach (swampy
brook) 80, 77, 122
Sultzbach, Sultzbaugh 159
(saltlick brook) 77
Sulz, Suls 159 (salt lick, salt
worker) 96
Sulzenbach, see Sultzenbach
Sulzer, Sulser 159, Sulzmann
(maker of jellied meat) 96
Sumwald, Sumwalt 159, see
Zumwald

Sundberg (southern mountain)
85, 68
Sunder, see Suende
Sundermann (southerner) 85
Sundheim (south hamlet) 85, 123,
122
Sundstrom, Sunstrom (southern
river) 85, 77
Surbaugh 159, see Sauerbach
Surland 159, see Sauerland
Suskind, Sussman, see Suesskind,
Suessman
Suss, see Suess
Suter, Sutor, Sutter (shoemaker,
fr Latin *Sutor*) 104
Sutorius (latinization of Sutor)
141
Sutter (swamp) 80, see also Suter
Sutterlin 55 (little shoemaker)
104
Sutterlin 55 (little swamp) 80
Sw ..., see under Schw ... Only a
sample given here.
Swab, see Schwab
Swaggert 159, see Schweiger
Swantner 159, see Schwander
Swantz 159, see Schwantz
Swarthout (dark skin) 114
Swarts 159, Swartz, see Schwartz
Swartsback 159, Swarzbaugh 159,
see Schwartzbach
Swarzwelder 159, see Schwartz-
waelder
Swauger 159, see Schwager
Swearer 153, see Schwoerer
Sweetman 153, see Suessman
Sweetser 159, see Schwytzer,
Schweitzer
Swek 159, see Zweck
Sweiger 159, Sweigert 74, Swei-
gart, see Schweiger
Sweitzer 159, see Schweitzer
Swerdlin 159, 55, see Schwertlein
Swiger 159, Swigger, Swiggert 74,
see Schweiger

Swindel 159, Swindle 159, Swin-
dler, Swindell, Swindall 159
(swindle, swindler) 151
Swinehart 159 < Schweinhart
(strong as a wild boar)
Swinghammer (Swing the ham-
mer!, blacksmith)
Switzer 159, see Schweitzer
Swob 159, Swope, Swopes 164,
see Schwab
Swonk, see Schwank
Swyger 159, Swygert 74, see
Schweiger
Sybel, Seybold < Siegbold
Sybert, see Siegbert
Syder 159, Sydnor, see Seider,
Seidner
Syfrett, Syford 159, see Siegfried
Sygrist, see Sigrist
Syler 159, see Seiler
Sylvester 159, see Silvester
Symon, see Simon
Synder 159, see Suender

**T**

Tabb, Taber, Tabbert < Dietbert
(people + famous) 46, 47
Taeger (day laborer) 96
Taenzer, see Tants
Taescher (purse maker) 96
Taeuber, see Teuber
Taffner (fr Taffingen, marsh
village) 80, 122
Tag, Tage, Tagg (day)
Taich, see Teich
Tallebach, Telebach (muddy
brook) 80, 77
Tanbusch (forest bush) 89, 72
Tanhauser (forest house, fir
house) 89, 65
Tanhof, see Tannhoeffer
Tanne (fir tree) 89
Tannebaum, Tannenbaum (fir
tree) 89

Tannenberg, Tannenberger (fr
Tannenberg 122, fir mountain)
89, 65
Tannenzapf (pine cone) 89
Tanner (dweller among the firs)
89
Tannhauser, see Tanhauser
Tannhoeffer (fr Tanhof 122, farm
among the firs, forest farm) 89,
92
Tants 159, Tantz, Tantzer, Tan-
zer (dance, dancer) 96
Tapfer (brave) 115
Tapp, Tapper (tap maker, ta-
verner) 96, 106
Tappert (wearers or makers of
long coats, fr Latin *tabardum*)
106
Tarnkappe (invisible cloak)
Tasch, Tascher, Taschner, see
Taescher
Tatelbaum, Dattelbaum (date
tree) 62, 89
Taub, Tauber (deaf, deaf man)
114
Taub, Taube (dove) 115
Taubenfeld (dove field) 84
Taubenheim (dove + hamlet) 123,
122
Taubenslag 159 (dove cote)
Tauber, Taubert 74, Taubermann
(cock pigeon, pidgeon raiser or
seller) 105, 143
Tauber (name of river) 83
Taubner, Taubman, Taupmann,
see Tauber
Tauchinbaugh 159 (Jump in the
brook!) 116, 77
Tauhauer (hawser maker) 100
Tausch (barter, trickster)
Tausendschoen (thousand beau-
tiful [thanks?]) 117
Taxler (badger hunter) 91
Taylor 153, see Schneider
Teagle 159, see Tiegel
Teale 159, see Thiel

Tederick < Dietrich
Teel 159, see Thiel
Teeter 159, see Dieter
Teets 159, see Dietz
Tegler, Tegele (tyler, brickmaker, fr Latin *tegula)* 96
Teich, Teichner, Teichman (pond, dweller by a pond) 82, 122
Teich (dough, baker's helper) 96
Teichgraeber (pond digger, ditch digger) 82, 96
Teichholtz (forest by a pond or dike) 82, 72
Teichmueller, Teichmoeller (miller on the pond) 82, 103
Teitelbaum, see Dattelbaum
Teitz 159, see Dietz
Telebach, see Tallebach
Teller, Tellermann (dish, dish-maker, fr Latin *talea)* 106
Tempel, Tempelman (temple, synagogue)
Tenberg, Tennenberg, Tennen-baum, see Tanberg, Tannen-berg, Tannenbaum
Tenberg, Tenberge, see Zumberg
Tenner, see Danner
Tenser 159, see Tants
Teobald 159, see Theobald
Tepel 53, Teppel < Theobald
Tepper, Tepperman (potter) 96
Terkeltaub 159, see Tuerkeltaub
Termoehlen (at the mill) 69, 103
Tesch 159, Tesche, see Taescher
Tessler, see Tischler
Tester 159, Testor, see Textor
Teubel, see Teufel
Teuber, Teuber, Teubner, see Tauber
Teufel, Teufell (devil) 131
Teufelbiss (the devil's bite) 131
Teufer (baptist)
Teutsch, see Deutsch
Textor, Textur (Latin for Weber) 141
Thal (valley) 76, 122

Thalberg, Thalberger (valley mountain) 76, 68
Thaler (coin from Joachimsthal) 117
Thalheim (valley hamlet) 76, 123
Thalhofer (valley farm) 76, 92
Thalmann (valley man) 76, 94
Thanhouser 159, see Tannhauser
Thankappan 159, see Tarnkappe
Theil (part)
Theis 53, Theiss 6, Theissen < Matthias
Theobald, Thebald (folk + bold) 46, 46
Theodor (Greek, gift of God) 143
Theologus (Latin, theologian) 141
Therman 159, see Thurmann
Theuerkauf (expensive purchase)
Theus 53 < Matthaeus or Timo-thaeus
Thiel 53, Thiele, Thielemann, Thielman < Dietrich
Thieman, see Dietman
Thiemer < Dietmar
Thier (animal)
Thierfelder 122 (animal field) 84, 122
Thiergarten (zoo, animal park), 84, 122
Thiess 53, Thiesse, Thiessen 122 < Matthias
Thilo 53 < Dietrich
Thiringer, see Thueringer
Thoene 53 < Antonius
Tholde 53 < Berthold
Thom 53, Thome < Thomas
Thomas, Tomas (St. Thomas) 131
Thomburn (at the spring) 69, 79
Thomsen (son of Thomas) 59
Thon (clay, potter) 96
Thons 53, Thonis, Thonges < St. Anthonius
Thor (door)
Thorbruggen, see Zurbrueck
Thormann (gate keeper) 96
Thorwart (door keeper) 96

Thron 122, Throne (throne)
Thueringer (Thuringian) 120
Thuermann (door man) 96
Thurm (tower, fr Latin *turris*)
Thurmherr (lord of the tower) 109
Thurneck (tower field) 85
Thussing, see Tussing
Thyssen 53 < Matthias
Tibbet < Theobald
Tice 159, see Theiss
Tidbal, see Dietbald
Tiebendorf, see Tiefendorf
Tiede 53, Tiedebohl, Tiedeman 94,
  Tiedemann, Tidemann <
  Dietbald
Tiefenbach (deep brook) 77, 122
Tieffenbrunn (deep well) 79, 122
Tiefendorf, Tiebenderf 159 (deep
  village) 123, 122
Tiefenwerth, Tieffenwert, Tiefen-
  worth (deep river island) 79
Tiegel (saucepan, crucible, fr
  Latin *tegula*) 106
Tielmann 53, 94, Tilman, Tillman
  < Dietrich
Tieman, see Dietman
Tier (animal)
Tierdorf (animal village) 123
Tiess 53 < Matthias
Tietz 53, Tietzer < Diedrich
Tiffenderfer 159, Tiffendarfer, see
  Tiefendorf
Tilgen, Till < St. Ilgen 131
Till, see Diehl
Tillich 53 < Dietrich
Tillinger, see Dillinger
Tillmann, see Tilgen
Tilly 53 < Dietrich
Tilo 53 < Dietrich
Timmer (timber, carpenter) 98,
  106
Timmerman, Timmermann, see
  Zimmermann
Timothaeus, Thimothee (St.
  Timothy) 131
Timke 55 (little Thimothaeus)

Tischler, Tischer, Tischmann
  (cabinet maker, fr Latin *discus*)
  106, 98
Tisher 159, see Tischler
Titshler 159, see Tischler
Titus (Latin name) 141
Tobel, Tobler (wooded gorge) 122
Tobias (OT name) 135
Tochtermann (son-in-law) 119
Tod, Todt (death)
Tod, Todt (godfather) 119
Toennies 53 < St. Anthonius
Toepfer, Toepfner (potter) 96
Toeplitz (Slavic place name) 146
Toericht (foolish) 115
Toerrenberger, see Duerrenberger
Togend, see Tugend
Tokayer (wine seller) 106, 96
Tolde 53 < Berthold
Toll, Tolle (mad) 115
Toll 53 < Berthold
Tollboom (custom's gate, toll
  collector) 109
Toller, Tollmann, Tolman, Tolner,
  Tollner (toll collector) 109
Toltzmann, Tolzman, see Tolde
Tombaugh 159 (at the brook) 69,
  77
Tonne, Tonnemacher (barrel,
  barrel maker) 96
Tonner, see Donner
Tonnewan (barrel, cooper) 106
Tontz 159, see Tantz
Toor, see Thor
Toothackers < Todenacker (ce-
  metery)
Topfer (potter) 96
Topp (forelock, pigtail) 112
Topper (potter) 96
Torbeck (at the brook) 69, 77
Torfstecker (peat digger) 95
Torgler, Torkler (wine presser, fr
  Latin *torculare)* 96
Tormoellen (at the mill) 69, 103
Torsch, see Dorsch

Tote, Toth (Death, in morality play) 111

Totenberg (swamp mountain) 80, 68

Totenberg (godfather's mountain) 68

Toth, see Tod

Toth, Thote, Totman (godfather) 119

Toubman 159, see Taubman

Towler 159, see Tauler

Trabant (fr Czech, infantryman) 109

Traber, Trabert 74 (trotter)

Trachsler, see Drechsler

Trachtehengst (packhorse, dray horse) 106

Trachtenberg (funnel mountain, fr Latin *tractarius*) 68

Traffley 159, see Trefflich

Trager 159, Traeger (porter, carrier) 96

Tran (whale oil) 106

Tranck (drink, taverner) 96

Trapp (bumpkin) 115

Trapp (bustard) 115

Traub (grape, vintner) 89, 96

Traugott (Trust God!) 116, 140

Traurig (sad) 115

Traut, Traud, Traudt, Trauth (dear) 48, 115

Trautmann (confidant) 48, 115

Trautwein (dear friend) 48, 48, 115

Trautwig (friend + battle) 48, 46

Traver, see Traber

Traver (dweller near the Trave) 83

Traxel, Traxler, see Drechsler

Trayer, see Dreier

Trefflich (excellent) 115, 117

Trefouse 159, see Dreifuss

Treger, see Trager

Treibel (mallet, cooper) 106

Tremoehlen, see Termoehlen

Trepp, Treppe (stairs)

Trescher, Treschner, Treshman 159, see Drescher

Tresp (broom plant) 89

Tressler, see Drechsler

Tretler (treader or treadmill)

Treu (loyal) 115

Treulieb (loyal and dear) 115

Treumann (loyal man) 115

Treut, Treuth (confidant) 115

Treutel, Treuttle (sweetheart) 48, 115

Treutlen, see Treutel 25

Trew 159, see Treu

Trexler, see Drechsler

Trieber (driver) 96

Triesler, see Drechsler

Trimbach (place name) 122

Trinkauf (Drink up!) 116

Trinkaus (Drink up!) 116

Trinker (drinker) 115

Trinkhaus, Trinkaus (tavern) 96

Tritt (step)

Trockenbrod, see Truckenbrodt

Trockenmiller (dry miller) 103

Troester (draff)

Troester (comforter) 115

Troll (goblin)

Trommer, Trommler (drummer) 96

Trompeter, Trumpeter (trumpeter) 96

Trootman 159, see Trautmann

Tropf (drop, simple person) 115

Tross (pack train) 107

Trost, Trostl 55, Trostle 159 (helper, comfort) 115

Trott, Trotter, Trottman (wine presser) 96

Trotz (defiance) 115

Troum 159 (dream)

Trout 159, see Traut

Troutman 159, see Trautmann

Troxel 159, Troxell, Troxler, see Drechsler

Troy 159, see Treu

Truckenberg (dry mountain)

Truckenbrodt (dry bread, baker) 96

Truckenmiller, see Trockenmiller

True 153, see Treu

Truhe (chest, trunk) 106

Trueb (sorrowful) 115

Truman 159, Trueman, see Treumann

Trumbower 159 (farmer at the end of the field) 91

Trumm (end of field) 84

Trump, Trumph (trump, drummer) 96

Trumpeter, see Trompeter

Trunk (drink)

Trupp (troop) 107

Trutmann, see Trautmann

Tsahn 159, see Zahn

Tschantz, see Schantze

Tschudi (judge) 109

Tschudi (foolish, tense person) 115

Tsvetshen 159, see Zwetschen

Tuch, Tuchman, Tuchmann, Tuchner (mercer) 106

Tuchscherer (cloth shearer) 96

Tuchmantel (cloth coat, tailor) 96

Tuefel 159, see Teufel

Tuerenberger, see Duerrenberger

Tuerk (Turk, one who has fought the Turks)

Tuerkeltaub (turtledove) 115

Tuerner (tower keeper, fr Latin *turris*) 109

Tullius (Latin name) 141

Tulman, Tulner, see Tollman, Tollner

Tulp (tulip) 89

Tunkel, see Dunkel

Turban 53 < St. Urbanus 131

Turc, Turk, Turkman, see Tuerk

Turinger, Thurringer, see Thueringer

Turkeltaub, see Tuerkeltaub

Turman, see Thuermann

Turn, see Thurm

Turnau (tower meadow) 84

Turner (tower keeper) 109

Turnbach (tower brook) 77

Turnbaugh 159, Turnbough, see Turnbach 151

Turnipseed 153, see Ruebsamen

Tussing (French, Toussaints) 144

Tutweiler, see Dutweiler

Tyce 159, see Theiss

Tyll, see Diehl

Tysen 159, Tyssen, Tyson, see Theissen

# U

Uberhoff (upper farm) 69, 92, 122

Uebel (evil, irascible obstinate person) 115

Ueber (over)

Ueberall (everywhere, ubiquitous) 115

Ueberholtz (upper forest, beyond the forest) 69, 72, 122

Ueberroth (upper clearing, beyond the clearing) 69, 126, 122

Uebersax (beyond Saxony, Upper Saxony) 121

Uehlein 55 (little owl) 115

Uffer, Ufner (dweller on the shore)

Uhl, Uhle, Uhll (owl) 115, see Ulrich

Uhland (lancer) 107

Uhlefelder, Uhlfelder (swamp field) 80, 84

Uhlenbeck (swamp brook) 80, 77

Uhlenberg (swamp mountain) 80, 68

Uhler, see Aulmann

Uhlich 53, Uhlig, Uhlik, Ulich, Uly < Ulrich

Uhlmann, Ullmann (dweller near the elms) 89

Uhlshafer (swamp farm) 89, 84

Uhrich, Urich, see Ulrich

Uhrmacher (clock maker) 96
Ulbrich < Uodalbrecht (inheritance + bright) 46, 47
Ulbright 159, see Ulbrich
Uli 53 < Ulrich
Ullman 53, 55, Ullmann, see Ulrich
Ulm, Ulmer (dweller by the elms) 89
Ulm, Ulmer (inhabitanht of Ulm) 122
Ulrich, Ullrich, Ulrik (inherited property + rule) 46, 46
Umbach 159, see Ambach
Umbaugh 159, see Umbach
Umberger 159, see Amberger
Umbreit, Umbright 159 (unwilling, incapable) 115
Umholtz 159 (at the forest) 69, 72
Umstad 159, Umstead < Amstad (at the landing)
Unangst, see Ohnangst
Unbescheiden (indiscrete, unknowledgeable) 115
Unclebach 159, see Unkelbach
Underkoffler, Underkofler, Underkaufer (middleman), see Unterkofler
Underweg (underway)
Unfried (disturber of the peace) 115
Unfug (mischief, impropriety) 115
Ungeheuer (monster) 115
Ungemach (inconvenient, unpleasant) 115
Unger, Ungerer (Hungarian) 121
Unkel, Unkle (toad) 115
Unkelbach (toad brook) 77, 122
Unkenholz (toad forest) 72
Unold, Unhold (monster, fiend) 115
Unrat, Unrath (rubbish)
Unrau, see Unruh
Unruh (disquiet) 115
Unselt, Unseldt, Unsoeld, Unsoelt (tallow dealer) 106

Unsinn (nonsense) 115
Unstruth (swamp on the One) 80, 79
Unterberg, Unterberger (below the mountain) 68, 122
Unterdenerd (under the earth) 69
Unterkofler (lower monticule) 67
Unterwalden (among the forests, below the forests) 69, 71, 122
Unterweger (the lower path) 65
Unverferth (unafraid) 115
Unversagt, Unferzagt (undaunted) 115
Uphoff (on the farm) 69, 92, 122
Upperman, see Obermann
Upperman, see Obmann
Upright 159, see Obrecht
Urbach 122, see Auerbach
Urban (St. Urbanus, name of pope) 134
Urich, Urick, see Ulrich
Urlaub (leave)
Urman, Urmann, see Uhrman
Utermohle, see Ausdermuehle
Utli 53, 55, Utley < Ulrich
Utterbach, Utterbaugh 159, see Otterbach
Uts 53, Utz, Utze < Ulrich

## V

Search also under W

Vaibel 159, see Weibel
Vaihinger (fr that city) 122
Valberg 159, see Wahlberg
Valck, Valck, see Falk
Valenstein 159, see Wallenstein
Valentin (St. Valentine) 131
Vannamacher 159, see Wannemacher
Vasbinder, see Fassbinder
Vass, see Fass
Vassler 53 < St. Gervasius 131
Vat (barrel, < St. Servatius) 131
Vater (father) 119

Vaught 159, see Vogt
Vauke, see Fauch
Vaytman 159, see Weitmann
Veit 53, Veicht < St. Vitus 131
Velte, Velten 122 < St. Valentin
  131
Venator (Latin, hunter) 141
Venholt 159, see Weinholt
Ventmuller 159, see Windmueller
Verch (wounded)
Verfuehrt (misled) 115
Verge, see Ferg
Verner, see Werner
Verber, see Faerber
Verleger (supplier for cottage
  industries)
Vetter, Vetters 164 (cousin,
  kinsman) 119
Vetterli 53, 55 (little cousin) 119
Veydt 159, see Weide
Victor (Latin, victor, name of
  pope) 134
Viebig, Viebing (cattle path) 65
Viehmann (husbandryman) 91
Viehmeyer (cattle farmer) 93
Viehweg, Vieweg (cattle path) 65
Viereck (quadrangle) 122
Vierengel (four angels, house
  name) 62
Vierheller (four pence) 117
Vierschilling (four shillings) 117
Viertel (one quarter)
Vietor (Latin: traveler) 141
Vincent (St. Vincent) 131
Vink, see Fink
Virts 159, see Wuertz
Vischer, Visher 159, see Fischer
Vitzthum 122, see Witzthum
Vleeschower 159, see Fleisch-
  hauer
Voegele 55, Voegeli, Voegelein
  (little bird)
Voelcker, Voelker, Voelkner, see
  Volker, Volkner
Voelkel 55 < Volkmar
Vogel, Vogl, Vogle 159 (bird) 115

Vogelberger (bird mountain) 68
Vogeler, Vogler, Voegeler (fowler)
  91, 96
Vogelgesang (birdsong)
Vogelhut (bird hat) 112
Vogelhut (bird watch)
Vogelius (latinized Vogel) 141
Vogelmann (fowler) 115
Vogelpohl (bird pool) 80, 12?
Vogelsang, see Vogelgesang
Vogelstein (bird mountain) 68
Vogt 122, Vogts 164, Voegt, Voigt,
  Voight 159, Vogtmann
  (governor, fr Latin *advocatus)*
  109
Volk, Volck, Volcks 164 (nation,
  folk) 46
Volkbrecht (folk + illustrious) 46,
  47
Volkel 55, Voelkel < Volkmar
Volkenstein, see Wolkenstein
Volker, Volcker, Volkner (people +
  army) 46, 46, also short for any
  of following
Volkhart, Volkert (folk + strong)
  46, 46
Volkmann (people + man) 46, 94
Volkmar (people + famous) 46, 47
Voll, Volle, Voller, Vollers 164
  (full)
Vollbert, Vollbrecht, see Volk-
  brecht
Vollenweide, Vollenweider, see
  Fuellenweide
Vollmer, Volmer, Volmar, see
  Volkmar
Vollmerhausen (Volkmar's hous-
  es) 65
Vollprecht, Volpert, see Volk-
  brecht
Vollrat, Volrath < Folkrat, folk +
  counsel)
Voltz, Volz, see Foltz
Vom Berg (fr the mountain) 69,
  70, 68
Vom Hoff (fr the court) 69, 92

In seeking a name preceded by *von*, look under the base name. Von Hagen appears under Hagen.

Von Berg (fr the mountain) 69, 70, 68

Von Burg (fr the castle) 69, 70, 73

Von Busch (fr the bush), see Busch 69, 70, 72

Vonderheid, Vonderheide (from the heath) 69, 70, 84

Vonderhorst (fr the hurst) 69, 70, 72

Von der Lind (fr the linden) 69, 70, 89

Vonderschmidt (fr the smithy) 69, 70, 96

Von der Weyt (fr the meadow) 69, 70, 84

Vonhagen (fr the enclosure) 69, 70, 123

Vonhoff (fr the farm) 69, 70, 92

Vonholt (fr the forest) 69, 70, 72

Vonniederhauser, Von Niederhaeuser (fr the lower houses) 69, 70, 65

Von Paris (Parisian, journeyman who trained in Paris) 69, 70, 122

Vonwald (fr the forest) 69, 70, 71

Vorberge, Vordemberge (before the mountain, piedmont) 69, 70, 68

Vorgang (process, proceedings)

Vorhenne (trout) 115

Vorhoff (atrium, before the farm) 69, 70, 92, 122

Vorkamp (before the field) 69, 70, 84

Vorman, see Fuhrmann

Vorm Walt (in front of the forest) 69, 71, 122

Vornfeld (before the field) 69, 84

Vorn Holt (before the forest) 69, 71

Vorspann (added team of horses)

Vosburg, Vosburgh (fox castle) 73

Voss (fox) 115

Vossberg (fox mountain) 68

Vosse 53 < Volkmar

Vosshage (fox enclosure) 123, 122

Vossloh (fox forest) 71, 72

Vought 159, see Vogt

Vries (Frisian) 121

Vroman, see Fromann

Vulkner, see Volkner

# W

Waag 122 (scales), see Wage

Waber, Waeber, see Weber

Wachenhut (sentry, guard) 96

Wachenschutz (guard) 107

Wachs, Wax, Wachsmann (wax dealer) 106

Wachsmuth (bright mind) 115

Wacht, Wachter, Wachtman, Wachterman (watchman) 96

Wachtel (quail) 115

Wachter, see Waechter

Wacker (brave, watchful) 115

Waeber, see Weber

Waechter, Wachter (watchman) 96

Waeger (official weigher) 109

Waesche (washing, bleaching) 106

Waffenschmidt (armorer) 108

Waffler, Wafler, Waffelaer (armorer) 108

Wage (scales) 106

Wageman (official weigher) 109

Wagener, see Wagner

Wagenfuehr (carter) 95

Wagenheim (marsh hamlet) 123

Wagenhorst (marshy hurst) 80, 72, 122

Wagenknecht (carter's helper) 95

Wagenmann (wainwright) 96

Wagenseil (wagon rope, carter)
106

Waggener, Waggner, Waggoner
159, see Wagner

Wagner, Wagener, Waagner,
Wagenaar (wainright) 96

Wagschal (scale, official weigher)
109

Wahl 122, Wall, Waal (choice)

Wahlberg (marsh mountain) 80,
68, 122

Wahlenfeld (marsh field) 80, 84

Wahrheit (truth, informant,
guarantor) 115

Wahrlich (honest) 115, 117

Waibel, see Weibel

Waiblinger (fr Waibling 122)

Waid 122, Waidner, see Weid,
Weidner

Waidmann, Waitmann, see
Weidmann

Wain, Wainberg, Wainstock, see
Wein, Weinberg, Weinstock

Waisman, see Weissmann

Waitz, see Weitzen

Waitzbauer, see Weitzbauer

Wajbel, see Weible

Wajer, see Weiher

Walbach (swamp brook) 80, 77

Waksmann, see Wachsmann

Walbaum (walnut tree) 89

Walber, Walberd, Walbert, Walbrecht (battlefield + bright) 46,
47

Walbrecher (wall breaker)

Walburg (battlefield + protection)
46, 47, see also Waldburg

Walch, Walcher (foreigner, non-
German) 145

Walchensee (foreigners' lake) 145,
80, 122

Walcker, see Walker

Wald, Waldt, Walde, Walt (forest)
71, or < Oswald or Walther

Waldbauer (forest farmer) 71, 91,
94

Waldberg (forest mountain) 71,
68, 122

Waldbrand (forest clearing) 71,
126

Waldburg, Waldburger (fr Waldburg 122, forest castle) 71, 73

Waldeck, Waldecker (fr Waldeck
122, forest place, German
province) 71, 85

Walden (forests) 71

Waldenberger (forest mountain)
71, 68

Waldhaus, Waldhausen, Wald-
hauser (fr Waldhausen 122,
forest houses) 71, 65

Waldhutter (forest guard) 96

Waldhutter (forest cotter) 71

Waldkirch (forest church) 71, 122

Waldkoenig (forest king, a bird?)

Waldman, Waldmann 122, Wald-
ner (forester, giant)

Waldmeier, Waldmayer (forest
farmer, fr the Waldhof) 71, 93,
94

Waldmueller (forest miller) 71,
103

Waldo < Waldau (forest meadow)
72, 84

Waldorf, Waldrop (forest village)
71, 123, 122

Waldschmidt, Waldschmitt (forest
smith, one who smelts his own
ore) 71, 96

Waldsee (forest lake) 71, 80, 122

Waldt, see Wald

Waldvogel (forest bird, carefree
person) 71, 115

Walheim (swamp hamlet) 80, 123,
122

Walk, Walker, Walkeman (fuller)
96

Wall (rampart, fr Latin *vallum*)
122

Wallach (gelding) 91, 122

Wallenborn (marsh spring) 80, 79

Wallendorf (marsh village) 80,
123, 122
Wallenhorst (marsh hurst) 80, 72,
122
Wallenser (Waldensian, fr Wall-
ensen 122)
Wallenstein (fortified mountain)
73, 122
Wallenstein (foreigners' moun-
tain) 145, 73, 122
Waller, Wallner (pilgrim)
Wallerstein (pilgrims' mountain)
73, 122
Walliser (Swiss fr Valais) 145,
121
Wallner (forest warden) 71
Wallrodt (marsh clearing) 80, 126,
122
Walpert (battlefield + brilliant)
46, 47
Walrath, Walrot, see Wallrodt
Walrath (battlefield + counsel) 46,
47
Walsch (Romance) 145
Walser, see Walliser
Walstein, see Wallenstein
Walt, see Wald
Waltemeyer, Waltimyer 159,
Waltemire 159 see Waldmeyer
Walter, Walters 164, see Walther
Walther, Walthers 164 (rule +
army) 46, 46
Walthorn (waldhorn) 96, 106
Waltmann, see Waldmann (forest
dweller, giant) 71
Waltz, Walz, Waltze 122, Waltzer,
Walzer (roll, roller), or <
Walther
Wambach, Wambaugh 159
(marsh brook) 80, 77
Wambold (hope + bold) 46, 122
Wamser, Wambescher (jerkin
maker) 96
Wand (cliff, bluff) 68
Wandel (Vandal) 121
Wandel (change) 115

Wanderer (wanderer) 115
Wanger (fr Wangen, damp sloping
meadow) 71, 122
Wankel (fickle) 115
Wankmueller (miller off the
beaten path) 103
Wann, Wanne 122 (vat) 106
Wannamacher, Wannemacher,
Wannermacher, Wannamaker
159 (winnowing basket maker,
vat maker, fr Latin *vannus*) 96
Wanner (tub maker) 96
Wantz (bedbug)
Wapner, see Waffner
Wapp, Wappe (weapon, armorer)
108
Wappaus (armory) 108, 65
Wardmann (watchmann) 96
Warkmeister, see Werkmeister
Warm (warm)
Warmkessel (warm kettle, cook)
106
Warmuth, see Wermuth
Warner (warner) 47
Warnke 53, 55, Warnecke,
Warneche, Warnek, Warneke <
Wernher
Warnold (guard + loyal) 47, 48
Warschauer, Warshauer 159 (fr
Warsaw) 122
Wartburg (lookout castle) 47, 73,
122
Warth, Warthmann, Wartmann,
Wartzmann 74 (lookout) 47
Waschke < Slavic: Vadislav 146
Washabaugh 159, see Wesche-
bach
Wasp (wasp)
Wasser (water) 122
Wasserbach (water brook) 77
Wasserkrug (water jug) 106
Wasserman (waterman, water
carrier) 96, also Aquarius 143
Wasserstrom (water stream) 79
Wasserzieher (bath attendant) 96
Waterman 153, see Wassermann

Watsack (clothes bag) 106
Watte (wadding, padding)
Wattenbach (swamp stream) 80,
   77, 122
Wattenberg (swamp mountain) 68
Waxler 159, see Wechsler
Waxmann, Wassmann, see
   Wachs, Wachsman
Wayer, see Weiher, Weyer
Weabel 159, see Webel, Weibel
Weaber 159, Weaver 153, see
   Weber
Wease 159, see Wiese
Weatherholtz, see Wedeholz
Webel (sergeant) 107, see Weibel
Weber, Webert 74, Webber 159,
   Webner, Webling (weaver) 96
Wechsler (money changer) 96
Weck, Wecker, Weckerle 55,
   Weckler, Weckerli, Weckerlin,
   Weckerling (baker or seller of
   rolls) 96
Weckesser (roll eater) 112, 115
Wecter 159, see Waechter
Wedekind (forest child) 72
Wedel, Weddel (whisk) 106, 122
Wedemann, Wedemeyer, Wede-
   mayer (forest dweller, farest
   farmer) 72, 93
Wedeholz (forest wood) 72
Weeber, see Weber
Weesenbeck 159, see Wiesenbach
Weesner 159, see Wiesner
Weg, Wege (way) 65, 122
Wegand, see Weigand
Wegener, Wegner, see Wagner
Weger, Wegerlein 55 (weigher)
Wegmann (dweller on a roadway)
   65
Wegner, see Wagner
Wegstein (guide post) 65 73
Weh, Wehe (woe, pain) 117
Wehmeyer, see Weidemeyer
Wehn 53, Wehner < Werner 122
Wehner, Wehnert 74, see Wagner
Wehr, Wehrs 164 (defense) 122

Wehrl 53, Wehrle 55, Wehrli,
   Wehrly 159 < Werner
Wehrstedt (fortified place)
Weibel, Weible 159 (village
   authority) 109, 107
Weich (soft) 115
Weichert < Wighard (battle +
   brave) 46, 46
Weichseldorf (Vistula village) 83,
   123
Weichseler (fr the Vistula) 83, see
   Wechsler
Weicker, Weickert, see Weichert
Weid 122, Weit, Weidt, Weide 122
   (pasture) 84
Weidebach (brook through mea-
   dow or willows) 84, 77
Weidemueller (miller on the
   meadow) 84, 103
Weidemann, Weidemeyer (mea-
   dow man 84), see also Weid-
   mann
Weidenauer (fr Weidenau 122,
   pasture meadow) 84, 84
Weidenbacher (fr Weidenbach
   122, meadow brook) 84, 77
Weidenbaum (willow tree) 89
Weidenfeld (willow field) 89, 84
Weidenhammer, Weidenhamer (fr
   the willow hamlet) 89, 123
Weidenhaus (meadow house,
   house in the willows) 84, 89, 65
Weidenhoefer (fr the Weidenhoff,
   willow farm, pasture farm) 89,
   92
Weidenmeyer (pasture farmer)
   84, 93
Weidenmueller (miller at the
   willows, at the pasture) 89, 103
Weiderholt 159, see Wiederholt
Weidmann, Wideman (hunter) 91
Weidner (hunter) 91
Weier 122, see Weiher
Weierbach (fish pond brook) 77,
   122

Weiermiller (fish pond miller) 77, 103

Weigand, Weygant (warrior) 107

Weigel, Weigels 164, Weigelt 74, Weigle 159 < Weigand

Weigert, see Weichert

Weihaus, see Weinhaus 102, 65

Weiher 122 (fish pond, fr Latin *vivarium*)

Weihermann (dweller at a fish pond)

Weihrauch (incense) 106

Weikert, see Weichert

Weil 122, Weile, Weill (village, fr Latin *villa*) 127, 148

Weiland, see Wieland

Weiler, Weilert 74 (inhabitant of a villa) 127

Weiman, see Weinmann

Weimar, Weimer, Weimert 74 (fr Weimar 122, holy spring) 79

Weimaster 159, Weinmeister (vintner) 96, 102

Wein, Wyn (wine, wine dealer) 102, 106

Weinacht (Christmas) 143

Weinbaum (wine tree, grape vine) 89, 102

Weinberg (vineyard) 102, 68, 122

Weinberger (vintner) 102, 68

Weinblatt (grape leaf) 102, 89

Weinbrecht (friend + brilliant) 48, 47

Weinbrenner (brandy distiller) 102, 96

Weiner, Weiners 164, see Wagner, Weinfeld (vine field) 102, 84

Weinflasch (wine flask, bottle) 106

Weingard, Weingarden, Weingart, Weingarten 122, Weingartz 74 (vineyard) 102, 84

Weingartner, Weingaertner, Weingertner (vintner) 102

Weinglass (wine glass) 106

Weinhandl (wine dealer) 102, 105

Weinhard (friend + strong) 48, 46

Weinhaus (tavern) 102, 65

Weinheimer (fr Weinheim 122, swamp hamlet) 80, 102, 123

Weinholt, Weinhold (friend + loyal) 48, 48

Weinhouse 153, see Weinhaus

Weininger (fr Weiningen) 122

Weinkauf, Weinkop (wine seller, drink to confirm a sale) 102, 106

Weinknecht (vineyard worker) 96

Weinland (wine country) 102

Weinmann (wine merchant) 102, 106

Weinreb (grape) 102

Weinreich, Weinrich (friend + rule) 68, 46

Weinschenk (taverner) 96

Weinstein (tartar in wine barrels)

Weinstock (grape vine) 102, 62

Weintraub, Weintrob (grape, wine dealer) 102, 62, 149

Weintraut (friend + dear) 48, 48

Weinzweig, Weintzweig (grape-vine twig) 89

Weir, see Weiher

Weirauch, see Weihrauch

Weis, see Weiss

Weisaecker, Waisacker (white field) 84, 85

Weisbacher, Weissbacher, Weisbeck, Weissbecker (fr Weissbach 122, white brook) 77

Weisbeck, see Weissbeck

Weisberg (white mountain) 68

Weisborn, Weisborrn (white spring) 79

Weisbrod, Weisbord, see Weissbrot

Weise (wise) 115

Weiselberger 159, see Wieselberger

Weisenborn 159, see Wiesenborn

Weisenmiller 159, see Weissmiller

Weller, Wellner, Wellmann (clay or loam mason) 96

Wels, Welss (catfish) 115

Welsch, Wellisch, Welser, Welsh 159, Welch 159 (Romance) 145

Welschhan (turkey) 145

Welter, Weltner, Weltz (fr Welt 122), see Walther

Wemming (fr Wemmingen) 122

Wendel, Wendl (Vandal, Wend) 121

Wendelmuth (vacillating) 115

Wendelspiess (Turn the spit!, cook) 96

Wengel (little cheek) 115

Wenger 122, Wengert 74, see Wanger

Wenholt, see Weinholt

Wenig (few, small)

Weniger (fewer, less)

Wenner 53, Wennert 74 < Werner

Wenrich, see Weinreich

Wentz 53, Wentzel 55, Wenz, Wenzel, Wentzle 159 < Werner

Weppler (armed soldier) 107

Weppner (armorer) 108

Werbel (legendary minstrel)

Werber (entrepreneur, recruiter) 96, 109

Werdebaugh 159 (river island creek) 79, 77

Werdmann, see Wertmann

Werdmueller (miller on river island) 79, 103

Werele 53, 55, Werle, Werli, Werlin, Werlein < Werner

Werfel 159, see Wurfel

Werkman (craftsman, artisan)

Werkmeister (foreman)

Wermuth (vermouth) 105

Wernegerode (swamp clearing) 80, 126, 122

Werner, Wernher, Warner (protection + army) 47, 46

Wernick, Wernicke, Wernecke < Werner 53, 54

Wernsdorfer (Werner's village)

Wert, Werth (island in river) 79

Werthamer, Wertheimer (German city, hamlet on river island) 79, 122

Wertmann, Werthmann (dweller on river island) 79

Werthmann (man of worth) 115

Wertmueller (miller on river island) 79, 103

Wertsch, see Wirtsch

Wertz 159, see Wuertz

Wesbrot, see Weissbrot

Weschenbach (laundry creek) 77

Weschler (fuller) 96

Wesenbach, 159 see Wiesenbach

Wess, Wessberg, see Weiss, Weissberg

Wessel 53 122, Wessel, Wessell < Werner

Wessler, see Weschler, Wechsler

Wesselhof (Werner's farm) 92

Wessner, 159 see Wiessner

West, see Wuest

Westbrock (west brake) 85, 72

Westdorf (west village) 85, 123

Westenberg, see Westerberg

Westendorf (west village) 85, 123, 122

Westenfeld, Westerfeld, Westerfield 152 (west field) 85, 84, 122

Westerberg (western mountain) 85, 68

Westerheide (western heath) 85, 84

Westerkamp, Westkamp (west field) 85, 84

Westerman, Westermann (westerner) 85

Westermeyer (fr the Westerhof, western farm) 85, 84, 93

Westfal, Westfalen (fr Westphalia) 121, 85

Westhafer, see Westhoff

Westheim (western hamlet) 85, 123

Westhoff (west farm, now sometimes Westcourt in America) 85, 84

Westinghouse 153 (house toward the west) 85, 65

Westkamp (west field) 85, 84

Westphal, Westphale, see Westfal 151

Westreich (western empire) 85

Wetter (weather, river name meaning "swamp") 80, 83

Wetterau (meadow on the Wetter) 83, 84

Wettstein, see Wetzstein

Wetzel 53, 55, Wetzler < Werner

Wetzelberger (Werner's mountain) 68

Wetzikon (Werner's village) 127

Wetzler (knife grinder) 96

Wetzstein, Wettstein (whetstone, knife grinder) 73, 106

Wexler 159, see Wechsler

Wey ..., see Wei ...

Weyand, Weyandt, Weygant, see Weigand

Weydenhauer (willow cutter) 89, 95, 100

Weydenmeyer, see Weidemeyer

Weydner, see Weidner

Weyer 122, Weyher, Weyerman, see Weiher

Weyerhausen (house on fish pond) 65

Weygand, Weygandt, Weygant, see Weigand

Weygel, see Weigel

Weyhinger, see Vaihinger

Weyhkamp (holy field) 84

Weyl, see Weil

Weyland, see Weiland

Weyman, see Weinman

Weyrauch, Weyhrauch, see Weihrauch

Weys, see Weiss

Whetsell 159, see Wetzel

Whetstone 152, see Wetzstein

White 153, see Witt, Weiss

Whitebread 153, see Weissbrot

Whitehard 159, see Weishard 151

Whiteman 159, see Wittmann, Weidmann

Whitesel 159, Whitesell, Whytsell, see Weitzel

Wibel, see Weibel

Wice 159, see Weiss

Wichert, Wichart < Wighard

Wichmann, see Wiechmann

Wicke (vetch, fr Latin *vicia*) 89

Wickenhoffer (vetch farm) 89, 92

Wickenmeyer (vetch farmer) 89, 103

Wicker, Wickert, see Wichert

Wickesser (vetch eater) 112

Wickheiser (vetch house) 89, 65, 66

Wickwier (vetch pond) 89

Wickes 53 < Ludowicus

Widder (ram) 91, 62

Widderkind, see Wederkind

Wideman 159, Widman, see Weidemann, Weidmann

Widemeyer 159, Widemayer, Widmaier, see Weidemeyer

Widener 159, Widenor, see Weidner

Widenhouse 153, see Weidenhaus

Widerholt 159, see Wiederholt

Widmann, Wideman 159, see Wittmann, Weidmann

Widmer, see Wittmann

Widmeyer, Weidemeyer

Widner 159, see Weidner

Wieboldt < Wicbald (battle + brave) 46, 46

Wiechert < Wighard

Wiechmann < Wigman (battle + man) 46, 94

Wied 122, Wiede (withe, willow tree) 89

Wiedbach (swamp brook) 80, 77

Wiedeck, Wiedecker (swamp field) 80, 84

Wiedefeld (swamp field) 80, 84

Wiedeman, Wiedenmann (dweller among the willows) 89, 94

Wiedeman, Wiedemann (dweller in the swamp) 80, 94

Wiedenheft, Wiedenhoeft (willow farm) 89, 92

Wieder, see Widder

Wiederholt (repeated, opponent)

Wiederkehr (return)

Wiedersprecher (gainsayer) 115

Wiedkamp (pasture field) 84, 84

Wiedman, Wiedmann, see Weidmann, Weidemann

Wiedmayer, Wiedmaier, see Weidemeyer

Wiedner < see Weidner

Wiedorfer (wine village) 102, 123

Wiedorfer (swamp village) 80, 123

Wiegand, Wigand, see Weigand

Wieger, Wiegert 74, Wiegner (official weigher) 109

Wiegman, Wiegmann (weigher) 109

Wiehoff (willow farm, swamp farm) 89, 92

Wiel, Wiele (marsh) 80

Wieland (name of legendary smith)

Wieman, Wiemann, see Wiechmann

Wiemer, Wiemers 164 < Wigmar, war + famous) 46, 47

Wien, Wiener, Wieners 164, Wienert 74 (fr Vienna, Viennese) 122

Wienhold, Wienholt, see Weinholt

Wienke 53, 55 < Wignand (battle + brave) 46

Wieprecht < Wigbrecht (battle + brilliant) 46, 47

Wier 159, see Weyher

Wies, Wiese (meadow) 84

Wiesbaum (hay pole) 84, 89

Wiesel, Wieseltier (weasel) 115

Wieselberger (fr Wieselberg 122, weasel mountain) 68

Wiesenbacher (fr Wiesenbach 122, meadow brook) 84, 77

Wiesenfeld (meadow field) 84, 84

Wiesenhoffer (meadow farm) 84, 92

Wiesent, Wiesendt (bison) 115

Wiesenthal (meadow valley) 84, 76, 122

Wiesenthal (bison valley) 115, 76

Wiesenthauer (bison meadow) 115, 84

Wiesman, see Wiesner

Wiesner, Wiessner (dweller on the meadow) 84

Wiess, see Wiese, Weiss

Wiest (fr Wieste 122), see Wuest

Wigand, see Weigand

Wigener < Weigand

Wighard (battle + strong) 46, 46

Wigle, see Weigel

Wightman 159, see Weidmann

Wikman, see Wiechmann, Wiegman

Wiland, see Wieland

Wilberger, see Wildberg

Wilbert (determination + bright) 46, 47

Wilcke 53, 55 (little William)

Wild, Wilde, Wilder (wild, game) 115

Wildbach (wild brook) 77

Wildberg 122, Wiltberger, Wildenberger (wild mountain) 68

Wilde (river name) 83

Wildeman, Wildemann (wild man) 115

Wildenmut, Wildermuth (wild disposition) 115

Wilder, Wilderer (hunter, poacher) 91

Wilderbach (wild stream) 77

Wildermuth (high spirits) 115

Wildfang, Wilfong 159 (tended forest, game, prey, tomboy) 115

Wildhengst (wild stallion) 91

Wildheyt (wildness) 115

Wildhorn (hunting horn)

Wildner (poacher) 91

Wildschuetz (hunter, poacher) 91

Wildt (game, hunter) 91

Wilfong, see Wildfang

Wilgar, Wilger (determination + spear) 46, 46

Wilhelm, Wilhelms 164, Wilhelmus 141 (determination + helmet) 46, 46, 136

Wilhelmi (son of Wilhelm) 142

Wilhelmsen (son of Wilhelm) 59

Wilhide 159, Wilhite, Wilhoit, see Wildheyt

Wilk 53, Wilke 55, Wilkes 74, Wilkens, Wilkins, Wilkie, Willikin < Wilhelm

Will, Wille (will, determination) 46

Willbach (village brook), see Wildbach

Willem, Willems 164, Willemsen 59 < Wilhelm

Willheim (village hamlet) 123, 123

Willhide 159, Willhite, see Wilhide

Willich, Willig, Willik, Willing (willing) 115

Willikon (Wilhelm's hamlet) 127

Williram (will + raven) 46, 48

Willkom (Welcome!) 117

Willmann, Willmanns 164 (determination + man) 46, 94

Willmer, Willmers 164, Wilmer, Wilmers (dertermination + famous) 46, 47

Willner, see Wildner

Willoch 53 < Wilhelm

Willowby 159, see Wilderbach

Willpert (determination + bright) 46, 47

Wilmann, see Willmann

Wilner, see Wildner

Wilpers 164, see Wilbert

Wilt, see Wild

Wiltrout 159 < Wiltraut, Wiltrud (determination + beloved) 46, 48

Wimert 74, Wimmer, Wimmers 164, see Widmer

Wimmler (marsh dweller) 80

Win, see Wein

Winacker, Winecker (grape field, vineyard) 102, 84

Winberg, see Weinberg

Winblat, see Weinblatt

Winchel 55, 159 see Wuensch

Winckler, Winckelmann, see Winkler

Wind (wind) 122

Wind, Winde (hunting dog, greyhound) 91

Windemuth, Windermuth, see Wendelmuth

Winder, Winders, see Winter, Winters

Windesheim (wind hamlet) 123

Windfeld (wind field) 84

Windheim, see Windesheim

Windhorst (wind hurst) 72

Windisch (Wendish, Slavic) 121

Windmiller, Windmueller (windmiller, dweller by a windmill) 103

Windstein (wind mountain) 73

Winebarger 159, see Weinberger

Winebrener 159, Winebrenner, Wineburner, see Weinbrenner

Winecoff 159, see Weinkauf

Winegard 159, Winegeard, see Weingard

Wineholt 159, see Weinhold

Wineman 159, see Weinman

Winfelder 159, see Weinfelder

Winfurth (fr Weinfurth) 122

Winhart (friend + strong) 48, 46

Winholt (friend + loyal) 48, 48

Winkel (corner, angle, wooded valley) 69, 122

Winkelbauer (farmer in a wooded valley) 69, 91

Winkelmeyer (farmer in wooded valley) 69, 93, or fr Winkel 122

Winkelstein (wooded mountain) 69, 73

Winkler, Winkelman, Winkelmann, Winklemann (storekeeper) 105

Winland, see Weinland

Winrich, see Weinreich

Winter 122, Winters 164 (winter)

Winter, see Wintzer

Winterberg (winter mountain) 68, 122

Winterberg (vintners' mountain) 102, 68

Wintermantel (winter coat) 112, 106

Wintermeyer (vintner) 102, 93

Winterstein (winter mountain) 73, 122

Winterstein (vintners' mountain) 102, 73

Wintner, Wintzer (vintner) 102

Wintsch 159, see Wuensch

Wintz, Winz 122, Winzer (vine dresser) 102

Winzell (tiny) 113

Wipbold, Wippel < Wigbald (battle + bold) 46, 46

Wipert, Wipprecht < Wigbert (battle + bright) 46, 47

Wirbel (whirl, vertebra)

Wireman 159, see Weiherman

Wirt, Wirth (host, proprietor) 96

Wirthlin 55 (little host) 96

Wirtsch < Wirt

Wirtz, Wuertz (spice) 106

Wisbrod, see Weissbrod

Wisch, Wischel (wiper) 96

Wise 159, see Wiese, Weiss

Wiseburg 159, see Weissburg

Wisel, see Wiesel

Wiseman 159, see Weissmann

Wisenauer (dweller on a meadow) 84

Wisenbaker 159, see Wiesenbacher, Weissenbacher

Wishard, Wishart, see Weisshart

Wisman, Wismann, see Weissman

Wismatt (white meadow) 84

Wisner, Wissner, see Wiessner

Wissant (bison, auerochs) 115

Wissel 53, Wissels 164 < Werner

Wissler, see Wechsler

Wist, see Wuest

Wisthoff (wilderness, uncultivated farm farm) 84

Withaar (white hair) 112

Witsel 159, see Witzel, Weitzel

Witt, Witte (white) 112

Wittbecker (fr Wittbeck 122, white brook, forest brook) 77

Wittekind, see Wedekind

Wittenbach (white brook, or forest brook) 77, 122

Wittenberg (white mountain) 68, 122

Wittfeld (white field) 84

Witthauer (woodchopper) 95, 100

Witthof (forest farm) 72, 92

Witthuhn (white chicken)

Witthuhn (grouse, forest hen)

Wittich, Wittig (legendary hero)

Wittmann, Wittmer (manager of church propety) 110, 139, or see Weidmann

Wittmayer, Wittmayer, Wittmyer 159 (manager of glebe land) 93, 110, 139

Wittstadt (white city) 122

Wittwer (widower) 119

Witz (wit, intelligence) 115, or < Witu, forest 72

Witzel 53, 55 < Ludwig, Wiegand

Witzthum (manager, fr Latin *vicedominus*) 109

Wizenbaker 159, see Weissenbacher

Wizeman 159, see Weissmann
Woeber, Wobner, Woebner see
    Weber
Woefel 55, Woefele, Woelffle (little
    wolf) 48, see Wolfhart
Woehrle, see Wehrl
Woehrmann (dweller on a dike)
Woelpert (wolf + bright 48, 47
Woelpert (rule + bright) 46, 47
Woerbel, see Werbel
Woerner, see Werner
Wohl (well-being) 115
Wohlfart, Wohlfahrt, Wohlfert
    (welfare)
Wohlfart, Wohlfahrt, Wohlfort <
    Wolfhart
Wohlfeil (inexpensive) 115, 105
Wohlgemut, Wohlgemuth,
    Wohlmut (happy disposition)
    115, 117
Wohlleben, Wohleben (the good
    life)
Wohlmut, Wohlmuter, see
    Wohlgemuth
Wohlschlaegel, Woleslagel 159 <
    Woolschlaegel (wool cleaner)
    106
Wohlust (joy) 115
Wohner (occupant)
Wolbert < Walbrecht
Wold, see Wald
Woldhouse 159, see Waldhaus
Woldorf, see Waldorf
Wolf 122, Wolfe, Wolff, Wolfs 164
    (wolf) 48, or < Wolfgang,
    Wolfhart
Wolfart, Wolfarts 164, 122,
    Wolfahrth, see Wohlfart
Wolfer, Wolfers 164, Wolfert 74 <
    Wolfher (wolf + army 48, 46),
    or Wolfhart
Wolffanger, Wolfanger (wolf
    catcher) 91
Wolfgang (wolf + gait) 48
Wolfhart (wolf + strong) 48, 46
Wolfisch < Walfisch (whale)

Wolfkamp, Wolfkampf (wolf field)
    48, 84
Wolfram (wolf + raven) 48, 48
Wolfshagen (wolf's enclosure) 48,
    123, 122
Wolfsheimer (wolf hamlet, Wolf's
    hamlet) 48, 123
Wolfskehl, Wolfskill 159 (wolf's
    throat) 48, 122
Wolhandler (wool dealer) 106
Wolk (cloud)
Wolkam (wool comb) 106
Wolkstein, see Wolkenstein
Wollenhaupt (wool head) 112
Wollenmacher (woolmaker) 96
Wollenschlaeger, Woolslager (wool
    beater) 96
Wollenweber, Wolweber (wool
    weaver) 96
Woller, Wollert 74, Wollner, see
    Wollenschlaeger
Wollf, see Wolf
Wollhuter (maker of wool hats) 96
Wollmershausen, see Vollmers-
    hausen
Woole (wool) 106
Woolman, Wolman (wool dealer)
    106
Woolsleger, see Woolenschlaeger
Wolpert < Walbrecht
Wolter, Wolters 164, see Walther,
    Walthers
Woltman, Woltmann, see Wald-
    mann
Woltz, see Waltz
Wombacher, see Wambach
Wonderly 159, see Wunderlich
Wool, Wolle (wool) 105, 106
Woolmaker 153, see Wollen-
    macher
Woost 122, see Wuest 159
Workman 153, see Werckmann
Workmester 159, see Werk-
    meister
Worms, Wormser (fr Worms) 122
Worst, see Wurst

Wrangel (querulous) 115
Wrighter 159, see Reiter
Wrights 159, 164, see Reitz
Wucher, Wucherer (usurer) 96
Wueller, Wuellner, see Wollner
Wuensch (wish)
Wuensch (Wendish) 121
Wuenschel < Wuenschelrute
    (divining rod)
Wuepper (river name) 83
Wuerfel (dice, gambler) 115
Wuertemberger, Wuerttemberger
    (fr Wurttemberg) 121
Wuertz (spice) 106
Wuest, Wueste (desert, waste-
    land, abandoned farm)
Wuestenberg (desert mountain)
    68
Wuetrich (maniac) 115
Wulf, Wulff, see Wolf, Wolff
Wulfhart, see Wolfhart
Wulfhorst (wolf horst) 72
Wuller (woolworker) 96
Wullschlaeger, see Woolen-
    schlaeger
Wullwever (wool weaver) 96
Wund (wound, wounded)
Wunder (wonder, miracle)
Wunderlich, Wunderlick 159,
    Wunderli, Wonderlich (quaint,
    odd, eccentric) 115
Wunsch, see Wuensch
Wurdeman (man of dignity) 115
Wurfel, Wuerfel (dice)
Wurmser, see Wormser
Wurst, Wurste (sausage) 106
Wurster (sausage maker) 96
Wurttemberger, Wurttenberger
    (fr Wurttemberg 122, reed
    mountain) 81, 68
Wurtz, Wurts, see Wuertz
Wurtzbach, Wurtzbacher, Wurtz-
    baugh 159 (spice brook) 77
Wurtzer (spice dealer) 106
Wurz 122, see Wuertz

Wurzburg, Wurtzburger (fr
    Wurtzburg 122, swamp castle)
    80, 73
Wurzel, Wurzell (root)
Wust 159, see Wuest
Wustfeld 159 (waste field) 84
Wycoff, Wyckoff (wine seller) 102,
    105
Wydman, see Weidmann
Wygand, see Weigand
Wygart, see Weingard
Wyl, Wyler, see Weil
Wyman, see Weinmann
Wynberg, see Weinberg
Wyner, see Weiner
Wyngarde, Wyngartner, Wynga-
    arden, see Weingard, Wein-
    gaertner
Wynkoop, see Wycoff
Wyrauch, Wyrouch, see
    Weihrauch
Wys, Wyss, see Weiss

### X

Xander < Alexander

### Y

For Y see also under J.

Yaeger 159, Yager, Yagermann,
    see Jaeger
Yaeter 159, see Jeter
Yahn 159, Yanke 55, see Jahn,
    Jahnke
Yahr 159, see Jahr
Yakel 159, 55, Yakeley, see
    Jaeckli
Yantz 159, see Jantz
Yauch 159, see Jauch
Yeager 159, Yager, see Jaeger
Yeaterman 159, see Jeter
Yenny 159, see Jenny
Yetter 159, see Jeter

Yingling 159, see Juengling
Yingst 159, see Juengst
Yoder 159, see Joder
Yon, see Jahn
Yonce 159, see Jantz
Yongman 159, see Jungman
Yonker 159, see Junker
Yoos 159, see Jost
Yorden 159, see Jordan
Yost 159, see Jost
Youngblood 153, see Jungblut
Younginger 159, see Junginger
Yssenhut, see Eisenhut
Yuengling 159, see Juengling
Yung 159, Yunger, see Jung,
    Junger
Yungmann 159 (young man)
Yungmeyer 159 (young farmer,
    heir to the farm) 93
Yunker 159, see Junker
Yustus 159, see Justus
Yutsi, see Uts

## Z

Zaber, Zaberer (fr Zabern) 122,
    129
Zach 53, 122, Zacharias (OT
    name) 135
Zachringer, Zaehringer (Swiss
    dynastic name)
Zachs 159, Zaks, see Sachs
Zaehringen (fr Celtic Tarodunum)
    129
Zaharias (OT name) 135
Zahl (number)
Zahler (teller, payer, debtor) 96
Zahm (tame, domestic)
Zahn (tooth, dentist) 114, 96
Zahringer, see Zachringer
Zaitman 159, see Seideman
Zaiss, see Zeiss
Zaller, Zalner, see Zahler
Zander, see Alexander
Zang 122, Zange (tongs, torturer,
    tooth puller) 106

Zanger 159 (lively, merry) 115,
    see Saenger 151
Zangmeister 159 (choir master)
Zank, Zanck, Zanker (quarrel,
    quarreler) 115
Zant (tooth) 114
Zapf (tap, taverner) 106
Zarncke (Slavic: black) 146, 112
Zart (tender) 115
Zassenhaus 159 (Saxons' house)
Zauberbuehler, Zouberbuhler, see
    Zuberbiller
Zaubermann (magician) 96
Zauberman (bucket maker) 96
Zaun, Zauner, Zuner (fence, fence
    maker) 96, 122
Zaydel 159, see Seidel
Zeagler 159, see Ziegler
Zech, Zecher, Zechman (tippler)
    115, 122
Zeder (cedar) 89
Zedler (scribe) 96
Zeender, see Zehender
Zegel 159, Zegal, see Siegel
Zeger 159, see Sieger
Zeh (toe) 114
Zehenbauer (tithe farmer) 91
Zehender, Zehnder, Zehnter (tithe
    collector) 109
Zehler, see Zahler
Zehn, Zehner (ten, tenth) 143
Zehntbauer, see Zehenbauer
Zehr (nourishment) 106
Zeichner (draftsman) 96
Zeidel 159, see Seidel
Zeiderman 159, see Seideman
Zeidler (honey gatherer) 95
Zeidner 159, see Seidner
Zeigenfuss, Zeigenfuse < Ziegen-
    fuss (goat foot) 114
Zeiger (hand of clock)
Zeigler 159, see Ziegler
Zeil, Zeile (line)
Zeiler 159, see Seiler
Zeiss (gentle, tender) 115
Zeit (time)

Zeitler, see Zeidler

Zeitung (tidings, announcement)

Zeits 159, Zeitz, see Seitz

Zelik 159, Zelikman, see Selig, Seligman

Zell (cell, fr Latin *cella*) 122

Zeller, Zellner, Zellmann (dweller near a shrine or cell)

Zellhofer (farm near a shrine or cell) 92

Zellner, see Zoellner

Zelt, Zelter, Zeltner (tent, tent-maker) 96

Zelter (palfrey) 92

Zeman 159, see Siemann

Zemel 159, see Semmel

Zenger (lively person) 115, see Saenger

Zenker (quarreler) 115

Zentgraf, Zentgraft (village magistrate) 109

Zentmyer 159 (tithing farmer) 93

Zentner (hundredweight) 114

Zents 53, Zentz < St. Vincentius 131

Zepp, see Zapf

Zepperfeld, Zeppenfeldt (threshing floor) 84

Zerbrock, see Zurbruek

Zercher, see Zuericher

Zerkel 159, see Zirkel

Zermatt (to the meadow, Swiss village) 69, 84, 122

Zetel (marsh) 80

Zetrower 159, see Zittrauer

Zettel (scrap of paper, note) 122

Zettelmeyer 159, Zettlemoyer, see Sattelmeyer

Zettler, see Zedler

Zeumer (bridle maker) 96

Zeuner (fence maker) 96

Zevenbergen 159 (seven mountains), see Siebenbuergen

Zickafoose 159, Zickefoose (Shake a leg!) 116, 151

Ziebenbuergen 159, see Siebenbuergen

Ziebli, Zieblin, see Zuebli

Ziebolt 159, see Siegbald

Zieg, Ziege, Ziecke (goat) 91, see Sieg

Ziegaus 159 < Zeughaus (armory) 65, 108

Ziegeheaver 159, see Ziegenhoff

Ziegel, Zieggel, see Zuegel

Ziegel 159, see Siegel

Ziegenbein (goat leg) 114

Ziegenfuss (goat foot) 114

Ziegenheim (goat hamlet) 123

Ziegenhoff (goat farm) 92

Ziegenmeyer (goat farmer) 93

Ziegenmilch (goat milk) 106

Ziegfeld, Ziegfield (goat field) 84

Ziegler, Zieglar, Zieglert 74 (tile setter or maker, fr Latin *tegulum*) 96, 101

Ziegman 159, see Siegmann

Ziel, Ziehl (goal)

Zielke 55 (little goal)

Zieman 159, see Sieman

Ziepold 159, see Siegbald

Zier (decoration) 115, 106

Zigel 159, see Siegel, Zuegel

Zigenfuss 159, see Ziegenfuss

Zigler 159, see Ziegler

Zilber 159, see Silber

Zimelman 159, see Semmel

Zimmer, Zimmerli 55 (timber, carpenter) 106

Zimmermann, Zimermann (carpenter) 96, 98

Zindel, see Zuendl

Zinder (silk worker) 96

Zinder, see Zuender

Zink (cornet player) 96

Zinn, Zinner, Zinnert 74 (pewterer) 96

Zinser, Zinsser (payer or receiver of rent)

Zinsmeister (tithe collector) 109

Zipfel, Zipfler (peak, peak
dweller) 68
Zintl, see Zuendl
Zipperer (thresher) 95
Zipprian (St. Cyprian) 131
Zircher, see Zuericher
Zirkel, Zirckel, Zirkle 159 (district) 122
Zirkelbach (circular brook) 77
Ziskind 159, see Sueskind
Zittrauer, Zittrower 159 (trembling mountain) 68
Zobel (hairknot, girl) 112
Zoberbiller, see Zuberbiller
Zobrist (uppermost)
Zoeller, Zoellner, Zeller (toll
collector, fr Latin *telonarius*)
109
Zoll (toll, fr Latin *teloneum*) 122
Zoll (club, log)
Zollbrueck (toll bridge) 122
Zoller, Zollner, see Zoeller, Zoellner
Zollikoffer, Zollicoffer, Zollickover
159 (place in Switzerland) 122
Zollinger (fr Zolling) 122
Zollmann, Zoellner (toll collector)
109
Zonderman 159, see Sondermann
Zooker 159, see Zucker
Zopf (forelock) 112
Zorbach, Zorbaugh 159 (at the
brook) 69, 77
Zorn (anger, also a place name)
115 122
Zornig (angry) 115
Zouberbuhler 159, see Zauberbuehler
Zuber (wooden bucket) 106
Zubly 159, see Zuebli
Zubrick, see Zurbrueck
Zuchtmann (disciplinarian) 115
Zucker, Zuckermann (sugar
seller) 106
Zuckerberg (sugar mountain) 68
Zuckerbrot (pastry baker) 96

Zuebli, Zueblin (mountain stream,
fr Latin *tubus*) 77
Zuegel (bridle) 106
Zuend, Zuender (fuse, harquebusier) 107
Zuend (at the end [of the village])
69
Zuendl (fuse, kindling, fire
tender) 96
Zuericher, Zuercher (Swiss fr
Zurich) 122, 129
Zuern, see Zorn
Zufall (incident, accident)
Zug (city in Switzerland) 122
Zugel 159, see Zuegel
Zulauf, Zulouf 159 (throng)
Zumberg (at or on the mountain)
68
Zumbrun, Zumbrunn, Zum
Brunnen (at the well) 69, 79
Zumbusch (at the bush) 69, 72
Zumdahl (at the valley) 69, 76
Zumlaub (at the foliage) 69
Zumstein, Zumstain (at the stone)
69, 73, 122
Zumwald (at the forest, cf. Eng.
Atwood) 69, 71, 122
Zunder (tinder, punk, harquebusier) 107
Zunft (guild)
Zupfer (wool or flax puller) 96
Zurbrueck (at the bridge) 69
Zurbuch, Zurbuechen (at the
beeches) 69, 89
Zurcher 159, see Zuericher
Zurgable 159 (at the fork) 69, 65
Zurheide (to the heath) 69, 84,
122
Zuskin 159, see Sueskind
Zwaig, see Zweig
Zwantzig, Zwanzger, Zwantziger
(twenty)
Zweback 159, see Zwieback
Zweck (nail, target, goal) 122
Zweibrucker 159, Zweibricher (fr
Zweibruecken) 121, 122

Zweifel (doubt) 115
Zweig (branch, twig, taverner) 96
Zweigle 55 (little branch, graft)
Zweigler (dweller at a crossroads) 65
Zwetsch, Zwetschen (plum) 89
Zwickel (gusset)
Zwicker (excutioner)
Zwiebach (zwieback, baker) 96

Zwiebbler (onion seller) 106
Zwiebel (onion, green grocer) 106
Zwieg 159, see Zweig
Zwiffler, see Zwiebbler
Zwigart 159, see Schweiger
Zwinger (castle) 73, 122
Zwirn (thread) 96, 106
Zygler, see Ziegler

# ADDENDA

The following names have been suggested by readers of the first edition of this book who did not find their names included. Those that arrived after the type for the revision had been set are presented here as an addendum. A large number of these names are merely variant spellings of names previously listed. The command *See* usually refers to the main body of names. I particularly wish to acknowledge the contributions of Mr. Edward J. Leyenaar, who showed an uncanny knack for recognizing American names of German origin.

## A

Aalrep (eel catcher) 91
Aar, Ahr (eagle) 48
Abendstern (evening star) 148
Aberhart, see Eberhard 151
Achleiter (land sloping down to water) 79, 71
Ahlhelm < Adelhelm (noble + helmet) 47, 46
Ahlschlaeger, see Ohlschlaeger
Ahlwart < Adelwart (noble + guardian) 47, 47
Ahnsorge, see Ansorge
Aisch (river name) 83
Albern < Adelbern (noble + bear) 47, 48
Alderman, see Altermann
Alletag (every day) 118
Alram < Adelram (noble + raven) 47, 48
Altenkirch (old church) 71
Ambos (anvil, blacksmith) 96
Amstutz, Amsturtz (on the steep slope) 71
Ankenbauer (butter farmer) 91
Annecker, see Anacker
Anwaerter (candidate) 109
Arant, see Arnd
Arg (mean, stingy) 115
Armut, Armuth (poverty) 114
Artmann, Artmeier (proprietor of tilled field) 84, 93

Aschenbrand (clearing in the ashtrees) 89, 126
Aschenfelter (ashtree fields) 89, 84
Aschenreiter (clearing in ash woods) 89, 126
Aspin (aspen) 89
Asser, Assmann (wainwright) 96
Asshauer (wainwright) 96, 95
Attenborn (at the well) 70, 79
Auchenbaugh, see Achebach 151
Aufrecht (upright) 115
Aulner, see Aulmann
Aultmann, see Altmann
Averdieck (beyond the dike) 70, 82
Awald, see Ewald 151

## B

Baarsch, see Barsch
Bache (ham, hog) 91, 82
Bachfeld (brook field) 122, 84
Bad, Bade, see Bader
Bainter, see Painter
Barchent (fustian weaver) 96
Bardenheuer (halbard maker) 108
Barthels, see Berthhold
Bastian, Bastmann (St. Sebastian) 134-136

Baumhauer (tree chopper) 95
Bechler, Beckmann (dweller by
a stream) 77, 94
Beerschank (pub, public house)
taverner) 96
Beichley, see Beichel 151
Beikler, see Beichler
Belser (swamp dweller) 80
Bemiller, see Buehlmueller 151
Bercht, see Berchthold
Bergdorf (mountain village)
68, 123
Bernhauser (swamp house) 80,
65
Berwig (bear + battle) 48, 46
Beseke (fr St. Basilius) 134-137
Besserdich (Better yourself!,
initiation name) 116
Bestheimer (for Westheimer,
Western hamlet) 123
Betcher, see Boettcher 151
Biegel, see Buhler
Biehn, see Bien
Bildhauer (sculptor) 96
Bimmiller, see Buehlmueller
Binns, see Bintz
Binsbacher (reed brook) 81, 77
Binzen, see Bintz
Birkbach, see Birkelbach
Birkhan (black grouse) 115
Birnstengel (pear stem) 89,
114, 118
Blaas, see Blass
Blasebalg (bellows,
blacksmith's helper) 96
Blaufuss (a kind of falcon,
falconer) 115, 96
Blaurock (blue coat, dandy,
coat maker) 112, 96
Bockhorst (beech grove) 41, 72
Bodenhamer, see Bodenheimer
Boeggeman, see Beckermann
Bollenbach (swampy brook) 77
Boltzmann, see Boltz
Bonzer, see Panzer 151
Borries (St. Liborius) 134-137

Bouck, see Buch, Bock
Bourgholtzer, see Burkhalter
151
Brackmann, see Brachmann
Bradfisch (fried fish) 112, 106
Braitenbah, see Breitenbach
Brandkamp (burned field) 126,
84
Brantz, see Brand
Breitkopf, see Breithaupt
Bridenbaugh, see Breitenbach
Brief, Brieftrager (letter
carrier) 96
Brinksitzer (owner of small
parcel of land near village) 74
Bronkhorst, see Brunkhorst
Brookhizer, see Brockhaus 151
Brookhouser, see Brockhaus
151
Broyle, Broyles, see Breul 151
Brugaman, see Brugge
Bruhl, see Bruehl
Bryfogel (porridge bird) 112
Buchenauer (beach meadow)
89, 84
Buchenhorst (beech hurst) 89,
72
Buchhalter (beech slope) 89, 71
Buchstab (letter, schoolmaster)
96, 109
Bulle (bull, cattle dealer) 91,
106
Buntrock (fur coat, furrier) 112,
96
Burchland (castle land) 118
Burenfeind, see Bauernfeind
Busler (penitent) 115
Buttermann (butter seller) 106
Butzke (little Burkhard) 54, 55


C

Cale, see Kehl 151
Calehuff (fr the Kehlhoff,
gorge farm) 92, 151

Elterman (dweller on the
  Elter) 83
Emery, see Emerich 151
Emmermann (bucket maker)
  96
Erdreich (kingdom of earth,
  see Erdmann)
Erlenmeyer (occupant of the
  Erlenhoff, alder farm) 89, 92
Esterly, see Oester, Oesterle
  151

Friichtenicht, fr Fuerchte
  nicht! (Fear not!) 116
Frohmader (corvée mower) 91,
  96
Frohwirth (jolly host) 115, 96
Froschheiser (frog house) 65,
  149
Fuerchtenichts (Fear nothing!)
  116
Fuendling, see Findling

### F

Fale, Fales, see Fehl 151
Faltin (St. Valentinus) 134-137
Farch, Farke (little pig) 91, 115
Fehlhaber (oat farmer) 91
Fehleisen (file maker) 96
Feinfrock, Finfrock (fine gown)
  96, 112
Feltenbarger, see Feldberger
Fengfisch (catch fish,
  fisherman) 91
Ferckel (shoat, pig raiser) 115,
  91
Feuerborn (fire spring) 79
Feuersang (burned clearing)
  126
Fiebach, Viehbach (cattle
  brook) 77
Finster (dark, gloomy) 115
Flachshaar (flaxenhaired) 112
Flager < Pfleger, governor)
  109, 151
Floesser, Pfloetner (raftsman)
  96
Foertner (dweller by a ford) 71
Fontane (fr French Fontaine,
  fountain) 114
Freeh, see Frueh
Fresenburg (Friesian castle)
  120, 73

### G

Garten (garden, gardener) 84
Gastgeber (host, inn-keeper) 96
Gauman (country dweller) 91
Geas, see Giese 151
Gebwein (gift + friend) 48
Genzer, see Gensler 151
Geppert < Gebhard
Gerwart (spear + guardian)
  46, 47
Gesche, see Giese
Gescheidt (clever, prudent) 115
Geselschap (company) 118
Getty, see Goethe 151
Gewehr (warrantor, sponsor)
  96, 109
Gewert, see Gebhard
Gideon (OT name) 135
Giebel (gable) 118
Gierhard, see Gerhard
Giessler (foundryman) 96
Gippe (jacket) 96, 106, 112
Glasenap (glass bowl) 96
Glasshof (glass factory) 96
Glitzenberg (glittering
  mountain) 68
Godehard < Gotthard
Godeluck (Good luck!) 117
Godeschalk, see Gottschalk
Godewald (god + rule) 48, 46,
  see Gottwald

Godschall, see Gottschalck
Goedhart, see Gotthard
Goerg, see Georg
Goessler, see Gessler
Goesswein, see Gooswein
Goethe, see Goedeke
Gohr (swamp) 80
Goldammer, see Goldhammer
Goldschlager (goldsmith) 96
Gosswein (Goth + friend) 121,
    48
Grabmann (dweller near a
    ditch) 80, 94
Grahmann (greyberd) 112
Granroth (clearing in the
    juniper trees) 89, 126
Grans (beak) 114
Grasmaeder (grass mower) 95
Grathewohl see Gerathewol
Graubart (greybeard) 122
Grauper (barley peeler) 96
Greble, see Kraehbuehl 151
Greilsamer (fr Crailsheim) 122
Griesbaum < Kriesbaum
    (cherry tree) 89
Grobecker (rye bread baker) 96
Gronhaeuser (occupant of a
    green house) 65
Gronhagen (green hedge, green
    enclosure) 123
Gronheim (green hamlet) 123
Gronloh (green forest) 71
Gronweg (green path) 65
Grosbush (large bush) 72
Grosmueck, see Grasmick
Grotewohl, see Gerathewohl
Gruetzner (grits grinder,
    dealer) 96, 106
Gruntal, see Gruenthal
Gubler (ridge dweller) 68
Gumpost (sauerkraut) 112
Gutbier (brewer) 96
Gutbrodt (baker) 96
Gutkind (good child) 115
Guttentag (Good day!) 117

Gutwasser (good water) 118
Gutwirt, Gutwirth (good host)
    96


# H

Haarer (flax dealer) 96, 106
Habedank (Many thanks!) 117
Hackenteufel (Hit the devil!)
    116
Haehnel < Johannes 55
Hahnke (little rooster) 55, 115
Haidler (heath dweller) 81
Hailer, Heiler (castrator) 96
Haiss < Matthias
Hambrick, Hambright, see
    Hambrecht 115
Haner (poultry dealer) 106
Halbhuber (peasant owning
    half a hide of land) 91
Halbscheffel (payer of half a
    bushel rent) 91
Halfkath, see Halbmeyer
Hambrick, Hambright, see
    Hambrecht 151
Hamfstengel (hemp stalk) 114
Handel < Johannes 55
Hanover (Hannover) 121
Harde (herdsman) 9
Harmon, see Herrmann
Harsch (iced snow) 118
Hartmaire, see Hartmeyer
Hartneid = Neidhart
Hassenkerl (Hate the rascal!)
    116
Hau (chop!, hew!) 116
Hau (timber area) 72
Haueisen (Hack the iron!,
    blacksmith) 116, 96
Hauenschild, see Hauschild
Hauptvogel (bird dealer) 96
Hausbalk (rafter, carpenter) 96
Havemeyer (oat farmer) 93

## N

## O

## P

Portmann, Portner, see
  Pfoertner
Prang, Prange (quarreler,
  brawler) 115
Presl (fr Breslau) 122
Profrock, Prufrock (Test the
  rye!, market official) 116, 109
Pursch (lad, youth) 151
Pyle, see Peil, Pfeil 151

### Q

Queck (lively) 115

### R

Radekopf (red head) 112
Rademann (councillor) 96, 109
Rapp (raven) 48
Rappert < Radbrecht (counsel
  + brilliant) 36, 46, 47
Rast (swamp) 80
Ratzenberger (rat mountain)
  68
Rauber (robber) 96
Rauer, see Rau
Rauhut (fur cap, milliner) 112,
  96
Rechenmacher (rake maker) 96
Redeke (cartwright) 96
Rehmer, see Roemer
Reicher < Reichart (rule +
  strong) 46, 46
Reighn, see Rhein 151
Remy < St. Remigius 134–137
Rettenbaugh (swamp creek) 80,
  77, 151
Reuber, see Rauber
Reuchlin (little smoke,
  blacksmith) 55, 96
Reuss (cobbler) 96
Rhodaback, see Rodabaugh 151
Rickabaugh, see Rickenbacher

Riedelbauer (fr Riedel's farm),
  see Riedel
Riedesel (marsh donkey) 81,
  115
Rieschel (little Rudolf) 53
Rindt (cattle, cow) 91, 106, 115
Rippel < Ruprecht 55
Rode, see Roth
Roeper, Roper (town crier) 96
Rollwagen (stagecoach) 96
Rorich, see Rohrig
Rosa, see Rose 151
Rosecrans, see Rosencrans 151
Rosefeld, see Rosenfeld 151
Rosemann, see Rossmann
Ross (horse dealer) 106
Rosshirt (horse herder) 95
Rossmiller (horse miller)
Rothmund (red mouth) 114
Roudenbach, see Rautebach 151
Ruckhaus (house on a ridge) 65
Ruckhorn (peak on the ridge)
  68
Ruecker, see Ruediger
Rule, see Ruhl 151
Rumbarger, see Ramberger
Runke (wrinkle) 114
Runner, see Renner 151
Ruth (OT name) 135
Rutsch < Rudolf 53

### S

Sager (sawyer) 96
Salm (salmon) 91, 106
Salman < Salomon (OT name)
  135
Saxonhouse (Sachsenhausen)
  120, 65, 122, 151
Schaaf, see Schaf
Schaatz, see Schatz
Schane, see Schoen 151
Scheibe (common pasture) 84

Scheidemann (arbitor, judge) 96, 109

Scheithauer (wood splitter) 96

Schellenbach (swamp brook) -80, 77

Schenkbier (Serve bier!, taverner) 116, 96

Scheuenpflug (Run from the plow!) 116, 115

Schield, see Schild 151

Schienbein (shin bone) 114

Schleimer (glue maker) 96

Schlussel, Schlussler (key bearer) 96

Schmeling (slender, slight) 114

Schnebly, Schneebeli, see Schnaebele 151

Schnegel (snail) 115

Schoenwand (cloth maker) 96

Schottenheimer (Scots' hamlet) 121, 124

Schriftgiesser (type founder) 96

Schrimpf (cut, scratch) 114

Schroepfer (bleeder, cupper) 96

Schulberg (school mountain) 68

Schweiker, Schweicker < Schwindger (skillful + spear) 46, 46

Schweinhard (swineherd) 91

Schwicker < Schwindger (swift + spear) 46, 46

Sechter (bushel) 96, 106

Seidenfrau (silk woman) 96

Seidl, see Seidel

Senske (little sickle) 96, 106, 54, 55

Seyboot, see Seybold

Shaneour, see Schoenauer 151

Sharsmith < Scharschmidt (plow smith) 151, 96

Sheidelower (meadow on watershed) 84

Shelhamer, Schellheimer (bell hamlet) 123

Schellhouse, see Schellhaus, Schellhaas 151

Shelmire (occupant of the Schelhof, swamp farm) 80, 93

Shetzline, see Schatzle 55

Shugart, see Schuch 151

Siebenrock (seven coats, clothier, taylor) 112, 96

Siegwein (victory + friend) 46 + 48

Simrock, see Siebenrock

Slick, see Schlick 151

Sligh, see Schley 151

Smearcase < Schmerkaes (soft cheese) 112, 151

Smitz, see Schmidt 151

Smoller, see Schmoller 151

Smoltz, see Schmaltz 151

Snatterbeck (chatterer, gossip) 115

Soldat (soldier) 108

Sollenberg, see Solberg

Sommerhausen (summer house) 65

Sonderegger (swamp field) 80, 85

Sonnabend (Saturday) 143

Sox, see Sachs 151

Spaatz, see Spatz

Spanner (bale binder) 96

Sparkuhl (sparrow pond) 81

Spener (cutter of wood chips) 96

Spexarth, see Speicher

Spielholz (parish forest, glebe woodland) 72

Spring (dweller near a spring), see Springer

Stahlkopf (steel merchant) 96

Stalbach (steel brook) 77

Stalcupp, see Stahlkopf 151

Staubach (dammed up stream) 77

Stegreif (stirrup) 96, 106

Stehr (ram) 91, 115

Steinbeiss (stone cutter) 96, 100

Wandschneider (clothier, mercer) 96

Warmbier (warm beer, brewer) 96, 112

Waschbaugh (washing brook) 77, 151

Wascher (linen washer) 96

Waschnicht (Don't wash!) 116

Wechsler (money changer) 96

Wefer, see Weber

Wegbrot (viaticum, traveler) 118

Wegel, see Wagner

Wehrmann (defender) 108

Weichbrod (soft bread, baker) 96

Weinbold (friend + brave) 48, 46

Weitzenfeld (wheatfield) 84

Weltmer (world sea, traveler) 118

Wenberg, see Weinberg

Wentzke (little Werner) 54, 55, see Wentz

Werley, see Wehrl 151

Werts, see Wuertz 151

Westerlacken (western lakes)

Whetsler, see Wetzel 151

Whitmoyer, see Weidemann 151

Wickram (battle + raven) 46, 48

Wiedinmeyer, see Weidenmeyer 151

Wiegard, Wieghard (battle + strong) 46, 46

Wienkoop, see Weinkauf

Wildhauer, see Waldhauer

Wile, see Weil 151

Wine, see Wein 151

Winelspecht (forest jay) 115

Wintercorn (winter grain) 105

Winterroth (winter clearing, vintner's clearing) 126

Wismar (place name) 122

Wisterfeld (abandoned field, see Wuest) 84

Witkop, see Weisskopf

Wittbrod (white bread, baker) 96, 112

Wittkamp (white field) 84

Wittrock (white coat) 112

Wittstein (white stone, white mountain) 73

Wocher, see Wucher

Woellenweber, see Wollenweber

Wolfger (wolf + spear) 48, 46

Wurm (dragon, house name) 149

# Y

Yancey, see Jantz 151

Yerke, Jerkes, see Joerg 151

Youngheim (young hamlet) 123, 151

Yunginger, see Junginger 151

# Z

Zagel (tail, penis) 118

Zane, see Zahn 151

Zaring, see Zehr

Zaunkoenig (wren) 115

Zearing, see Zehr

Zenner, see Zentner

Zentner, see Zehender

Zering, Zehrung (nourishment, victualer) 106, 96

Zibel (onion) 91, 106

Zile, see Seil 151

Zipperer (prune grower or dealer) 91, 106

Zobel (sable, furrier) 96, 106, 112

Zober (bucket) 96, 106

Zumwinkel (at the corner) 70, 106

ligourian
Salzburg
ex crescent tsp. 53

Privacy Rights Clearing house